Low-Fat Living Cookbook

SKILLPOWER NOT WILLPOWER

by Leslie L. Cooper

RODALE PRESS, INC.

EMMAUS, PENNSYLVANIA

Cover and Book Designer: Debra Sfetsios
Cover Photographers: Angelo Caggiano, Donna Turek
Interior Illustrators: Michael Gellatly, Celia Johnson
Front Cover Recipe: Asparagus Risotto with Sun-Dried Tomatoes, page 207

Library of Congress Cataloging-in-Publication Data

Cooper, Leslie L.
    Low-fat living cookbook : 250 easy, great-tasting recipes / by
  Leslie L. Cooper ; with foreword by Robert K. Cooper.
        p.   cm.
    Includes index.
    ISBN 0–87596–435–4   hardcover
    1. Quick and easy cookery.   2. Low-fat diet—Recipes.   I. Title.
TX833.5.C665   1998
641.5'12—DC21   97–41540

Distributed in the book trade by St. Martin's Press

2 4 6 8 10 9 7 5 3 1 hardcover

—— OUR PURPOSE ——

*"We inspire and enable people to improve
their lives and the world around them."*

*This book is dedicated to my
husband, Robert K. Cooper, the love
of my life, my deepest friend, mentor,
and guiding star. Your extraordinary
talents, passion, intelligence,
courage, abundant energy, endless
love, and commitment to me, our
family, our life, and your work is an
inspiration to us all.*

*In all Rodale Press cookbooks, our mission is to provide
delicious and nutritious low-fat recipes. Our recipes also
meet the standards of the Rodale Test Kitchen for
dependability, ease, practicality, and, most of all, great
taste. To give us your comments, call 1-800-848-4735.*

CONTENTS

ACKNOWLEDGMENTS

Although many hours were spent alone creating, designing, researching, writing, editing, cooking (and cooking some more), I always looked forward to the wonderful company, unconditional support, enthusiasm, and constructive criticism that close family and friends shared while dining on my new creations for this book. This was among the most valuable of contributions.

A very close second to this was the great patience and understanding given by my editor, David Joachim. Believing that I would meet all my deadlines with or without a "date" and learning when to leave me on my own and when a marathon call was in order took knowledge and skill. His dedication to this book and amazing attention to detail are matched only by his ability to craft and shape my words and ideas into exciting prose. For this I am extremely grateful.

My gratitude to Linda Miller, for her many hours of detailed recipe editing and lovely wit that kept me smiling and laughing through long conversations. To Linda R. Yoakam, M.S., R.D., for providing the nutritional analyses quickly and accurately. And a special thanks to others at Rodale Books for their enthusiasm and support for Low-Fat Living—Pat Corpora, Peter Igoe, Debora T. Yost, Jean Rogers, Susan Massey, Cindy Ratzlaff, Dennis Lockard, Kathy Everleth, Christine Dreisbach, Debra Sfetsios, Thomas P. Aczel, Edward Claflin, Patrick T. Smith, Tom Ney, JoAnn Brader, and Nancy Zelko.

A very special, heartfelt thanks to my dedicated recipe testers, extraordinary supporters, and grand inspirers: Lynn and Larry Taylor, Dr. Robert and Renae Allen, Becka Lessard, Ambrose Lessard, Dottie Williams, Linda Weidmayer, Margaret Cooper, Hugh Cooper, Dan and Bobbie Marsh, Debbie Eisner, Clay and Deena Loecher, Jerry and Ana Loecher and the entire Loecher clan, Mary Hershberger, Ruth Hapgood, Suzanne Price, and the staff at Sunshine Special school.

And finally, to my dear husband, Robert, and children Shanna, Chelsea, and Chris. My utmost gratitude for continually supporting and challenging me at every moment to sacrifice what I am for what I can become. I love you all beyond imagination.

FOREWORD

It's all well and good to praise the value of low-fat cuisine; millions of Americans are doing that these days. But beneath the rhetoric and good intentions, it's quite another thing to love low-fat meals and snacks, to want to eat them every day, and to count low-fat recipes among the ones that you can't wait to share with your friends and neighbors.

Yet that's what this book can do for you and your family. I've eaten every recipe in this book at least twice, and I continue to enjoy these meals and snacks. In fact, I crave many of them. Which is all the more astonishing because these are good-for-you foods that boost metabolism, increase energy, and burn fat.

Ever since Leslie and I wrote *Low-Fat Living* and she began writing this cookbook, I've heard regular reports of how the staff of Rodale Books and *Prevention* magazine has been testing the recipes in this book. I've been told that there has never been such clamoring for more. Beyond this, a stream of our colleagues, neighbors, friends, and friends of friends—a number of whom told us that they had turned cynical after eating the usual low-fat fare being served up in restaurants and other cookbooks—gave Leslie's new meals and snacks a try. They and their families reported "oohs" and "aahs" as they enjoyed Leslie's delicious dishes. The result: Every one of these people requested an advance copy of the *Low-Fat Living Cookbook*.

This high praise for healthful food is worth pondering. Truth be told, there's not a lot of oohing and aahing going on in America when people eat low-fat foods. We eat low-fat because it's good for us. And that's too bad. Because you'll never stick with an eating plan that you don't love. None of us can.

So what's the answer? Call on willpower to eat foods that taste bland or boring? Not for long. Willpower eventually gives way. What holds strong for good is skillpower—the ability and the desire to make smart food choices. If you know what to eat when—and why—and have great-tasting food at your fingertips, low-fat living is a cinch. This book gives you that skillpower. It teaches you a simple set of eating strategies that make a low-fat lifestyle fun and satisfying. This book shows you how to switch off the high-fat kitchen and switch on the low-fat kitchen to make healthy eating an automatic part of your life. Once that's done, low-fat living is as simple as opening the kitchen door and turning on the light switch.

What's the payoff for eating this way? Quite simply, it's a lean, healthy body. This eating strategy (along with the other strategies that I outlined in *Low-Fat Living*) helps you burn off excess fat 24 hours a day—even while you sleep. We know from scientific research that low-fat, high-fiber foods are one of the keys to revving up the body's metabolism and turning on its fat-burning "switches." Turn these switches on, and you can start enjoying the benefits of a slim body, increased energy, and increased resistance to disease.

Another word about Leslie's recipes: I admit being biased. But here's why. Leslie and I have traveled extensively and have eaten low-fat cuisine prepared by a number of the best chefs in the world, which puts me in a pretty good position for comparison. But I would still—with or without a blindfold—choose the meals and snacks in this book. No one I've ever met has Leslie's touch for envisioning low-fat, high-taste, healthy homestyle recipes and getting them right the first time she tries them from scratch. This carries forward the tradition that she started with her first cookbook, *America's New Low-Fat Cuisine*, which was selected as "one of the best of the year" by *Cooking Light* magazine.

To put it simply, Leslie has an artist's gift for combining everyday ingredients and seasonings in ways that dazzle the palate. Once you try these recipes, I'm convinced that you'll agree.

Leslie also has a nutritionist's skill for packing recipes with important nutrients. The meals and snacks in the *Low-Fat Living Cookbook* meet the latest health guidelines of major health organizations like the American Heart Association, the National Cancer Institute, and the Food and Nutrition Board.

Best of all, the majority of the recipes are quick and easy. We're a busy family and don't have time to spend hours in the kitchen. No matter how hectic our lives have been this past year, the meals and snacks that you'll discover on the pages ahead have been the most steady and enjoyable parts of our days. To keep you ahead of the game in today's busy world, Leslie shares her timesaving secrets throughout the book.

In our home, this book has made the everyday implementation of fat-burning principles more achievable—and enjoyable—than I ever imagined it could be. This book is your invitation to building a new foundation for a healthy, low-fat, high-energy lifestyle, day in and day out. What greater gift can you give yourself and those you love?

—Robert K. Cooper, Ph.D.

PART ONE

Welcome

TO THE LOW-FAT LIVING KITCHEN

CHAPTER 1

"Laughter is brightest where food is best."

—IRISH PROVERB

FAT-BURNER SWITCH #1
MAKE THE MOVE TO A LOW-FAT LIFESTYLE

All across America, there is a growing movement toward low-fat living. It's a way of life. A lifestyle. Not a trend. Not another diet. Millions of us want to learn the simplest—and most effective—ways to eliminate excess fat from our plates and our bodies. Since the publication of *Low-Fat Living*, which I co-authored with my husband, Robert, we have received hundreds of letters. The message is loud and clear: People enjoy the Low-Fat Living Program. They find that it fits easily into their busy lives. And it works. Simple, gradual changes in the choices that you make can help control your weight and improve your health forever. But people want to know more about applying the principles of *Low-Fat Living* in the kitchen. For many of us, low-fat food is the central concern. Will it taste good? Will it be easy to make? Will I be able to stick with it? Here are the answers to these and other questions.

Will It Taste Good?

The answer is a resounding yes! You don't have to leave behind flavor when you make the move to low-fat cooking. Take it from the taste-testers across the country who tried all the recipes in this book. They found that low-fat food is bursting with fresh flavors and creamy textures. Many testers reported that the *Low-Fat Living* recipes expanded the range of flavors that they appreciate and enjoy. They loved the variety of familiar dishes, ethnic favorites, and sweet treats in the book. Most were surprised to learn that you can enjoy chocolate in the Low-Fat Living Program. Another surprise: Some recipes use butter. Many recipes include cheese. Some even use half-and-half (in small amounts) to rev up the flavor with less fat than heavy cream.

You won't go hungry on the Low-Fat Living Program. The food tastes good, and the portions are more generous than in most low-fat cookbooks. Testers told me that the serving sizes satisfied the most hungry eaters. And they were shocked to hear that eating sweet and savory snacks every day is a pivotal part of the program. It's more than okay to grab a chewy brownie for a mid-afternoon snack. It's one of the simplest ways to fire up fat-burning. Hungry for a muffin in the morning? Go for it. It'll help boost your metabolism before lunch. Of course, we're talking about brownies and muffins that are low in fat and high in fiber. I have recipes for these and more in this book.

As you make the move to a low-fat lifestyle, consider this other important aspect of flavor: time. Americans eat about 93 billion fat grams a year. Over time, we've grown accustomed to the flavor of fat. It creates a creamy feel in the mouth. And we've come to expect that flavor from our food. Acquiring a taste for lower-fat foods may take a little time. How much? If low-fat foods are new to you, give yourself a grace period of about eight weeks. That will give your taste buds a chance to adjust. Take it slow. If you're used to whole milk, switch to 2 percent low-fat milk at first. Get familiar with the texture and taste for a few weeks. Then try 1 percent low-fat milk when you're up to it. A slow progression will result in the biggest payoffs because you're more likely to stick with the changes that you make.

Will It Be Easy?

Today's hectic lifestyles demand that nothing be difficult, fussy, or time-consuming. My life is a good example. I'm busy. I have a family of five and I work. I don't have time to spend all day in the kitchen.

Over the years, I've developed a number of strategies to save time while staying on the low-fat track. The big time-savers are in chapters 5 and 9. That's where you'll find out how to shop fast and stock your kitchen with quick meals that burn fat and don't take hours to prepare. Throughout the recipes, you'll also find cooking shortcuts that make meal preparation a breeze.

Another timesaving bonus is the cooking time listed with each recipe. I included both "hands-on time" and "unattended time" so that you can find recipes that meet your needs at a glance. Skim the recipes and you'll see that hands-on time is kept to a minimum. Most recipes cook on the stove, bake in the oven, or chill in the refrigerator—while you're doing something else. In addition, most of the ingredients are widely available in grocery stores. You can get everything you need from your supermarket or, in some cases, a health food store. For those who live in very rural

SWITCHBREAK

Skillpower Not Willpower

Think for a minute right now about a healthy goal that you'd like to achieve. Do you want to lose weight? Sleep better? Have more energy? Grab a pen and paper and write down the one goal that you'd like to achieve most. Put it under the heading "Healthy Goal." Make another heading on the page called "How to Get There." Now think for a moment about your goal. What small steps can you take to achieve it? For instance, if you want to lose weight, what one thing can you do today to start? Jot down small, specific actions—like eating a bagel as a morning snack instead of a doughnut. Or going for a short walk after dinner instead of watching TV. After writing down a few, pick the one action that looks easiest and do it today. This is the hard part, so take it slow. Do just that one thing today—even if it's as simple as putting jam on your bagel instead of cream cheese. Then do it again tomorrow. After a few days, you'll notice that this one thing will start to become automatic. Tack the healthy goal list on your refrigerator. When that first action becomes automatic, move on to the next action step that you wrote down. These small steps will put you on the road to low-fat living.

areas, there is a list of mail-order sources in the back of the book. Several recipes come with step-by-step illustrations, too. They show you exactly what the dish is supposed to look like as you're making it. Each of these features makes it easy to start cooking and eating the Low-Fat Living way today.

Will It Be Low-Fat—And Healthy?

The Low-Fat Living approach to eliminating excess fat from your body is firmly rooted in healthy eating. It's not a crash diet. If, like so many of us, you've tried to lose weight by dieting, skipping meals, and basically starving yourself, you know that it doesn't work. Eventually, all the weight comes back. Research suggests that yo-yo dieting could even cause you to gain weight. People who repeatedly lose weight and gain it back tend to accumulate more abdominal fat than those who reach a certain weight and stay there, according to a study published in the *International Journal of Obesity*. That's the exact opposite of what dieting is supposed to achieve.

Habitual dieting can also lead to lower bone density and increased risk of osteoporosis in both women and men, according to researchers at the University of California, San Diego, department of community and family medicine. What's more, a study conducted by Case Western Reserve University School of Medicine and the department of medicine at Saint Luke's Medical Center, both in Cleveland, found that weight cycling—continually losing and gaining weight—can elevate your blood pressure and increase your risk of developing diabetes. It's clear that dieting is a dead end. And it could be downright dangerous to your health.

The Low-Fat Living Program is designed for safe, healthy weight loss that lasts. It can get you off the dieting roller-coaster for good.

Unlike fad diets and questionable weight-loss schemes, the Low-Fat Living recipes and tips are based on a balanced eating strategy that you can count on. The meals and snacks in this book are backed by dietary recommendations made by the American Cancer Society, the American Heart Association, the National Cancer Institute, the National Academy of Sciences, and the Food and Nutrition Board. Most recipes derive between 20 and 25 percent of calories from fat. They're high in fiber and complex carbohydrates, moderate in protein, and limited in saturated fat, cholesterol, and sodium.

What are the health payoffs of a low-fat lifestyle? Researchers in the United States and Germany reviewed more than 200 worldwide studies and concluded that eating a low-fat diet high in fruits and vegetables can cut your cancer risk in half. Numerous studies link a low-fat lifestyle to lower blood pressure. Reducing the saturated fat in your diet is the number-one way to lower blood cholesterol and cut heart disease risk, according to Henry N. Ginsberg, professor of medicine at Columbia University College of Physicians and Surgeons in New York City. To put it simply, less fat in your diet means less fat on your body and reduced risk of diseases linked to obesity. Once you start cooking the Low-Fat Living way, you can stop worrying about your weight, obsessing about eating, or feeling deprived. And you can start enjoying the benefits of a lean, healthy body, including feeling younger and having increased vitality, energy, alertness, and greater resistance to a wide range of illnesses and diseases.

Will I Be Able to Stick with It?

The Low-Fat Living Program is a simple set of strategies that you can use for the rest of your life. It's easy and enjoyable. The strategies are called switches. They are not only principles but things that you can do right now—and every day—to boost your body's metabolism and burn more body fat. Water is a great example. Drink a glass of water right now and you'll make a major move toward low-fat living. It's that simple. See page 13 to find out why water has such a powerful effect.

The key to lasting weight loss, increased energy, and prevention of disease is right under your nose. In fact, it's right in your kitchen. This book shows you how to switch *off* the high-fat kitchen and switch *on* the low-fat kitchen so that you are in control of your body's fat-burning potential. Once it becomes automatic in the kitchen, it'll be a snap to take your low-fat lifestyle out the door—to restaurants, to work, or wherever you are. And that's when you'll know that you've made lasting changes. Living a low-fat lifestyle will become automatic.

Renae Allen, an early childhood educator and mother of two, is a good example of this. She has tested recipes for both *Low-Fat Living* and this cookbook. Renae is a living testimonial of how low-fat living can become automatic. "I'm food savvy now. Just living it has taught me that the more you do it, the more you learn," she says. Renae recalls growing up in a midwestern family and learning to cook from her mom, whom she describes as a very good, but basic, traditional cook—mostly meat and potatoes, with fish and noodles on Fridays. For the first seven years of her marriage, Renae's husband, Rob, a physician, asked her to cook healthier meals using less or no meat. Her response to him was always, "I'd be happy to, but I just don't know how."

I started Renae off slowly—by showing her how to transform her favorite recipes. Then I asked her if the transition to low-fat cooking was hard. She told me, "It's been easy because everything I make tastes so good, and Rob is really appreciative. He tells me, 'Renae, you are the best cook.' And that's not something that he said before."

Renae quickly learned how to cook low-fat food that tastes great. Before, if she didn't have an ingredient, she wouldn't make the recipe.

Now, she tries a variety of recipes and substitutes low-fat ingredients for high-fat ones. Or she substitutes foods that she knows her family will like. "I've learned how to look at any recipe and make it low-fat and high-flavor," she says. As a result, she has a whole new repertoire of recipes that her family considers favorites.

Renae, Rob, and their kids have all acquired a taste for healthy eating and a low-fat lifestyle. They love to entertain now, too. They have fun building low-fat menus "that will blow the guests away," as she puts it. And for Renae, it's a kind of coming home. "I'm my mom now—only a different generation," she says. "People are enjoying my food and being comforted by it, but they're also getting the benefits of health that will carry them far into the future."

Where Do I Start?

The inspiring thing about the Low-Fat Living Program is that you can start anywhere you like. Start with whatever sparks your interest or makes your mouth water. Begin by skimming the chapters that interest you most right now. Or pick a recipe that sounds good to you. The Fat-Burner Switches, Switchbreaks, Switch Tips, and recipes are designed to be easy and accessible. They give you the skillpower to make smart choices, to live a more active lifestyle, and to increase your body's fat-burning power 24 hours a day. We're talking about simple tools that you can use to improve your quality of life.

"It has always seemed strange to me that people can be vague and casual about what they put into their mouths as food and drink."

—PAMELA VANDYKE PRICE, BRITISH WINE BOOK AUTHOR

FAT-BURNER SWITCH #2

TURN *OFF* THE FAT-MAKERS AND TURN *ON* THE FAT-BURNERS

Losing weight, beating disease, and boosting your energy level may seem an insurmountable task. But in the Low-Fat Living Program, it's only a matter of making a few simple switches. The most important theme of this program is turning off the body's fat-making "switches" and turning on the fat-burning ones. This easy, effective method brings together the latest insights of scientists and clinicians around the world. My family has successfully used this approach for more than a decade. It has been endorsed by a number of health authorities, including Dean Ornish, M.D., preventive medicine researcher and author of *Eat More, Weigh Less* and *Dr. Dean Ornish's Program to Reverse Heart Disease*. These switches help you steer clear of the hidden pitfalls that can shift your body chemistry toward producing and storing excess fat. In *Low-Fat Living*, we explained these principles in detail. Here's a brief recap of your body's 10 fat-makers.

1. High-fat meals or snacks

2. Stuffing yourself—even with low-fat or nonfat foods

3. Low-fiber or no-fiber meals or snacks

4. Vanishing muscle tone

5. Alcohol—two or more drinks per day

6. Skipping meals or snacks

7. Hidden dehydration

8. Inactivity

9. Poor-quality sleep

10. Mismanaged stress

Turn off these 10 fat-making switches and you'll be halfway toward permanent weight control and lasting good health. By turning off these fat-makers, you'll be switching on your body's natural fat-burning power. Your body has the amazing ability to burn fat. And you can help it along by turning on your body's fat-burning switches. We're talking about easy things that you can do to increase your metabolism, raise your energy level, and burn excess fat all day long. Here are some of the switches that you can turn on today.

Quick-Start Your Morning Metabolism

You just woke up. You're feeling groggy. Don't go back to bed—here is an ideal place to begin low-fat living. Turn on this one switch, and you'll increase your energy level and fat-burning power for the rest of the day.

Researchers have found that from the moment you get out of bed, your brain cues your body's metabolism to match your current and anticipated physical demands. According to national surveys, most of us are pretty sedentary in the morning hours, and this keeps our metabolism sluggish. Yet, as little as five minutes of light morning activity is enough to kick-start your morning metabolism. You can do it before or after breakfast. Go through a gentle warmup period, then do a few minutes of light physical activity. Take an easy five-minute stroll. Watch the morning news as you pedal at a relaxed, moderate pace on a stationary cycle. We're not talking about jogging 10 miles.

Even some smooth, balanced oar strokes on a rowing machine is enough to get your motor running.

For variety, do some moderate strength training with heavy objects. Or try abdominal toning exercises. These brief moments of active time increase your energy level for the entire day. I've come to enjoy this morning activity so much that on some days, I find myself spending 15 to 20 minutes at it. The longer you go, the more all-day fat-burning power you'll have.

Eat Low-Fat, High-Fiber Snacks between Meals

Good news! Snacking is healthy. Now, hold on. That doesn't mean munching down a whole bag of chocolate chip cookies after lunch. But it does mean eating smaller amounts more often throughout the day to pump up your energy level. According to research, eating healthy between-meal snacks can help you boost your metabolism, shed body fat, lower blood cholesterol levels, and improve digestion. Eating snacks actually energizes your body by producing heat and burning calories.

The typical American three-squares-a-day eating pattern leaves you with two major lulls in energy—one mid-morning and another after lunch. The Low-Fat Living 3-plus-4 Eating Plan eliminates the notorious afternoon slump and helps you burn fat all day. Here's the plan: Eat three moderate-size meals plus two to four low-fat, high-fiber snacks throughout the day. Keep some healthy snacks in the kitchen or at your desk. Have one mid-morning, about 10:00 A.M. Have another mid-afternoon, about 3:00 P.M. If you feel like having a snack before dinner, munch on another. And if you're hankering for a little something after dinner, go ahead and have another. What kind of snacks are we talking about? Here are some examples.

- 1 apple, orange, banana, or other piece of fruit

- 1 low-fat granola bar

- 1 cup nonfat plain yogurt with fruit or low-fat granola

- 4 ounces nonfat frozen yogurt

- 1 whole-wheat English muffin, whole-grain bagel, or 5 whole-grain crackers with nonfat cream cheese and all-fruit spread

- Fresh-cut vegetables or fruit with nonfat dip and 3 whole-grain crackers

- 1 cup nonfat or low-fat canned vegetable or bean soup

- 1 slice whole-grain bread with 1 teaspoon nonfat mayonnaise and 2 ounces water-packed tuna

- 1 whole-grain bagel with 1 teaspoon mustard, 1 teaspoon nonfat mayonnaise, and 2 thin slices turkey breast or part-skim cheese

For more fat-fighting snacks, see the "Slimming Snacks for People on the Go" recipes, beginning on page 124. Also see the "Fat-Burning Dips, Spreads, and Sauces" recipes, beginning on page 356.

Drink Ice Water and Other Fat-Fighting Beverages

Do you ever reach the end of a workday and feel completely exhausted? The fatigue, headaches, lack of concentration,

---

SWITCHBREAK

Skillpower Not Willpower

Want to start low-fat living right now? Turn to page 356 and make the Herb Butter Spread. You'll need a few fresh herbs, a little butter, and some nonfat cream cheese. Don't have them? Make a quick trip to the store. If the store is nearby, walk or ride your bike instead of driving. When you get back, whip up the spread. Toast a slice of your favorite bread and top it with the spread. Now pour yourself a tall glass of ice water. Find a comfortable chair, have a seat, and start nibbling.

Believe it or not, you've just revved up your fat-burning power in two—possibly three—very important ways.

First, you've hydrated your body with cold water. Drinking water helps you feel full, which satisfies your appetite so you don't binge on high-fat snacks. Plus, you've burned a few calories warming up the water to your body temperature of 98.6°F.

Second, you've chosen a low-fat snack instead of a high-fat one. Healthy snacking is one of the keys to firing up fat-burning all day long.

And third, if you walked to the store, you began a process of physical activity that could be your ticket to lasting weight control. Staying active is another key to low-fat living and burning body fat 24 hours a day.

and dizziness that you feel can result simply from not drinking enough water. And, contrary to popular belief, the best way to rid your body of excess retained water is to drink more water. That's right. When you cut back on your water intake, your body goes into starvation mode. It responds by retaining even more fluid. Studies show that a decrease in water intake may cause fat deposits in the body to increase. On the other hand, an increase in water intake may help reduce fat deposits.

Here's why. When your body is fully hydrated, it helps release the fatty acids in your fat cells so they can be delivered to the muscles for burning. To maximize this calorie burn even further, "keep the water ice cold," recommends Ellington Darden, Ph.D., exercise scientist and researcher for Biotest Laboratories, Colorado Springs, CO. One gallon of ice-cold water (40°F) requires more than 200 calories of heat energy to warm it to the core body temperature of 98.6°F. Even if you drink only a glass or two, your body will spend extra calories warming up the water. So get out a glass of ice water right now and sip it as you read the rest of this passage. Fat-burning couldn't be more simple. For a change of pace, try iced herb tea, iced decaffeinated black tea, or iced decaffeinated coffee. The key is to avoid beverages with added sugar.

Engage in Do-It-Anywhere "Active Minutes" and Low-Intensity Aerobics

Few of us love to do hour-long exercise sessions, at least not every day. But the truth is, you don't have to get out there and do a full-scale formal workout to reap the benefits of exercise. Just add a few "active minutes" here and there throughout the day. Take the stairs instead of the elevator. Walk an extra block or two. Do some gardening. Rake the leaves. Or sweep the floor. These active minutes increase your metabolism so that you can steadily burn off excess body fat. Plus, they boost your control of dietary fat intake by neutralizing natural cravings for high-fat foods. The big payoff is that these active minutes can reduce your risk of heart disease, high blood pressure, osteoporosis, obesity, and breast and colon cancer, according to a panel of experts convened by the Centers for Disease Control and Prevention and the American College of Sports Medicine. Small amounts of exercise throughout the day may also help alleviate depression, anxiety, and stress.

To reap even more benefits, extend these activities to 20 to 30 minutes. In my household, we try to go for a brisk 30-minute walk after dinner three times a week. Our 4-year-old and 6-year-old daughters sometimes tag along or play on playground equipment within sight nearby. Our 17-year-old son even heads out the door with us on occasion and goes for a run or shoots baskets. Don't let the weather stop you. When it's cold or rainy outside, take your low-intensity aerobics into the family room or living room. Ride a stationary cycle, use a treadmill, or step on a stair-climber. Or try dancing. Our goal is always to make this after-dinner time fun for us and the kids. Do we do this seven days a week? No, yet we always try to spend some active time after dinner, even if it's just 10 minutes of playing "chase" or other get-up-and-go games with the girls.

These active minutes play an important role in the Low-Fat Living Program. The metabolism-boosting effect of any physical activity (including eating) usually returns to a near-resting level within an hour after you've finished the activity. This means that aerobic exercise within 30 minutes of the evening meal will help recharge P.M. fat-burning right as your metabolism begins to fall. Research shows that the combined metabolic lift of eating and exercise within a half-hour of each other may extend P.M. calorie-burning for up to 10 hours.

Use on-the-Spot Distress Blockers

The less distress you hang on to, the greater your metabolic power may be, according to obesity researchers. Why? Because anxious, angry, or hostile people metabolize fats more slowly than others. When you're hit with increased stress, your body responds by releasing adrenaline. That adrenaline stimulates the release of fat from cells throughout the body. In the moments that follow this stress response, you can do one of two things: You can diffuse the stress with relaxation techniques, or you can lapse into a prolonged period of tension in which the stress hormone cortisol is released. When cortisol is released,

BURN CALORIES WITH ACTIVE MINUTES

Think it takes a regimented exercise program to burn calories? Not so. Your body burns calories all day long. Just take a sip of cold water and you'll burn a few. Here's a list of common activities and how many calories you could burn by doing the activity for 30 minutes. If you are a 150-pound woman, you can burn nearly 100 calories just by getting in the kitchen and cooking for a half-hour. When you sit down and eat, you'll burn about 50 calories more.

ACTIVITY	CALORIES BURNED IN 30 MIN.	
	123-LB. PERSON	150-LB. PERSON
Bowling	162	198
Calisthenics (warmups)	126	143
Car washing	117	144
Cooking	75	93
Cycling (9.4 mph)	168	203
Dancing	174	210
Eating	39	48
Food shopping	105	126
Housecleaning	105	126
Ironing clothes	54	66
Playing piano	66	81
Running (10 min. per mi.)	276	336
Typing	45	54
Walking	135	162

it dampens your body's fat-burning processes and may even trigger you to store excess fat in your abdomen. Feel a little tension creeping up your neck? Block it immediately by taking a few deep breaths, briefly stretching, listening to calming music, or any other relaxation technique that works for you. These on-the-spot distress blockers can have a direct impact on your energy level and fat-burning power.

Rely on Fast Firm-Ups for Easy Muscle Toning

Your body is comprised of more than 400 muscles that help make your body look firm and keep it from sagging. If your muscles aren't strong and balanced in relation to each other, they slowly wither away. The biggest price you pay is reduced metabolism. One of the most important fitness discoveries is that well-toned muscles serve a vital role in low-fat living. Well-toned muscles act as fat-burning furnaces, providing a remarkable metabolic boost. "To wage war effectively against body fat," explains Bryant A. Stamford, Ph.D., exercise physiologist and director of the health promotion program at the University of Louisville, "you need to be a good calorie-burning machine 24 hours a day, and having adequate muscle tissue is the only way to do that."

If you're over 40 years of age, muscle-making resistance exercise may be your most effective weapon against weight gain, according to research conducted by William Evans, Ph.D., director of the Noll Physiological Research Center at Pennsylvania State University in University Park. Toning your muscles will raise your resting metabolic rate. That means you'll burn more fat even when you're just sitting around.

Both men and women benefit from muscle-strengthening exercises, says Barbara Drinkwater, Ph.D., past president of the American College of Sports Medicine. "It's healthy that women are now accepting muscles as part of a normal human body."

Like many Americans, you may think that muscle tone requires hours in the gym. The truth is, it doesn't. You can do quick firm-ups like situps and pushups almost anywhere. Try gentle strength training with light weights in your living room. And when you're seated at work, maintain good posture to keep your lower back muscles strong. With simple exercises like these, you'll see and feel quick results.

Get Deeper, High-Metabolism Sleep and Awake Invigorated

Many people think that their muscles grow while they're exercising. Guess again. During exercise, your muscle tissue actually breaks down. Your muscles get the full benefit of that exercise while you're fast asleep. During rest (the deeper, the better), your muscle fibers gain tone and increase their metabolic capacity. That's why it's so important to sleep well. And here's the flip side of the equation: The best way to get deeper, high-metabolism sleep is to do some moderate after-dinner exercise. Research shows that when you increase your physical activity, you improve your quality of sleep. It's no wonder that physical inactivity ranks among the prime causes of insomnia among Americans.

Why is exercise so beneficial to high-quality sleep? "Because exercise raises your body temperature," says Peter Hauri, Ph.D., director of the Mayo Clinic insomnia program in Rochester, Minnesota. "If you increase your body temperature three to six hours before going to bed, the temperature will drop down the most just as you are ready to go to sleep. Then the biological 'trough' deepens, and sleep becomes deeper, with fewer wakenings."

You can achieve this temperature-raising effect just by taking a hot bath or shower within three hours of bedtime, says James A. Horne, Ph.D., a sleep scientist at Loughborough University in Great Britain. But exercise has many other fat-burning benefits, too. So plan on doing a little after-dinner activity whenever possible.

Rev Up Fat-Burning in the Kitchen

Staying active is a key factor in weight control and good health. But being aware of what, when, and how much you eat is the cornerstone of low-fat living. If you can face this challenge and win—all the while enjoying the foods you eat—you'll make the kind of real-world changes that result in increased energy, resistance to disease, and weight loss for the rest of your life. That's where this cookbook comes in. This book takes the fat-trimming, metabolism-revving process of low-fat living into the kitchen. On the following pages, you'll find hundreds of Cooking Hints, Switchbreaks, and Switch Tips—plus great-tasting recipes—that will give you the skillpower to burn fat without even thinking about it.

"One cannot think well, love well, sleep well, if one does not eat well."
—Virginia Woolf, British author

Fat-Burner Switch #3
Fire Up Fat-Burning While You Eat

What did you have for breakfast this morning? Take a minute to think back. Was it a bagel with cream cheese? A bowl of cereal? Eggs, bacon, and toast? You may not realize it, but what you ate this morning influenced the way you are feeling right now—as you read this sentence. Everything you eat over the course of a day—and when and how much you eat—affects your mood, energy level, and brain power for the rest of that day. As you can imagine, over the course of several years, your eating patterns have a huge impact on your overall health.

Researchers have discovered a strong link between diet and disease. Many studies show that you can prevent some of our nation's most widespread illnesses just by eating better. According to the National Cancer Institute, dietary change can prevent 70 to 75 percent of most major cancers. Evidence is mounting to suggest that the healthiest diets include a wide variety of plant foods (vegetables, fruits, legumes, and grains) and only moderate amounts of meat, fish, poultry, and dairy products (especially high-fat ones). The U.S. Department of Agriculture, the American Heart Association, the American Cancer Society, the American Health Foundation, and the National Cancer Institute all endorse such an eating plan.

Have you been trying to lose weight for some time now? Healthy food is a key player in your battle. One of the best ways to burn excess body fat is to rely on whole foods as part of your daily meals and snacks. Since my family and I adopted a low-fat lifestyle in the early 1980s, I have steadily reduced my weight from a size 12 to my natural size 4. And I shed the weight without dieting in just two short years. After each of my pregnancies, I was back into my jeans in under six weeks. Over the years, I realized that permanent weight control requires a balance of four important factors.

- A steady low-fat diet
- Occasional higher-fat treats for emotional comfort
- Regular snacking on healthy nibbles
- Frequent exercise and other activity

The key is balance. Since cooking and eating the Low-Fat Living way, I can consume a little more one night or enjoy a higher-fat favorite (like chocolate) on another night. But the next day, I'm back to my regular eating pattern. And when I do need to shed a few extra pounds, I step up the exercising a bit, limit the high-fat treats, and make sure that I'm snacking on healthy foods. The best thing about the Low-Fat Living eating plan is that it squelches random food cravings, keeping weight in check and appetite under control. Often, there's no temptation to resist.

Go Whole-Grain

Whole-grain foods are a dietary staple for fat-burning and optimum lifelong health. They provide health-boosting fiber, complex carbohydrates for long-lasting energy, and an abundance of vitamins and minerals. "When you eat whole grains, you get more micronutrients like folate, magnesium, and vitamin E," says Walter Willett, chairman of the nutrition department at the Harvard School of Public Health.

SEVEN WAYS TO GET MORE WHOLE GRAINS

Whole grains are the building blocks of healthy diets around the world. We're talking about the basics—things like bread, rice, pasta, and cereal. Here are seven easy ways to make whole grains a healthy habit.

1. Substitute brown rice for white rice (brown rice has a pleasant, nutty flavor).
2. Substitute whole-wheat or whole-grain bread for white bread.
3. For baking, use whole-wheat flour and whole-wheat pastry flour instead of white flour or unbleached flour.
4. Snack on whole-wheat, whole-grain, or rye crackers.
5. Go for whole-grain cold cereals (also, check out the muesli recipes beginning on page 110).
6. Choose hot cereals that are whole grain, like oatmeal, oat bran, and multigrain.
7. Cook up whole-wheat varieties of pasta and couscous (check your local health food store if your supermarket doesn't carry these items).

Studies show that whole grains can help protect your heart by lowering blood cholesterol and blood pressure, controlling blood sugar, and lowering blood triglycerides.

At Harvard University, researchers reported that women who ate more whole grains had a lower risk of diabetes. Studies show that 80 percent of Americans eat whole grains less than once a day. But it's almost effortless to go whole-grain. Pick up some whole-grain crackers instead of the plain white-flour ones. Use whole-wheat tortillas, whole-wheat bread, and other whole-grain breads. When cooking, choose whole grains like brown rice and whole-wheat pastry flour. Unlike refined grains such as white rice and white flour, whole grains still have the beneficial outer layers of the grain intact—along with a majority of the vitamins, minerals, and fiber.

Five to Nine a Day

Here's a slogan worth remembering: "Five to nine a day keeps the doctor away." That's five to nine servings of fruits and vegetables. These easy-to-eat foods are loaded with fiber, vitamins, and some minerals. Researchers have found that people who eat more vegetables are generally healthier. According to a study sponsored by the National Heart, Lung, and Blood Institute, a low-fat diet rich in fruits and vegetables can significantly lower your blood pressure.

Fruits and vegetables are generally good sources of vitamins A and C plus dozens of phytochemicals. These "plant chemicals" are natural antioxidants, which means that they help prevent the undesirable free radicals in your body from damaging healthy cells. In other words, they boost your immune system and help you ward off disease. Researchers at the State University of New York at Buffalo studied premenopausal women in their forties and found that the more vegetables they ate, the less likely they were to develop breast cancer. They con-

TOP SOURCES OF VITAMIN-RICH VEGETABLES

Nutrition experts recommend getting your vitamins from food instead of pills. The main reason? Researchers have discovered that the nutrient compounds in vegetables work together to deliver health benefits. Pills, on the other hand, isolate nutrients from one another. Strive to eat a variety of vegetables over the course of each week. Go heavy on these nutritional standouts.

- Dark leafy greens, like spinach, kale, and Swiss chard
- Deep orange-yellow vegetables, like sweet potatoes and carrots
- Cruciferous vegetables, like broccoli, cauliflower, and brussels sprouts
- Green and sweet red peppers

cluded that various components in the vegetables may have a synergistic effect. Eating five to nine fruits and vegetables a day may also:

- Give you a healthy dose of folate and reduce your risk of cancer
- Increase your intake of beta-carotene and other antioxidants, cutting cancer risk even further
- Increase the soluble fiber and flavonoids in your diet, helping reduce your risk of heart disease
- Pump up your potassium profile so that you're less likely to have a stroke

Bean Cuisine

Eat beans. They are indeed good for your heart, say nutrition experts. Beans and other legumes have been shown to lower cholesterol and triglycerides and help stabilize blood sugar. One cup of beans also provides nearly a full day's supply of folate (400 micrograms), which is great news for pregnant women. A good supply of folate can help prevent birth defects, low birth weight, and premature deliveries. If you're pregnant or nursing, plan a few bean meals for a healthy baby.

What's the difference between a bean and a legume? All beans are legumes, but not all legumes are beans. Legumes, by definition, are the mature edible seeds that grow inside the pods of leguminous plants. Under this large umbrella of legumes falls a wide variety of beans, peas, lentils, and even peanuts. So lentils are legumes, but they're not beans.

Legumes have been known for centuries as poor people's meat because they are an inexpensive source of protein. They're also high in fiber, low in fat, and satisfying. And they keep well. You may want to cash in on the many benefits of this simple foodstuff. Studies show that legumes are a staple in the diets of the world's healthiest and longest-lived people.

Many people avoid beans and legumes because they produce intestinal gas. You can put a lid on most of the gas by soaking dried beans in water and discarding the water before cooking. Soaking helps break down the indigestible carbohydrates on the surface of the beans. Or try lentils and split peas. These legumes don't need presoaking and are often less gas-producing than soybeans and black beans. Experiment with the recipes in this book. The next time you go shopping, look for these legume varieties.

- Adzuki (azuki) beans: small red beans often used in Asian cooking
- Black beans (turtle beans): oval-shaped black beans used in Latin American and Asian dishes
- Black-eyed peas (cowpeas): tan beans with a black spot used often in Southern cooking
- Cannellini beans: large kidney-shaped white beans
- Chickpeas (garbanzo beans, ceci): round, tan beans the size of a hazelnut used in Middle Eastern, Indian, and Latino cooking
- Cranberry beans: small, tan, oval beans that are great in salads and casseroles
- Fava beans (broad beans): similar to lima beans but bigger and very popular in Italian dishes
- Flageolets: pale green baby kidney beans often used in French cooking
- Great Northern beans: largest of the mild-flavored white beans
- Kidney beans: available in a variety of colors and used in many types of dishes from chili to salads

- Lentils: small disk-shaped legumes that don't need presoaking and come in a variety of colors
- Lima beans (butterbeans, Fordhooks): pale green when fresh and white when dried; popular in soups
- Mung beans: very small green beans that are usually eaten sprouted
- Pinto beans: medium beans with faint red and tan specks and the most fiber of any bean
- Red beans: small deep red beans used in Southern dishes, such as red beans and rice
- Soybeans: small, round, tan-colored beans that are eaten fresh or dried; made into baby formula, soybean oil, soy protein, tofu, tempeh, miso, soy sauce, and a variety of other products
- Split peas: small, green, disk-shaped legumes that don't need presoaking and are often used to make soup

Wing It

Poultry can be a high-quality source of lean protein. It's also high in iron and zinc. For the least fat, choose skinless chicken and turkey breasts. Thighs and drumsticks—even without the skin—can have as much saturated fat as red meat. Before cooking, trim any visible fat to reduce your exposure to pesticides and other substances that accumulate in fatty tissues. When possible, buy poultry that is labeled "organic," "free-range," or "naturally raised." These tend to be healthier birds with fewer additives.

Look for ground poultry, too. But watch those package labels—many companies grind a selection of poultry parts, including the skin.

This type of ground poultry can have 10 times as much fat as the ground skinless breast meat. Buy only ground chicken or turkey breasts. Or buy boneless, skinless chicken and turkey breasts and ask your butcher to grind them for you.

Then what do you do with it? Use it to replace half the ground beef in your favorite meat loaf or meatball recipe. You'll save loads of fat grams, and most people can hardly tell the difference. For even more fat savings, replace all of the ground beef with ground turkey. Ground turkey makes a great-tasting burger when combined with chopped onions, garlic, peppers, herbs, spices, and steak sauce.

Go Fishing

More and more Americans are enjoying the bounty of the sea—and for good reason. Many varieties of fish contain a special type of fat called omega-3 fatty acids. Experts say that omega-3's can help lower blood cholesterol, prevent hypertension (high blood pressure), reduce your risk of stroke, and stave off heart disease. A study at the University of Washington in Seattle found that eating 5.5 grams of omega-3 fatty acids a month (about four 3-ounce servings of salmon) can reduce risk of cardiac arrest by 50 percent. A good supply of omega-3's may also reduce the risk of breast cancer and rheumatoid arthritis. Eating fish is good for the soul, too. U.S. government researchers have linked low intakes of omega-3 fatty acids with depression. So give yourself a lift and eat more fish. (Check out the seafood recipes, beginning on page 238, and the pasta-seafood recipes, beginning on page 220.)

Fats, Oils, and Other Spoils

Not all fats are created equal. The secret to eating smart is knowing which types of fat to avoid and relying on the healthier fats. There are three main categories: saturated, monounsaturated, and polyunsatu-

OMEGA FINDER

Nutrition experts recommend omega-3 fatty acids for a strong heart. The best sources are fatty fish like salmon and tuna. You can also find omega-3's in certain vegetable oils, particularly flaxseed oil, which is available in most health food stores.

THIS SEAFOOD (3½ OZ., COOKED)...	HAS THIS AMOUNT OF OMEGA-3'S (G.)...
Atlantic mackerel	2.5
Atlantic herring	1.6
Lake trout	1.6
Anchovies, canned in olive oil	1.4
Albacore tuna (canned tuna)	1.3
Lake whitefish	1.3
Atlantic salmon	1.2
Red sockeye salmon	1.2
Pink salmon	1.0
Atlantic halibut	0.9
Coho (silver) salmon	0.8
Atlantic mussels	0.5
Pacific halibut	0.4
Yellowfin tuna	0.4
Cod	0.3
Shrimp, mixed varieties	0.3
Sea trout	0.3
Walleye pike	0.3
Clams	0.2
Flounder	0.2
Lobster	0.2
Red snapper	0.2
Scallops	0.2
Swordfish	0.2
Sole	0.1
Mahi mahi	0.1
Northern pike	0.1

rated. Saturated fat is the artery-clogging type found in things like cooled pan drippings, lard, shortening, meats, cheese, butter, coconut oil, and palm oil. The American Heart Association recommends limiting saturated fats to 10 percent of your total calorie intake. For most Americans, that means cutting back on this type of fat. Choose lean meats instead of fatty ones and use olive oil instead of butter.

Monounsaturated and polyunsaturated fats are the healthier choices, according to nutritionists. These fats should make up the bulk of your dietary fat intake. Monos and polys are usually liquid at room temperature and are found in things like olive oil, canola oil, sesame oil, nut oils, and avocados. Which one is better—mono or poly? The jury is still out. Researchers at Stanford University School of Medicine analyzed 14 comprehensive studies comparing the effects of monounsaturated and polyunsaturated fats on blood cholesterol. They found that both have similar effects: They lower the sinister low-density lipoprotein, or LDL, cholesterol and leave alone the helpful high-density lipoproteins, or HDLs. The best advice for now is to split the difference between the two, perhaps leaning a little heavier on monounsaturated fats like olive oil and canola oil. I use canola for baking and cooking when recipes need a mild-tasting oil. For dressings, sauces, and sautéing, olive oil is my first choice. Look for unrefined oils, often labeled "cold pressed." These oils are rich in antioxidant vitamin E, which acts as a natural preservative. Heavily refined oils generally have less vitamin E and contain artificial preservatives.

Through the miracle of modern food production, there is yet another type of fat called trans fatty acids. Trans fats are created when liquid oil is hydrogenated (or artificially hardened) by adding extra hydrogen atoms. This process transforms a liquid fat like vegetable oil into a solid fat like margarine, which helps prevent the fat from becoming rancid. The latest research indicates that trans fats may act much like saturated fat in your body, raising your total blood cholesterol. The American Heart Association recommends limiting trans fats as you would limit saturated fat. Go easy on the margarine. Or choose a soft tub-style margarine instead of the stick variety. Tub-style margarine has fewer trans fatty acids.

All fats and oils will spoil or become rancid when exposed to light, heat, or air for extended periods of time. You'll know rancid oils by their off smell and bitter taste. Discard rancid oils. To prevent rancidity, buy smaller quantities of lesser-used oils. For the longest shelf life, store oils in the refrigerator.

Fill Up on H$_2$O

It has virtually no nutritional value. Yet water is one of the most important ingredients in the Low-Fat Living Program. Weight-loss experts agree that a generous daily supply of water can help you lose weight. "Water helps reduce your appetite," says George L. Blackburn, M.D., Ph.D., associate professor of surgery at Harvard Medical School and chief of the Nutrition Metabolism Laboratory at Beth Israel Deaconess Medical Center in Boston. And studies show that drinking water throughout the day can keep your energy level up.

SWITCHBREAK
Skillpower Not Willpower

Here's a supereasy way to maximize your body's fat-burning power. If you read Fat-Burner Switch #2 (see page 9), you know that water curbs your appetite, keeps your body hydrated, and burns a few calories when you drink it ice cold. So get yourself a 16-ounce plastic cup with a wide mouth. (You'll need a wide-mouth cup to fit the ice in comfortably.) If you don't have one, make a note to buy one. This is your special water cup. Don't use it for anything but water. Fill the cup with ice and water and place it right next to you at your workspace. The water will be ice cold, so you might want to rest the cup on a coaster or paper towel to absorb any condensation. Take a few sips of the cold water as soon as you fill the cup. Take a few more sips whenever you feel thirsty, hungry, anxious, or bored. When it's empty, get up and refill the cup with ice and water. Do this four times a day, and you won't have to think about getting the recommended 64 ounces of water a day. You'll do it automatically. If you don't like to get up often, use a 32-ounce plastic cup. You'll only have to fill that twice.

YOUR DAILY CALORIE LIMIT

How many calories should you eat? Use this table to find out. Pick the activity level that best describes you day in and day out. If you're in doubt, choose the lesser of the two. Next, write your ideal healthy weight in the second column (be realistic). Then multiply by the number in the third column. The result is your average daily calorie limit. For instance, if you are a moderately active woman and you want to weigh 140 pounds, your daily limit is 2,100 calories.

IF YOU ARE A...	AND WANT TO WEIGH...	MULTIPLY THE WEIGHT BY...	YOUR DAILY CALORIE LIMIT IS...
Sedentary woman	____lb.	12	____
Sedentary man	____lb.	14	____
Moderately active woman	____lb.	15	____
Moderately active man	____lb.	17	____
Very active woman	____lb.	18	____
Very active man	____lb.	20	____

How much should you drink? Nutritionists recommend getting about 64 ounces of water a day (that's eight 8-ounce cups). More is better, especially if you are exercising, are in hot weather, are in a dry environment (such as an airplane), are drinking caffeine or alcohol, or have a fever. All of these situations can be dehydrating. And if you feel a hunger pang coming on, grab a glass of water. You may not be hungry. You may just be thirsty.

Nutrition Know-How

A little nutrition knowledge goes a long way toward good health. It helps you understand food labels, make smart food choices, and maintain a low-fat lifestyle. It also helps you pick recipes and build menus that meet your health goals. Every recipe in this book comes with a detailed nutritional analysis, including calories, total fat, saturated fat, protein, carbohydrates, fiber, cholesterol, and sodium. Let's take a look at the importance of each nutrient in your diet.

Calories. These are the basic unit of energy found in all foods. No matter what you eat, if your calorie intake is higher than your outflow (if you eat more calories than you burn off), those extra calories will probably be stored as body fat. The first step to lasting weight control is knowing how many calories to eat in a day. It varies from person to person based on activity level, sex, and ideal weight. See "Your Daily Calorie Limit" on facing page to see what's right for you.

The next step is sticking to that calorie level. Here's where a little know-how comes in handy. Fats (like butter and oil) have the most calorie density—about 9 calories per gram. Proteins (like meats and beans) and carbohydrates (like bread, rice, and cereal) both have about 4 calories per gram. So the calories add up faster when you eat fats. Here's the good news: You can eat more volume of food—and take in less calories—if you stick with proteins and carbohydrates.

Total fat. Fats play an important role in body functioning. They carry the fat-soluble vitamins A, D, E, and K to the cells in your body. Plus, some fats (or fatty acids) are necessary to metabolize cholesterol and form hormones such as estrogen. But most Americans consume far more than their bodies' daily requirements.

Health officials recommend limiting dietary fat to no more than 25 to 30 percent of your total daily calories. Generally, that translates into

FAT BUDGETING

The U.S. Department of Agriculture recommends that Americans limit dietary fat intake to no more than 30 percent of total calories. Some health authorities, including the American Heart Association and the American Dietetic Association, say that 20 to 25 percent is more realistic for fat-burning and optimal health. Pick a percentage goal that you're comfortable with, then use the chart below to find your daily fat budget. Your daily calorie intake and percentage goals will determine the total number of fat grams that you can consume in a day.

DAILY CALORIE INTAKE	DAILY FAT BUDGET (G.)		
	20% GOAL	25% GOAL	30% GOAL
1,400	31	39	47
1,500	33	42	50
1,600	36	44	53
1,700	38	47	57
1,800	40	50	60
1,900	42	53	63
2,000	44	56	67
2,100	47	58	70
2,200	49	62	73
2,300	51	64	77
2,400	53	67	80

anywhere from 30 to 80 grams of fat per day, depending on your caloric intake and activity level. But don't go by percentages alone. The percent of calories from fat may be high in a healthy dish that is low in both calories and fat. Here's an example: The typical grilled portobello mushroom (marinated in vinaigrette) has about 1.5 grams of fat and 15 calories per serving. With so few calories and so little fat, the percentage of calories from fat is very high—90 percent. Does that make the mushroom unhealthy? Absolutely not. Its high percentage of calories from fat will be balanced by other foods eaten throughout the day. And that's the key to understanding percentages. The 25 to 30 percent recommendation is a daily or even weekly goal. It's not meant to apply to every food you eat. Generally, it's safer to judge individual foods by fat grams instead of percentages. Look for foods that are low in fat grams and very low in saturated fat grams. (See "Fat Budgeting" on facing page to see how many grams of fat you can eat in a day.)

Protein. Moderate amounts of protein can raise your energy level, quicken thinking, promote attention to detail, and improve reaction time. But studies show that 30 percent of Americans eat too much protein, especially those who indulge in lots of meat, poultry, seafood, and dairy products. How much protein do you need? It varies with sex, activity level, and calorie intake. Women should get between 50 and 80 grams of protein a day. Men need between 60 and 90 grams. If you are very active and have a high calorie intake, shoot for the upper ranges of these numbers. Nutritionists say that it's easy to meet protein needs with a varied low-fat diet (unless you are eating too little food). The American Dietetic Association also reports that vegetarians who eat a variety of foods satisfy their daily protein needs. When you do eat meat, enjoy realistic portion sizes—about 3 ounces of cooked meat, poultry, or seafood per meal. Look for lean cuts of beef and pork, such as tenderloin, top loin, and sirloin. Or take a tip from the American Cancer Society and move these foods to the side of the plate rather than relying on them as the centerpiece. For the most fat-burning power, put the focus on beans, grains, and vegetables.

Carbohydrates. Complex carbohydrates are the mainstay of the Low-Fat Living Program. They provide a lasting source of energy and are good sources of fiber. Look to foods like fresh fruits, vegetables, legumes, and grains. It takes eight times as many calories to turn these foods into body fat as it does to turn dietary fat into body fat.

FIBER: WHERE TO FIND IT

Researchers have found that dietary fiber can lower undesirable low-density lipoprotein, or LDL, cholesterol and reduce your risk of heart disease. Strive for 20 to 35 grams a day. Fiber-rich foods include whole grains (like whole-wheat bread, whole-grain cereal, and brown rice), fresh fruits, vegetables, and legumes (like beans and lentils).

Here are the top sources and their fiber contents.

THIS MUCH FOOD...	PROVIDES THIS MUCH FIBER (G.)...
1 cup cooked navy beans	6.9
1 cup cooked fresh peas	6
1 cup red raspberries	5.8
1/2 cup cooked canned red beans	5
3/4 cup cooked regular oatmeal	4
1/2 cup cooked canned pumpkin	4
1 cup cooked spinach	4
1 baked sweet potato, with skin	3.9
1 cup strawberries	3.8
1/2 cup cooked chickpeas	3.2
2 slices whole-wheat bread	3.2
1 cup cooked pasta	3.1
1 cup cooked brown rice	3
1 raw carrot	3
1 cup cooked corn	3
1 packet instant oatmeal, cooked	3
1/4 cup peanuts	2.9
1 cup sliced peaches	2.8
1 cup cooked wild rice	2.4
1/2 ounce (about 3 tablespoons) sunflower seeds	2.2
1 boiled potato, without skin	2.1

Simple carbohydrates are another story. They provide calories but little or no nutritional value—they are "empty calories." Simple carbohydrates include all types of sugar: refined white sugar, brown sugar, raw sugar, and natural sugars such as maple syrup and honey. Use sugars only in moderation to enhance the flavor of more healthful foods. When it comes to prepared foods, avoid sugary sodas and supersweet snacks. Try fruit juice–sweetened iced teas, juices, and sparkling water.

Dietary fiber. Some people say that it keeps you regular. And it's true. Dietary fiber does help keep your digestive system healthy. According to studies, it may also lower cholesterol levels and reduce colon cancer risk. Fiber has the added advantage of making you feel full and satisfied for extended periods of time, so you get hungry less often. What better way to control calories and reduce fat intake? Health officials recommend getting 20 to 35 grams of fiber a day. That's the equivalent of about four ears of corn or three bowls of whole-grain cereal. Most whole grains, fruits, vegetables, and legumes are good sources of fiber. Eat plenty of these foods and you just can't go wrong. If fiber is new to your diet, add these foods gradually to give your body time to adjust.

Cholesterol. You might avoid it like the plague, but your body needs some to have cholesterol. This waxy lipid substance is essential for the digestion of fat, the formation of estrogen and testosterone, and the internal production of vitamin D. Luckily, the body makes most of the cholesterol that it needs. The rest is dietary cholesterol that you get from foods. And you can get too much. The American Heart Association and the National Institutes of Health recommend getting no more than 300 milligrams of dietary cholesterol per day. That's about one fast-food sausage-and-egg sandwich. Other sources of cholesterol include dairy foods (especially cheese and ice cream), poultry, fish, and meats. To keep your cholesterol in check, use moderate amounts of these cholesterol-containing foods. Note that cholesterol is found only in animal foods, not in plant foods.

Sodium. Sodium is necessary to balance body fluids. But if you get too much, it could result in high blood pressure readings. A high-salt diet has also been linked to osteoporosis because excess sodium causes calcium to be lost from your bones. Yet some health officials say that we've overemphasized salt restriction for Americans as a whole. That's because high blood pressure from salt occurs mostly in people who are salt-sensitive. Researchers say that a high-fat diet, inactivity, and stress are more important risk factors. And osteoporosis is a health issue mostly for postmenopausal women.

So how much sodium is too much? There's no official daily recommendation, but most health experts suggest limiting total intake to 2,400 milligrams a day. That's the equivalent of about 1 teaspoon of salt. Canned goods and salty snacks are among the biggest sources of salt in the American diet. If you're used to canned vegetables, try frozen. The flavor and nutrient content are comparable. To reduce the sodium in canned beans, rinse and drain them before using.

Note: Many of the recipes in this book include the phrase "season to taste" with regard to salt. I usually use just a pinch or two of salt. Most of the flavor comes from other seasonings and condiments. If you are accustomed to using salt as your primary seasoning, check out chapter 7 for easy ways to use other healthy spices and condiments. Once you start using these high-flavor seasonings, you'll find yourself using less salt.

CHAPTER 4

"There is no love sincerer than the love of food."
—GEORGE BERNARD SHAW, IRISH-BORN PLAYWRIGHT

FAT-BURNER SWITCH #4
REVAMP YOUR PANTRY

You just got home. You're starving. You rummage through the cupboards and find a bag of potato chips. Bag in hand, you crack open the refrigerator, and a tub of sour cream dip calls to you. In two seconds, you're seated at the table, plunging a chip into the dip. Half a bag later, you realize that the dip is gone, your fingers are all greasy, and you feel guilty about what you just did to your body.

One of the keys to a successful low-fat lifestyle is knowing your own eating habits. If snack attacks always hit when you get home from a long day's work, plan ahead. Stock the kitchen with fat-fighting snacks like baked tortilla chips and salsa instead of fat-making foods like greasy potato chips and sour cream dip.

Let's take a peek into your lifestyle to get a handle on what foods you should keep on your shelves. Do you leave the house early in the morning and come home late in the evening? Do you work at home? What kinds of foods do you like to eat?

Here's an example: My husband, Robert, works long, intense hours and likes to have fast snacks that include protein for alertness. He often eats muesli for breakfast, varying the fruit with the seasons. For lunch, he loves last night's leftovers reheated in the microwave. I also keep the freezer stocked with vegetarian and turkey burgers, salmon cakes, and crab cakes. In minutes, Robert can enjoy a healthy sandwich with lettuce, tomato, onions, and his favorite condiments. For snacks, he likes whole-grain crackers or homemade bread with dips and spreads like roasted red-pepper hummus. Robert likes cookies, too. The cookie jar in our house is never empty. I fill it with homemade low-fat peanut butter cookies, double chocolate chip cookies, and other low-fat treats that he can nibble on throughout the day.

My typical day is quite different. I have to get the kids to school in the morning, care for the cat and orchids, and see that the house is in decent order. Breakfast is usually on the run. I often have a piece of fresh fruit, a slice or two of homemade bread with low-fat cream cheese, and some low-fat or nonfat yogurt. My snack time is also more structured than Robert's. I usually have one morning snack, such as yogurt or an energy bar. The protein helps boost my alertness in the early hours. For my afternoon snack, I often go with complex carbohydrates like crackers or pretzels. These slightly sweet, whole-grain treats tend to calm me down and get me emotionally ready to meet the kids' needs when they get home. Unlike Robert, I'm able to cook in the kitchen when I feel like eating. He relies mostly on the freezer and microwave for lunch, whereas—on some days—I might have a moment to fix tuna pasta salad or roasted garlic soup. I plan ahead for these types of dishes if I know that I'll have a few extra minutes.

Take a moment now to think about your typical day. Here's a quick quiz.

1. Where do you spend most of your day?

2. What kind of work do you do?

3. Do you prefer sweet snacks or savory snacks? Or both?

4. How much time do you usually have for lunch?

5. Do you have access to a refrigerator? Microwave? Toaster oven?

The answers are crucial. They will determine what kinds of foods you should keep around the house. If you work on the road all day with absolutely no appliances and have only a half-hour for lunch with no other breaks throughout the day, you need ready-to-eat snacks—things like apples, bananas, pretzels, and crackers. Be sure to put plenty of low-fat finger foods on your weekly shopping list. Or make up a batch of spicy tortilla crisps, crunchy pita crisps, or low-fat brownies. All of these dishes travel and keep well without refrigeration.

If your workplace has a few basic appliances, you'll have a lot more flexibility. With a refrigerator, you can keep salads and other foods cold. A microwave opens up a whole world of possibilities for reheating foods, such as crab and corn chowder and tortellini primavera.

Find the low-fat foods that fit your lifestyle and taste preferences. Then stock your kitchen with those foods.

Fill the Shelves with Fat-Burning Foods

Tracking down your eating patterns is one thing. Finding low-fat ways to satisfy your food cravings is quite another.

SWITCHBREAK
Skillpower Not Willpower

Are you at home? Here's a fat-fighting tactic that you can switch on right now. Go to the kitchen. Open up your cupboard or pantry. Take a look at each shelf. Poke through the first layer of foods. Try to get to those items lurking behind everything else. Look for that two-year-old can of cream of mushroom soup. Or that ancient tub of shortening. If you see something with a layer of dust on it, pull that out, too. Seek out the items—especially high-fat or high-sodium foods—that you haven't used in years. Pull them off the shelves and put them in a pile. There's a reason why these items are so far back on the shelf.

Now ask yourself: "Do I need these things? Will I ever use them?" You may find one or two that you might like to keep. Put those back. Throw away the rest. (Save unopened containers for a food drive, homeless shelter, or other charitable organization.) When they're out of the house, those potentially fat-making foods won't be a temptation. What's more, that space on your shelves is prime real estate. Now you'll have room for the fat-burning foods that you use day in and day out. Let's call it spring cleaning—an easy way to switch off the high-fat kitchen and switch on the low-fat kitchen.

Many nonfat products on the market today are bland, overly sweet, or have a bad aftertaste. And some fat-free items are still sky-high in fat-making calories. Shop around for good-tasting low-fat versions of the foods that you use often. You may find that many reduced-fat and low-fat foods taste just as good as the original—especially in the context of other flavors in a recipe. For instance, low-fat mayonnaise tastes great combined with roasted eggplant and garlic in a creamy spread.

Below is a step-by-step tour of the Low-Fat Living kitchen, including the refrigerator, freezer, pantry, and spice rack. That makes it easy to go through your kitchen and revamp each area as needed. Some of the items are staples. Others are flavor-boosters that help you whip up tasty meals in minutes. This list is by no means complete. But it does include ingredients used throughout the Low-Fat Living recipes.

Restock the Refrigerator

The refrigerator houses some of the most important fat-burning ingredients—things like fresh vegetables and fruits, low-fat cheeses and other dairy products, and a variety of flavor-boosting condiments. I stock up on many of these items every week. Make it a habit to plan meals for the week so that you know what fresh produce to buy on your regular shopping trip.

Vegetables, fruits, and herbs. Some staple vegetables in our house include carrots, celery, broccoli, and sweet red peppers. For fruits, I always keep fresh apples, oranges, and grapes on hand. When they're in season, stock up on berries, too. As for herbs, plan on keeping fresh basil, cilantro, and parsley in stock. If you have room for them on your kitchen windowsills, buy herb seedlings from a nursery. You'll have fresh herbs for months.

MAKE IT LAST

Fresh herbs can spoil quickly. To keep herbs fresh for up to two weeks, snip one-quarter inch off the stems and store the whole bunch (stems down, bouquet-style) in a glass of water in the refrigerator. Cover loosely with a plastic bag. To keep vegetables and fruits fresher longer, store them in special green plastic bags designed for this purpose. The green bags are made with a mineral called oya, which absorbs ethylene gas as vegetables and fruits exhale it. The bags help keep refrigerated produce dry and prevent the growth of bacteria. They also reduce vitamin C loss. Produce stored in these bags stays fresh for up to two weeks. Ask for the bags at your grocery store. Two makers of the bags include Frieda's and Evert-Fresh.

Dairy products. Stock up on skim milk, low-fat milk, and nonfat yogurt. (Skim and low-fat milk are higher in calcium than whole milk.) Have small amounts of unsalted butter and half-and-half on hand. If you're used to using whole milk, try 2 percent low-fat milk at first. Once you've adjusted to it, give 1 percent a shot. Gradual changes are the easiest to make.

Cheeses. Keep a variety of part skim–milk cheeses on hand. They're versatile and last well in the refrigerator. I regularly buy part-skim mozzarella, provolone, Cheddar, and Swiss (Jarlsberg light is my favorite). For special dishes, try hot-pepper Monterey Jack and Havarti light cheeses. Small amounts of higher-fat cheeses also come in handy when crumbled onto salads and such. I use feta cheese, blue cheese, Gorgonzola, and Roquefort. For soft cheese, rely on low-fat or nonfat ricotta cheese, cream cheese, and cottage cheese (if you choose nonfat, shop around for a good-tasting brand). Don't forget the Parmesan cheese. I grate it over pasta and salads to pump up the flavor. It has only 1.5 grams of fat per tablespoon.

Condiments and perishables. Here are a few other things to keep in your refrigerator (the condiments will vary according to your tastes): eggs, active dry yeast, low-fat or fat-free tortillas (corn and flour), mustards, low-fat mayonnaise, ketchup, chili-garlic puree (for Asian cooking), natural peanut butter, tahini (sesame seed butter), walnut oil, and low-fat tofu and tempeh (for making vegetarian dishes).

Fill the Freezer

The freezer is every kitchen's little-recognized best ally. I keep mine well-stocked. If I need a meal on the table fast, it's the first place I look.

Poultry. Always keeps some frozen poultry on hand, like skinless chicken breasts (boneless and bone-in), ground turkey breast, a variety of turkey sausages, and sliced turkey breast.

Fish. Frozen fish is occasionally useful, especially if you live in a rural area and have few fresh fish markets nearby. Freeze shrimp and scallops in single-portion containers. Talk to your local fishmonger, too. Some freeze fish like halibut right on the boat. You may be able to buy it fresh-frozen and take it directly to your freezer.

Vegetables, fruits, and herbs. Some frozen vegetables are staples in our house. Corn, peas, and spinach are incredibly versatile and easy to use. During the summer months, we pick fresh fruit (like blueberries, raspberries, and peaches) and freeze it for the winter months. I often freeze fresh herbs, too. They taste better than dried—particularly in soups, sauces, and other cooked dishes. Place your favorite whole fresh herbs in freezer bags and pop them into the freezer. When they're frozen, crunch up the bag to chop the herbs.

Breads. We couldn't live without frozen bread in our house. Bread stays fresh-tasting in the freezer and is available every day of the week. Keep a supply of pita bread, multigrain sandwich bread, and burger buns. Thaw before using. Phyllo dough is also useful to have on hand.

BREAK OUT OF THE RICE MOLD

Whole grains aren't limited to brown rice. Look for unusual varieties in health food stores or in the grain and ethnic-foods aisles of large supermarkets. As for whole-grain flours, try a mixture instead of using all white flour. Whole-wheat pastry flour has a very fine texture that's perfect for desserts and quick breads. Or try a combination of oat flour, brown rice flour, soy flour, millet flour, or barley flour.

UNIQUE VARIETIES
OF RICE

- Black japonica
- Brown basmati
- Jasmine
- Wehani
- Wild rice

UNIQUE GRAINS

- Amaranth
- Buckwheat
- Bulgur
- Kamut
- Millet
- Quinoa
- Spelt

Other freezables. Pack your freezer with these items, too: fat-free egg substitute, low-fat and nonfat frozen yogurt or ice cream, and pastas like tortellini, ravioli, and lasagna sheets. Leave room for leftovers and make-ahead meals.

Pad the Pantry

The pantry offers a wide variety of fat-trimming foods. These items keep so well that there's no reason not to stock up. Refrigerate any items that need to be kept cold after opening. Check the label if in doubt.

Grains and flours. These foods are the foundation of low-fat living. Here are the ones used regularly in the recipes throughout this book: whole-wheat flour, whole-wheat pastry flour, unbleached flour, cornmeal, semolina, rolled oats, brown rice, wild rice, couscous, and barley. Popcorn is also technically a grain, and one of my favorite treats. Use an air popper to make popcorn without added fat.

Pasta. Tastes vary here. Find your favorite pastas and keep them on the shelves. I try to always have some strand pasta (like spaghetti) and some shaped pasta (like ziti). Other favorites include linguini, orzo, fusilli, and Chinese noodles. I always have whole-wheat pasta in the house.

Whole-grain cereals. A variety of low-fat, whole-grain cereals make breakfast a snap. Some cereals make tasty midday snacks, too. Read the labels to find words like "whole-grain," "whole-wheat," and "whole-oat flour."

Whole-grain crackers. These are popular munchies in our house. The kids love them for quick bites. They're great alone or with low-fat dips and spreads. Again, check the label to see that "whole-wheat" or other whole grains are listed early on in the ingredient list. (Food labels list ingredients in the order of quantity used.)

Legumes. Beans make great side dishes, salads, and vegetarian main dishes like chili. Stock up on black beans, chickpeas, kidney beans, pinto beans, black-eyed peas, lentils, and white beans (like Great Northern, navy, and cannellini). Canned and dried nonfat re-fried beans are great for last-minute burritos or snack dips.

Fresh vegetables and fruits. Some fresh fruits and vegetables don't belong in the refrigerator. I keep onions, garlic, and shallots in one basket in a cool, dry, dark place. Potatoes and sweet potatoes are tucked away in another basket. A third holds tomatoes, bananas, and other fruits that ripen at room temperature. (Store potatoes away from onions. The potatoes give off moisture that can cause the onions to sprout.)

Canned vegetables and fruits. Many canned vegetables and fruits make superb flavor-boosters. Artichoke hearts (packed in water), olives, capers, roasted red peppers, mild green chili peppers, salsas, water chestnuts, applesauce, pitted prunes (to make prune puree for low-fat baking), fruit spreads and jams, unsweetened pumpkin, and fruits packed in fruit juice are good examples. Most of these need refrigeration after opening.

Canned tomato products. A definite staple in the low-fat kitchen. Use regular and reduced-sodium varieties of diced tomatoes, whole peeled tomatoes, fat-free tomato sauces, tomato juice, tomato paste, and crushed tomatoes.

Canned seafood products. These come in handy for soups, salads, and sandwiches. I periodically buy quantities of canned tuna, salmon, chopped clams, and bottled clam juice.

Dried fruits. In winter, dried fruits are perfect for baked treats. Lay in a supply of raisins, cherries, cranberries, apricots, prunes, currants, and blueberries.

Nuts and seeds. Small amounts of nuts and seeds add flavor and texture to many foods—especially baked goods. Keep small bags of unsalted almonds, cashews, peanuts, pecans, poppy seeds, pumpkin seeds, sesame seeds, sunflower seeds, and walnuts on hand.

Sweeteners. Sugar, brown sugar, honey, molasses, maple syrup, and confectioners' sugar are all useful in cooking.

Oils. Olive oil is the oil of choice in my kitchen. Use good-quality extra-virgin olive oil for sautéing, for dressings, and special dishes. When a flavorless oil is needed, canola oil fits the bill. Both types are high in heart-healthy monounsaturated fat. If you eat a lot of salads, walnut oil is excellent for dressings—especially those made with fruit vinegars where olive oil tends to be too strong. Toasted sesame oil is indispensable in Asian stir-fries and sauces. Both of these oils are highly perishable and keep best in the refrigerator after opening.

Vinegars. These add a shot of flavor to an array of dishes. Balsamic vinegar is used most often in our house. You may find it useful to have these vinegars as well: white vinegar, red-wine vinegar, white-wine vinegar (it has a milder flavor than red-wine vinegar, so you can use more vinegar and less oil for salad dressing), sherry-wine vinegar, raspberry vinegar, and rice-wine vinegar (for Asian dishes).

Wines and nonalcoholic wines. Wines add flavor when cooking low-fat. I use dry red, dry white, and sherry as flavor-enhancing ingredients. Nonalcoholic varieties make a fine substitute if alcohol is a problem for you.

Dry goods. These include baking basics like baking powder, baking soda, arrowroot or cornstarch, unsweetened cocoa powder, and Dutch-process cocoa powder (for richer chocolate desserts).

Miscellaneous items. The pantry shelves are home to several other timesaving and flavor-boosting items. These keep well, so be sure to have them on hand: no-stick spray (canola oil and olive oil), nonfat chicken and vegetable broths, dried hot chili peppers, dried mushrooms, sun-dried tomatoes, evaporated skim milk, vanilla extract, almond extract, lemon extract, unflavored gelatin, soy sauce, Worcestershire sauce, hot-pepper sauce, and taco shells.

Spice Rack

Now, to the seasonings. Following are the dried spices and herbs used most often in my recipes. You may come across a few others as you try different dishes. Stock up on those when you need to. I keep dried grated lemon rind and orange rind in my spice rack for the occasions when I don't have fresh ones. For maximum flavor and shelf life, store dried spices and herbs in a cool, dry place away from the stove and out of the light.

MUST-HAVE SEASONINGS

Here's what I keep in my spice rack at all times. These seasonings create flavor without fat.

SPICES

- Allspice, ground
- Chili powder
- Cinnamon, ground
- Cloves, ground
- Coriander, ground
- Cumin, ground
- Curry powder
- Garlic powder
- Ginger, ground
- Mustard powder
- Nutmeg, whole and ground
- Paprika
- Pepper, ground red
- Peppercorns, black for grinding
- Red-pepper flakes
- Saffron

HERBS

- Basil
- Bay leaves
- Chives
- Dill
- Italian herb seasoning
- Marjoram
- Oregano
- Rosemary
- Sage
- Tarragon
- Thyme

CHAPTER 5

"Hunger is the teacher of the arts and the bestower of invention."
—PERSIUS, ROMAN POET

FAT-BURNER SWITCH #5
SHOP SMART TO SAVE TIME, MONEY, AND ENERGY

Americans spend an average of 99 minutes a week shopping for food, according to the Food Marketing Institute. And most of us go into the store without knowing what we want to buy. That means we spend more than an hour and a half each week on "splurchases"—or unplanned splurge purchases—say food industry analysts. What's the secret to avoiding high-fat impulse purchases, spending less time in the store, and slashing your grocery bill? Shop the Low-Fat Living way. Here's how.

Make a plan. It may sound daunting, but the trick to quick shopping is planning ahead for the week's meals, according to Renee Bessinger, clinical dietitian at Duke University's Diet and Fitness Center in Durham, North Carolina. "That way you won't waste time in the store thinking about what to buy." Keep it simple. Jot a few notes like "Monday: turkey burgers and mashed potatoes. Tuesday: bean burritos and rice. Wednesday: spaghetti and salad." If the whole week seems too far ahead, start by planning just three dinners.

Shop once a week. Constantly driving to and from the store is a big time-waster. It also wastes gasoline and money. Plan on one weekly shopping trip. Here's where jotting down meals for the week comes in handy. You'll know exactly what you need to buy so you don't have to run back for a single ingredient.

Don't be listless. A shopping list saves mountains of time in the grocery store. Most stores carry more than 30,000 items. You could spend days just looking at them all. Go in with a list and you'll know just what to buy. I keep a running list on the refrigerator door. Whenever we run out of something, it gets added to the list. My family has learned that if they want something, they have to write it down. The list also helps me avoid impulse buys, which saves money and calories. Want to cut your shopping time even further? Organize your shopping list by your supermarket's layout.

Eat before you shop. Never go to the store hungry. Everything looks and sounds delicious when you're hungry, and you can end up buying high-fat foods that you wouldn't buy otherwise. Have a snack like a bagel or some crackers before you head out.

Shop after dinner. You can avoid both the crowds and the cravings by shopping right after the evening meal. That's when most people are at home cleaning up or relaxing. "Tuesday through Thursday after 7:00 P.M. is your best bet," says Dayle Hayes, nutrition consultant at the Deaconess Medical Center in Billings, Montana. "On Mondays, many stores still haven't restocked their shelves after the weekend rush."

Go local. Shop the same store whenever possible. You'll know where everything is and won't waste time hunting down items. If you go to a new store, ask the manager for a printed layout of the store so you can see at a glance where specific items are kept.

SWITCHBREAK
Skillpower Not Willpower

Grab a pen and some paper. Believe it or not, these are important fat-burning tools. Think about what you'd like to eat in the next few days. Don't think too hard. Just let your taste buds be your guide. Let yourself crave foods. Think of one or two dinners that you'd enjoy eating. Add items to the list as they come to mind. If you know of low-fat versions of the foods that you crave, write them down. Hungry for chocolate? Write down cocoa powder. Dreaming of nachos piled high with cheese? Jot down whole-wheat tortillas and low-fat Monterey Jack cheese. Thinking about what you'd like to eat before you go into the store helps you find low-fat ways to satisfy those desires.

BE A LABEL READER

Federal regulations require most foods to carry a Nutrition Facts label that tells all. A quick glance can tell you whether to add the item to your cart or put it back on the shelf. Here's what to look for.

Nutrition Facts

Serving Size
Servings Per Container

Amount Per Serving

Calories 0	Calories from Fat 0

	% Daily Value*
Total Fat 0g	**0**%
Saturated Fat 0g	**0**%
Polyunsaturated Fat 0g	
Monounsaturated Fat 0g	
Cholesterol 0mg	**0**%
Sodium 0mg	**0**%
Total Carbohydrate 0g	**0**%
Dietary Fiber 0g	**0**%
Sugars 0g	
Protein 0g	

Vitamin A 0%	•	Vitamin C 0%
Calcium 0%	•	Iron 0%

* Percent Daily Values are based on a 2,000 calorie diet. Your daily values may be higher or lower depending on your calorie needs:

	Calories:	2,000	2,500
Total Fat	Less than	0g	0g
Sat Fat	Less than	0g	0g
Cholesterol	Less than	0mg	0mg
Sodium	Less than	0mg	0mg
Total Carbohydrate		0g	0g
Dietary Fiber		0g	0g

Check the serving size. Serving size is listed right at the top. Make sure that it's the amount you will actually eat. For instance, the standard serving size on many ice cream packages is $^1/_2$ cup. Most folks eat at least twice that, which means doubling the rest of the numbers on the label.

Stay to the left. The numbers on the left side of the label give grams per serving rather than "percent Daily Value." Once you know the basic range of calories and fat grams that you want to stay within every day, these numbers tell you instantly where you stand.

Look at calories per serving. Calories *do* count. Even fat-free items can be sky-high in fat-making calories. According to experts, most women should eat 2,000 calories a day—or less—to maintain body weight.

Check for fat and saturated fat grams. Be sure that the number of fat grams fits within your daily eating plan. Nutritionists say that most women should get fewer than 60 total fat grams a day.

Stock up on nonperishable favorites. Many of us eat the same foods each week, says Michele Tuttle, director of consumer affairs at the Food Marketing Institute in Washington, D.C. Here is Tuttle's tip for saving time and cutting your weekly shopping list by as much as 50 percent: Buy your favorite nonperishables monthly instead of weekly. "If you eat pasta twice a week, buy 10 boxes of pasta and 10 jars of sauce at once."

Keep an eye on cholesterol. Experts recommend getting fewer than 300 milligrams of cholesterol a day.

Watch out for sodium. Many low-fat foods—like some brands of baked tortilla chips—add flavor by loading on the salt. Strive to keep total sodium intake to fewer than 2,400 milligrams a day.

Be a fiber finder. The National Cancer Institute recommends getting 20 to 35 grams of fiber a day. When buying cold cereal, look for those that supply at least 5 grams of fiber per serving. Other good sources include whole-grain bread and pasta.

Get your vitamins. Nutrients like calcium, iron, and vitamins A and C are listed at the bottom. Look for foods that supply at least 20 percent of the Daily Value.

Scan the ingredient list. Ingredients are usually listed outside the Nutrition Facts label, but they are important. They're listed from the greatest quantity to the least, which can reveal whether the food has more sugar than flour in it, for instance. The list is especially useful when buying whole-grain foods like bread and crackers. Check to see that the whole grain is listed first. If not, the food may contain only trace amounts.

Avoid the fat-free fallacy. Foods labeled fat-free are not always a dream come true. Many are loaded with calories. That said, keep in mind that many reduced-fat, nonfat, and low-fat products can help you create good-tasting, healthy meals. Low-fat varieties of milk, cheese, and other dairy products keep fat consumption down while adding smooth, creamy textures.

Buy low-fat foods. There's no doubt that a hunk of meat will cost you more money than a box of pasta. You can even buy a few dozen oranges for the price that one tub of double-chocolate-chunk ice cream will cost you. The bottom line is, if you buy plenty of grains, fruits, and vegetables, you will save money while you fire up fat-burning.

Get What You Need

Don't waste time searching the aisles for items that you can't find. Ask for help. Don't settle for substandard fare. If the produce that's on the shelf isn't up to par, for instance, ask if there's more in the back (often, they haven't unpacked their whole order).

If you would like your store to carry a new item, ask for the grocery manager. This person is responsible for buying all the items stocked on the grocery store shelves. Tell this person that you could go to another store for the item but that you'd rather shop at their store. Many grocery managers are very willing to stock items that you buy regularly.

Here's where to locate some harder-to-find items in the typical grocery store.

- Roasted red peppers are usually stocked with the olives, capers, and pickles in the canned goods aisle. Some stores also stock them in the international aisle.
- Evaporated skim milk is often found with the condensed milk in the baking aisle.
- Fat-replacers (such as prune puree and Lighter Bake) are often stocked with the oils in the baking aisle.
- Buttermilk powder is great when you don't need an entire container of fresh buttermilk. It keeps well and you just add water to get the amount that you need.
- Some large supermarkets carry whole-wheat pastry flour with other specialty flours in the baking aisle. If you can't find it, your local health food store is sure to have it.

"Cooking with love means never having to feel chained to your stove, never feeling that getting dinner on the table is a teeth-gritting experience rather than a charming interlude."

—FRANCIS ANTHONY, THE "LOVE CHEF," ITALIAN-AMERICAN COOKBOOK AUTHOR

FAT-BURNER SWITCH #6
GET KITCHEN SAVVY WITH FAT-TRIMMING TOOLS AND SAFETY TIPS

Time can be a powerful fat-burning ally. Many folks slip into old high-fat habits because they don't have the time to cook healthfully. When you're armed with timesaving tools and fat-cutting techniques, low-fat cooking gets a lot easier. Take it from the taste-testers who worked on this book. Many found that once they got used to these methods, low-fat cooking was as quick and simple as high-fat cooking.

Imagine wanting a rich chocolate brownie. If you have within reach a food processor and some no-stick spray (and a few other simple in-gredients), you can whip up my Chewy Brownies in 15 minutes of hands-on time. Just the simple physical activity of preparing the snack raises your metabolism and burns more fat, too. That's the greatest thing about the Low-Fat Living Program. Every recipe doubles your fat-burning power. Your body burns fat as you move around the kitchen preparing the food. And the food itself is low-fat. You can eat more of the fresh food that you love and shed pounds at the same time.

Seven Timesaving Tools for the Low-Fat Kitchen

Most of the items that you need for low-fat cooking are right in your local supermarket, department store, or kitchen store. I consider the following to be indispensable.

No-stick pans. No-stick cookware dramatically cuts the amount of fat required when cooking and baking. I recommend three basic no-stick pans: a deep 12-inch skillet for sautéing, pan-searing, and browning meats; a medium saucepan for sauces and soups; and a griddle for pancakes and burgers. If you stir-fry often, you may want to stock a large wok. For baking, a no-stick loaf pan, muffin pan, cake pans, or baking sheets will do the trick. The rest of your pots and pans needn't be no-stick since you'll use them mostly for dishes that have plenty of liquid.

Sharp knives. Good-quality knives are a great asset to quick low-fat cooking. Chopping and slicing is much faster (and more fun) when your knives are sharp and easy to use. Find knives that feel good in your hands. Most cooks use just three: an 8-inch chef's knife for slicing and chopping, a paring knife, and a serrated knife for bread or tomatoes. To keep knives sharp, pick up an inexpensive handheld sharpener.

Food processor. You'll thank yourself for investing in this timesaving appliance—it makes most cooking jobs a breeze. I use mine for chopping, slicing, and grating vegetables; pureeing soups and sauces; chopping fresh herbs and nuts; mixing salad dressings; making bread crumbs; and making bread dough.

SWITCHBREAK

Skillpower Not Willpower

Take a moment right now to peek inside your cutlery drawer or to look at your knife rack. Take this book with you. Find your favorite knife—the one you use most often for slicing and chopping. Pull this page away from all the other pages in this book. Hold this page in one hand and the knife in your other hand. With a quick slicing motion, make a small slit at the top of this page. Did your knife make a clean, quick cut? If not, it could turn simple cutting tasks into time-consuming chores. What's more, dull knives are a potential safety hazard because they slip off foods easily.

Spend the next minute sharpening your knife. If you don't have a sharpener, make a note to buy an inexpensive one. After sharpening the knife, return it to the rack. (If you have a knife drawer, cut a piece of cardboard the size of the blade to make a protective sheath for the blade.)

What's the purpose of all this? Quite simply, a sharp knife makes low-fat cooking easier. Chopping vegetables and trimming fat from chicken are a breeze with a well-kept blade. Keep your knives sharp and you'll be more willing to whip up low-fat food rather than rely on a high-fat favorite. The slit at the top of this page makes a great reminder.

Garlic press. I use a fair amount of garlic in my recipes for flavor. And why not? Studies show that garlic can help lower your cholesterol and blood pressure levels. A garlic press takes away the chore of mincing the fresh cloves. Many presses don't even need the cloves to be peeled. Just pop the unpeeled cloves into the press and squeeze.

Salad spinner. Drying fresh greens like lettuce and spinach can eat up lots of kitchen time. A salad spinner is the perfect solution. With a few spins, the greens are dry. No more wet towels or drying the leaves one by one. The spinner is an ideal place to store salad greens, too. Just leave the greens in the spinner and store the whole thing in the refrigerator. The spinner will keep greens fresh and dry for up to two weeks.

Citrus juicer. This tool is the quickest, least expensive way to enjoy the zesty flavors of fresh lemon, lime, and orange juices. Most plastic juicers fit neatly over a 2-cup glass measure to catch the juice. An added bonus is that the juicer screens out the seeds.

Small-holed citrus zester. Citrus rind, or zest, adds refreshing flavor to many low-fat recipes. Rather than mincing the rind, this inexpensive kitchen tool finely grates the rind in seconds.

Low-Fat Living Cooking Techniques

Most home cooks habitually use large amounts of butter, margarine, or oil in their cooking. There are alternatives to cooking with loads of fat. Sometimes just a small amount of fat and high heat will achieve similar results. A few other tricks come in handy, too. Here are the techniques that I use most often.

Toasting. Briefly toasting nuts and spices intensifies their flavors. With nuts, that means you can save fat grams by using less to get the same amount of flavor. The easiest way to toast nuts and spices is to place them in a dry skillet over medium-high heat for 2 to 4 minutes, or until lightly browned and fragrant. Shake the pan often to avoid burning.

Roasting. Like toasting, roasting brings out rich flavors, but in the oven instead of on the stove. I use this method mostly for vegetables. Here's the basic technique: Place the oven rack on the lowest shelf and heat the oven to 500°F. Place the vegetables in a single layer in a baking dish and coat them with no-stick spray or a small amount of olive oil. Add herbs, salt, pepper, and other seasonings as desired. Cook the vegetables on the bottom rack of the oven until slightly soft and golden brown. Most root vegetable like potatoes, carrots, and turnips need about 30 minutes. Tomatoes, peppers, and eggplant take a little less time. This roasting technique is featured in many of my recipes, including Roasted Winter Vegetables, Roasted New Potatoes, and Pineapple Salsa.

Steaming. This moist-heat cooking method is perfect for delicate foods like fish and some vegetables. The food cooks gently over boiling water without a drop of added fat. Bring one inch of water to a boil in a saucepan. Place the food in a steamer basket and insert the basket into the pan. Cover and steam until the food is cooked through—it's that simple. To steam foods in the oven, use parchment paper or foil. Wrap a piece of fish or poultry in parchment paper or foil and bake at 350° to 400°F until the food is cooked through. The food steams in its own juices (and whatever flavorings you choose to add, such as herbs, spices, citrus juice, or stock).

Poaching. I use this technique often for fish. It imparts light, fresh-tasting flavors without added fat. Poaching is similar to steaming, except that the food cooks right in the liquid. For the most flavor, season the poaching liquid with fresh herbs, spices, citrus juice, broth, or wine.

Pan-searing. Frying takes on a whole new look in the Low-Fat Living kitchen. In place of the traditional deep-frying pan filled with oil, I achieve similar results with a no-stick skillet, medium-high heat, and a small amount of oil or no-stick spray. Known as pan-searing, this method creates a crispy brown outer layer while the food stays moist and tender inside. For a taste, try my Pan-Seared Crab Cakes.

Oven-frying. Here's another fantastic low-fat alternative to traditional frying. Coat the food with no-stick spray and bake it in a hot oven (450° to 500°F) until brown and crispy. You can oven-fry most foods that are typically deep-fried in oceans of fat—like french fries, breaded chicken, and batter-dipped vegetables. For breaded foods, coat the food with egg whites first (leave the yolks out to avoid the fat and cholesterol). Dredge the food in the breading, then generously coat with no-stick spray. Place the food on a baking sheet and bake until crisp. This method works wonders in recipes like Chicken Parmesan Strips and Buttermilk-Batter Baked Chicken.

Sautéing. I usually sauté in a no-stick skillet with a small amount of oil or no-stick spray. There's no need for tablespoon upon tablespoon of fat. I sometimes combine a little oil with broth or sherry. If the food starts to stick, add a bit more broth. To prevent the food from absorbing too much oil before it is cooked, heat the oil in the pan before adding the food. You should hear a sizzle right as the food goes into the pan.

Cooking Safety

Food-related poisoning is an increasing concern among today's home cooks. Twenty-five Americans will die today—and another 16,000 will become ill—from something they ate. There's no need for a scare, but simple precautions can help reduce risk of contamination in your own kitchen. Red meats, chicken, turkey, fish, and eggs are the most likely culprits. To fend off food-borne illness, here's what health experts at the Centers for Disease Control and Prevention and the U.S. Department of Agriculture advise.

Eggs. These kitchen staples are used in everything from breakfast to dessert. So it's important to handle them with care.

- Buy eggs refrigerated and store them in the refrigerator. The greatest risk of contamination occurs in eggs that have not been refrigerated.

- Avoid foods and beverages containing raw or undercooked eggs. Steer clear of eggnog, soft-boiled or runny eggs, Caesar salad made with raw eggs, and mousses and uncooked pie fillings containing raw eggs. No matter how much they beg, don't let the kids lick the spoon after making a batter that contains raw eggs.

- Always cook eggs until the white is set and the yolk begins to thicken (about 145°F).

- Eat eggs immediately after cooking them.

- Wash hands, utensils, and surfaces with soap and hot water after contact with raw eggs.

Poultry. At least 25 percent of the chickens sent to market contain enough salmonella bacteria to make you sick. Some contain enough bacteria to kill you. Take these simple steps to avoid getting pecked by salmonella poisoning.

- Thaw frozen poultry in the refrigerator—not at room temperature.

- Store thawed poultry in the refrigerator until ready to use.

- Never leave raw poultry out on the counter—even when marinating.

- Never baste poultry with uncooked marinade.

- High heat kills bacteria. If you plan to serve the marinade as a sauce, bring it to a boil first.

- Cook poultry thoroughly. When fully cooked, the juices will run clear when you pierce the flesh with a fork, and the inner thigh will no longer be pink. For surefire safety, insert a meat thermometer into the thickest part of the inner thigh without touching bone. It should read at least 180°F.

- Stuff your bird with caution. Experts advise against it. Even though the poultry may have gotten hot enough to kill bacteria, the stuffing inside may not have. Here's a safe alternative: Put that stuffing into a baking dish instead and bake it alongside the bird. Baste the stuffing occasionally with chicken stock to get that cooked-in-the-bird flavor. If stuffing the turkey is an important tradition in your household, take steps to avoid contamination. Stuff the bird just before it goes in the oven. That gives bacteria very little time to move from the poultry to the stuffing. Place the stuffing in loosely so that heat can circulate easily. To check for doneness, insert a meat thermometer into the center of the stuffing. It should reach a temperature of 165°F.

- If you plan to eat poultry leftovers, get them into the refrigerator immediately.

Meat. Like poultry, meat can become contaminated with bacteria such as salmonella and *E. coli*. Contamination occurs most often in ground beef because bacteria on the surface of the meat ends up in the entire mixture when it gets ground. Handle meats as you would handle poultry (see the tips above). For added safety, experts also recommend the following.

- Avoid eating raw meats in dishes like steak tartare and carpaccio.

- Avoid undercooked meats like very rare steaks and hamburgers. The meat should reach an internal temperature of 165°F to kill bacteria.

Seafood. Raw and undercooked shellfish is, by far, the biggest seafood safety hazard. Raw shellfish accounts for more than 90 percent of seafood poisoning cases, according to the Food and Drug Administration. So don't be intimidated by all seafood. Some of the most popular seafood is also the safest, like shrimp, cod, flounder, haddock, salmon, and canned tuna. It's also a good idea to keep fish on the menu because many varieties are high in omega-3 fatty acids, which help protect your heart. To avoid problems from seafood, take these tips from the pros.

- Avoid raw fish such as the fish found in sashimi and some sushi (when ordering sushi, ask that it be made with vegetables instead of raw fish).
- Avoid raw undercooked shellfish like oysters and clams.

Kitchen Safety

Smart food handling is the best way to keep bacteria from spoiling your party. It also helps to be a clean cook. Germs left on countertops, sponges, and towels can migrate to your hands and utensils. Keep germs out of your kitchen by cleaning up regularly. Here are some other kitchen pointers from food professionals.

- Use antibacterial soap and hot water to clean surfaces that have come in contact with raw fish, eggs, poultry, and meat.
- Use an antibacterial (or self-disinfecting) sponge. Rinse with hot water and squeeze dry when not in use. Don't wait until the sponge falls apart to replace it. I replace mine about once a week.
- For maximum safety, use wooden instead of plastic cutting boards. Heat old wooden boards in the microwave for 5 minutes to kill any bacteria deep inside the wood (don't worry; there are no ill side effects from microwaving your wooden cut-

ting board). If you use a plastic board, clean it in the dishwasher after each use. Or scrub it well with antibacterial soap and hot water.

- Use a separate cutting board for meats, poultry, and seafood. If you only have one board, mark one side for meats and the other for vegetables.

- Clean seafood and trim poultry in the sink. That makes washing up and disinfecting a cinch.

- Wash dish towels regularly. Moist and warm dish towels—especially those used to wipe up remnants of food—make an ideal breeding ground for bacteria. In a few hours, hundreds of bacteria multiply into millions and may be transferred to your hands, dishes, utensils, and food. Keep a good supply of clean dish towels in the kitchen. Launder damp or soiled towels regularly in hot water and dry them in a hot dryer. Or use disposable paper towels for cleaning up spills from milk, eggs, meats, poultry, and raw seafood.

CHAPTER 7

"Spice a dish with love and it pleases every palate."

—PLAUTUS, ROMAN PLAYWRIGHT

FAT-BURNER SWITCH #7
SPICE UP YOUR LIFE WITH WINNING FLAVOR COMBINATIONS

A common fear about low-fat food is that it tastes bland and boring. There's no doubt that fat enhances flavor in foods, but many other nonfat, high-flavor ingredients can do the same thing. I'm talking about taste-ticklers like fresh citrus, hot chili peppers, balsamic vinegar, and sun-dried tomatoes. These foods are fat-free yet packed with flavor. The secret to the Low-Fat Living Program is using herbs, spices, and other seasonings that make up for the absence of fat. These flavor-boosters can make the difference between enjoying low-fat food and falling back on your high-fat habits. In many cases, you end up with even more flavor than you'd get with traditional high-fat dishes. And here's the kicker: Some of the spices used in the Low-Fat Living recipes actually raise your metabolism and help burn more body fat.

More Ingredients, Not More Work

It's no wonder that high-fat recipes often have few ingredients. Just one or two high-fat items will do the trick. For low-fat recipes, the reverse is often true. More ingredients are needed to create the intense flavors that most folks are used to. But just because a recipe has a lot of ingredients doesn't mean that it's difficult to prepare or is more work. It's really no trouble to add a few more herbs and spices as you put a dish together.

Take a traditional pasta recipe, for example. The sauce is often made using mostly oil, butter, or cream—with a touch of an herb or spice. In a low-fat recipe, the pasta can be sauced with just a tablespoon of oil or butter, some nonfat chicken or vegetable broth, and an abundance of herbs, spices, and other seasonings—things like fresh basil, fresh parsley, saffron, grated lemon rind, and freshly ground black pepper. The result is a low-fat, high-flavor dish. No more steps are required. Just adding a few extra flavorings pumps up the volume on your taste buds.

Using Dried Herbs and Spices

Dried herbs and spices are the workhorses of the Low-Fat Living kitchen. Countless savory and sweet dishes depend on their flavors. Can you imagine zucchini bread without ground ginger and ground cloves? Here's how to get the most bang for your buck when using dried herbs and spices.

Buy only a little. Herbs and spices begin to lose potency after about a year. For maximum flavor, buy only small quantities. Avoid the jars at the grocery store when possible; they cost a small fortune. To save money, go to the bulk bins at your local health food store and get only as much as you need. Most health food stores sell a large quantity of herbs, so they should be fresh. If in doubt, ask the staff when the herbs were last restocked.

Keep 'em tight; no heat, no light. To prolong the shelf life of dried herbs and spices, store them in tightly covered containers. Keep the containers away from heat, moisture, and light. In other words, away from the stove.

Crush herbs for more flavor. To release the essential oils (and flavor) of dried herbs, crush them between your fingers as you add them to the dish.

Add them early. Dried herbs, especially bay leaves, are best added early on in the cooking process. That gives the herbs time to rehydrate and release their flavor.

Add them late. Some spices such as cinnamon and black pepper can taste bitter when subjected to high heat. If you're using high heat with these spices, add them toward the end of cooking time.

Toast them first. Toasting dried spices like cumin and curry powder heightens their flavor. Heat the spices in a dry skillet over medium-high heat for 2 to 4 minutes, or until fragrant and slightly browned. Be careful not to burn the spices, especially if they're already ground. If using whole spices, crush them in a mortar and pestle after toasting.

Using Fresh Herbs

Fresh herbs are nature's fat-free condiments. They're packed with bright, clean tastes that make low-fat food a symphony on your tongue. Whenever you can, go for fresh herbs instead of dried. Maximize flavor with these hints.

Buy 'em green. Look for bright green leaves with no traces of moisture or browning. If the leaves look wilted, the herbs are about to lose their flavor.

Store them like flowers. Fresh-cut herbs last longest in the refrigerator. Place the whole bunch—stems down, bouquet-style—in a container filled halfway with water. Cover loosely with plastic wrap and refrigerate. Stored this way, fresh herbs last for up to two weeks.

Deep-freeze them. Herbs like basil can be hard to find fresh in winter. The next best thing is frozen. When you have the chance, freeze fresh herbs. Place the fresh leaves in plastic freezer bags and press out the air. Seal the bags and freeze. Just squeeze the bag to crumble the frozen leaves, then add them to soups, stews, sauces, and casseroles.

CILANTRO GETS THE LEAD OUT

Fresh cilantro is a key flavoring ingredient in salsa and other foods in Mexican, Thai, and Vietnamese cooking. The herb is also a potential remedy for lead and mercury poisoning—and may even aid in cancer treatment, according to research conducted by Yoshiaki Omura, M.D., Sc.D., director of medical research at the Heart Disease Research Foundation and president of the International College of Acupuncture and Electro-Therapeutics in New York City. Dr. Omura discovered that cilantro is a powerful chelating agent, which means that it binds to heavy metals and helps flush them from your system—without requiring injections. He also found that cancer cells contain mercury and can be better treated if the mercury is eliminated. As a preventive measure against lead and mercury poisoning, Dr. Omura recommends adding 1 to 2 teaspoons of chopped fresh cilantro to your everyday cooking.

Grow your own. Many herbs grow well on sunny windowsills during the winter. I keep a pot of basil in my kitchen all winter long.

Toss them in late. Fresh herbs taste best when added toward the end of the cooking process. Most need only a minute or two to heat up and release flavor. Of course, if you're making an uncooked marinade, dressing, or salsa, add the herbs with the rest of the ingredients.

Fresh out? Use dried. When fresh herbs aren't available, use dried but reduce the amount by a third. For instance, if the recipe calls for 1 tablespoon of fresh oregano, use 1 teaspoon dried. This is a general guideline, not a steadfast rule. Some herbs are more intense than others. Let your taste buds have the final say.

Sweet Stuff

Sugar has the unique quality of neutralizing bitter, sour, and salty tastes. Small amounts of sugar can greatly improve the flavor of foods

SUGAR DOESN'T MAKE YOU FAT BUT CALORIES CAN

New research suggests that sugar itself doesn't make you fat or hyperactive. Researchers at Duke University Medical Center's Steadman Nutrition Center in Durham, North Carolina, found that a diet high in sugar has no effect on weight, mood, or behavior. Cavities are the biggest health problem linked to sugar consumption. However, a sugar-laden diet can cause weight gain if you exceed healthy daily calorie limits. Lots of sweet snacks and soda add empty calories that can be stored as body fat if the calories aren't worked off.

without adding loads of calories. That's why many savory recipes call for a teaspoon of sugar (which has only 15 calories). Here are some uses for a pinch of the sweet stuff.

Tomato sauce. Tomato-based sauces often taste acidic from the natural acids in tomatoes. A pinch of sugar mellows the acidity and makes a much better-tasting sauce.

Spinach dishes. The big leaves of spinach sold in most grocery stores are grown in hot, dry weather, which can give them a bitter taste. A sprinkling of sugar added during cooking takes off the bitter edge and rounds out the flavor.

Salty soup. Oversalted your soup or stew? Try adding a pinch of sugar. It counterbalances the salty flavor. Remember to add just a pinch. If you toss in too much, the calories will add up quickly, and the soup will begin to taste sweet.

Salt—Friend and Foe

Salt has been a flavor-enhancer and food preservative for thousands of years. It inhibits the growth of bacteria and mold in canned and pickled foods, cheeses, and meats. Salt also controls the rate of yeast development when raising bread dough. And it helps stabilize color, flavor, and texture in vegetables. What's more, it tastes good.

Unfortunately, the great taste of salt has gotten us into trouble. Almost every processed food on the market contains salt. Every restaurant and diner in America has a saltshaker on the table. Every bag of fast food contains a few packets of salt. Americans consume three times the amount of salt established as healthy by the Senate Select Committee on Nutrition. Here's how to keep a lid on salt consumption in your kitchen.

A little dab'll do ya. Salt is a powerful seasoning. When using it in savory recipes or at the table, add just enough to bring out the other flavors in the dish. For whole recipes, that usually means adding less than ½ teaspoon. At the table, a pinch (or ¹⁄₁₆ of a teaspoon) is all that you need.

Expand your palate. Get into the habit of reaching for other flavorings instead of salt. Balsamic vinegar, lemon juice, soy sauce, mustard, or salsa may have the flavor punch that your taste buds are after. If you're used to highly salted foods, give yourself a few weeks to get used to the taste of these other seasonings.

Leave it in the baked goods. Some added salt is necessary in baked goods. Most recipes call for less than ½ teaspoon, so there's no need to make adjustments.

Be a Pepper

Pepper does exactly what its name implies: It gives dishes pep. But pepper has its more complicated side, too. There is a big difference between peppercorns and hot chili peppers. They come from completely different plant species. Let's tackle everyone's favorite pepper first.

Peppercorns are berries that grow on the climbing vines of the pepper plant (*Piper nigrum*). Most home cooks use black peppercorns. They are picked slightly immature, then dried whole and ground. I recommend buying peppercorns whole rather than preground. The preground variety loses flavor very quickly. With whole black peppercorns on hand, your pepper will always be fresh-tasting. Place the peppercorns in a peppermill and grind them as needed. Most folks use pepper in savory dishes for a slightly hot, slightly sweet flavor. But pepper tastes great on strawberries, too. Sprinkle fresh strawberries with balsamic vinegar and a pinch each of ground pepper and sugar for an early summer treat.

Now to the hot stuff. Hot peppers (or chili peppers) are the pungent pods of the *Capsicum* plant. They come in an endless variety of shapes, sizes, flavors, and degrees of hotness. If you like hot food, experiment with the many hot-pepper varieties available in your grocery store. Most people become accustomed to spicy food the more they eat it. If you want the basics, here are the core four that I keep around the house to turn up the heat.

1. Ground red pepper (cayenne): for soups, stews, chili, rice, and beans
2. Red-pepper flakes: to perk up pizza and pasta
3. Canned mild green chili peppers: for Mexican dishes like quesadillas and tortilla casserole
4. Fresh jalapeño peppers: for burritos, tacos, and fresh salsa

HOT FOODS BURN CALORIES

Foods made with hot spices may help you lose weight. Chili peppers and mustard have been shown to help boost the body's metabolic rate and actually burn more calories—an average of 25 percent more than if you left out the spices. Chilies can also aid in digestion by accelerating the flow of gastric juices. Most chili peppers are good sources of vitamins A and C, too. So give yourself a shot of the hot stuff. It does a body good.

Low-Fat Flavor-Boosters

A few special seasonings are used throughout the Low-Fat Living recipes. These are the secret to transforming low-fat food into a high-flavor feast. Make these ingredients a part of your cooking and you'll always know how to rev up the flavor when you need to.

Citrus juice. A squeeze of lemon or lime brightens the taste of almost any hot or cold bean dish. For cold dishes like white bean dip, add a splash along with the rest of the ingredients. For hot dishes like black bean soup, add the juice toward the end of cooking time. Try lemon juice with white beans and lime juice with black beans. Use lemon juice to flavor seafood dishes, too.

Citrus rind. Grated lemon, lime, or orange rind gives low-fat muffins and quick breads a fresh, zesty taste. A sprinkle of grated lemon rind also works wonders in light pasta dishes.

Sun-dried tomatoes. Soften these in hot water for 15 minutes and you'll have deep tomato flavor at your fingertips. Chop the softened tomatoes for pizza, pasta, dips, spreads, pesto, and salads.

Dried mushrooms. Here's another dried food wonder. Supermarkets are teeming with dried mushrooms, which keep in your pantry for months. I mainly use dried shiitake and porcini mushrooms. Soften them in hot water and add them to soups, sauces, pasta, pizza, polenta, burgers, meatballs, or in anything else where you want deep, earthy flavor.

Dried fruit. Surprise! Dried fruit is a fantastic flavor-booster. Dried apricots, cranberries (craisins), blueberries, cherries, currants, and raisins lend mellow, fruity flavors to muffins, quick breads, cookies, and salads. Soften them in hot water before using.

Soaking liquid. Don't forget the soaking liquid from sun-dried tomatoes and dried mushrooms, fruit, or chili peppers. The liquid has a flavor all its own. Add it to the recipe right along with the other ingredients. Or freeze it in an airtight container. It makes a great base for soups, stews, and sauces.

The Condiments Basket

Why rely on salt and pepper when other exciting flavors await you? In our house, we grab a variety of liquid seasonings instead. We keep them in a basket right on the table. These jump-start the taste of tuna and turkey sandwiches, cooked grains and beans, or anything else that needs more zip. Check the condiment section of your grocery store or health food store to make up your own condiments basket. Most condiments are nonfat and need no refrigeration. Read the labels to make sure. If they need refrigeration, make up two smaller baskets—one at room temperature and one cold. Here's what to keep in your baskets at all times.

- Hot-pepper sauce (several varieties)
- Mustard (brown, Dijon, honey-mustard, whole-grain)
- Prepared horseradish
- Salsa (fruit, tomato)
- Soy sauce
- Vinegar (balsamic, raspberry)
- Worcestershire sauce

SWITCHBREAK

Skillpower Not Willpower

Good-tasting food is your ticket to staying on the low-fat track. Here's a way to make it a little easier. Look around your kitchen for the condiments. Look in the cupboards. Look in the refrigerator. Pull out the ketchup, the salsa, and the mustard (get every variety if you have more than one). Put them on a table. Now take a peek inside the containers of each one. Is that Dijon mustard looking a little old? Inspect the lids closely. Are they so caked up that they won't stay on the jar? When was the last time you used the ketchup? Throw out any condiments that look past their prime and restock your shelves with fresh jars of your favorite flavor-boosters. These are your weapons against bland-tasting food. Put these condiments in a place that's easy to reach. Next time you're tempted by a high-fat dish, reach for these flavors instead. They make low-fat food fun. If you like spicy condiments, you get an extra payoff. Mustards and hot sauces have been shown to raise your metabolism and burn extra calories.

Cooking with Spirit

Wine adds flavor to foods without a trace of fat. If you avoid alcohol, nonalcoholic wines make a fine substitute. Remember that alcohol has a relatively low boiling point (about 175°F). If the wine is heated in an uncovered pot for more than a short time, the alcohol will begin to evaporate. The best part is that the flavor stays behind.

I use small amounts of white wine, red wine, and sherry for cooking. Sherry is a key flavor ingredient in many creamy soups and sauces, especially those made with mushrooms. It lends a subtle aroma and dry, fruity flavor that's hard to duplicate. For the best results, add just a tablespoon or two of sherry after the soup or sauce is removed from the heat.

When buying wines, don't skimp on quality just because you're using a small amount. There's an old saying: "Never cook with a wine you wouldn't drink." Avoid the bottles labeled "cooking wine" found near the vinegars on your grocer's shelf. These wines are often spiked with strong flavoring ingredients like salt and monosodium glutamate, or MSG, that can throw off the taste of a recipe. Go for an inexpensive dry red, white, or pale sherry instead.

CHAPTER 8

"If the purpose of flavor is to arouse a special kind of emotion, that flavor must emerge from genuine feelings about the materials you are handling. What you are, you cook."

—MARCELLA HAZAN, ITALIAN COOKBOOK AUTHOR

FAT-BURNER SWITCH #8
RESCUE YOUR FAVORITE RECIPES WITH LOW-FAT KNOW-HOW

You don't have to abandon your family's favorite recipes. I've rescued dozens of recipes from fat-making pitfalls with the low-fat techniques outlined in this chapter. Once you get a handle on some cooking basics and pick up a few tricks, transforming recipes from high-fat to low-fat can become automatic—as it did for many of the recipe testers who worked with me on this book. I heard countless success stories of recipe rescues from testers who applied Low-Fat Living techniques to their all-time favorites.

Of course, some things just don't transform well and are better left alone. Or there may be an important emotional trigger linked to your original recipe, so you don't want to change it. For me, this is the case with Lindy's New York–Style Cheesecake. Sure, I've created lots of delicious low-fat cheesecakes. I love them and know that they can be a regular addition to my meal plans. But I won't attempt to lighten Lindy's because the 2½ pounds of full-fat cream cheese, ½ cup butter, 5 whole eggs, 3 egg yolks, and ¼ cup heavy cream *are* the cake. These ingredients create the flavor and texture that low-fat substitutions can't match. What's more, I have a special fondness for a Lindy's cheesecake that I prefer not to tinker with. Maybe it's the 69 grams of fat per slice! Knowing how fatty it really is, I rarely have any. But when I'm in New York, I share a piece (one piece) with a friend and savor each and every morsel. Then I'm back to my everyday routine.

This occasional indulgence is acceptable in the context of a low-fat eating plan. It helps prevent feelings of deprivation, which can lead to bingeing on more food than you would have eaten in the first place. Just remember the important concepts here: "occasional" and "moderation."

How to Revamp a Recipe

Turning a high-fat favorite into a low-fat treat is not as hard as you might think. Flavor and texture are the two main considerations. Some recipes rely on a certain amount of fat for texture and structure. These are often recipes made with flour—like baked goods and desserts. Other recipes need a bit of fat for flavor—like the olive oil in pesto or the cream in cream soups. Here's how to lower the fat in a recipe from start to finish. Look at the recipe on paper first. Ask yourself the questions outlined below and make notes on the recipe. Once you've planned a few adjustments, get in the kitchen and try it out. Where possible, taste the recipe as you prepare it, adding seasonings or making other changes as necessary. Note these on the recipe, too.

WHAT IS THE COOKING METHOD?

Look at the recipe directions to see how the dish is cooked. In many cases, you can cut fat just by changing the cooking method. If the directions say to deep-fry in oil, try this alternative: Coat the surface of the food with no-stick spray, place the food on a baking sheet and bake at 450° to 475°F until browned and crispy. By skipping the oil for frying, you save dozens of fat grams. For sautéing,

FAT-TRIMMING SWAPS

Don't abandon your favorite recipes. Many high-fat ingredients have low-fat and nonfat alternatives that retain the textures and flavors that you're used to. Here are some substitutions that I use to keep my family's favorite recipes on the menu. Try different brands (especially for cheeses and other dairy products) to find the ones that taste good to you. Remember that you can use butter, oil, and other fats if you cut way back on the amount, especially for sautéing and other cooking methods.

REPLACE THIS...	WITH THIS...
Butter	No-stick spray, for coating pans Small amounts of unsalted butter or canola oil, combined with applesauce or prune puree, for baking Low-Fat Living butter spreads, for spreading (see page 356)
Cheese	Part skim–milk cheese (such as mozzarella, ricotta, Cheddar, Monterey Jack, American, Swiss)
Chocolate	Cocoa powder combined with prune puree
Chocolate chips	Small amounts of mini chocolate chips
Cottage cheese	1% or 2% low-fat cottage cheese
Cream	Evaporated skim milk Small amounts of half-and-half

you can often cut the amount of fat called for by a third. If the recipe says to sauté in 3 tablespoons butter, you can get similar results with just a tablespoon of canola oil and a no-stick pan. By jettisoning the butter, you avoid saturated fat, too. Vary the flavors when you sauté by replacing some of the fat with vegetable broth or chicken broth.

REPLACE THIS...	WITH THIS...
Cream cheese	Nonfat cream cheese or Neufchâtel cheese
Eggs	Egg whites Fat-free egg substitute
Ground beef	Ground skinless turkey breast
Mayonnaise	Nonfat, low-fat, or cholesterol-free mayonnaise
Nuts	Small amounts of toasted and finely chopped nuts
Oil	No-stick spray, for coating pans Small amounts of extra-virgin olive oil or canola oil, combined with broth or wine, for sautéing
Pork	Chicken
Sausage	Turkey sausage, chicken sausage, or tofu sausage
Shortening	Small amounts of butter, canola oil, or olive oil
Sour cream	Nonfat or low-fat sour cream Nonfat or low-fat plain yogurt
Whole milk	Skim milk, for cereal and drinking Evaporated skim milk, for baking, soups, sauces, and casseroles

HOW MANY SERVINGS DOES IT MAKE?

Before perusing the ingredients, take a peek at the number of servings. This tells you how the ingredients will be divided up in the end and how low in fat you can go. For instance, if a recipe makes four servings and calls for ¾ cup butter (12 tablespoons), that means 3 tablespoons of butter per serving. Here's an ideal place to start reducing fat. Remember, it may be important to retain some fat in certain recipes—especially baked goods and desserts.

HOW MUCH BUTTER OR OIL DOES IT CALL FOR?

Fats like butter, oil, margarine, and shortening are the focus of most adjustments when lowering the fat in a recipe. In general, a recipe that serves four should be limited to just 1 to 2 tablespoons of these fats. That averages out to about 1½ teaspoons per serving (or 6.5 grams of fat). By keeping the principal fats low, you can add small amounts of other high-fat ingredients that have more flavor—like cheeses, nuts, and eggs. In savory recipes, try replacing some of the butter or oil with nonfat chicken broth or vegetable broth. For baking and desserts, replace some of the butter or shortening with applesauce or prune puree (pitted prunes pureed with hot water).

WHAT ARE THE OTHER HIGH-FAT INGREDIENTS? CAN THEY BE REDUCED?

Scan the recipe for other high-fat ingredients like eggs, cheese, and nuts. Reduce the amount wherever possible. In many cases, a recipe will taste just as good with a little less cheese, fewer nuts, or just one egg instead of two.

WHAT LOW-FAT SUBSTITUTIONS CAN BE MADE?

Milk, eggs, cheese, mayonnaise, cream, sour cream, chocolate, ground beef, and sausage all have lower-fat substitutions. Four egg whites replaces two whole eggs for a fat savings of 10 grams. Part skim–milk cheeses easily stand in for full-fat cheese and save 4 grams of fat per ounce (or 32 fat grams for every 2 cups). Ground turkey makes a good substitute for some of the ground beef in a recipe. And flavored turkey sausage is hardly distinguishable from pork sausage in most recipes.

WHAT HERBS, SPICES, AND SEASONINGS CAN INTENSIFY THE FLAVOR?

When taking the fat out of a recipe, you also take out some flavor. Be sure to add flavor back with nonfat ingredients like fresh herbs, additional spices, grated citrus rind, balsamic vinegar, wine or sherry, sun-dried tomatoes, dried mushrooms, ground red pepper, mustard, and Worcestershire sauce.

Don't Ban All High-Fat Ingredients

Small amounts of high-fat ingredients can make low-fat food satisfying. You won't need much. High-fat ingredients tend to have strong flavors. The key here is using just a little. Here's how to stay smart about high-fat ingredients while creating great-tasting low-fat dishes.

Butter. Everyone's favorite culinary vice is high in saturated fat. But small amounts of butter can create a satisfying texture and flavor—especially in low-fat baked goods and desserts. When used as part of the Low-Fat Living Program, sparse amounts of butter will not raise the saturated fat in your diet over the recommended 10 percent of calories. Strive for no more than 1 to 2 teaspoons of butter per serving in a recipe.

Cheese. If you're like me, you love cheese. It adds unmatched flavor and texture to a variety of foods. To keep fat and cholesterol down, use part skim–milk versions of mozzarella, ricotta, Cheddar, provolone, Monterey Jack, Havarti, and Swiss (Jarlsberg light is wonderful). Steer clear of the nonfat cheeses. Most don't melt well when heated, and they don't pass the taste-bud test for most folks. The two exceptions are nonfat cottage cheese and nonfat cream cheese, which can be useful in creating texture in casseroles and desserts. Some full-fat cheeses can be useful, too. A little strong-flavored cheese goes a long way and won't pile on the fat and calories. Grated Parmesan and Romano cheeses add flavor highlights to pasta, salads, and savory pies. Crumbled blue cheese, Roquefort, Gorgonzola, and feta make great additions to salads, pasta dishes, and toasted bread.

Eggs. One egg yolk contains 5 grams of fat and 213 milligrams of cholesterol. Only about a third of the fat is the saturated kind. The other two-thirds are polyunsaturated. Saturated fat is the main culprit in raising blood cholesterol, possibly even more than dietary cholesterol, according to researchers. Plus, eggs are complete proteins, containing all the amino acids as well as iron, phosphorus, potassium, calcium, and vitamins A and D. What this boils down to is that, when used sparingly, eggs can be part of a low-fat diet. I often combine one or two whole eggs with egg whites or egg substitute to reduce fat but retain flavor and texture. This method works well in breakfast entrées, desserts, and baked products.

Half-and-half. It's lower in fat than cream yet produces similar results in most recipes. Plus, it keeps well, so it's always around if I need just a touch. Small amounts of half-and-half help create the creamy texture that people come to expect in smooth sauces, cream soups, and rich casseroles.

Nuts. Toast nuts in a dry skillet over medium-high heat for 2 to 3 minutes, or until golden and fragrant. Toasting intensifies the flavor so that you can use less. You can also use less by chopping them small so that their flavor distributes throughout the recipe.

Let's Rescue a Brownie Recipe

To put these principles into practice, here's a recipe rescued from my own kitchen. I turned my family's favorite high-fat brownies into dark and delicious chewy brownies with less than 3 grams of fat per serving.

The original recipe had a buttercream frosting, which sent the fat profile off the charts. For starters, I eliminated the frosting. To make a fair comparison with the new recipe, the figures shown here do not include the frosting, which had contributed 38 grams of fat to the brownies. Let's take a look at the old and new brownie recipes side by side.

Here's what I did. The original recipe has ½ cup butter as the principal fat. To reduce the fat, I replaced the butter with 1 tablespoon canola oil and ½ cup prune puree (pitted prunes blended with hot water). These substitutions maintain the moist texture and rich flavor that the butter would have created. They also leave plenty of room in the fat profile for some real chocolate chips, which add more fudgy flavor.

ORIGINAL BROWNIES

MAKES 16

½	cup butter
2	whole eggs
1	cup sugar
⅓	cup cocoa powder
1	teaspoon vanilla
½	cup all-purpose flour
¼	teaspoon baking powder
⅛	teaspoon salt
½	cup chopped nuts

PER BROWNIE: 150 CALORIES, 8.8 G. TOTAL FAT, 3.9 G. SATURATED FAT, 2.5 G. PROTEIN, 17.2 G. CARBOHY-DRATES, 0.3 G. DIETARY FIBER, 42 MG. CHOLESTEROL, 89 MG. SODIUM

LOW-FAT CHEWY BROWNIES

MAKES 16

⅓	cup boiling water
⅓	cup pureed prunes
½	cup milk chocolate chips, melted
1	tablespoon canola oil
1¼	cups sugar
½	cup packed brown sugar
4	egg whites
½	cup cocoa powder
1	tablespoon vanilla
1¼	cups unbleached flour
1	teaspoon baking powder
½	teaspoon salt

PER BROWNIE: 181 CALORIES, 2.7 G. TOTAL FAT, 0.1 G. SATURATED FAT, 2.9 G. PROTEIN, 38.2 G. CARBOHY-DRATES, 0.6 G. DIETARY FIBER, 1 MG. CHOLESTEROL, 110 MG. SODIUM

STRESS CAN BE A FAT-MAKER

Strive to avoid stress around the holidays (and other times, too). Stress can put your body's fat-making processes into overdrive and cause you to store extra body fat. Studies show that stress triggers the body's "starvation response," which prompts the internal storage of food as if the body were preparing for famine. Plus, hormones like cortisol and epinephrine are released in stressful situations and may jolt your body into storing even more fat. Plan ahead to avoid unnecessary frustration. Whenever you feel stress coming on, take a moment to counteract it. Draw in a deep breath. And then another. Focus your mind on practical ways to resolve the situation. If it can't be resolved, take another deep breath and do some simple stretching or light exercise. Defusing the stress will turn off this fat-maker before it makes a big impact on you.

For further fat savings, I replaced the two whole eggs with four egg whites. The egg whites provide the same binding and leavening qualities of whole eggs, but without the fat. Because prune puree is so moist, I added ¾ cup more flour, resulting in a larger, more filling brownie. To pump up the rich flavors, I added about 3 tablespoons more cocoa, 2 teaspoons more vanilla, and ¼ cup more sugar. I also omitted the nuts.

Total fat savings is 6 grams per brownie. More important, the new recipe saves nearly 4 grams of artery-clogging saturated fat per brownie (thanks to eliminating the butter). The percentage of calories from fat comes down from 53 percent to just 13 percent. In the new recipe, most of the calories come from carbohydrates instead of from fat. That's exactly where they should be coming from in the Low-Fat Living Program.

While some of your favorite recipes may need extensive adjustments like these, most recipes need only one or two changes. Often, a simple switch or two does the trick—like replacing 3 tablespoons butter for sautéing with 1 tablespoon olive oil. Or using ¼ cup nuts instead of ½ cup, and toasting the nuts for more flavor. Make simple changes like these to the recipes that you serve day in and day out, and the fat savings will add up significantly.

Lighten the Load during Holidays

It's easy to lose sight of low-fat goals around the holidays. After all, celebrations are meant for a little indulgence. To fight fat during these times, emphasize light and festive flavors rather than heavy foods that put you in the classic after-dinner slump. Of course, if Grandma walks in with her famous pecan pie or holiday cookies, be sure to graciously accept them. And truly enjoy the small bites that you do take. It's not what you eat today that matters most but how you eat tomorrow, next week, and for the rest of your life. Here are some things that you can do to lighten up the holidays while retaining the satisfaction of time-honored traditions.

- Give your favorite holiday recipes a low-fat profile by using the rescue techniques throughout this chapter.

- Instead of cookies, chocolates, and nuts, fill holiday bowls with fresh vegetable crudités, homemade chips, whole-grain crackers, and low-fat dips for munching.

- If the usual holiday centerpiece is a brisket or ham, try switching to

SWITCHBREAK

Skillpower Not Willpower

Here's a quick way to cut fat from your diet. Keep a simple food record. Make four columns on a sheet of paper: Breakfast, Lunch, Dinner, Snacks. For the next two weeks, eat as you normally would but write down what you eat. Make entries once in the afternoon and once at night so that you don't leave anything out. After two weeks, look over the record. Sniff out the high-fat patterns. For instance, most people eat the same thing for breakfast on weekdays. Think of ways to make these regular meals healthier. Do you always have bacon with your morning eggs and toast? Try switching to Canadian bacon. It has only 2 grams of fat per ounce (regular bacon has 14 grams of fat per ounce). Use the food record to take stock of your eating habits and make small changes. Over time, these changes will add up to big fat savings.

turkey, fish, or even Cornish hens. Baste the hens with a mix of broth, wine, ground sage, and garlic instead of butter or oil. If turkey is your number-one holiday main dish, try this fat-trimming glaze: Combine ⅔ cup honey with 12 ounces thawed frozen apple juice concentrate and 2 tablespoons dry mustard powder. Baste the turkey every 15 minutes with the glaze and a small amount of pan drippings. Don't forget to remove the skin when you serve the bird, for extra fat savings.

- Make a reduced-fat gravy. Use a fat separator to skim the fat from pan juices. Add some nonfat chicken broth and evaporated skim milk mixed with flour to thicken the gravy as it cooks. A splash of sherry adds pleasant flavor.

- Create side dishes that emphasize fiber-rich vegetables, grains, and fruits. Mashed potatoes, roasted mixed vegetables, wild rice salad, mushroom-barley pilaf, and fresh cranberry relish are good examples.

- Serve a lower-fat vinaigrette with salad. Traditional vinaigrette proportions call for three parts oil to one part vinegar. Replace some of the oil with nonfat chicken or vegetable broth. Add extra vinegar and stir in some chopped fresh herbs and mustard to boost the flavor.

- Offer two desserts instead of one. For those with endless appetites, serve low-fat pumpkin pie or chocolate cake. For others who want just a little something, serve a lighter dessert like cookies or vanilla ice cream with fruit sauce.

CHAPTER 9

"I always plan dinner first thing in the morning. That's the only way I can get through the day—having a specific meal to look forward to at night."

—ALAN KING, AMERICAN COMEDIAN

FAT-BURNER SWITCH #9

REINVENT MEALS-IN-A-MINUTE FOR CONVENIENCE WITHOUT COMPROMISE

Everybody loves shortcuts, especially when it comes to low-fat meals and snacks. You've probably experienced the frustration of opening the refrigerator at mealtime and just staring inside, wondering what to fix. It's one of the main reasons why most folks reach for high-fat convenience foods. Planning ahead, making double batches, using the freezer, and having the right ingredients can help you avoid the dinnertime dilemma. Turn off the fat-maker of convenience foods by reinventing homemade meals-in-a-minute.

Plan Ahead to Dodge the Last-Minute Struggle

There's no doubt about it. Planning is the number-one way to avoid falling back on high-fat habits. Think of it as an investment. A few moments of planning now will save you time, frustration, and unwanted fat later.

Make lists. Whether it's every few days or once a week, create a short list of recipes that sound interesting to you. Pick recipes that you've been wanting to try, ones that use seasonal ingredients, or old favorites that you'd like to make again. Jot down the recipe titles or mark the pages in books or magazines so that you can refer to them easily.

Pick quick recipes. Plan for at least two super-rushed evenings per week. For these nights, pick recipes that are ready from start to finish in 30 minutes or less. Check the hands-on time and unattended time. If a recipe takes only 10 minutes of hands-on time and 20 minutes in the oven, it could meet your needs perfectly.

Stock up on ingredients. As you choose recipes, jot down any ingredients that you may need. Add them to your shopping list and pick them up the next time you shop.

Let taste be your guide. When mealtime arrives, let your taste buds do the talking. Look at your list of recipes and pick the one you feel like making most that night. You've planned ahead, so you know that you'll have all the ingredients. The meal will be ready in a jiffy.

Stay Organized

A well-organized kitchen is the quick cook's greatest asset. It saves time and helps you feel in control of your diet. Here's what I do to keep stress levels down when time is short.

Keep a regular dinnertime. Eating dinner at the same time every day helps you plan accordingly and avoid last-minute scrambling. Set a time that works for the whole family. For instance, my family likes to eat at about 6:00 in the evening. I know that by 5:00, I need to be easing out of work, settling the kids into a project, and heading into the kitchen. If 5:30 rolls around and I'm not making dinner, I'll have to rely on one of my super-quick meal options.

Delegate responsibilities. More hands make light work. Whether you cook for two or a large family, delegate some kitchen responsibilities. Kids can set and clear the table, help wash the dishes, or make a salad. There's no reason that the cook should do all the work.

Keep things nearby. Keep frequently used appliances, utensils, and ingredients within easy reach. Cutting boards, knives, pans, no-stick spray, oil, spices, and other seasonings should all be right at your fingertips.

Clear a space. Make sure that your workspace for chopping and mixing ingredients is uncluttered. If dishes are in the way, move them into the sink or somewhere else away from your workspace before you start cooking.

Prep Ahead When You Can

Today's busy lifestyles make the family dinner hour more important than ever. The evening meal may be the one time of day when the whole family gets together to relax, reconnect, and share news of the day. But finding the time and energy to make this meal can be tough. Here's my secret to preserving this family tradition: advance preparation. Whenever you have a few moments, do some simple cooking tasks to save time later. These few moments could make the difference between a healthy meal enjoyed by the whole family and another night of delivery pizza.

Cook on the weekend. If you have a spare hour on weekends, cook some of the dishes or foods that you'll need throughout the week. Make up a batch of rice or beans and store it in the freezer. Or simmer a pot of soup and freeze it in individual portions.

Chop extra. Double up on common tasks like chopping onions. If you're making a recipe that calls for half an onion, chop the whole thing anyway. Store the remainder in the refrigerator or freezer. You'll thank yourself the next time you have only a few minutes to get dinner together.

Make part of the recipe. If you're planning to have pizza, pasta, or a casserole later in the week, prepare part of it ahead of time. Make the pizza dough, pasta sauce, or part of the casserole when you have time. (Or assemble the whole casserole.) Then freeze or refrigerate the items. Only a few steps will be left when it comes time to fix supper.

Double the recipe. Many home cooks make the same recipes week after week. Get two meals for the work of one by doubling the recipe and freezing half. Cool the food, wrap it well, and label it with the contents, date, and approximate number of portions before freezing. Think of these foods as "planned-overs." On a day that you know you won't have time to cook, thaw the dish and it'll be ready for a low-fat meal in minutes.

Stock the fridge. Whip up a salad dressing or two, some dips and spreads for snacks, and cookies or brownies for sweet treats. Store them in the refrigerator. Having these foods ready will make dinner prep easier and satisfy predinner hunger pangs throughout the week.

Stock up on lunches. For fast midday meals, keep some of your family's favorite lunch foods on hand. I always keep a supply of frozen vegetarian or turkey burgers, salmon cakes, crab cakes, and slices of turkey meat loaf in plastic freezer bags. These foods can be quickly reheated in a microwave and made into sandwiches with lettuce, tomato, onions, and condiments.

Make It Mexican

Mexican is often my first choice when I need a fresh meal in minutes. My kids love it, and so do I. Most Mexican dishes are packed with fat-burning beans and grains. What's more, Mexican food is fast and open to endless variations.

Low-fat nachos. Spread a layer of baked tortilla chips in a 13" × 9" baking dish. Top with 1 can (16 ounces) warmed nonfat or low-fat re-fried beans, chili beans, or leftover chili. Sprinkle on 1 cup shredded part skim–milk Cheddar, Monterey Jack, or hot-pepper cheese. Broil until the cheese is melted. Top with ½ cup chopped lettuce, ½ cup chopped tomatoes, and ½ cup chopped scallions or onions. Serve with nonfat sour cream and salsa.

Tacos. Use the same ingredients as for nachos. Replace the tortilla chips with hard corn taco shells. Place the ingredients in separate bowls and set on the table.

Burritos. Use the same ingredients as for nachos. Replace the tor-tilla chips with large flour tortillas. Place the ingredients in separate bowls and set on the table.

Tostadas. Use the same ingredients as for nachos. Replace the tor-tilla chips with large flour tortillas. Bake the tortillas in a single layer for 5 minutes, or until crispy. Layer the beans and cheese on top. Broil until the cheese is melted. Top with the lettuce, tomatoes, and scal-lions. Serve with nonfat sour cream and salsa.

Beanwiches. Use the same ingredients as for nachos. Replace the tortilla chips with whole-wheat pita bread. Stuff the ingredients in-side the pita pockets for a quick lunch.

Quesadillas. Coat a large no-stick skillet with no-stick spray. Place a flour tortilla in the skillet. Spread the tortilla with a layer of cooked beans, refried beans, vegetables, rice, chicken, turkey, or seafood. Sprinkle with shredded Cheddar or Monterey Jack cheese. Top with another tortilla and cook over medium heat until the bottom begins to brown. (As the cheese melts, it holds everything else to-gether.) Flip the quesadilla over and cook until the other side begins to brown and the cheese melts. Transfer to a plate and cut into wedges. Serve with nonfat sour cream and salsa.

Breakfast burrito. Coat a large no-stick skillet with no-stick spray. Add onions and sweet red peppers and cook over medium heat for 2 minutes. Add shredded potatoes and cook until the potatoes are browned. Transfer to a plate to keep warm. In the same skillet, cook eggs and/or fat-free egg substitute until scrambled. Place the potato mixture and eggs in a large flour tortilla. Top with shredded Cheddar or Monterey Jack cheese. Roll up and serve with salsa.

Fix Hot Pasta in Minutes

Pasta is a regular standby for fast meals in our house. It usually cooks in 10 minutes or less, and I always have several shapes in stock. I also keep low-fat ravioli and tortellini in the freezer. You can freeze sauces, too. Tomato and pesto sauces keep well for months. Here are some other swift ideas for pasta.

Quick tomato sauce. Pour a jar of low-fat or nonfat tomato sauce into a medium saucepan. Add cooked vegetables, chicken, ground turkey, or turkey sausage. Heat through. Serve over your favorite pasta with grated Parmesan cheese.

Seafood pasta. Instead of vegetables or meat, add canned salmon, tuna, crabmeat, or clams to the tomato sauce.

Pasta with pink sauce. For a creamy pink sauce, add evaporated skim milk to the tomato sauce.

Light pasta from the freezer. Thaw frozen chicken, turkey sausage, or seafood in the microwave. Warm a little butter or olive oil and some nonfat chicken or vegetable broth in a no-stick skillet. Add the thawed ingredients and sprinkle with herbs and spices. Heat through. Meanwhile, cook the pasta (fusilli and rotini are my favorites). Drain and return to the pot. Pour the sauce over the pasta.

Add additional broth to moisten the pasta. Sprinkle with grated Parmesan cheese, salt, and pepper. Toss to mix. (For a vegetarian version, replace the chicken, turkey sausage, or seafood with a can of rinsed and drained white beans.)

Stuff a Pita Pocket Full of...

Pita bread helps get lunches and light suppers on the table fast. I always keep a package of whole-wheat pita bread in the freezer. In 10 minutes, the pitas can be thawed, cut, and baked into pita strips. Served with dips and spreads, they make a nutritious snack. Or use the pockets for your favorite fillings.

Pita sandwiches. Fill pita pockets with leftovers like chili, couscous, tabbouleh, Spanish rice, risotto, or grilled chicken with peanut sauce. Be creative. And don't forget traditional fillings like tuna salad, chicken salad, or canned salmon with lettuce and tomato.

Pita pizzas. Bake whole pitas at 400°F until slightly crispy (make a small slit in each pita to allow steam to escape). Spread with tomato sauce and top with shredded part skim–milk mozzarella cheese. Bake for 5 to 8 minutes more, or until the cheese melts. To vary the flavor, add your favorite toppings before adding the cheese. Try mushrooms, peppers, olives, artichoke hearts, or turkey sausage.

Build Better Burgers

Burgers make a fast meal option, and they freeze well. To cut the fat and cholesterol of ground beef, replace some or all of the ground beef with ground turkey breast. To kick up the flavor, add a few seasonings. Here's my favorite recipe: Combine 1 pound ground skinless turkey breast with ½ cup finely chopped onions, ½ cup finely chopped green or sweet red peppers, and 3 tablespoons steak sauce. Mix well and form into patties. Freeze the patties between layers of wax paper.

Thaw the burgers and grill or broil until cooked through. Serve on whole-wheat buns with traditional toppings like lettuce, tomatoes, onions, and ketchup.

Brown-Bag It

Many folks eat their lunches away from home. A smart brown-bag lunch can save you time and money and enhance your performance for the rest of the day. Even those who don't have access to appliances needn't rely on high-fat fast foods for lunch. Here are a few ideas.

Warm up to leftovers. If you have access to appliances like a refrigerator, microwave, and toaster oven, you have almost all the comforts of the kitchen. You can easily microwave leftovers for lunch. Soups, casseroles, pasta, poultry, and grains all reheat well. Or pack a sandwich for the refrigerator. Don't forget the snacks, like baked tortilla chips with black bean dip, rice pudding with fruit, oatmeal-raisin cookies, or whole-grain crackers with one of my butter spreads (see recipes beginning on page 356).

Take along instant foods. Many packaged foods are nutritious and ready in a snap. Dried soups, refried beans, frozen vegetarian burgers, and turkey or tofu hot dogs need only a microwave, some water, and 2 minutes of cooking time. Look for other fast and filling lunches in the soup aisle and freezer case of your grocery store or health food store.

Take it on the road. Do you work on the road without seeing an office during the lunch hour? Pack a Thermos with hot soup. Pack another with cold water or iced tea. Pack a low-fat sandwich like turkey breast and part-skim Swiss cheese with lettuce, tomato, and mustard on rye bread. For snacks, fill your bag with crackers, pretzels, fresh fruit, and low-fat cookies. Use a thermal lunch bag or mini-cooler to keep foods chilled.

Pack plenty of water. A good supply of cold water is a must. It helps you feel full longer and burns calories when your body warms up the water. Pass up the sugary sodas and flashy soft drinks. Good old water is the best thing for you. Store it in a Thermos to keep it cold.

Eat fast food, not fat food. Sometimes fast food is the only option. When you go to a fast-food restaurant, eat smart by finding the healthy choices. Avoid fatty foods like burgers and fries. Opt for grilled chicken or a baked potato instead. Choose a bean burrito or vegetable-and-cheese sandwich. Make full use of the salad bar, especially if it includes pasta salads, grain salads, and cut fresh fruit. Look for pasta and grain salads that aren't swimming in oil.

"When pleasures to the eye and palate meet, that cook has rendered his work complete."

—MARIA J. MOSS, COOKBOOK AUTHOR

FAT-BURNER SWITCH #10

BUILD MEALS THAT BURN FAT ALL DAY LONG

Picture a plateful of grilled chicken, brown rice pilaf, and steamed cauliflower. It's low-fat and nutritionally balanced and includes a variety of flavors. So what's wrong with this picture? Visualize the meal again. Can you see it? It's all bland shades of off-white. As a whole, the meal lacks color and excitement. And that may be enough to make you feel unsatisfied after eating it.

Great-tasting low-fat meals are satisfying on several levels: visual, emotional, and nutritional as well as the level of flavor. If a meal falls short in just one area, it may leave you hungry and prompt you to reach for a high-fat snack. The trick to burning fat all day long is building low-fat meals that work on every level. It's the only way that you'll be truly satisfied. Think about how each meal will look as a whole. Consider how the flavor of the side dishes will match that of the main dish. Don't forget to build in a few between-meal snacks. Healthy snacks can keep a low-fat day from turning into a high-fat nightmare. Here's how to make fat-burning meals a simple and automatic part of your everyday life.

Strive for Nutritional Balance

When building main meals like breakfast, lunch, and dinner, nutritional balance should be a priority. In general, each meal should account for 30 percent of your total calories for the day. That leaves another 10 percent for snacks. For instance, if you eat 2,000 calories a day, that means limiting breakfast, lunch, and dinner to 600 calories each. Of course, if you eat fewer calories at breakfast, you can eat a few more at dinner. Here are some other nutritional considerations.

Don't go by fat grams alone. Watching fat intake is a key concern. But a low-fat meal can end up turning *on* your body's fat-making processes instead of turning them *off*. If the meal is too low in calories, you may end up feeling deprived and hungry soon after eating it. That could lead to high-fat bingeing later in the day. Here's an example: Let's say that you decide to have a light lunch. You choose a large mixed-vegetable salad with vinaigrette dressing. For something to drink, you choose iced tea. You're feeling weight-conscious, so you end the meal right there. This lunch seems healthful because it's loaded with vegetables, high in fiber, and low in calories. But the meal is *too* low in calories. Plus, the majority of those calories are coming from the fat in the salad dressing. The best way to make it more healthful is to add more food like bread or cooked grains for carbohydrates or cooked beans, cottage cheese, or shredded part-skim Cheddar cheese for protein.

Go heavy on the carbohydrates and proteins. Complex carbohydrates and proteins are important foods in the Low-Fat Living Program. If your main meals are short on these foods, they may not give you the energy that you need to last for the rest of the day. Most of the calories in Low-Fat Living main meals should come from carbohydrates and proteins rather than fats. What kinds of foods are we talking about? Here's a quick checklist.

Complex carbohydrates

- Grain foods like bread, crackers, pasta, rice, and cereal
- Vegetables
- Fruits

Eat More throughout the Day

Hungry and trying to lose weight? The trick may not be eating less but pacing yourself over the course of a day. Evenly spacing your meals and snacks throughout the day reduces the hormonal signal that causes fat cells to divide and multiply, according to Peter D. Vash, M.D., endocrinologist and eating disorders specialist at the University of California, Los Angeles, Medical Center. Guard against the generation of new fat cells by avoiding large intakes of food at one sitting. Instead, eat smaller amounts more frequently.

Proteins

- Low-fat dairy products like milk, cheese, and yogurt
- Beans
- Poultry
- Fish

Pay attention to portion size. A low-fat meal can go astray if the portion sizes are too large. If you double or triple the serving size to satisfy your appetite, you'll also bump up the number of calories and fat grams.

To prevent this phenomenon, the serving sizes in the *Low-Fat Living Cookbook* recipes are generous. If you find that a portion size is too large or too small for you, adjust the nutritional figures to match what you eat.

Think of Taste and Texture

If low-fat food doesn't taste good, you won't come back for more. Part of making low-fat meals taste great is balancing flavors and textures. If the dishes are well-matched, the interplay of flavors can make the whole meal taste better than the individual dishes. Think of the dishes in a meal as singers in a choir. When they harmonize, the whole meal comes off beautifully. Here's how to get your low-fat meals in tune.

Avoid extremely sharp contrasts. Choose side dishes that complement rather than compete with the main dish. If burritos are on the menu, you probably won't want to serve them with Asian noodles. Pick a complementary side dish like Spanish rice instead.

Match hearty to hearty. Suppose you'd like to make mushroom-barley pilaf or roasted garlic mashed potatoes as side dishes. The main dishes should match these flavors. I'd pair the pilaf with a poultry dish like chicken breasts sautéed with onions, garlic, mushrooms, and peppers. The rich flavors of the chicken dish will complement the earthy flavors of the barley. Likewise, the potatoes would go well with thick broiled tuna steaks marinated in a richly flavored cherry sauce.

Pair mild with mild. If a more mild-flavored main dish is on the menu, plan on delicate side dishes. Let's say that you're making steamed salmon fillets with fresh tomato sauce. Look for a side dish with mellow flavors and soft textures, like saffron buttered noodles. The side dishes should play supporting roles instead of dominating the rest of the tastes on the plate.

Play Up Presentation

One of the pleasures of dining out at a nice restaurant is the moment when the plates arrive at the table. Everyone oohs and aahs at how beautiful they look. That's because we taste with our eyes first. If a plate comes to the table looking bland, dull, or colorless, it makes the whole meal less enjoyable. The same holds true at home. Get creative and make your meals look as good as they taste. Here are a few tips from top chefs.

Call on color. Think back to that plate of grilled chicken, brown rice, and steamed cauliflower mentioned earlier. It's all bland shades of off-white. Now picture the same grilled chicken breast served with bright yellow polenta and steamed green broccoli. By choosing more vibrant side dishes, the plate comes alive with color. Make color a part of your meal planning and your food will taste good before you even take a fork to it.

Get saucy. Sauces do double duty. They add both important flavors and visual excitement to a meal. Imagine a plain swordfish steak with no sauce. Sounds pretty dull. Now, add a colorful salsa made with pineapple and jalapeño peppers. The whole dish gets a jolt of flavor and color. Be creative when using sauces. Instead of just drowning the food in sauce, drizzle it on artfully. Or drizzle the sauce around the food in a decorative pattern. For dessert sauces, spread the sauce on the plate first and serve the dessert on top. For soups, swirl low-fat sour cream or cooked pureed vegetables into the soup just before serving.

Sprinkle on chopped herbs. Here's another burst of color and flavor for low-fat cooking. A sprinkling of chopped fresh basil makes pasta dishes look fresh and inviting. For Asian meals, perk up rice with chopped cilantro. Toss some chopped fresh parsley on pasta, risotto, steamed vegetables, and just about any other savory dish. Fresh tarragon blends well with egg dishes.

Go with garnishes. Most fruits and vegetables can be used to make beautiful garnishes. Make a series of diagonal cuts around the circumference of radishes or tomatoes to create a jagged edge that will make the halves look like crowns. Or peel the skin off a tomato in a continuous strip, then roll it into a spiral to make a tomato rose. Cut a pomegranate in half and use the seeds for a beautiful fruit-salad garnish. Looking for more spectacular color and flavor? Serve your dish with edible flowers. Calendulas and nasturtiums are particularly eye-catching and tasty. Herb sprigs are always appropriate. So are herb flowers.

Use edible bowls. Instead of serving soup in conventional bowls, try using hollowed-out squashes or melons. For winter soups, cut an acorn squash or other round squash in half, scoop out the seeds, and fill with the soup. (If you cook the squash first, it can also be eaten when the soup is finished.) For fruit soups, hollow out a cantaloupe or honeydew melon half for a bowl. Melons make great salad bowls, too. For fruit salad, cut a cantaloupe in half and make diagonal cuts around the edge to form a decorative crown. Or try your hand at a watermelon basket. Cut the watermelon in half lengthwise, leaving a crosswise center strip for the handle. Scoop out the watermelon flesh and use it for the fruit salad. Serve the fruit salad in the basket.

Plan Snacks That Energize the Body and Soothe the Soul

Adults make an average of 20 to 30 food decisions a day, according to George L. Blackburn, M.D., Ph.D., associate professor of surgery at Harvard Medical School and chief of the Nutrition Metabolism Laboratory at Beth Israel Deaconess Medical Center in Boston. Many of the foods that we decide on are snacks because we eat them so often and rarely plan for them. Planning ahead for snacks is an important part of the Low-Fat Living Program. These between-meal foods play a pivotal role in turning off the fat-makers and turning on the fat-burners. They help curb your appetite, and studies show that one nutritious mid-morning snack and one mid-afternoon snack can promote better health by lowering blood cholesterol and boosting energy.

What's more, every food you eat has an effect on the neurotransmitters in your brain, according to Judith J. Wurtman, Ph.D., a researcher at the Massachusetts Institute of Technology in Cambridge.

A FULL DAY OF FAT-BURNING FOOD

Here's an example of a full-day meal plan that turns off the fat-makers and turns on the fat-burners. It's balanced nutritionally, includes fat-burning snacks, and makes the most of taste, texture, and presentation. Use this as a model when creating your own fat-burning meals.

BREAKFAST
    Northern Summers Muesli (page 111)
    Orange juice (4 ounces)

MID-MORNING SNACK
    Orange-Currant Scones (page 141)
    Apple

LUNCH
    Crab and Corn Chowder (page 187)
    Soft Semolina Rolls (page 379)
    Pesto Butter Spread (page 356)
    Mixed greens (1¹/₂ cups) with Creamy Basil Dressing (page 146)

MID-AFTERNOON SNACK
    Seasoned Tortilla Chips (page 353)
    Spicy Black Bean Dip (page 364)

DINNER
    Stuffed Pizza (page 284)
    Light Caesar Salad (page 157)

DESSERT OR LIGHT EVENING SNACK
    Chewy Brownies (page 134)

Per serving, this menu provides the following nutrients for the entire day: 1,897 calories, 38.9 g. total fat, 12.9 g. saturated fat, 86.5 g. protein, 323.2 g. carbohydrates, 31.1 g. dietary fiber, 104 mg. cholesterol, 2,583 mg. sodium.

These neurotransmitters, in turn, affect your mental alertness, concentration, attitude, mood, and performance. Here's how researchers recommend making the food-mood connection work for you instead of against you.

Grab high-protein snacks for alertness. Studies show that foods high in protein may contribute to increased energy, greater attention to detail, and improved alertness for up to three hours after eating. Choose high-protein snacks when you need an extra lift or want to get energized for work or exercise. Good choices include yogurt, cottage cheese, turkey, chicken, fish, skim milk, part skim–milk cheese, beans, or even a few almonds. Protein snacks are often hard to travel with because they need to be kept cold. When I'm away from home, I get protein from energy bars. I usually have three options: the energy bar in my car, the one in my backpack, or the one in my briefcase. Look for a bar that's low in calories and fat. Buy a few different brands to find your favorite. My favorites include BTU Stoker and Cliff Bar. These are available in most health food stores and many supermarkets.

Choose high-carbohydrate snacks for a calming effect. Researchers say that foods high in complex carbohydrates may help foster a calm, focused state of mind for up to three hours after eating. If you feel tense or stressed, munch on complex carbohydrates to relax your emotions. Try bready foods like whole-grain cereal, bagels, muffins, low-fat cookies, pretzels, or crackers.

These bread snacks travel well, so when I leave the house, I take along a muffin or bagel for moments when I feel like calming down.

Match snacks to your daily routine. Choosing which snacks to eat when can be the key to controlling how you feel throughout the day. Plan snacks around your daily routine. I usually have a high-

> ## SWITCHBREAK
> *Skillpower Not Willpower*
>
> Do you have a sweet tooth? Here's a fat-fighting strategy for you. Reach for fat-free hard candies instead of candy bars or chocolate. Hard candies have about 100 calories per ounce and almost no fat or cholesterol (chocolate has about 150 calories and 10 grams of fat per ounce). But remember that the calories in hard candy are still on the high side. If you constantly crave sweets, look for other ways to get your fix. An ounce of candied ginger makes a tasty treat and has 95 calories and no fat. One large marshmallow has only 23 calories and no fat. Or try fresh fruit. Apples, bananas, oranges, grapes, figs, and berries are loaded with fruit sugar—or fructose—that can satisfy your sweet tooth. Plus, they add fat-fighting fiber to your diet.

protein snack mid-morning and a high-carbohydrate snack mid-afternoon. The morning snack kick-starts my day with a boost in mental alertness. The afternoon snack calms me down, so when the kids come home, I'm relaxed and ready to meet their needs. You may want to plan an additional light snack if you have a long commute home, to help take the edge off your appetite. Don't be shy about using this snack-planning strategy for your children, too. When the kids are tired and sluggish, offer them high-protein snacks like yogurt or part-skim cheese for an energy lift. When they're bouncing off the walls, calm them down with whole-grain cereal, pretzels, or baked tortilla chips.

"Cooking is an act of love."

—ALAIN CHAPEL, FRENCH CHEF AND RESTAURATEUR

LOW-FAT LIVING MENUS FOR SPECIAL OCCASIONS

The weather often dictates what I feel like eating and cooking. A cool, fresh gazpacho tastes great on a hot summer day. On cold winter evenings, I look to hot and hearty bean soups instead. Many foods are seasonal, such as fruits and vegetables, so I plan menus around what's readily available.

Below are some of my favorite Low-Fat Living menus. Each menu is coordinated for visual appeal, nutritional balance, and great taste. As you create your own menus, jot down your favorites so that you can call on them again when the occasion arises.

SOMETHING SPECIAL

Salmon Fillets with Fresh Tomatoes (page 244)

Brown Basmati and Orzo Pilaf (page 205)

Asparagus with Lemon-Hazelnut Sauce (page 336)

Bibb Lettuce with Raspberry Vinaigrette (page 153)

PER SERVING FOR ENTIRE MEAL: 559 CALORIES, 18 G. TOTAL FAT, 3.3 G. SATURATED FAT, 43.8 G. PROTEIN, 59.3 G. CARBOHYDRATES, 2.8 G. DIETARY FIBER, 91 MG. CHOLESTEROL, 606 MG. SODIUM

SUNDAY BRUNCH

Mexican Eggs in Phyllo Cups (page 114)

Hash-Brown Potatoes with Rosemary (page 108)

PER SERVING FOR ENTIRE MEAL: 535 CALORIES, 12.3 G. TOTAL FAT, 3.3 G. SATURATED FAT, 30.5 G. PROTEIN, 80.2 G. CARBOHYDRATES, 1.8 G. DIETARY FIBER, 155 MG. CHOLESTEROL, 572 MG. SODIUM

LIGHT LUNCH

Chilled Seafood Soup (page 190)

Spinach and Strawberry Salad (page 152)

Apricot-Almond Oatmeal Bread (page 386)

PER SERVING FOR ENTIRE MEAL: 421 CALORIES, 12.8 G. TOTAL FAT, 2.5 G. SATURATED FAT, 35 G. PROTEIN, 38.8 G. CARBOHYDRATES, 6.1 G. DIETARY FIBER, 114 MG. CHOLESTEROL, 419 MG. SODIUM

EASY PICNIC

Couscous Tabbouleh (page 173)

Black-Eyed Pea Salad (page 170)

Crunchy Pita Strips (page 352)

White Bean and Walnut Dip (page 363)

PER SERVING FOR ENTIRE MEAL: 524 CALORIES, 15 G. TOTAL FAT, 2.2 G. SATURATED FAT, 16.6 G. PROTEIN, 84.4 G. CARBOHYDRATES, 17 G. DIETARY FIBER, 2 MG. CHOLESTEROL, 314 MG. SODIUM

SEASIDE FEAST

Pan-Seared Crab Cakes (page 248)

Zippy Tartar Sauce (page 368)

All-American Potato Salad (page 164)

Whole-Wheat Buttermilk Biscuits (page 372)

PER SERVING FOR ENTIRE MEAL: 509 CALORIES, 12.3 G. TOTAL FAT, 4.5 G. SATURATED FAT, 32.9 G. PROTEIN, 66.9 G. CARBOHYDRATES, 3 G. DIETARY FIBER, 303 MG. CHOLESTEROL, 1,727 MG. SODIUM

HOT SUMMER'S NIGHT

Fruity Gazpacho (page 191)

Spinach Salad with Orange Vinaigrette (page 151)

Spicy Black Bean Dip (page 364)

Seasoned Tortilla Chips (page 353)

PER SERVING FOR ENTIRE MEAL: 541 CALORIES, 18.1 G. TOTAL FAT, 2.1 G. SATURATED FAT, 18.4 G. PROTEIN, 91.4 G. CARBOHYDRATES, 14.6 G. DIETARY FIBER, 0 MG. CHOLESTEROL, 761 MG. SODIUM

QUICK PASTA DINNER

Ziti with Creamy Walnut Sauce (page 232)

Chopped Salad (page 160)

Cottage Cheese and Dill Biscuits (page 373)

PER SERVING FOR ENTIRE MEAL: 557 CALORIES, 16.3 G. TOTAL FAT, 3.9 G. SATURATED FAT, 23.5 G. PROTEIN, 80.9 G. CARBOHYDRATES, 4.2 G. DIETARY FIBER, 12 MG. CHOLESTEROL, 398 MG. SODIUM

MEXICAN IN MINUTES

Chicken Tacos (page 303)

Easy Black Beans (page 212)

Mexican Vegetable Salad (page 155)

PER SERVING FOR ENTIRE MEAL: 442 CALORIES, 9.7 G. TOTAL FAT, 1.6 G. SATURATED FAT, 33.7 G. PROTEIN, 77.8 G. CARBOHYDRATES, 15.3 G. DIETARY FIBER, 28 MG. CHOLESTEROL, 932 MG. SODIUM

SOUP SUPPER

White Bean and Escarole Soup (page 195)

Multigrain Italian Herb Bread (page 381)

Romaine with Roasted-Garlic Dressing (page 150)

PER SERVING FOR ENTIRE MEAL: 629 CALORIES, 15.7 G. TOTAL FAT, 4.1 G. SATURATED FAT, 33.8 G. PROTEIN, 90.9 G. CARBOHYDRATES, 6 G. DIETARY FIBER, 10 MG. CHOLESTEROL, 1,379 MG. SODIUM

FAMILY-STYLE DINNER

Greek Macaroni and Cheese (page 316)

Crispy Steamed Vegetable Salad (page 161)

Quick Herb-Crusted Bread (page 378)

PER SERVING FOR ENTIRE MEAL: 603 CALORIES, 13.4 G. TOTAL FAT, 4.8 G. SATURATED FAT, 42.8 G. PROTEIN, 78.7 G. CARBOHYDRATES, 4.4 G. DIETARY FIBER, 47 MG. CHOLESTEROL, 852 MG. SODIUM

SUPER-BOWL SUNDAY

Super-Bowl Chili (page 198)

Green Chili and Roasted Pepper Cornbread (page 374)

Crunchy Winter Salad (page 163)

PER SERVING FOR ENTIRE MEAL: 552 CALORIES, 12.8 G. TOTAL FAT, 2.7 G. SATURATED FAT, 39.2 G. PROTEIN, 79 G. CARBOHYDRATES, 16.4 G. DIETARY FIBER, 65 MG. CHOLESTEROL, 1,204 MG. SODIUM

ROMANTIC DINNER

Seafood Cannelloni with Pink Sauce (page 292)

Soft Semolina Rolls (page 379)

Mixed Greens with Pecan Vinaigrette (page 152)

PER SERVING FOR ENTIRE MEAL: 500 CALORIES, 13.4 G. TOTAL FAT, 2.3 G. SATURATED FAT, 37.4 G. PROTEIN, 59.2 G. CARBOHYDRATES, 5.3 G. DIETARY FIBER, 100 MG. CHOLESTEROL, 864 MG. SODIUM

FOR THE KIDS 'N' US

Chicken Parmesan Strips (page 258)

Corn on the cob with Herb Butter Spread (page 356)

Chili Fries (page 349)

PER SERVING FOR ENTIRE MEAL: 620 CALORIES, 11.6 G. TOTAL FAT, 3.7 G. SATURATED FAT, 38.9 G. PROTEIN, 92.8 G. CARBOHYDRATES, 9.4 G. DIETARY FIBER, 79 MG. CHOLESTEROL, 330 MG. SODIUM

Fresh~Start

LOW-FAT LIVING RECIPES

RECIPES

12

"A simple enough pleasure, surely, to have breakfast alone with one's husband, but how seldom married people in the midst of life achieve it."
—ANNE MORROW LINDBERGH, AMERICAN AVIATOR AND WRITER

WAKE UP TO LOW-FAT LIVING

You're pressed for time and getting ready to dash out the door. But, wait. You've forgotten the most important thing: breakfast.

A satisfying, good-for-you breakfast fires up fat-burning for the entire day. Scientists have discovered that what we eat (or don't eat) in the morning impacts our energy levels all day long—including how we feel at supper time.

Get off to a good start with a high-quality, low-fat breakfast. If the morning is a rush, plan your breakfast the night before. (And if there's simply no time to sit down for a meal, keep foods on hand that you can drop into your purse or briefcase.) Here are a few quick ideas that go beyond a bowl of dry cereal with milk.

- Orange-Currant Scones (page 141) made the day before
- Whole-grain toast or a bagel with jam and a piece of fresh fruit
- Raisin-Pecan Wheat Bread (page 384) with low-fat cream cheese
- One of last night's biscuits with nonfat yogurt, low-fat cottage cheese, or skim milk and fresh fruit
- Brown Rice Pudding with Fruit (page 142)

The key is to rev up your natural energy and appetite when the sun comes up. What's the payoff? All-day energy and fat-burning power.

HASH-BROWN POTATOES WITH ROSEMARY

You'll think that a short-order cook from the local diner prepared these tasty spuds. They're just as crispy but don't cook in oceans of fat, so you can enjoy them often—even for dinner.

HANDS-ON TIME: 15 MINUTES
UNATTENDED TIME: 10 MINUTES

2½	pounds potatoes, cut into bite-size pieces
1	teaspoon olive or canola oil
1	onion, thickly sliced
1	teaspoon crushed dried rosemary
	Salt and ground black pepper

MAKES 4 SERVINGS
PER SERVING

258	CALORIES
2.6 G.	TOTAL FAT
0.4 G.	SATURATED FAT
4.9 G.	PROTEIN
55.2 G.	CARBOHYDRATES
0.7 G.	DIETARY FIBER
0 MG.	CHOLESTEROL
14 MG.	SODIUM

Bring a large pot of water to a boil over high heat. Add the potatoes and bring the water back to a boil. Reduce the heat to medium and cook for 5 to 8 minutes more, or until the potatoes begin to get tender. Drain and set side.

While the potatoes are cooking, warm the oil in a large no-stick skillet over medium heat. Add the onions and cook for 5 minutes. Gently stir in the potatoes and rosemary. Coat the potatoes with no-stick spray and season with salt and pepper to taste.

Cook, stirring gently, for 15 minutes, or until the potatoes are browned and soft inside.

BREAKFAST IN A BREAD BOWL

Take a large dinner roll. Stuff it with scrambled eggs, cheese, and sautéed vegetables. Now that's a simple, satisfying breakfast. You can even toss in fresh herbs or leftover cooked vegetables, chicken, fish, or beans. If you prefer, use 8 smaller rolls (1½ ounces each) in place of the 4 larger ones.

HANDS-ON TIME: 20 MINUTES
UNATTENDED TIME: NONE

MAKES 4 SERVINGS
PER SERVING
427   CALORIES
6.8 G. TOTAL FAT
2.6 G. SATURATED FAT
34.3 G. PROTEIN
53.1 G. CARBOHYDRATES
1.4 G. DIETARY FIBER
10 MG. CHOLESTEROL
820 MG. SODIUM

1	small red onion, chopped
½	green or sweet red pepper, chopped
1	small zucchini, chopped
4	mushrooms, chopped
1	cup packed fresh spinach, torn into pieces
3	cups fat-free egg substitute
	Salt and ground black pepper
1	cup shredded low-sodium part-skim Swiss or Cheddar cheese
4	large crusty French or Italian-style rolls (3 ounces each)

Coat a large no-stick skillet with no-stick spray. Set over medium heat until warm. Add the onions and peppers and cook for 2 minutes. Add the zucchini, mushrooms, and spinach. Cook and stir for 7 to 10 minutes. Transfer to a plate.

Again coat the skillet with no-stick spray and set over medium heat until warm.

In a medium bowl, beat the egg substitute. Season with the salt and pepper. Pour into the skillet and cook for 2 to 3 minutes, or until scrambled. Add the reserved vegetables. Cook and stir for 1 to 3 minutes, or until the eggs are almost cooked. Add the Swiss or Cheddar and stir until melted.

Slice the top off each roll and gently press the bread inside to form a bowl shape. Spoon the egg filling into the bread bowls and cover with the tops of the bread.

COOKING HINT

- When making scrambled eggs or omelets, combine the eggs with a little water instead of milk. Water makes the eggs more fluffy when cooked.

Basic Swiss Muesli

Tired of commercial cereals for breakfast? Make your own! It's simple, and you can tailor the cereal to suit your tastes. Plus, you'll avoid the preservatives, colorings, and sugar that are added to most commercial cereals. The cereal known as muesli appeared on American breakfast tables years ago, but credit goes to the Swiss for its origins. In German, the term muesli means mixture. And that's the most specific definition that you'll find anywhere. The main ingredient is rolled oats, but after that, the sky's the limit. Rolled wheat flakes, rolled rye flakes, corn flakes, nuts, and dried fruits can be included in various amounts.

Here's the easiest way to make muesli: Buy your favorite rolled grain flakes (like oats), nuts, and dried fruits from the bulk bins at your supermarket or health food store. Chop the nuts and fruits, then mix up the cereal to your liking and store it in an airtight container. At breakfast time, scoop some into a bowl, add low-fat milk, and let the cereal rest for 5 minutes to absorb the milk and soften the grains.

For a softer cereal, I like to soak the grain overnight. Then in the morning, I just add whatever other ingredients I want. Here's the basic recipe and some ingredient options to get you started. For more specific combinations, see the muesli recipes starting on the facing page.

For each serving, place about ½ cup rolled oats (or rolled wheat or rolled rye) in a serving bowl. Add just enough water or low-fat milk to cover the grain. Cover the bowl and refrigerate overnight. In the morning, stir in your favorite ingredients, like these.

- Dried fruit, chopped (apricots, cherries, cranberries, currants, dates, papaya, raisins)
- Nuts and seeds, chopped (almonds, brazil nuts, cashews, hazelnuts, macadamia nuts, pecans, pistachios, pine nuts, walnuts, pumpkin seeds, sesame seeds, sunflower seeds)
- Yogurt (nonfat plain or flavored)
- Sweetener (brown sugar, honey, maple syrup)
- Spices and flavorings (ground cinnamon or nutmeg, vanilla)
- Fresh fruit, chopped (apples, bananas, berries, citrus fruit, grapes, kiwifruit, mango, melons, papaya, peaches, pears, pineapple, plums)

NORTHERN SUMMERS MUESLI

This is one of my favorite warm-weather muesli recipes. It features the fresh fruits and berries of summer. To make 4 servings, double the amounts and use separate bowls for each serving.

½ cup rolled oats
1 tablespoon dried tart cherries or currants
1 tablespoon nonfat vanilla or lemon yogurt
1 teaspoon sunflower seeds
1 teaspoon ground almonds
1 teaspoon maple syrup
    Pinch of ground cinnamon
¼ cup raspberries
¼ cup blueberries
¼ cup chopped strawberries
1 peach, peeled, pitted, and chopped

Divide the oats between 2 serving bowls and add just enough water to cover. Cover the bowls and refrigerate overnight.

In the morning, divide the cherries or currants, yogurt, sunflower seeds, almonds, maple syrup, and cinnamon between the bowls. Mix well. Top with the raspberries, blueberries, strawberries, and peaches.

HANDS-ON TIME: 5 MINUTES
UNATTENDED TIME: OVERNIGHT

MAKES 2 SERVINGS

PER SERVING

153	CALORIES
3 G.	TOTAL FAT
0.4 G.	SATURATED FAT
5 G.	PROTEIN
28.5 G.	CARBOHYDRATES
4.3 G.	DIETARY FIBER
0 MG.	CHOLESTEROL
7 MG.	SODIUM

SWITCH TIP

Do you drink the milk left over in the bottom of the cereal bowl? You should. Many of the important vitamins and minerals used to fortify the cereals end up in the milk.

AUTUMN FRUIT AND NUT MUESLI

Apples, pears, walnuts, and dates add delicious fall flavors and textures to this muesli.

HANDS-ON TIME: 5 MINUTES
UNATTENDED TIME: OVERNIGHT

¾   cup rolled oats
1   tablespoon nonfat vanilla or plain yogurt
2   teaspoons brown sugar or honey
    Ground cinnamon
    Ground nutmeg
2   dates, pitted and chopped, or 2 tablespoons raisins
2   teaspoons chopped walnuts
1   apple, cored and chopped
1   pear, cored and chopped

MAKES 2 SERVINGS

PER SERVING
267	CALORIES
3.9 G.	TOTAL FAT
0.5 G.	SATURATED FAT
6.5 G.	PROTEIN
55.4 G.	CARBOHYDRATES
7.5 G.	DIETARY FIBER
0 MG.	CHOLESTEROL
8 MG.	SODIUM

Divide the oats between 2 serving bowls and add just enough water to cover. Cover the bowls and refrigerate overnight.

In the morning, divide the yogurt and sugar or honey between the bowls. Add cinnamon and nutmeg to taste. Mix well. Stir in the dates or raisins, walnuts, apples, and pears.

WINTER FRUIT MUESLI

The extra oats in this cold-weather cereal are crowned with a generous fruit topping for extra vitamin C. Choose a big cereal bowl for this hearty breakfast. For variety, use different nuts, seeds, dried fruit, and citrus fruit.

1	cup rolled oats
2	tablespoons nonfat vanilla or flavored yogurt
1	tablespoon honey or maple syrup
1	tablespoon dried cranberries
1	teaspoon chopped cashews
1	teaspoon pumpkin seeds
1	kiwifruit, peeled and sliced
1	banana, sliced
1	tangerine, peeled and separated into sections

Divide the oats between 2 serving bowls and add just enough water to cover. Cover the bowls and refrigerate overnight.

In the morning, divide the yogurt, honey or maple syrup, cranberries, cashews, and pumpkin seeds between the bowls. Top with the kiwifruit, bananas, and tangerines.

HANDS-ON TIME: 5 MINUTES
UNATTENDED TIME: OVERNIGHT

MAKES 2 SERVINGS
PER SERVING
303	CALORIES
3.9 G.	TOTAL FAT
0.7 G.	SATURATED FAT
8.4 G.	PROTEIN
62.1 G.	CARBOHYDRATES
7.5 G.	DIETARY FIBER
0 MG.	CHOLESTEROL
10 MG.	SODIUM

113

MEXICAN EGGS IN PHYLLO CUPS

The traditional version of this dish, *huevos rancheros*, is a layered combination of fried beans, fried eggs, and full-fat cheese on fried tortillas. To cut the fat, I use phyllo dough instead of fried tortillas, a combination of eggs and egg substitute, and reduced-fat cheese.

HANDS-ON TIME: 20 MINUTES
UNATTENDED TIME: 20 MINUTES

MAKES 6 SERVINGS
PER SERVING
277   CALORIES
9.7 G.   TOTAL FAT
2.9 G.   SATURATED FAT
25.6 G. PROTEIN
25 G.   CARBOHYDRATES
1.1 G.   DIETARY FIBER
155 MG. CHOLESTEROL
558 MG. SODIUM

4 ounces frozen phyllo dough, thawed (see hint)
1 cup fat-free egg substitute
4 eggs
   Salt and ground black pepper
2 cups shredded low-sodium reduced-fat sharp Cheddar or Monterey Jack cheese
1 can (15½ ounces) reduced-fat chili beans or refried beans, warmed

Preheat the oven to 400°F. Coat a 6-cup jumbo muffin pan with no-stick spray.

Cover the phyllo dough with plastic wrap to prevent it from drying out as you work. Carefully pick up 1 square of dough and set it on a piece of wax paper. Coat with no-stick spray. Top with another square of dough at a slightly different angle

(so that the corners are not on top of one another). Coat with no-stick spray. Repeat with the dough and no-stick spray to make 5 sheets of dough in a pile. Working quickly, repeat with the remaining dough and no-stick spray to make 6 piles of 5 sheets each.

Transfer the piles of dough to the prepared muffin pan; gently push the center of each pile inside a cup so that the edges stick up. Bake for 10 minutes, or until lightly browned and crispy.

Meanwhile, in a medium bowl, beat the egg substitute and eggs until foamy. Season with the salt and pepper. Coat a

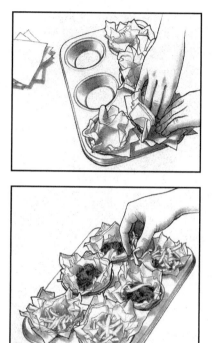

large no-stick skillet with no-stick spray. Set over medium heat until warm. Add the egg mixture and stir for 5 minutes, or until the eggs are cooked through. Remove from the heat.

Sprinkle about 2 tablespoons of the Cheddar or Monterey Jack into each phyllo cup. Divide the eggs evenly among the cups. Top with equal amounts of the beans. Sprinkle with the remaining cheese. Bake for 10 minutes, or until the cheese is melted.

SWITCH TIP

Here's an easy way to cut down on cholesterol and fat: Switch from eggs to egg substitute. You'll save 100 calories, 10 grams of fat, and 430 milligrams of cholesterol for every two eggs. You'll still get important nutrients like folate, iron, vitamin A, and vitamin B12. Buy fat-free egg substitute. It's made mostly of egg whites, so the taste and texture are close to real eggs. If you want to ease into the switch, start out using a combination of egg substitute and whole eggs. I like to keep a few cartons of egg substitute in the freezer. They thaw quickly in the microwave or overnight in the refrigerator.

COOKING HINTS

- To get the right amount of phyllo dough for this dish, cut a 1-pound package of phyllo dough in half crosswise. Return half of the dough to the freezer. Unroll the remaining half and cut in half again to form squares.

- If you don't have a 6-cup jumbo muffin pan, you can use six 8-ounce custard baking cups.

QUICK SWITCHES

Mexican Tofu in Phyllo Cups: Replace the eggs and egg substitute with 1 pound tofu (drained and crumbled). Sauté in the skillet for 5 minutes, or until heated through.

Vegetable Mexican Eggs in Phyllo Cups: Before adding the eggs, sauté ½ cup chopped onions, ½ cup chopped peppers, and ¼ cup corn kernels for 5 minutes, or until tender. Add the eggs to the skillet and proceed as directed.

STEWED FRUIT

Stewing may sound old-fashioned, but you'll love the rich, sweet flavor of stewed fruit. Use your favorite dried fruit and serve this compote by itself or on top of cooked cereal, yogurt, cottage cheese, or pancakes. It also makes a good dessert on top of frozen yogurt.

3	cups mixed dried fruit
3	cups water
1	cinnamon stick

In a large saucepan, mix the fruit, water, and cinnamon stick.

Bring the mixture to a boil over high heat. Reduce the heat to medium-low and simmer for 20 minutes, or until the fruit is plump and the liquid is slightly thickened. Remove and discard the cinnamon stick before serving. Serve warm. Or refrigerate the fruit in an airtight container for up to 3 days and serve cold.

COOKING HINT

• If you prefer a little more sweetness, add 1 to 2 tablespoons brown sugar to the mixture as it simmers.

HANDS-ON TIME: 2 MINUTES
UNATTENDED TIME: 20 MINUTES

MAKES 4 CUPS
PER ½ CUP

154	CALORIES
0.4 G.	TOTAL FAT
0 G.	SATURATED FAT
1.9 G.	PROTEIN
40 G.	CARBOHYDRATES
2 G.	DIETARY FIBER
0 MG.	CHOLESTEROL
4 MG.	SODIUM

CINNAMON WHOLE-GRAIN FRENCH TOAST

For healthier French toast, I use egg substitute to cut the cholesterol and whole-grain bread to increase fiber. Try using leftover Raisin-Pecan Wheat Bread (page 384). Top with maple syrup or fruit syrup instead of butter.

HANDS-ON TIME: 15 MINUTES
UNATTENDED TIME: 5 MINUTES

MAKES 4 SERVINGS
PER SERVING
198   CALORIES
1.1 G.   TOTAL FAT
0.1 G.   SATURATED FAT
15.8 G. PROTEIN
43.6 G. CARBOHYDRATES
4 G.   DIETARY FIBER
1 MG.   CHOLESTEROL
284 MG. SODIUM

1   cup fat-free egg substitute
1   egg
1   can (5 ounces) evaporated skim milk
1   teaspoon vanilla
½   teaspoon ground cinnamon
⅛   teaspoon ground nutmeg
8   slices whole-grain Italian or sourdough bread (1" thick)
1   teaspoon unsalted butter or margarine (optional)

In a 13" × 9" glass baking dish, combine the egg substitute, egg, milk, vanilla, cinnamon, and nutmeg. Beat with an electric mixer until foamy. Add the bread and turn to coat with the egg mixture. Soak for 5 minutes.

Place a no-stick griddle or large no-stick skillet over medium heat until warm. Coat with no-stick spray. Add the butter or margarine (if using) and swirl to coat the pan.

Lift the bread from the egg mixture, allowing the excess to drip off. Transfer the bread to the griddle or skillet. Cook for 2 to 3 minutes per side, or until browned and cooked through.

QUICK SWITCHES

Orange French Toast: Add 1 teaspoon frozen orange juice concentrate or orange liqueur and ½ teaspoon grated orange rind to the egg mixture. Dust the finished French toast with cocoa powder.

Stuffed French Toast: Cut a slit in the side of each piece of bread to form a pocket. In a small bowl, mix together ½ cup softened low-fat or nonfat cream cheese, ½ teaspoon ground cinnamon, and ¼ cup raspberries or sliced bananas. Divide the filling equally among the bread pockets. Coat with the egg mixture and cook as directed.

WHOLE-WHEAT BUTTERMILK PANCAKES

This pancake batter makes great waffles, too.

HANDS-ON TIME: 25 MINUTES
UNATTENDED TIME: NONE

2½	cups whole-wheat pastry flour or unbleached flour
2	teaspoons baking powder
1	teaspoon baking soda
¼	teaspoon salt
2½	cups nonfat or low-fat buttermilk
¼	cup honey or maple syrup
1	egg or 2 egg whites, lightly beaten
1	tablespoon canola oil
1	teaspoon vanilla

MAKES 14

PER PANCAKE
122   CALORIES
1.8 G.   TOTAL FAT
0.3 G.   SATURATED FAT
4.9 G.   PROTEIN
22.8 G. CARBOHYDRATES
2.7 G.   DIETARY FIBER
16 MG.   CHOLESTEROL
227 MG. SODIUM

Coat a no-stick griddle or large skillet with no-stick spray. Set over medium heat until hot.

In a large bowl, mix the flour, baking powder, baking soda, and salt.

In a small bowl, mix the buttermilk, honey or maple syrup, egg or egg whites, oil, and vanilla. Add to the flour mixture and stir until just moistened (the batter will be lumpy).

Drop the batter by spoonfuls onto the hot griddle. Cook for 2 to 4 minutes, or until the bottoms are light brown and bubbles appear on top. Using a spatula, flip the pancakes and cook for 1 to 2 minutes more, or until browned.

Transfer to a covered serving plate to keep warm. Repeat with the remaining batter.

QUICK SWITCHES

Buckwheat Buttermilk Pancakes: Replace 1 cup of the flour with buckwheat flour.

Multigrain Buttermilk Pancakes: Replace 2 cups of the flour with a mixture of the following: oat, millet, brown rice, barley, rye, or triticale flour; cornmeal or blue cornmeal; or oat bran.

Fruit-Filled Buttermilk Pancakes: Fold 1 cup chopped fruit into the batter. Blueberries, raspberries, strawberries, blackberries, peaches, and bananas are favorites in our house.

INDIVIDUAL FRUIT HOTCAKES

Ho-hum about regular breakfast fare? Try these fruit-filled baked hotcakes from the French countryside that are easy to make and low in fat and calories. You could even serve this sweet dish as a late-night snack.

HANDS-ON TIME: 10 MINUTES
UNATTENDED TIME: 25 MINUTES

2	cups chopped fresh fruit
1	cup nonfat lemon or vanilla yogurt
¼	cup honey or sugar
2	eggs or ½ cup fat-free egg substitute
½	cup whole-wheat pastry flour or unbleached flour
1	teaspoon vanilla
¼	teaspoon ground cinnamon
⅛	teaspoon salt

MAKES 4 SERVINGS

PER SERVING

211	CALORIES
3.1 G.	TOTAL FAT
0.8 G.	SATURATED FAT
7.6 G.	PROTEIN
39.9 G.	CARBOHYDRATES
3.8 G.	DIETARY FIBER
106 MG.	CHOLESTEROL
137 MG.	SODIUM

Preheat the oven to 400°F. Coat four 6-ounce custard baking cups with no-stick spray. Divide the fruit equally among the cups.

Place ¾ cup of the yogurt in a medium bowl. Whisk in the honey or sugar, eggs or egg substitute, flour, vanilla, cinnamon, and salt. Pour over the fruit.

Bake for 25 to 30 minutes, or until the tops are lightly browned. Serve warm or at room temperature. Top each serving with 1 tablespoon of the remaining yogurt.

COOKING HINT

• Any type of fruit may be used in this recipe. In winter, try bananas and pears. In summer, take advantage of seasonal favorites like strawberries, blueberries, raspberries, blackberries, peaches, cherries, and plums.

Low-Calorie Pancake Toppings

Commercial pancake syrups are usually made with
high-calorie corn syrup, colorings, and additives. Here
are two low-calorie toppings that come together
quickly. Fresh (or frozen) fruit gives them a sweet
flavor and a bit of fiber.

Raspberry Sauce

Fresh-tasting and mildly sweet, this sauce is 90 percent fruit
and only 10 percent sweetener. Try it spooned over pancakes,
French toast, frozen yogurt, cakes, fresh fruit salads, even toast.
I recommend leaving in the raspberry seeds for their texture
and fiber, although you can strain them out if preferred.

HANDS-ON TIME: 5 MINUTES
UNATTENDED TIME: 15 MINUTES

MAKES 1¼ CUPS
PER 4 TEASPOONS

62	CALORIES
0.3 G.	TOTAL FAT
0 G.	SATURATED FAT
0.6 G.	PROTEIN
15.4 G.	CARBOHYDRATES
2.7 G.	DIETARY FIBER
0 MG.	CHOLESTEROL
0 MG.	SODIUM

3	**cups raspberries**
¼	**cup sugar or honey**
1	**tablespoon raspberry liqueur (optional)**

In a medium saucepan, combine the raspberries, sugar or
honey, and liqueur (if using). Cook over medium heat, stirring
occasionally, for 20 minutes, or until the fruit is very soft and
the liquid is slightly thickened.

Pour the sauce into a serving bowl. Serve warm or cover and
refrigerate for up to 1 week.

Cooking Hint

• Experiment with other fruits such as blueberries, strawberries,
peeled and finely chopped peaches, apricots, or plums. Even
frozen unsweetened fruit can be used.

FRUIT SAUCE

Making your own fruit sauce is a breeze. All you need is unsweetened fresh, frozen, or canned fruit and a little honey or sugar. Good choices include strawberries, blueberries, raspberries, peaches, pineapple, and apricots. Use the sauce over pancakes, French toast, waffles, or frozen yogurt.

HANDS-ON TIME: 5 MINUTES
UNATTENDED TIME: 15 MINUTES

MAKES 2 CUPS
PER ½ CUP

57	CALORIES
0.4 G.	TOTAL FAT
0 G.	SATURATED FAT
0.7 G.	PROTEIN
14 G.	CARBOHYDRATES
2.1 G.	DIETARY FIBER
0 MG.	CHOLESTEROL
1 MG.	SODIUM

1	**pound fruit, chopped into bite-size pieces**
1–3	**tablespoons honey or sugar**
1–3	**tablespoons arrowroot or cornstarch**
	Ground cinnamon or nutmeg (optional)

In a medium saucepan, mix the fruit, 1 tablespoon of the honey or sugar, and 1 tablespoon of the arrowroot or cornstarch. Season with the cinnamon or nutmeg (if using). Add additional honey or sugar if necessary to sweeten the fruit.

Bring to a boil over high heat. Reduce the heat to medium-low and simmer for 10 to 15 minutes, or until slightly thickened. (If necessary to thicken the sauce, dissolve additional arrowroot or cornstarch in a small amount of cold water. Add to the sauce and stir until thickened.) Serve warm or cover and refrigerate for up to 1 week.

COOKING HINT

• Adjust the amount of sweetener and thickener to match the type of fruit you use. For example, fruit that's extra sweet and juicy will require less honey or sugar for sweetening and more arrowroot or cornstarch for thickening.

RECIPES

"No man can be wise on an empty stomach."

—GEORGE ELIOT, BRITISH NOVELIST

SLIMMING SNACKS FOR PEOPLE ON THE GO

Here's an amazing fact: Snacks help you burn fat. Studies show that every time you eat healthy, low-fat foods, your body gets a metabolic lift that turns on your fat-burning power. If you skip between-meal snacks to "save calories," you actually reduce your body's fat-burning potential and increase its fat-making machinery. Plus, you go hungry.

Plan on snacking two or three times throughout the day, say researchers. Most folks find it convenient to have two snacks—one mid-morning and one mid-afternoon. If you eat your evening meal early (before 6:00 P.M.), plan on another light snack after dinner. These nibbles reduce the urge to overeat at main meals, and keep your metabolism up all day long. And that translates into more energy for you.

If you like sweet snacks, find a few treats in this chapter and make them a daily habit. The Almond Ahhs are especially good, and they're a snap to prepare. Chocoholics will love the Double Chocolate Chip Cookies, Chocolate-Almond Biscotti, and Chewy Brownies. Most of these snacks can be prepared ahead and stored at room temperature until you're ready to eat them. So there's no excuse not to have them with you throughout the day. If you prefer salty over sweet, check out the savory snacks in chapters 22 and 23.

ALMOND AHHS

These light, airy cookies have an irresistibly soft, melt-in-your-mouth feel. The secret is a creamy meringue that has absolutely no fat. The only fat in this recipe comes from what's naturally in the almonds.

HANDS-ON TIME: 10 MINUTES
UNATTENDED TIME: 20 MINUTES

3	egg whites
⅛	teaspoon salt
1	cup sugar
1	tablespoon vanilla
½	cup finely chopped toasted almonds

MAKES 40

PER COOKIE

31	CALORIES
0.8 G.	TOTAL FAT
0.1 G.	SATURATED FAT
0.6 G.	PROTEIN
5.5 G.	CARBOHYDRATES
0.1 G.	DIETARY FIBER
0 MG.	CHOLESTEROL
11 MG.	SODIUM

Preheat the oven to 250°F. Coat 2 baking sheets with no-stick spray.

Place the egg whites in a medium bowl. Using an electric mixer, beat until soft peaks form. Add the salt. Gradually beat in the sugar and then the vanilla. Beat until the egg whites are stiff but not dry. Gently fold in the almonds.

Drop teaspoonfuls of the batter onto the prepared baking sheets; lift the spoon as you drop the batter to create a peak in the center. Do not allow the batter to spread.

Bake for 20 to 30 minutes, or until the cookies are light brown and hard to the touch on top. Carefully remove the cookies from the baking sheets and cool on a wire rack.

COOKING HINT

• You can replace the almonds with pecans, walnuts, pistachios, pine nuts, or other nuts.

COCOA MERINGUES

These cookies make great housewarming or holiday gifts.

HANDS-ON TIME: 10 MINUTES
UNATTENDED TIME: 25 MINUTES

3	egg whites
1	cup sugar
1	tablespoon vanilla
6	tablespoons unsweetened Dutch process cocoa powder

MAKES 40
PER COOKIE
23	CALORIES
0.1 G.	TOTAL FAT
0 G.	SATURATED FAT
0.4 G.	PROTEIN
5.6 G.	CARBOHYDRATES
0 G.	DIETARY FIBER
0 MG.	CHOLESTEROL
5 MG.	SODIUM

Preheat the oven to 250°F. Coat 2 baking sheets with no-stick spray.

Place the egg whites in a medium bowl. Using an electric mixer, beat until soft peaks form. Gradually beat in the sugar and then the vanilla. Beat until the egg whites are stiff but not dry. Gently fold in the cocoa.

Drop teaspoonfuls of the batter onto the prepared baking sheets; lift the spoon as you drop the batter to create a peak in the center. Do not allow the batter to spread (see illustration on the facing page).

Bake for 25 to 30 minutes, or until the cookies are light brown and hard to the touch on top. Carefully remove the cookies from the baking sheets and cool on a wire rack.

COOKING HINTS

- For a more crunchy cookie, bake for another 5 to 10 minutes.

- Dutch process cocoa powder has a richer flavor than regular unsweetened cocoa powder. Look for it next to the regular cocoa powder in your grocery store. If necessary, regular unsweetened cocoa powder can be substituted.

QUICK SWITCHES

Cocoa-Nut Meringues: Fold in ½ cup finely chopped walnuts, pecans, or almonds along with the cocoa.

Double Chocolate Meringues: Fold in ½ cup mini chocolate chips along with the cocoa.

CINNAMON SUGAR COOKIES

These sugar cookies are a favorite in our house. I usually double the recipe because they go fast and keep for up to a week in an airtight container.

HANDS-ON TIME: 15 MINUTES
UNATTENDED TIME: 20 MINUTES

¼	cup unsalted butter or margarine, softened
¼	cup packed brown sugar
2	egg whites
2	tablespoons light corn syrup
1½	teaspoons vanilla
⅓	cup + 1 tablespoon sugar
1½	cups whole-wheat pastry flour or unbleached flour
½	teaspoon baking powder
¼	teaspoon baking soda
	Pinch of salt
1	teaspoon ground cinnamon

MAKES 48
PER COOKIE
36   CALORIES
1.1 G.   TOTAL FAT
0.7 G.   SATURATED FAT
0.7 G.   PROTEIN
6.3 G.   CARBOHYDRATES
0.5 G.   DIETARY FIBER
3 MG.   CHOLESTEROL
17 MG.   SODIUM

Preheat the oven to 375°F. Coat 2 baking sheets with no-stick spray.

Place the butter or margarine in a large bowl. Using an electric mixer, beat until creamy. Add the brown sugar, egg whites, corn syrup, vanilla, and ⅓ cup of the sugar. Beat until smooth.

In a medium bowl, combine the flour, baking powder, baking soda, salt, and ½ teaspoon of the cinnamon. Mix well. Add to the butter mixture and mix well.

In a cup, combine the remaining 1 tablespoon sugar and the remaining ½ teaspoon cinnamon. Mix well.

Drop the dough by teaspoons onto the prepared baking sheets about 2" to 3" apart. Sprinkle with the cinnamon-sugar mixture.

Bake 1 sheet at a time for 10 minutes, or until light brown. Remove the cookies from the baking sheets and cool on a wire rack.

BANANA-NUT COOKIES

When you have a craving for sweets and need quick relief, these treats won't disappoint. A little butter or margarine goes a long way to create soft cookies with big banana flavor.

HANDS-ON TIME: 15 MINUTES
UNATTENDED TIME: 25 MINUTES

MAKES 42
PER COOKIE

57	CALORIES
1.4 G.	TOTAL FAT
0.6 G.	SATURATED FAT
1 G.	PROTEIN
10.7 G.	CARBOHYDRATES
0.9 G.	DIETARY FIBER
2 MG.	CHOLESTEROL
32 MG.	SODIUM

2	ripe bananas
1	cup packed brown sugar
3	tablespoons unsalted butter or margarine, softened
2	teaspoons vanilla
¼	teaspoon salt (optional)
2	cups whole-wheat pastry flour or unbleached flour
1	teaspoon baking soda
¼	cup chopped toasted walnuts

Preheat the oven to 350°F. Coat 2 baking sheets with no-stick spray.

In a large bowl, combine the bananas, brown sugar, butter or margarine, vanilla, and salt (if using). Using an electric mixer, beat until well-combined.

In a small bowl, combine the flour and baking soda. Mix well. Add to the banana mixture. Stir until well-combined. Fold in the walnuts.

Drop the dough by rounded teaspoons onto the prepared baking sheets about 2" to 3" apart.

Bake 1 sheet at a time for 12 to 15 minutes, or until lightly browned. Remove the cookies from the baking sheets and cool on a wire rack.

Oatmeal-Raisin Chocolate Chip Cookies

If you'd rather pass on the chocolate chips, substitute dried cherries, strawberries, or dates. I also like these cookies with dried blueberries and a little cinnamon and nutmeg.

HANDS-ON TIME: 10 MINUTES
UNATTENDED TIME: 20 MINUTES

1¾	**cups rolled oats**
1½	**cups whole-wheat pastry flour or unbleached flour**
½	**teaspoon baking soda**
¼	**teaspoon salt**
2	**egg whites**
½	**cup honey**
5	**tablespoons unsweetened applesauce**
3	**tablespoons unsalted butter or margarine, melted**
1	**tablespoon vanilla**
½	**cup raisins**
2	**tablespoons mini chocolate chips**

MAKES 26

PER COOKIE
93	CALORIES
2.1 G.	TOTAL FAT
1 G.	SATURATED FAT
2.3 G.	PROTEIN
17.2 G.	CARBOHYDRATES
1.6 G.	DIETARY FIBER
4 MG.	CHOLESTEROL
31 MG.	SODIUM

Preheat the oven to 325°F. Coat a baking sheet with no-stick spray.

In a large bowl, combine the oats, flour, baking soda, and salt. Mix well.

Place the egg whites in a medium bowl and whisk lightly. Whisk in the honey, applesauce, butter or margarine, and vanilla. Add to the flour mixture and stir until well-combined. Fold in the raisins and chocolate chips.

Drop the dough by rounded teaspoons onto the prepared baking sheet about 2" to 3" apart. If desired, flatten the cookies slightly with a fork.

Bake for 16 to 18 minutes, or until lightly browned. Remove the cookies from the baking sheet and cool on a wire rack.

Cooking Hint

• Mini chocolate chips are great fat-savers. Their small size helps distribute the chocolate flavor throughout recipes so you don't need to use as much.

DOUBLE CHOCOLATE CHIP COOKIES

Egg substitute and prune puree slash the fat in these chewy cookies. Freeze them in airtight containers for sweet treats anytime.

HANDS-ON TIME: 15 MINUTES
UNATTENDED TIME: 30 MINUTES

2½	**cups whole-wheat pastry flour or unbleached flour**
¼	**cup unsweetened cocoa powder**
1	**teaspoon baking soda**
½	**teaspoon salt**
¼	**cup unsalted butter or margarine, softened**
¾	**cup prune puree (see hint)**
¾	**cup sugar**
¾	**cup packed brown sugar**
½	**cup fat-free egg substitute**
1	**tablespoon vanilla**
1	**cup mini chocolate chips**

MAKES 68
PER COOKIE
58   CALORIES
1.5 G.   TOTAL FAT
0.5 G.   SATURATED FAT
1 G.   PROTEIN
10.7 G.   CARBOHYDRATES
0.7 G.   DIETARY FIBER
2 MG.   CHOLESTEROL
41 MG.   SODIUM

Preheat the oven to 375°F. Coat 3 baking sheets with no-stick spray.

In a medium bowl, combine the flour, cocoa powder, baking soda, and salt.

Place the butter or margarine in a large bowl. Using an electric mixer, beat until creamy. Add the prune puree, sugar, brown sugar, egg substitute, and vanilla. Beat until smooth. Gradually beat in the flour mixture. Stir in the chocolate chips.

Drop the dough by rounded teaspoons onto the prepared baking sheets about 2" to 3" apart.

Bake 1 sheet at a time for 9 to 10 minutes, or until the cookies look firm on top. Remove the cookies from the baking sheets and cool on a wire rack.

COOKING HINT

• To make ¾ cup prune puree, cover ½ cup pitted prunes with ½ cup hot water and soak for 5 minutes, or until plump. Process in a blender or food processor until smooth.

CRUNCHY PEANUT BUTTER COOKIES

These cookies are like the ones I bought at school as a kid. To keep them slightly chewy inside, don't flatten them too much, and bake them just until the bottoms are lightly browned.

HANDS-ON TIME: 15 MINUTES
UNATTENDED TIME: 15 MINUTES

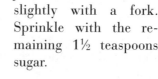

2	tablespoons unsalted butter or margarine, softened
¾	cup packed brown sugar
½	cup crunchy peanut butter
2	egg whites
2	tablespoons light corn syrup
1	tablespoon vanilla
¼	cup + 1½ teaspoons sugar
1½	cups whole-wheat pastry flour or unbleached flour
½	teaspoon baking soda
¼	teaspoon salt

MAKES 48

PER COOKIE

53	CALORIES
1.7 G.	TOTAL FAT
0.5 G.	SATURATED FAT
1.3 G.	PROTEIN
8.5 G.	CARBOHYDRATES
0.7 G.	DIETARY FIBER
1 MG.	CHOLESTEROL
29 MG.	SODIUM

SWITCH TIP

Peanut butter is an American favorite. We consume more than a million pounds of the stuff every day. To avoid added sugar, oils, and salt, choose natural peanut butter. For variety, try different types of nut butter such as almond butter and cashew butter. These are available at health food stores and some large supermarkets.

Preheat the oven to 375°F. Coat 2 baking sheets with no-stick spray.

Place the butter or margarine in a large bowl. Using an electric mixer, beat until creamy. Add the brown sugar, peanut butter, egg whites, corn syrup, vanilla, and ¼ cup of the sugar. Beat until smooth.

In a medium bowl, combine the flour, baking soda, and salt. Add to the peanut butter mixture and beat well.

Drop the dough by rounded teaspoons onto the prepared baking sheets about 2" to 3" apart. Flatten the cookies

slightly with a fork. Sprinkle with the remaining 1½ teaspoons sugar.

Bake 1 sheet at a time for 7 to 9 minutes, or until the bottoms just begin to brown. Remove the cookies from the baking sheets and cool on a wire rack.

CHOCOLATE-ALMOND BISCOTTI

Biscotti are twice-baked Italian cookies. They're slightly sweet and ideal for dipping in a cup of hot tea or coffee. Kids love to dunk them in cold milk.

HANDS-ON TIME: 20 MINUTES
UNATTENDED TIME: 1¼ HOURS

2	cups whole-wheat pastry flour or unbleached flour
1½	cups sugar
¼	cup unsweetened cocoa powder
½	teaspoon baking soda
¼	teaspoon salt
3	eggs
1	egg white
¾	cup chopped toasted almonds
2	teaspoons vanilla

MAKES 40
PER BISCOTTO
71	CALORIES
1.8 G.	TOTAL FAT
0.3 G.	SATURATED FAT
2 G.	PROTEIN
12.8 G.	CARBOHYDRATES
1 G.	DIETARY FIBER
16 MG.	CHOLESTEROL
36 MG.	SODIUM

Preheat the oven to 325°F. Coat a baking sheet with no-stick spray.

In a large bowl, combine the flour, sugar, cocoa, baking soda, and salt. Mix well.

Place the eggs and egg white in a medium bowl and whisk lightly. Whisk in the almonds and vanilla. Add to the flour mixture and stir until well-combined.

Shape the dough into 2 logs, about 5" × 11". Place the logs on the prepared baking sheet.

Bake for 35 to 40 minutes, or until a toothpick inserted in the center of a log comes out dry. Remove from the oven and cool on a wire rack for 10 minutes.

Slice each log crosswise into ½" pieces. Place each piece on the baking sheet, cut side down.

Bake for 15 minutes. Turn the biscotti and bake for 15 minutes, or until dry. Remove the biscotti from the baking sheet and cool on a wire rack.

OATMEAL LACE COOKIES WITH CHOCOLATE DRIZZLES

This is the fanciest and prettiest drop cookie you'll ever make. Just promise not to bake them for company only. These light, crunchy treats are great for family snacking.

HANDS-ON TIME: 5 MINUTES
UNATTENDED TIME: 25 MINUTES

1	egg
¼	cup packed brown sugar
¼	cup sugar
1	cup rolled oats
1	tablespoon unsalted butter or margarine, melted
½	teaspoon vanilla
¼	teaspoon salt
3	tablespoons chocolate chips
2	tablespoons skim milk

MAKES 30
PER COOKIE
36 CALORIES
1.1 G. TOTAL FAT
0.3 G. SATURATED FAT
0.8 G. PROTEIN
6 G. CARBOHYDRATES
0.3 G. DIETARY FIBER
8 MG. CHOLESTEROL
22 MG. SODIUM

Preheat the oven to 325°F. Line 3 baking sheets with parchment paper or foil and coat with no-stick spray.

In a medium bowl, combine the egg, brown sugar, and sugar. Using an electric mixer, beat until thick and creamy. Stir in the oats, butter or margarine, vanilla, and salt until well-combined.

Drop the batter by half-teaspoons onto the prepared baking sheets about 3" apart. Using the back of a spoon, flatten and spread out each cookie.

Bake 1 sheet at a time for 7 to 9 minutes, or until golden around the edges. Cool the cookies on the baking sheets on a wire rack.

In a small saucepan, combine the chocolate chips and milk. Stir over low heat until the chips are melted. Dip a knife into the chocolate and drizzle a thin stream of chocolate over each cookie. Remove the cookies from the baking sheets and let stand until the chocolate hardens.

CHOCOLATE-WALNUT CHEESECAKE BARS

These yummy snacks whip up fast, so make lots. They keep well in the refrigerator, but don't expect to have many leftovers.

HANDS-ON TIME: 10 MINUTES
UNATTENDED TIME: 1 HOUR

12	ounces nonfat cream cheese, softened
2¼	cups sugar
1	cup fat-free egg substitute
1	tablespoon vanilla
1	cup whole-wheat pastry flour or unbleached flour
½	cup milk chocolate chips, melted
3	tablespoons unsweetened cocoa powder
⅓	cup chopped walnuts

MAKES 16
PER BAR
206   CALORIES
3.2 G.   TOTAL FAT
0.1 G.   SATURATED FAT
6.5 G.   PROTEIN
39.1 G. CARBOHYDRATES
1 G.   DIETARY FIBER
1 MG.   CHOLESTEROL
159 MG. SODIUM

Preheat the oven to 325°F. Coat an 8" × 8" baking dish with no-stick spray.

Place the cream cheese in a large bowl. Using an electric mixer, beat until smooth. Add the sugar and beat well. Beat in the egg substitute and vanilla. Slowly beat in the flour until well-combined.

Pour 1½ cups of the batter into a small bowl.

Stir the melted chocolate and cocoa into the remaining batter until well-combined. Pour into the prepared baking dish. Pour the reserved batter evenly over the chocolate layer. Sprinkle with the walnuts.

Bake for 55 minutes, or until lightly browned. Cool completely, cover, and chill.

COOKING HINT

• Here's an easy way to melt chocolate chips. Place the chocolate in a glass measuring cup. Microwave on high for 30 seconds. Stir. Repeat until the chocolate is just melted. (Be careful not to overcook the chocolate or it will become chalky. The chips will not change shape as they soften, so you can't go by appearance.)

CHEWY BROWNIES

Chocolate chips, cocoa powder, and prune puree make these brownies moist, rich, and low in fat. Chocoholics will love them!

HANDS-ON TIME: 15 MINUTES
UNATTENDED TIME: 2 HOURS

1¼	cups unbleached flour
1	teaspoon baking powder
½	teaspoon salt
1¼	cups sugar
½	cup packed brown sugar
½	cup milk chocolate or semi-sweet chocolate chips, melted
½	cup unsweetened cocoa powder
4	egg whites
1	tablespoon canola oil
1	tablespoon vanilla
½	cup prune puree (see hint)

MAKES 16

PER BROWNIE
181	CALORIES
2.7 G.	TOTAL FAT
0.1 G.	SATURATED FAT
2.9 G.	PROTEIN
38.2 G.	CARBOHYDRATES
0.6 G.	DIETARY FIBER
1 MG.	CHOLESTEROL
110 MG.	SODIUM

Preheat the oven to 350°F. Coat an 8" × 8" baking dish with no-stick spray. Sprinkle lightly with flour.

In a medium bowl, combine the flour, baking powder, and salt. Mix well. Set aside.

In a large bowl, combine the sugar, brown sugar, melted chocolate, cocoa, egg whites, oil, and vanilla. Using an electric mixer, beat until smooth. Beat in the prune puree.

Add the flour mixture to the chocolate mixture and beat until well-combined. Pour the batter into the prepared baking dish.

Bake for 45 to 50 minutes, or until a toothpick inserted into the center comes out moist but not wet. Cool on a wire rack for 1 hour before cutting.

COOKING HINTS

- To make ½ cup prune puree, cover ⅓ cup pitted prunes with ⅓ cup hot water and soak for 5 minutes, or until plump. Process in a blender or food processor until smooth.

- Here's an easy way to melt chocolate chips. Place the chocolate in a glass measuring cup. Microwave on high for 30 seconds. Stir. Repeat until the chocolate is just melted. (Be careful not to overcook the chocolate or it will become chalky. The chips will not change shape as they soften, so you can't go by appearance.)

CHOCOLATE CUPCAKES

The kids will never guess that these little gems are low-fat.

HANDS-ON TIME: 15 MINUTES
UNATTENDED TIME: 20 MINUTES

CUPCAKES

1	cup whole-wheat pastry flour or unbleached flour
¼	cup unsweetened cocoa powder
1	teaspoon baking soda
⅛	teaspoon salt
3	tablespoons soft unsalted butter or margarine
¾	cup packed brown sugar
2	eggs
½	cup prune puree (see hint)
1	teaspoon vanilla

FROSTING

4	ounces nonfat cream cheese, softened
¾	cup confectioners' sugar
1	tablespoon unsweetened cocoa powder

MAKES 12

PER CUPCAKE

160	CALORIES
3.5 G.	TOTAL FAT
1.8 G.	SATURATED FAT
3.6 G.	PROTEIN
30.7 G.	CARBOHYDRATES
1.8 G.	DIETARY FIBER
35 MG.	CHOLESTEROL
180 MG.	SODIUM

To make the cupcakes: Preheat the oven to 375°F. Line a 12-cup muffin pan with paper cups.

In a large bowl, combine the flour, cocoa, baking soda, and salt.

Place the butter or margarine and brown sugar in a medium bowl. Using an electric mixer, beat until smooth. Add the eggs, prune puree, and vanilla. Beat until smooth. Stir into the flour mixture. Stir to combine. Spoon the batter into the prepared cups.

Bake for 20 minutes, or until a toothpick inserted into the center comes out clean. (Be careful to not overbake.) Remove the cupcakes from the pan and cool on a wire rack.

To make the frosting: In a medium bowl, combine the cream cheese, confectioners' sugar, and cocoa. Beat until smooth. Spread over the cooled cupcakes.

COOKING HINT

- To make ¾ cup prune puree, cover ½ cup pitted prunes with ½ cup hot water and soak for 5 minutes. Process in a blender or food processor until smooth.

JUMBO CHOCOLATE-CHERRY MUFFINS

These chocolate treats taste incredibly decadent.

HANDS-ON TIME: 15 MINUTES
UNATTENDED TIME: 35 MINUTES

¾	**cup water**
¾	**cup dried cherries**
1	**cup unbleached flour or whole-wheat pastry flour**
¾	**cup sugar**
½	**cup unsweetened cocoa powder**
¼	**cup packed brown sugar**
1½	**teaspoons baking powder**
½	**teaspoon baking soda**
⅛	**teaspoon salt**
4	**egg whites**
¼	**cup skim milk**
1	**tablespoon canola oil**
1	**tablespoon vanilla**
⅔	**cup prune puree (see hint)**
2	**tablespoons mini chocolate chips**

MAKES 6

PER MUFFIN

341	CALORIES
4.4 G.	TOTAL FAT
0.4 G.	SATURATED FAT
8.2 G.	PROTEIN
3.4 G.	DIETARY FIBER
73.7 G.	CARBOHYDRATES
0 MG.	CHOLESTEROL
289 MG.	SODIUM

Preheat the oven to 350°F. Coat a 6-cup jumbo muffin pan with no-stick spray.

Bring the water to a boil in a small saucepan. Add the cherries and remove from the heat. Let soak until needed.

In a large bowl, combine the flour, sugar, cocoa, brown sugar, baking powder, baking soda, and salt. Mix well.

In a medium bowl, whisk together the egg whites, milk, oil, and vanilla. Add the prune puree and mix well. Add to the flour mixture and stir just until combined; do not overmix.

Drain the cherries. Fold the cherries and chocolate chips into the batter. Spoon the batter into the prepared muffin pan.

Bake for 35 minutes, or until a toothpick inserted in the center of a muffin comes out moist but not wet. Remove the muffins from the pan and cool on a wire rack.

COOKING HINT

- To make ⅔ cup prune puree, cover a scant ½ cup pitted prunes with ⅓ cup hot water and soak for 5 minutes. Process in a blender or food processor until smooth.

CARROT-PUMPKIN MUFFINS WITH ORANGE

Pumpkin and carrots are loaded with beta-carotene, an antioxidant vitamin that the body converts into vitamin A. Snack on these tasty, high-fiber muffins and you'll help boost your immune system.

HANDS-ON TIME: 15 MINUTES
UNATTENDED TIME: 25 MINUTES

MAKES 12
PER MUFFIN
147   CALORIES
2 G.   TOTAL FAT
0.3 G.   SATURATED FAT
2.9 G.   PROTEIN
31.4 G.   CARBOHYDRATES
2.9 G.   DIETARY FIBER
18 MG.   CHOLESTEROL
130 MG.   SODIUM

1½	cups whole-wheat pastry flour or unbleached flour
1	teaspoon ground cinnamon
1	teaspoon baking soda
½	teaspoon baking powder
½	teaspoon ground cloves
¼	teaspoon ground nutmeg
1	egg
1	cup unsweetened canned pumpkin
¾	cup honey
2	tablespoons unsweetened applesauce
1	tablespoon canola oil
1	teaspoon grated orange rind
1	cup shredded carrots

Preheat the oven to 350°F. Coat a 12-cup muffin pan with no-stick spray.

In a large bowl, combine the flour, cinnamon, baking soda, baking powder, cloves, and nutmeg. Mix well.

Place the egg in a medium bowl and whisk lightly. Whisk in the pumpkin, honey, applesauce, oil, and orange rind. Add to the flour mixture and stir just until combined; do not overmix. Fold in the carrots. Spoon the batter into the prepared muffin pan.

Bake for 25 minutes, or until a toothpick inserted in the center of a muffin comes out almost clean. Remove the muffins from the pan and cool on a wire rack.

APPLESAUCE CAKE WITH WALNUTS AND RAISINS

This remake of classic applesauce cake cuts way back on the oil, using just 2 tablespoons. The cake is plenty moist from the applesauce. Raisins and walnuts add sweetness and crunch.

HANDS-ON TIME: 15 MINUTES
UNATTENDED TIME: 45 MINUTES

MAKES 18 SERVINGS
PER SERVING
283 CALORIES
5.1 G. TOTAL FAT
0.4 G. SATURATED FAT
6.3 G. PROTEIN
56.7 G. CARBOHYDRATES
4.4 G. DIETARY FIBER
0 MG. CHOLESTEROL
201 MG. SODIUM

4 **cups whole-wheat pastry flour or unbleached flour**
1 **tablespoon ground cinnamon**
2 **teaspoons baking powder**
1 **teaspoon baking soda**
½ **teaspoon ground nutmeg**
½ **teaspoon salt**
¼ **teaspoon ground cloves**
¼ **teaspoon ground allspice**
4 **apples, peeled, cored, and chopped**
¾ **cup coarsely chopped walnuts**
⅓ **cup raisins**
2 **cups unsweetened applesauce**
2 **cups packed brown sugar**
1 **cup fat-free egg substitute**
2 **tablespoons canola oil**
1 **tablespoon vanilla**

Preheat the oven to 350°F. Coat a 13" × 9" baking dish with no-stick spray.

In a large bowl, combine the flour, cinnamon, baking powder, baking soda, nutmeg, salt, cloves, and allspice. Mix well.

In a small bowl, combine the apples, walnuts, and raisins. Mix well.

In a medium bowl, combine the applesauce, brown sugar, egg substitute, oil, and vanilla. Mix well. Add to the flour mixture and stir just until combined. Fold in the apple mixture. Spoon the batter into the prepared baking dish.

Bake for 45 minutes, or until a toothpick inserted in the center comes out clean. Cool on a wire rack.

LEMON-LIME POPPY SEED LOAF

I turned an old family recipe for lemon cake into this poppy seed loaf. It has a light texture and a lively lemon-lime taste.

HANDS-ON TIME: 10 MINUTES
UNATTENDED TIME: 1 HOUR

CAKE

1½	cups whole-wheat pastry flour or unbleached flour
¾	cup sugar
2	tablespoons poppy seeds
1	teaspoon baking powder
½	teaspoon salt
¾	cup fat-free egg substitute
3	tablespoons unsweetened applesauce
2	tablespoons canola oil
1½	teaspoons grated lemon rind
1½	teaspoons grated lime rind
½	teaspoon vanilla

TOPPING

¼	cup sugar
1½	tablespoons lemon juice
1½	tablespoons lime juice

MAKES 1 LOAF;
10 SLICES
PER SLICE
191   CALORIES
3.7 G.   TOTAL FAT
0.3 G.   SATURATED FAT
3.8 G.   PROTEIN
36.2 G.   CARBOHYDRATES
0.6 G.   DIETARY FIBER
0 MG.   CHOLESTEROL
172 MG.   SODIUM

To make the cake: Preheat the oven to 350°F. Coat an 8" × 4" loaf pan with no-stick spray.

In a large bowl, combine the flour, sugar, poppy seeds, baking powder, and salt. Mix well.

In a medium bowl, combine the egg substitute, applesauce, oil, lemon rind, lime rind, and vanilla. Mix well. Add to the flour mixture and stir just until combined. Spoon the batter into the prepared pan.

Bake for 40 to 45 minutes, or until a toothpick inserted in the center comes out dry. Place the pan on a wire rack.

To make the topping: In a cup, combine the sugar, lemon juice, and lime juice. Mix well.

Prick the top of the warm loaf all over with a toothpick. Pour the topping over the loaf. Let stand for 15 minutes. Remove from the pan and cool on the wire rack.

ORANGE DATE-NUT BREAD

Fresh citrus rind makes this bread fragrant and refreshing. Try it as a snack any time of the day.

½	**cup water**
1	**cup chopped pitted dates**
2	**cups whole-wheat pastry flour or unbleached flour**
¾	**cup sugar**
1½	**teaspoons baking powder**
½	**teaspoon baking soda**
¼	**teaspoon salt**
⅓	**cup finely chopped walnuts or pecans** **Grated rind of 2 oranges**
1	**egg**
⅓	**cup orange juice**
2	**tablespoons unsalted butter or margarine, melted**
2	**teaspoons lemon juice**
2	**teaspoons vanilla**

HANDS-ON TIME: 10 MINUTES
UNATTENDED TIME: 1 HOUR

MAKES 1 LOAF;
15 SLICES
PER SLICE
170   CALORIES
3.9 G. TOTAL FAT
1.3 G. SATURATED FAT
3.6 G. PROTEIN
32.5 G. CARBOHYDRATES
3.3 G. DIETARY FIBER
19 MG. CHOLESTEROL
116 MG. SODIUM

Preheat the oven to 350°F. Coat a 9" × 5" loaf pan with no-stick spray.

Bring the water to a boil in a small saucepan. Stir in the dates and remove from the heat. Let soak until needed.

In a large bowl, combine the flour, sugar, baking powder, baking soda, and salt. Mix well. Stir in the walnuts or pecans and orange rind.

Place the egg in a medium bowl and whisk lightly. Whisk in the orange juice, butter or margarine, lemon juice, and vanilla. Add the dates and water. Add to the flour mixture and stir just until combined. Spoon the batter into the prepared pan.

Bake for 50 to 60 minutes, or until a toothpick inserted in the center comes out dry. Cool on a wire rack.

ORANGE-CURRANT SCONES

A small amount of butter or margarine is the secret to these flaky scones. If currants aren't your favorite fruit, replace them with any other dried fruits, nuts, or even chocolate chips.

HANDS-ON TIME: 20 MINUTES
UNATTENDED TIME: 15 MINUTES

1¾	cups unbleached flour
1	cup whole-wheat pastry flour
1	teaspoon baking powder
½	teaspoon baking soda
½	teaspoon salt
2	tablespoons + 2 teaspoons sugar
3	tablespoons unsalted butter or margarine
½	cup currants
¼	teaspoon grated orange rind
¾	cup + 2 tablespoons low-fat or nonfat buttermilk
1	tablespoon skim milk

MAKES 16
PER SCONE
122	CALORIES
2.7 G.	TOTAL FAT
1.5 G.	SATURATED FAT
3.1 G.	PROTEIN
22.1 G.	CARBOHYDRATES
1.7 G.	DIETARY FIBER
7 MG.	CHOLESTEROL
142 MG.	SODIUM

SWITCH TIP

Looking for a mid-morning snack to hold you over until lunch? Pass up that butter-laden croissant. The typical croissant has 14 grams of fat (much of it saturated). Instead, go for an English muffin with fruit spread. An English muffin has only 1 gram of fat, and the spread has none.

Preheat the oven to 400°F. Coat a baking sheet with no-stick spray.

In a large bowl, combine the unbleached flour, whole-wheat flour, baking powder, baking soda, salt, and 2 tablespoons of the sugar. Using a pastry blender or 2 knives, cut in the butter or margarine until the mixture forms fine crumbs. Stir in the currants and orange rind.

Make a well in the center of the flour mixture and pour in the buttermilk. Using a fork, stir just until combined. Turn the dough out onto a lightly floured surface and knead 10 times; do not overhandle.

Roll the dough ½" thick. Using a 2" biscuit cutter or the rim of a glass, cut the dough into rounds and place on the prepared baking sheet. Continue rolling and cutting until all the dough is used. Brush the tops with the skim milk and sprinkle with the remaining 2 teaspoons sugar.

Bake for 12 to 15 minutes, or until the scones just begin to brown slightly. Remove from the baking sheet and cool on a wire rack.

BROWN RICE PUDDING WITH FRUIT

Make this recipe ahead of time and refrigerate it for snack attacks or even breakfast. Family and guests always ask for seconds, so this batch makes enough for a crowd.

HANDS-ON TIME: 30 MINUTES
UNATTENDED TIME: 1½ HOURS

3	cups water
1	cup short-grain brown rice
½	teaspoon salt
2	cups 1% low-fat milk
¾	teaspoon ground cinnamon
¾	cup sugar
1	tablespoon vanilla
4	cups sliced fruit
1	cup nonfat vanilla yogurt

MAKES 12 SERVINGS
PER SERVING
172   CALORIES
0.9 G.   TOTAL FAT
0.4 G.   SATURATED FAT
3.8 G.   PROTEIN
38 G.   CARBOHYDRATES
1.2 G.   DIETARY FIBER
2 MG.   CHOLESTEROL
122 MG.   SODIUM

Bring the water to a boil in a medium saucepan over high heat. Stir in the rice and salt. Reduce the heat to medium-low, cover, and cook for 45 minutes. Uncover and cook for 10 minutes, or until the rice is tender and the water is absorbed.

Stir in the milk, cinnamon, and ½ cup of the sugar. Increase the heat to medium-high. Stir constantly until the mixture begins to bubble (watch closely to prevent burning). Reduce the heat to medium-low and cook, stirring frequently, for 30 minutes, or until the mixture is very thick and creamy.

Remove from the heat and stir in the vanilla. Allow to cool. Divide among serving dishes.

In a small bowl, combine the fruit and the remaining ¼ cup sugar. Spoon over the pudding. Top with the yogurt.

COOKING HINT

• Use your favorite fruit for this recipe, such as apples, pears, peaches, oranges, cherries, or dried cranberries. Try different flavors of yogurt, too, such as lemon. You can even sprinkle chopped walnuts, pecans, or almonds over the pudding.

DOUBLE LAYER CHOCOLATE PUDDING

Double your pleasure with two layers of chocolate. The top layer is light and creamy, like chocolate mousse. Underneath rests a thick layer of rich old-fashioned chocolate pudding. The layers form naturally as the pudding cools.

HANDS-ON TIME: 30 MINUTES
UNATTENDED TIME: 1 HOUR

MAKES 8 SERVINGS
PER SERVING
239   CALORIES
5.5 G.   TOTAL FAT
2.8 G.   SATURATED FAT
8.4 G.   PROTEIN
43.4 G. CARBOHYDRATES
0.3 G.   DIETARY FIBER
32 MG.   CHOLESTEROL
93 MG.   SODIUM

1	egg
1	cup sugar
¾	cup unsweetened cocoa powder
⅛	teaspoon ground cinnamon
1	cup 1% low-fat milk
3	ounces milk chocolate, chopped
1	tablespoon vanilla
1	envelope unflavored gelatin
1	can (12 ounces) evaporated skim milk

Place the egg in a medium saucepan and whisk lightly. Whisk in the sugar, cocoa, cinnamon, and ¾ cup of the low-fat milk. Cook over medium heat, whisking constantly, for 5 minutes, or until thickened. Remove from the heat. Whisk in the chocolate and vanilla until smooth. Let cool for 5 minutes, then set in the freezer to cool further until ready to use.

Place the remaining ¼ cup milk in a small saucepan. Sprinkle with the gelatin. Set aside to soften for 5 minutes. Cook over medium heat, stirring constantly, for 2 to 3 minutes, or until the gelatin has dissolved. Remove from the heat and slowly stir in the evaporated milk. Transfer to a large bowl.

Using an electric mixer, beat on high speed for 7 minutes, or until thickened and greatly increased in volume.

Remove the chocolate mixture from the freezer. Beat 1 cup of the gelatin mixture into the chocolate until well-combined. Beat the chocolate mixture back into the bowl until thoroughly combined.

Divide among serving dishes and refrigerate for 1 hour.

COOKING HINT

• Vegetarian and kosher gelatin is available in many grocery stores and health food stores.

RECIPES

"You can put everything, and the more things the better, into a salad, as into conversation; but everything depends on the mixing."
—Charles Dudley Warner, American writer and editor

Ready-in-a-Minute Salads and Dressings

Eating more vegetables may help you look and feel younger. Researchers say that certain compounds in vegetables may slow down the aging process and help protect you against degenerative diseases like cancer and heart disease. That's reason enough to start eating more salads.

Of course, you have to watch what you put on your salad, too. High-fat salad dressing is a leading source of fat in the diets of American women between the ages of 19 and 50, according to the U.S. Department of Agriculture Human Nutrition Information Service and the National Cancer Institute. Rely on low-fat dressings instead. They're quick and easy, and the flavor comes from vinegars, fruits, and herbs instead of fat. For great-tasting creamy dressings, I use low-fat dairy products and sometimes a small amount of strong cheese like feta or Roquefort.

Don't forget about bean, grain, and pasta salads. They make easy picnic dishes and lunches or light dinners that are high in fiber and complex carbohydrates. One of my favorites is Curried Lentil Salad. It's refreshing and keeps for days, so you can make a batch ahead of time.

CREAMY BASIL DRESSING

To Italians, basil is a symbol of love.

HANDS-ON TIME: 5 MINUTES
UNATTENDED TIME: NONE

½ cup packed fresh basil
3 tablespoons grated Parmesan cheese
1 clove garlic
6 tablespoons skim milk
2 tablespoons white-wine vinegar
2 tablespoons nonfat sour cream
1 tablespoon olive oil
    Salt and ground black pepper

MAKES ¾ CUP
PER 2 TABLESPOONS
44   CALORIES
3.2 G.   TOTAL FAT
0.9 G.   SATURATED FAT
2.2 G.   PROTEIN
1.9 G.   CARBOHYDRATES
0 G.   DIETARY FIBER
3 MG.   CHOLESTEROL
69 MG.   SODIUM

In a food processor or blender, combine the basil, Parmesan, and garlic. Process until the basil is finely chopped. Add the milk, vinegar, sour cream, and oil. Season with the salt and pepper. Process until smooth. Transfer to a covered container and refrigerate until ready to use.

ROQUEFORT DRESSING

The trick to lean Roquefort dressing is a mixture of low-fat cottage cheese, sour cream, and buttermilk.

HANDS-ON TIME: 5 MINUTES
UNATTENDED TIME: 1 HOUR

¼ cup nonfat or 1% low-fat cottage cheese
¼ cup nonfat sour cream
3 tablespoons low-fat or nonfat buttermilk
¼ teaspoon garlic powder
2 teaspoons lemon juice
3 ounces Roquefort cheese
    Ground black pepper

MAKES 1 CUP
PER 2 TABLESPOONS
51   CALORIES
3.3 G.   TOTAL FAT
2.1 G.   SATURATED FAT
3.9 G.   PROTEIN
1.6 G.   CARBOHYDRATES
0 G.   DIETARY FIBER
10 MG.   CHOLESTEROL
222 MG.   SODIUM

In a food processor or blender, combine the cottage cheese, sour cream, buttermilk, garlic powder, lemon juice, and 2 ounces of the Roquefort. Season with the pepper. Process until smooth. Transfer to a small bowl.

Crumble the remaining 1 ounce Roquefort into the bowl and mix well. Cover and refrigerate for at least 1 hour or up to 2 days to allow the flavors to blend.

POPPY SEED–TAHINI DRESSING

Tahini is a paste made from ground sesame seeds. Look for it in the international aisle of your grocery store or in health food stores. Here, it's made into a slightly sweet dressing studded with poppy seeds. Try it over mixed greens or spinach salads.

HANDS-ON TIME: 5 MINUTES
UNATTENDED TIME: NONE

MAKES 1¼ CUPS
PER 2 TABLESPOONS

47	CALORIES
3.6 G.	TOTAL FAT
0.2 G.	SATURATED FAT
1.2 G.	PROTEIN
2.8 G.	CARBOHYDRATES
0 G.	DIETARY FIBER
0 MG.	CHOLESTEROL
42 MG.	SODIUM

½   **cup water**
3   **tablespoons lemon juice**
2   **tablespoons tahini**
2   **tablespoons nonfat sour cream**
1   **tablespoon olive oil**
1   **tablespoon vegetable juice or tomato juice**
1   **tablespoon honey**
1   **teaspoon soy sauce**
1   **tablespoon poppy seeds**

In a food processor or blender, combine the water, lemon juice, tahini, sour cream, oil, vegetable juice or tomato juice, honey, and soy sauce. Process until smooth. Add the poppy seeds and process briefly. Transfer to a covered container and refrigerate until ready to use. If necessary, thin with a small amount of water before serving.

SWITCH TIP

Vegetable juice and tomato juice are often loaded with salt. To keep sodium to a minimum, buy low-sodium varieties. They taste just as good—if not better. When you're using only small amounts, buy the juice in small cans (6 ounces) to avoid waste.

147

GREEK FETA VINAIGRETTE

This dressing tastes great on any green salad.

HANDS-ON TIME: 10 MINUTES
UNATTENDED TIME: NONE

1	clove garlic, minced
¼	cup packed fresh parsley
6	large fresh basil leaves
½	cup fat-free chicken broth or vegetable broth
¼	cup balsamic vinegar
2	ounces feta cheese, crumbled
2	tablespoons olive oil
½	teaspoon dried oregano
½	teaspoon grated lemon rind
⅛	teaspoon ground black pepper

MAKES ABOUT 1¼ CUPS
PER 2 TABLESPOONS

48	CALORIES
3.9 G.	TOTAL FAT
1.2 G.	SATURATED FAT
1.2 G.	PROTEIN
2.1 G.	CARBOHYDRATES
0 G.	DIETARY FIBER
5 MG.	CHOLESTEROL
82 MG.	SODIUM

In a food processor or blender, combine the garlic, parsley, and basil. Process until finely chopped. Add the broth, vinegar, feta, oil, oregano, lemon rind, and pepper. Process until well-mixed. Transfer to a covered container and refrigerate until ready to use.

DRIED-CHERRY VINAIGRETTE

Try this zippy dressing in the autumn months.

HANDS-ON TIME: 10 MINUTES
UNATTENDED TIME: NONE

¾	cup boiling water
½	cup dried cherries
2	tablespoons walnut oil or canola oil
1	tablespoon raspberry vinegar
½	teaspoon sugar

MAKES ABOUT ¾ CUP
PER 2 TABLESPOONS

75	CALORIES
4.7 G.	TOTAL FAT
0.4 G.	SATURATED FAT
0.7 G.	PROTEIN
8.5 G.	CARBOHYDRATES
0.1 G.	DIETARY FIBER
0 MG.	CHOLESTEROL
2 MG.	SODIUM

In a small bowl, combine the water and cherries. Let soak for 5 minutes.

Transfer to a food processor or blender. Process until smooth. Add the oil, vinegar, and sugar. Process until well-mixed. Transfer to a covered jar and store in the refrigerator. Serve at room temperature.

COOKING HINT

- Walnut oil and raspberry vinegar are available in most large supermarkets and health food stores. To order them by mail, see page 416.

SUN-DRIED TOMATO VINAIGRETTE

Sun-dried tomatoes lend a rich flavor to this thick dressing. It really livens up mixed greens and even steamed vegetables.

HANDS-ON TIME: 10 MINUTES
UNATTENDED TIME: NONE

10	sun-dried tomatoes
¼	cup boiling water
1	tablespoon fresh parsley leaves
1	tablespoon fresh basil leaves
1	clove garlic
¾	cup spicy vegetable juice or tomato juice
2	tablespoons balsamic vinegar
1	tablespoon olive oil
2	teaspoons honey
	Salt and ground black pepper

MAKES 1 CUP
PER 3 TABLESPOONS

77	CALORIES
2.9 G.	TOTAL FAT
0.4 G.	SATURATED FAT
2 G.	PROTEIN
12.2 G.	CARBOHYDRATES
0.3 G.	DIETARY FIBER
0 MG.	CHOLESTEROL
388 MG.	SODIUM

In a small bowl, combine the tomatoes and water. Let soak for 5 minutes.

Transfer to a food processor or blender. Add the parsley, basil, and garlic. Process until a paste forms. Add the vegetable juice or tomato juice, vinegar, oil, and honey. Season with the salt and pepper. Process until well-mixed. Transfer to a covered container and refrigerate until ready to use.

ROASTED RED PEPPER VINAIGRETTE

Classic Italian ingredients make a light dressing that goes well with almost any crunchy salad.

HANDS-ON TIME: 5 MINUTES
UNATTENDED TIME: NONE

1	cup chopped roasted red peppers
1	clove garlic
¼	cup packed fresh parsley
8	fresh basil leaves
2	tablespoons olive oil
2	tablespoons balsamic vinegar
	Salt and ground black pepper

MAKES 1¼ CUPS
PER 3 TABLESPOONS

33	CALORIES
2.8 G.	TOTAL FAT
0.4 G.	SATURATED FAT
0.3 G.	PROTEIN
2 G.	CARBOHYDRATES
0.4 G.	DIETARY FIBER
0 MG.	CHOLESTEROL
2 MG.	SODIUM

In a food processor or blender, combine the red peppers, garlic, parsley, basil, oil, and vinegar. Season with the salt and black pepper. Process until smooth. Transfer to a covered container and refrigerate until ready to use.

Romaine with Roasted-Garlic Dressing

Crisp romaine lettuce blends perfectly with creamy roasted-garlic dressing.

Hands-on time: 10 minutes
Unattended time: 20 minutes

5	cloves garlic, unpeeled
5	toasted almonds
2½	tablespoons water
1	tablespoon nonfat sour cream
2¼	teaspoons lemon juice
1½	teaspoons olive oil
¾	teaspoon white-wine vinegar
⅛	teaspoon sugar
⅛	teaspoon dry mustard
	Pinch of grated lemon rind
	Salt and ground black pepper
8	cups torn romaine lettuce
1½	tablespoons grated Parmesan cheese

Makes 4 servings

Per serving

87	CALORIES
5.6 G.	TOTAL FAT
1 G.	SATURATED FAT
4.2 G.	PROTEIN
6.2 G.	CARBOHYDRATES
2.5 G.	DIETARY FIBER
2 MG.	CHOLESTEROL
134 MG.	SODIUM

Preheat the oven to 500°F.

Place the garlic on a piece of foil in a single layer and mist with no-stick spray. Bake for 20 minutes. Remove from the oven and cool slightly.

Peel the garlic and transfer to a food processor or blender. Add the almonds, water, sour cream, lemon juice, oil, vinegar, sugar, mustard, and lemon rind. Season with the salt and pepper. Process until smooth. If necessary, add more water to achieve the desired consistency.

Place the lettuce in a large bowl. Add the dressing and Parmesan. Gently toss to mix.

SPINACH SALAD WITH ORANGE VINAIGRETTE

Spinach and oranges blend well together. To enhance the combination, I added dried cranberries, walnuts, and endive leaves.

HANDS-ON TIME: 10 MINUTES
UNATTENDED TIME: NONE

2	tablespoons orange juice
2	tablespoons walnut oil
2	tablespoons white-wine vinegar
½	teaspoon grated orange rind
	Salt and ground black pepper
4	heads Belgian endive, separated into leaves
5	ounces fresh spinach, thick stems removed
2	navel oranges, peeled and cut into bite-size pieces
½	cup dried cranberries
¼	cup chopped toasted walnuts

MAKES 6 SERVINGS
PER SERVING

121	CALORIES
7.8 G.	TOTAL FAT
0.7 G.	SATURATED FAT
3.3 G.	PROTEIN
11 G.	CARBOHYDRATES
4.3 G.	DIETARY FIBER
0 MG.	CHOLESTEROL
34 MG.	SODIUM

In a small bowl, combine the orange juice, oil, vinegar, and orange rind. Season with the salt and pepper. Whisk to combine.

In a large bowl, combine the endive, spinach, oranges, cranberries, and walnuts. Toss to mix. Add the vinaigrette and toss gently to mix.

COOKING HINT

- You can replace the spinach with arugula or radicchio. The oranges can be replaced with strawberries, raspberries, or other juicy fruit. The walnut oil can be replaced with olive oil.

SWITCH TIP

Walnut oil is an excellent salad oil that has advantages over milder-tasting oils. It marries well with vinegars and has a pronounced nutty flavor, so you can use just a small amount and save on fat grams. Store walnut oil in the refrigerator to keep it fresh. Look for it with the other oils in your grocery store or health food store.

SPINACH AND STRAWBERRY SALAD

This vibrant salad is a feast for the eyes and the palate.

HANDS-ON TIME: 10 MINUTES
UNATTENDED TIME: NONE

2 tablespoons low-fat mayonnaise
1 tablespoon white-wine vinegar
⅛ teaspoon ground cinnamon
⅛ teaspoon ground ginger
17 large strawberries
   Salt and ground black pepper
6 cups packed fresh spinach, torn into pieces
6 tablespoons chopped walnuts

MAKES 6 SERVINGS

PER SERVING	
88	CALORIES
6.1 G.	TOTAL FAT
0.5 G.	SATURATED FAT
4 G.	PROTEIN
6.7 G.	CARBOHYDRATES
3.3 G.	DIETARY FIBER
2 MG.	CHOLESTEROL
50 MG.	SODIUM

In a food processor or blender, combine the mayonnaise, vinegar, cinnamon, ginger, and 5 of the strawberries. Season with the salt and pepper. Process until smooth.

Divide the spinach, walnuts, and the remaining 12 strawberries among individual serving plates. Drizzle with the dressing.

MIXED GREENS WITH PECAN VINAIGRETTE

The tender, young greens in this salad are known as mesclun. They range in flavor from sweet to nutty to pleasantly bitter. Many stores carry prepared mesclun mix in the produce aisle. Or create your own mix with your favorite baby lettuces. If you don't have walnut oil, substitute canola.

HANDS-ON TIME: 5 MINUTES
UNATTENDED TIME: NONE

12 toasted pecan halves
¼ cup apple juice
1 tablespoon walnut oil or canola oil
1 tablespoon white-wine vinegar
   Salt and ground black pepper
8 cups mesclun greens or mixed baby lettuce

MAKES 4 SERVINGS

PER SERVING	
101	CALORIES
8.2 G.	TOTAL FAT
0.7 G.	SATURATED FAT
2.3 G.	PROTEIN
5.9 G.	CARBOHYDRATES
2.4 G.	DIETARY FIBER
0 MG.	CHOLESTEROL
9 MG.	SODIUM

In a food processor or blender, combine the pecans, apple juice, oil, and vinegar. Season with the salt and pepper. Process until smooth.

Place the greens in a large bowl. Add the dressing and toss gently to mix.

BIBB LETTUCE WITH RASPBERRY VINAIGRETTE

The sweet, mild flavor of Bibb lettuce beats plain iceberg lettuce by a mile. A splash of raspberry vinaigrette makes it even better.

HANDS-ON TIME: 10 MINUTES
UNATTENDED TIME: NONE

1	tablespoon raspberry vinegar
1	tablespoon walnut oil
1	tablespoon water
⅛	teaspoon dried tarragon
⅛	teaspoon dried basil
⅛	teaspoon sugar
	Salt and ground black pepper
4	raspberries
2	heads Bibb lettuce, torn into bite-size pieces
¼	cup dried cherries
4	teaspoons toasted pine nuts

MAKES 4 SERVINGS
PER SERVING

109	CALORIES
5.4 G.	TOTAL FAT
0.6 G.	SATURATED FAT
2.4 G.	PROTEIN
15.2 G.	CARBOHYDRATES
1.1 G.	DIETARY FIBER
0 MG.	CHOLESTEROL
6 MG.	SODIUM

In a small bowl, combine the vinegar, oil, water, tarragon, basil, and sugar. Season with the salt and pepper. Whisk well to combine. Add the raspberries and mash slightly.

Divide the lettuce among individual serving plates. Sprinkle with the cherries and pine nuts. Drizzle with the dressing.

BIBB LETTUCE WITH APPLE-MINT DRESSING

A dressing from The Inn at Woodstock in Woodstock, Connecticut, inspired me to create this salad. It has quite a few ingredients but comes together quickly in a food processor or blender. Try it in Autumn when apples are in their prime.

HANDS-ON TIME: 15 MINUTES
UNATTENDED TIME: NONE

MAKES 6 SERVINGS
PER SERVING
99	CALORIES
7 G.	TOTAL FAT
1 G.	SATURATED FAT
0.3 G.	PROTEIN
9.9 G.	CARBOHYDRATES
2.1 G.	DIETARY FIBER
0 MG.	CHOLESTEROL
47 MG.	SODIUM

2	small apples
10	leaves fresh mint
1½	teaspoons fresh dill
⅛	teaspoon dried thyme
2	leaves fresh basil
2	tablespoons low-fat mayonnaise
1½	tablespoons olive oil
1½	teaspoons white-wine vinegar
¼	teaspoon horseradish
¼	teaspoon Worcestershire sauce
⅛	teaspoon garlic powder
	Salt and ground black pepper
1	tablespoon chopped fresh chives
2	heads Bibb lettuce, torn into bite-size pieces
⅓	cup dried cranberries
¼	cup coarsely chopped pecans

Peel, core, and chop 1 of the apples. Place in a food processor or blender. Add the mint, dill, thyme, and basil. Process until finely chopped. Add the mayonnaise, oil, vinegar, horseradish, Worcestershire sauce, and garlic powder. Season with the salt and pepper. Process until smooth. Add the chives and process briefly.

Divide the lettuce, cranberries, and pecans among individual serving plates. Chop the remaining apple and divide among the plates. Drizzle with the dressing.

BEET SALAD WITH RASPBERRY VINAIGRETTE

Beets and raspberries are a flavor match made in heaven.

HANDS-ON TIME: 5 MINUTES
UNATTENDED TIME: 15 MINUTES

2	cans (13¼ ounces each) sliced small beets, drained
1	sweet onion, thinly sliced
2	tablespoons olive oil
2	tablespoons raspberry vinegar
1	tablespoon balsamic vinegar
1	small clove garlic, minced
	Salt and ground black pepper
2	tablespoons chopped fresh chives (optional)

MAKES 4 SERVINGS

PER SERVING
106	CALORIES
3.7 G.	TOTAL FAT
0.5 G.	SATURATED FAT
2.2 G.	PROTEIN
17.7 G.	CARBOHYDRATES
3.9 G.	DIETARY FIBER
0 MG.	CHOLESTEROL
517 MG.	SODIUM

Place the beets and onions in a large bowl.

In a cup, combine the oil, raspberry vinegar, balsamic vinegar, and garlic. Season with the salt and pepper. Whisk to combine. Pour over the beet mixture and toss well. Sprinkle with the chives (if using). Cover and refrigerate for at least 15 minutes or up to 3 days.

MEXICAN VEGETABLE SALAD

Jícama is known as the Mexican potato. It tastes like a cross between a potato and an apple. It has a crisp, juicy texture and a slightly sweet flavor. South of the border, they eat it with a squirt of lime and a dash of chili powder. Here, a little cucumber and sweet red pepper enhance its mild flavor.

HANDS-ON TIME: 5 MINUTES
UNATTENDED TIME: NONE

1	small jícama, peeled and cut into thin strips
1	cucumber, peeled and diced
½	sweet red or green pepper, sliced
	Juice of 1 lime
	Salt and ground black pepper
	Chili powder

MAKES 4 SERVINGS

PER SERVING
30	CALORIES
0.2 G.	TOTAL FAT
0 G.	SATURATED FAT
1.2 G.	PROTEIN
6.9 G.	CARBOHYDRATES
0.5 G.	DIETARY FIBER
0 MG.	CHOLESTEROL
2 MG.	SODIUM

In a medium bowl, combine the jícama, cucumbers, sliced peppers, and lime juice. Season with the salt, black pepper, and chili powder. Toss to mix.

PANZANELLA

Panzanella is an Italian vegetable salad with fresh croutons. It tastes best at the height of summer when tomatoes, peppers, cucumbers, and basil are at the peak of ripeness. For an extra touch of flavor, add a little crumbled feta or goat cheese.

HANDS-ON TIME: 20 MINUTES
UNATTENDED TIME: NONE

MAKES 8 SERVINGS
PER SERVING
187   CALORIES
5.1 G.   TOTAL FAT
0.7 G.   SATURATED FAT
5.3 G.   PROTEIN
32.2 G.   CARBOHYDRATES
2.2 G.   DIETARY FIBER
0 MG.   CHOLESTEROL
229 MG.   SODIUM

1   loaf whole-grain French or Italian bread, cubed
     Garlic powder
2   sweet red, yellow, or green peppers, thickly sliced
1   large red onion, thickly sliced
3   cloves garlic, chopped
1   cucumber, diced
30   cherry tomatoes, halved
½   cup packed fresh basil, shredded
¼   cup balsamic vinegar
2   tablespoons olive oil
     Salt and ground black pepper

Preheat the oven to 350°F. Coat a baking sheet with no-stick spray. Place the bread cubes on the sheet in an even layer. Sprinkle with garlic powder and coat with no-stick spray. Bake for 10 minutes, or until lightly browned. Transfer to a large bowl.

Coat a large no-stick skillet with no-stick spray and set over medium-high heat. Add the sliced peppers, onions, and garlic. Cook, stirring constantly, for 4 minutes. Add to the bowl with the bread. Add the cucumbers, tomatoes, and basil. Toss to mix.

In a cup, mix together the vinegar and oil. Season with the salt and black pepper. Whisk to combine. Pour over the salad and toss to mix.

COOKING HINT

• Here's an easy way to shred basil. Stack 4 or 5 leaves on top of one another. Roll up the stack starting from one of the long ends. Slice the roll crosswise to make shreds.

LIGHT CAESAR SALAD

Caesar salad can have as much as 40 grams of fat in a single serving. This lightened version cuts the fat with pasteurized egg substitute instead of the traditional raw egg and a lot less olive oil. The salad weighs in at only 6.6 grams of fat.

HANDS-ON TIME: 10 MINUTES
UNATTENDED TIME: NONE

MAKES 4 SERVINGS
PER SERVING
131	CALORIES
6.6 G.	TOTAL FAT
1.9 G.	SATURATED FAT
7.5 G.	PROTEIN
11.9 G.	CARBOHYDRATES
2.3 G.	DIETARY FIBER
6 MG.	CHOLESTEROL
440 MG.	SODIUM

¼	cup fat-free egg substitute
3	tablespoons low-fat mayonnaise
1½	tablespoons Dijon mustard
1½	tablespoons lemon juice
1½	tablespoons white-wine vinegar
1	tablespoon olive oil
1	teaspoon anchovy paste or finely chopped anchovies
1	teaspoon Worcestershire sauce
1	small clove garlic, minced
¼	teaspoon ground black pepper
1	large head romaine lettuce, torn into bite-size pieces
1	cup nonfat croutons or Garlic Croutons (page 351)
¼	cup grated Parmesan cheese

In a food processor or blender, combine the egg substitute, mayonnaise, mustard, lemon juice, vinegar, oil, anchovy paste or anchovies, Worcestershire sauce, garlic, and pepper. Process until smooth.

Place the lettuce in a large bowl. Add the dressing and toss to mix. Sprinkle with the croutons and Parmesan. Toss lightly.

COOKING HINTS

- Anchovy paste is available in the canned fish section of most supermarkets. It has a bit more flavor than chopped anchovies because the paste is mixed with spices.

- For a vegetarian version, replace the anchovy paste with ¾ teaspoon reduced-sodium soy sauce.

THAI CUCUMBER SALAD

This refreshing salad packs a bite but not a five-alarm fire. Expect a nice mix of slightly sweet and spicy flavors. If you're skeptical, try half a jalapeño at first.

HANDS-ON TIME: 10 MINUTES
UNATTENDED TIME: NONE

4	cucumbers, peeled and diced
6	scallions, chopped
¼	cup peanuts
1	cup packed fresh parsley
½	cup packed fresh cilantro
1	jalapeño pepper, seeded (wear plastic gloves when handling)
¼	cup rice vinegar
1	tablespoon canola oil
1½	teaspoons curry powder
1	teaspoon sugar
1	clove garlic, minced
	Salt and ground black pepper

MAKES 8 SERVINGS

PER SERVING	
65	CALORIES
4.2 G.	TOTAL FAT
0.4 G.	SATURATED FAT
2.2 G.	PROTEIN
5.8 G.	CARBOHYDRATES
0.6 G.	DIETARY FIBER
0 MG.	CHOLESTEROL
16 MG.	SODIUM

In a large bowl, combine the cucumbers, scallions, and peanuts. Toss to mix.

In a food processor or blender, combine the parsley, cilantro, and jalapeño pepper. Process until finely chopped. Add to the cucumber mixture and toss to mix.

In a cup, combine the vinegar, oil, curry powder, sugar, and garlic. Season with the salt and black pepper. Whisk to combine. Pour over the cucumber mixture and toss to mix.

COOKING HINT

• If you don't have a food processor or blender, you can use a sharp knife to finely chop the parsley, cilantro, and jalapeño pepper.

FARMERS' MARKET SALAD

Make this simple salad in the heart of summer when fresh vegetables are overflowing in market bins. Add a small amount of thinly sliced mozzarella cheese or goat cheese for an extra shot of flavor and a little more protein.

HANDS-ON TIME: 10 MINUTES
UNATTENDED TIME: NONE

MAKES 4 SERVINGS
PER SERVING
98   CALORIES
4 G.   TOTAL FAT
0.6 G.   SATURATED FAT
2.6 G.   PROTEIN
15.2 G.   CARBOHYDRATES
2.3 G.   DIETARY FIBER
0 MG.   CHOLESTEROL
16 MG.   SODIUM

4	ripe tomatoes, sliced
2	English cucumbers, peeled and thinly sliced
1	red onion, thinly sliced
¼	cup packed fresh basil, shredded
	Salt and ground black pepper
2	tablespoons balsamic vinegar
1	tablespoon olive oil

Divide the tomatoes, cucumbers, and onions on individual serving plates. Sprinkle with the basil. Season with the salt and pepper.

In a cup, combine the vinegar and oil. Whisk to combine. Drizzle over the salads.

COOKING HINT

• English cucumbers have a thinner and less bitter skin than regular cucumbers. They're nearly seedless and grow up to 2 feet in length. Look for them wrapped in plastic in the produce section. If English cucumbers are unavailable, substitute regular peeled cucumbers.

CHOPPED SALAD

This is a quick and simple salad with a great taste. Feel free to vary the ingredients to suit your own preference.

5	cups chopped romaine lettuce
1	cup finely chopped radicchio or cabbage
1	small red onion, chopped
½	cup chopped roasted red peppers
1	tablespoon olive oil
1	tablespoon balsamic vinegar
	Salt and ground black pepper
	Grated Parmesan or Romano cheese (optional)

In a large bowl, combine the romaine, radicchio or cabbage, onions, and red peppers. Toss to mix. Sprinkle with the oil and vinegar. Season with the salt and black pepper. Toss to mix. Sprinkle with the Parmesan or Romano (if using).

COOKING HINT

• Radicchio is an Italian form of chicory. It has a slightly peppery and pleasantly bitter flavor. Look for reddish-purple leaves and white ribs in a small round head.

HANDS-ON TIME: 10 MINUTES
UNATTENDED TIME: NONE

MAKES 4 SERVINGS
PER SERVING

60	CALORIES
3.6 G.	TOTAL FAT
0.5 G.	SATURATED FAT
1.7 G.	PROTEIN
6 G.	CARBOHYDRATES
2 G.	DIETARY FIBER
0 MG.	CHOLESTEROL
9 MG.	SODIUM

SWITCH TIP

Roasted red peppers are a wonderful flavor-booster for salads, pasta, rice, or pizza. But don't buy the kind that are swimming in oil. Read the label to make sure that the peppers are packed in water instead. Or make your own at home. Cut 2 large red peppers in half; remove and discard the ribs and seeds. Place the peppers, skin side up, on a foil-lined baking sheet. Broil 3" from the heat until the skins begin to bubble and blacken. Remove the peppers from the oven and place in a paper bag. Seal and let sweat for 15 minutes. When cool enough to handle, remove and discard the skins. Then chop the flesh and use as desired.

CRISPY STEAMED VEGETABLE SALAD

This salad can accommodate a variety of different combinations. Steam your favorite vegetables until crisp-tender, then allow them to come to room temperature. Serve the salad with a thick, flavorful dressing like the one called for here. Or try Sun-Dried Tomato Vinaigrette (page 149) or Roquefort Dressing (page 146).

HANDS-ON TIME: 20 MINUTES
UNATTENDED TIME: 30 MINUTES

MAKES 4 SERVINGS
PER SERVING
75   CALORIES
3.3 G.   TOTAL FAT
0.5 G.   SATURATED FAT
3.9 G.   PROTEIN
10.6 G.   CARBOHYDRATES
3.2 G.   DIETARY FIBER
0 MG.   CHOLESTEROL
66 MG.   SODIUM

2½   cups cauliflower florets
1   cup baby carrots, quartered
2½   cups broccoli florets
¾   cup Roasted Red Pepper Vinaigrette (page 149)

Place the cauliflower in a steamer basket. Steam over boiling water in a large covered saucepan for 5 minutes. Add the carrots and steam for 2 minutes. Add the broccoli and steam for 5 minutes. Transfer the vegetables to a large bowl. Cool to room temperature.

Add the dressing to the bowl and toss to mix.

WALDORF SALAD WITH BLUE CHEESE

When Waldorf salad was created about 100 years ago, nobody cared about the fat in real mayonnaise. Here, a small amount of blue cheese adds flavor, while nonfat or low-fat mayonnaise gives the dish a creamy finish.

HANDS-ON TIME: 10 MINUTES
UNATTENDED TIME: NONE

MAKES 4 SERVINGS
PER SERVING
203   CALORIES
7.1 G.   TOTAL FAT
1.7 G.   SATURATED FAT
4.3 G.   PROTEIN
34.9 G.   CARBOHYDRATES
7.7 G.   DIETARY FIBER
5 MG.   CHOLESTEROL
252 MG.   SODIUM

4   cups chopped red apples
1   stalk celery, chopped
¼   cup chopped toasted walnuts
6   dried figs, chopped
3   tablespoons nonfat or low-fat mayonnaise
     Ground black pepper
1   ounce blue cheese, crumbled

In a large bowl, combine the apples, celery, walnuts, figs, and mayonnaise. Season with the pepper. Mix well. Add the blue cheese and toss gently.

COBB SALAD

Cobb salad was created in 1936 by Robert Cobb at the Brown Derby Restaurant in Hollywood. It's usually layered with hard-cooked eggs, bacon, tomatoes, and blue cheese. In this lighter rendition, chicken breast takes the place of bacon, and I've reduced the amount of blue cheese.

4	cups torn romaine lettuce
2	cups Crunchy Pita Strips (page 352) or low-fat croutons (optional)
1½	cups shredded cooked chicken breast
½	small red onion, thinly sliced
4	scallions, chopped
1	ounce blue cheese, crumbled
2	tomatoes, cubed
4	hard-cooked eggs, cubed
	Ground black pepper
½	cup Creamy Basil Dressing (page 146)

In a large bowl, combine the lettuce, pita strips or croutons (if using), chicken, onions, scallions, and blue cheese. Toss to mix.

Add the tomatoes and eggs. Toss gently. Divide among individual serving plates. Season with the black pepper. Drizzle with the dressing.

HANDS-ON TIME: 15 MINUTES
UNATTENDED TIME: NONE

MAKES 4 SERVINGS
PER SERVING
257 CALORIES
12.3 G. TOTAL FAT
4.3 G. SATURATED FAT
28.1 G. PROTEIN
8 G. CARBOHYDRATES
2 G. DIETARY FIBER
265 MG. CHOLESTEROL
277 MG. SODIUM

CRUNCHY WINTER SALAD

The ingredients for this salad store well, so they're easy to keep on hand. I like a thick, flavorful dressing like low-fat Roquefort dressing. Roasted Red Pepper Vinaigrette (page 149) would also work nicely.

1½ **cups small broccoli florets**
1½ **cups small cauliflower florets**
1 **small red onion, chopped**
1 **carrot, shredded**
1 **cup finely chopped cabbage**
½ **cup Roquefort Dressing (page 146)**

In a large bowl, combine the broccoli, cauliflower, onions, carrots, and cabbage. Add the dressing and toss to mix.

HANDS-ON TIME: 5 MINUTES
UNATTENDED TIME: NONE

MAKES 4 SERVINGS
PER SERVING
89   CALORIES
3.6 G.   TOTAL FAT
2.1 G.   SATURATED FAT
6.3 G.   PROTEIN
9.7 G.   CARBOHYDRATES
2.2 G.   DIETARY FIBER
10 MG.   CHOLESTEROL
252 MG. SODIUM

SWITCH TIP

Cruciferous vegetables like broccoli, brussels sprouts, cabbage, cauliflower, collard greens, kale, kohlrabi, mustard, rutabaga, and turnips contain nitrogen compounds that have been found to play a role in reducing your risk of cancer. Plus, most are high in vitamin C and folate, other valuable nutrients. Give yourself a health boost and make the switch to eating more cruciferous vegetables.

ALL-AMERICAN POTATO SALAD

A friend asked me to create a potato salad that tasted as good as his mother used to make—only low-fat. The original included lots of full-fat mayonnaise and quite a few eggs. Here's my rendition. It passed his taste test with flying colors.

HANDS-ON TIME: 15 MINUTES
UNATTENDED TIME: NONE

MAKES 6 SERVINGS
PER SERVING
207   CALORIES
3.7 G.   TOTAL FAT
1.1.G.   SATURATED FAT
6.9 G.   PROTEIN
36.9 G.   CARBOHYDRATES
0.6 G.   DIETARY FIBER
142 MG.   CHOLESTEROL
568 MG.   SODIUM

2	**pounds red potatoes, cut into 1" cubes**
2	**stalks celery, chopped**
6	**scallions, chopped**
1	**cup nonfat or low-fat mayonnaise**
1	**tablespoon chopped fresh parsley**
1½	**teaspoons dry mustard**
1	**teaspoon white-wine vinegar**
¼	**teaspoon grated lemon rind**
¼	**teaspoon dried dill**
4	**hard-cooked eggs, chopped**
	Salt and ground black pepper

Place the potatoes in a large saucepan and add cold water to cover. Bring to a boil over high heat. Reduce the heat to medium and cook for 10 minutes, or until just soft enough to pierce with a fork. Drain.

In a large bowl, combine the celery, scallions, mayonnaise, parsley, mustard, vinegar, lemon rind, and dill. Mix well. Add the potatoes and eggs. Season with the salt and pepper. Mix well.

ASIAN COLESLAW WITH ORANGE-GINGER DRESSING

Asian napa cabbage makes fantastic coleslaw. It's also called Chinese cabbage, Chinese celery cabbage, or Peking cabbage. It has a conical shape with long, pale green leaves similar to romaine lettuce.

HANDS-ON TIME: 15 MINUTES
UNATTENDED TIME: 30 MINUTES

2	pounds napa cabbage, thinly sliced
1	carrot, shredded
½	red onion, thinly sliced
½	cup orange juice
3	tablespoons rice vinegar
1½	tablespoons reduced-sodium soy sauce
1	tablespoon toasted sesame oil
1½	teaspoons minced fresh ginger
1½	teaspoons chopped fresh cilantro
	Salt and ground black pepper

MAKES 4 SERVINGS

PER SERVING
101   CALORIES
4 G.   TOTAL FAT
0.5 G. SATURATED FAT
5.5 G. PROTEIN
11.5 G. CARBOHYDRATES
2.4 G. DIETARY FIBER
0 MG.   CHOLESTEROL
244 MG. SODIUM

In a large bowl, combine the cabbage, carrots, and onions. Toss to mix.

In a food processor or blender, combine the orange juice, vinegar, soy sauce, oil, ginger, and cilantro. Process until smooth. Pour over the cabbage mixture. Season with the salt and pepper. Toss to mix. Let stand for 30 minutes before serving.

SHRIMP AND CRAB SALAD

This shrimp and crab salad will perk up your plate. Stuff it inside pita pockets with a touch of mustard and salad greens. Or pile it high on a bagel.

HANDS-ON TIME: 10 MINUTES
UNATTENDED TIME: NONE

1	**pound peeled and cooked small salad shrimp**
4	**ounces lump crabmeat**
½	**cup finely chopped celery**
1	**shallot, finely chopped**
1	**teaspoon chopped fresh dill**
⅓	**cup low-fat or nonfat mayonnaise**
2	**tablespoons lemon juice**
1	**teaspoon Dijon mustard**
	Hot-pepper sauce
	Salt and ground black pepper

In a large bowl, combine the shrimp, crab, celery, shallots, and dill. Toss to mix.

In a small bowl, combine the mayonnaise, lemon juice, and mustard. Season with the hot-pepper sauce, salt, and black pepper. Mix well. Add to the seafood mixture and mix well.

MAKES 4 SERVINGS
PER SERVING
184   CALORIES
4.5 G.   TOTAL FAT
0.7 G.   SATURATED FAT
29.7 G.   PROTEIN
4.4 G.   CARBOHYDRATES
0.3 G.   DIETARY FIBER
253 MG.   CHOLESTEROL
500 MG.   SODIUM

SWITCH TIP

Mayonnaise can pack as much as 11 grams of fat in 1 tablespoon. The "light" versions have about 5 grams. For the least fat, buy nonfat mayonnaise. If that's a tad too low for you, choose cholesterol-free mayonnaise. It has only 1 gram of fat per tablespoon. And the flavor tends to be better than many of the nonfat varieties.

TUNA SALAD WITH APPLES AND CASHEWS

Here's a new twist on tuna salad. Apples add sweet crunch; toasted cashews and curry powder lend rich flavor. Try it with whole-grain crackers or Crunchy Pita Chips (page 352). If you don't have cantaloupe on hand, serve the salad in pita pockets as a sandwich.

HANDS-ON TIME: 10 MINUTES
UNATTENDED TIME: NONE

MAKES 4 SERVINGS

PER SERVING
415   CALORIES
7 G.   TOTAL FAT
1.4 G. SATURATED FAT
29.7 G. PROTEIN
65.6 G. CARBOHYDRATES
9.3 G. DIETARY FIBER
35 MG. CHOLESTEROL
650 MG. SODIUM

2   **cans (6 ounces each) water-packed albacore tuna, drained and flaked**
2   **small apples, chopped**
¼   **cup nonfat or low-fat mayonnaise**
¼   **cup chopped cashews**
1   **teaspoon curry powder**
    Ground black pepper
2   **small cantaloupe**

In a medium bowl, combine the tuna, apples, and mayonnaise. Mix well.

Place the cashews in a small skillet. Stir over medium heat for 1 to 2 minutes, or until the nuts are fragrant and golden. Add the curry powder and stir for 30 seconds, or until the cashews are well-coated. Add to the tuna mixture. Season with the pepper. Mix well.

Cut the cantaloupe in half and remove the seeds. Spoon the tuna salad into the melon halves.

CHICKEN AND TORTELLINI SALAD

Pile this chunky chicken salad atop a bed of fresh green lettuce or stuff it inside a pita pocket. Look for low-fat cheese tortellini in your grocer's refrigerated or frozen foods aisle.

HANDS-ON TIME: 15 MINUTES
UNATTENDED TIME: NONE

MAKES 4 SERVINGS

PER SERVING
250	CALORIES
8.2 G.	TOTAL FAT
2.8 G.	SATURATED FAT
17.5 G.	PROTEIN
27.2 G.	CARBOHYDRATES
1 G.	DIETARY FIBER
44 MG.	CHOLESTEROL
544 MG.	SODIUM

8	ounces low-fat cheese tortellini
8	ounces boneless, skinless chicken breast
2	stalks celery, chopped
½	cup red seedless grapes
¼	cup chopped toasted pecans
½	cup nonfat or low-fat mayonnaise
1	tablespoon white-wine vinegar
1	teaspoon honey
1	teaspoon Dijon mustard
	Salt and ground black pepper

Cook the tortellini in a large pot of boiling water according to the package directions. Drain and place in a large bowl.

Coat a large no-stick skillet with no-stick spray. Add the chicken. Cover and cook over medium heat for 5 minutes per side, or until the chicken is no longer pink in the center when tested with a sharp knife. Cool and cut into bite-size cubes. Add to the bowl with the tortellini.

Add the celery, grapes, and pecans. Mix well.

In a small bowl, combine the mayonnaise, vinegar, honey, and mustard. Mix well. Pour over the chicken mixture and mix well. Season with the salt and pepper.

THREE-BEAN SALAD WITH BALSAMIC VINAIGRETTE

This easy bean dish is overflowing with fiber. You can use almost any combination of beans you like. For the best flavor, serve the salad at room temperature.

HANDS-ON TIME: 10 MINUTES
UNATTENDED TIME: 2 HOURS

MAKES 6 SERVINGS
PER SERVING
251   CALORIES
6.9 G.   TOTAL FAT
0.8 G.   SATURATED FAT
14.9 G. PROTEIN
43.1 G. CARBOHYDRATES
12.5 G. DIETARY FIBER
0 MG.   CHOLESTEROL
511 MG. SODIUM

1	can (15 ounces) chickpeas, rinsed and drained
1	can (15 ounces) red kidney beans, rinsed and drained
1	can (15 ounces) cannellini beans, rinsed and drained
1	red onion, thinly sliced
½	cup chopped fresh parsley
¼	cup chopped fresh basil or cilantro
⅓	cup fat-free chicken broth or vegetable broth
¼	cup balsamic vinegar
2	tablespoons olive oil
2	cloves garlic, minced
1	teaspoon molasses
½	teaspoon grated lemon rind
¼	teaspoon ground cumin
¼	teaspoon ground coriander
	Salt and ground black pepper

In a large bowl, combine the chickpeas, kidney beans, cannellini beans, onions, parsley, and basil or cilantro. Toss to mix.

In a small bowl, combine the broth, vinegar, oil, garlic, molasses, lemon rind, cumin, and coriander. Season with the salt and pepper. Mix well. Pour over the bean mixture and toss to mix. Cover and refrigerate for at least 2 hours.

COOKING HINT

- For lunch, serve this salad on a bed of mixed greens with crispy bread. For dinner, try it as a side dish or first course served in cabbage or radicchio leaves. It also makes a great picnic dish.

169

BLACK-EYED PEA SALAD

This Southern-inspired salad is high in fiber from the black-eyed peas, which are also known as cowpeas or China beans. For best results, use freshly cooked or canned black-eyed peas; the frozen ones are too mushy when thawed.

HANDS-ON TIME: 10 MINUTES
UNATTENDED TIME: 1 HOUR

MAKES 6 SERVINGS
PER SERVING

150	CALORIES
5 G.	TOTAL FAT
0.7 G.	SATURATED FAT
3.5 G.	PROTEIN
23.7 G.	CARBOHYDRATES
7.2 G.	DIETARY FIBER
0 MG.	CHOLESTEROL
79 MG.	SODIUM

3	cups cooked or canned (rinsed and drained if canned) black-eyed peas
1	red onion, sliced
½	sweet red pepper, chopped
1	carrot, shredded
1	can (4 ounces) chopped green chili peppers
¼	cup chopped fresh parsley
2	tablespoons chopped fresh basil or cilantro
¼	cup lime juice
2	tablespoons olive oil
1	clove garlic, minced
¼	teaspoon ground cumin
	Salt and ground black pepper

In a large bowl, combine the black-eyed peas, onions, red peppers, carrots, chili peppers, parsley, and basil or cilantro. Toss to mix.

In a small bowl, combine the lime juice, oil, garlic, and cumin. Mix well. Add to the salad and toss to mix. Season with the salt and black pepper. Refrigerate for at least 1 hour or up to 3 days.

COOKING HINT

- For a more filling salad, add cooked grains, chicken, turkey hot dogs, or turkey sausage.

CURRIED LENTIL SALAD

This ingredient list is on the long side, but the hands-on time is only 10 minutes. The flavor is refreshingly light. Serve this lentil salad over a bed of greens with whole-grain crackers.

HANDS-ON TIME: 10 MINUTES
UNATTENDED TIME: 45 MINUTES

MAKES 4 SERVINGS
PER SERVING
372   CALORIES
7.9 G.   TOTAL FAT
1 G.   SATURATED FAT
22.4 G. PROTEIN
56.6 G. CARBOHYDRATES
13.9 G. DIETARY FIBER
0 MG.   CHOLESTEROL
203 MG. SODIUM

3	cups water
1½	cups lentils
½	cup fat-free chicken broth or vegetable broth
2	tablespoons olive oil
2	tablespoons sherry vinegar or white-wine vinegar
1	tablespoon reduced-sodium soy sauce
1	clove garlic, minced
2	tablespoons lemon juice
1	teaspoon grated lemon rind
½	teaspoon chili powder
½	teaspoon curry powder
2	cups shredded carrots
1	red onion, thinly sliced
2	tablespoons chopped fresh cilantro
¼	cup chopped roasted red peppers
	Salt and ground black pepper

Bring the water to a boil in a medium saucepan over high heat. Add the lentils and return to a boil. Reduce the heat to medium-low. Cover and cook for 45 minutes, or until the water is absorbed.

In a large bowl, combine the broth, oil, vinegar, soy sauce, garlic, lemon juice, lemon rind, chili powder, and curry powder. Mix well.

Add the carrots, onions, cilantro, red peppers, and lentils. Season with the salt and black pepper. Toss gently to mix.

WILD RICE SALAD WITH PECANS AND CHERRIES

This salad is delicious warm, at room temperature, or chilled. Even the leftovers taste great the next day.

HANDS-ON TIME: 10 MINUTES
UNATTENDED TIME: 45 MINUTES

2½   cups water
1¼   cups wild rice, rinsed
1½   cups shredded carrots
¾   cup dried cherries
⅓   cup coarsely chopped pecans
6   scallions, chopped
¼   cup fat-free chicken broth or vegetable broth
2   tablespoons olive oil
2   tablespoons balsamic vinegar
1   clove garlic, minced
1   teaspoon dried thyme
       Salt and ground black pepper

MAKES 6 SERVINGS

PER SERVING
263   CALORIES
9.3 G.   TOTAL FAT
1 G.   SATURATED FAT
6.9 G.   PROTEIN
41.3 G.   CARBOHYDRATES
2 G.   DIETARY FIBER
0 MG.   CHOLESTEROL
30 MG.   SODIUM

Bring the water to a boil in a medium saucepan over high heat. Add the rice and return to a boil. Reduce the heat to medium-low. Cover and cook for 45 minutes, or until the liquid has been absorbed. Transfer to a large bowl.

Add the carrots, cherries, pecans, and scallions. Toss to mix.

In a small bowl, combine the broth, oil, vinegar, garlic, and thyme. Pour over the salad. Season with the salt and pepper. Toss to mix.

SWITCH TIP

White rice is a great grain, but wild rice is even better. Wild rice contains twice as much protein as white rice, and it's high in B complex vitamins. In addition, wild rice has a wonderful nutty flavor and a firm, chewy texture. Go wild for a boost of flavor and health.

COOKING HINT

• Vary the flavors by replacing the cherries with dried cranberries and the pecans with walnuts or almonds.

COUSCOUS TABBOULEH

Fluffy couscous steps in for traditional bulgur wheat in this colorful version of tabbouleh. It makes a refreshing light lunch or supper. Or serve it alongside chicken or fish. To intensify the flavors, let the dish marinate in the refrigerator for up to 3 days.

HANDS-ON TIME: 10 MINUTES
UNATTENDED TIME: NONE

MAKES 6 SERVINGS
PER SERVING
266   CALORIES
6 G.   TOTAL FAT
1.1 G.   SATURATED FAT
8.1 G.   PROTEIN
46.3 G.   CARBOHYDRATES
9.3 G.   DIETARY FIBER
1.7 MG.   CHOLESTEROL
29 MG.   SODIUM

2¼	cups water
1	teaspoon + 2 tablespoons olive oil
1½	cups couscous
8	scallions, chopped
1	cup packed finely chopped fresh parsley
1	sweet red pepper, finely chopped
1	cup shredded carrots
1	zucchini, diced
1	cucumber, diced
2	tomatoes, diced
	Salt and ground black pepper
¼	cup lemon juice
1	large clove garlic, minced
1	teaspoon minced fresh mint or ½ teaspoon dried

Bring the water and 1 teaspoon of the oil to a boil in a medium saucepan over high heat. Stir in the couscous. Remove from the heat, cover, and let stand for 5 minutes, or until the liquid is absorbed.

In a large bowl, combine the scallions, parsley, red peppers, carrots, zucchini, cucumbers, and tomatoes. Season with the salt and black pepper. Toss to mix. Fluff the couscous with a fork and add to the bowl. Toss to mix.

In a small bowl, combine the lemon juice, garlic, mint, and the remaining 2 tablespoons oil. Mix well. Add to the salad and toss to mix.

GREEK ORZO SALAD

Orzo is small rice-shaped pasta that's tender yet firm when cooked. Here, it blends with classic Greek ingredients in a tangy side salad. Make it a day ahead for the most flavor.

HANDS-ON TIME: 15 MINUTES
UNATTENDED TIME: NONE

1	pound orzo pasta
4	ounces feta cheese, crumbled
¼	cup chopped fresh parsley
¼	cup chopped roasted red peppers
1	red onion, thinly sliced
10	cherry tomatoes, halved
	Ground black pepper
½	cup fat-free chicken broth or vegetable broth
2	tablespoons white-wine vinegar
2	tablespoons lemon juice
2	tablespoons olive oil
1	clove garlic, minced
1	teaspoon dried oregano

MAKES 8 SERVINGS

PER SERVING
306 CALORIES
7.6 G. TOTAL FAT
2.7 G. SATURATED FAT
10.4 G. PROTEIN
49 G. CARBOHYDRATES
0.9 G. DIETARY FIBER
13 MG. CHOLESTEROL
185 MG. SODIUM

Cook the orzo in a large pot of boiling water according to the package directions. Drain and rinse with cold water. Drain well and place in a large bowl.

Add the feta, parsley, red peppers, onions, and tomatoes. Season with the black pepper. Toss to mix.

In a small bowl, combine the broth, vinegar, lemon juice, oil, garlic, and oregano. Add to the orzo mixture and toss to mix.

TUNA PASTA SALAD

This pasta salad gets even better as it stands, so you can make it up to 2 days ahead and keep in the refrigerator. It makes a great picnic dish or quick lunch.

HANDS-ON TIME: 20 MINUTES
UNATTENDED TIME: NONE

8	ounces bow-tie or rotini pasta
2	potatoes, cubed
4	ounces green beans
1	clove garlic, minced
½	cup fat-free chicken broth or vegetable broth
2	tablespoons lemon juice
2	tablespoons olive oil
1	tablespoon balsamic vinegar
1	tablespoon chopped fresh chives
1	can (19 ounces) cannellini or white beans, rinsed and drained
1	can (6 ounces) water-packed albacore tuna, drained and flaked
1	small red onion, thinly sliced
1	large tomato, diced
¼	cup sliced roasted red peppers
1	tablespoon drained capers
¼	cup thinly sliced fresh basil
	Salt and ground black pepper

MAKES 4 SERVINGS
PER SERVING
534   CALORIES
10.2 G. TOTAL FAT
1.4 G. SATURATED FAT
31.6 G. PROTEIN
90 G.   CARBOHYDRATES
10.5 G. DIETARY FIBER
17 MG. CHOLESTEROL
562 MG. SODIUM

Bring a large pot of water to a boil over high heat. Add the pasta and potatoes. Reduce the heat to medium and cook for 6 minutes. Add the green beans and cook for 5 minutes, or until the vegetables and pasta are tender, yet firm. Drain and transfer to a large bowl.

In a small bowl, combine the garlic, broth, lemon juice, oil, vinegar, and chives. Pour over the pasta mixture and toss to mix. Add the beans, tuna, onions, tomatoes, red peppers, capers, and basil. Season with the salt and pepper. Toss to mix.

QUICK SWITCH

Salmon Pasta Salad: Replace the tuna with canned pink salmon.

RECIPES

"Whoever tells a lie cannot be pure in heart—and only the pure in heart can make good soup."

—LUDWIG VAN BEETHOVEN, GERMAN COMPOSER

FLAVOR-RICH SOUPS AND STEWS THAT SATISFY

Soup is good food. A steaming bowl of soup can take the chill off an icy winter day. And during the dog days of summer, a cup of cold soup is like a breath of fresh air.

Most soups and stews are not especially high in fat. But some—like cheese soups, bisques, and chili—can tip the scale if you're not careful. I use evaporated skim milk or small amounts of half-and-half to replace the heavy cream in rich-textured soups. For hearty and healthy chili, look to low-fat turkey sausage instead of regular ground beef. If you're a die-hard beef lover, start out by replacing half of the ground beef with low-fat turkey sausage in your favorite soup and stew recipes. Once you get used to the flavor, switch to all low-fat turkey sausage. To achieve a rich texture without the fat in your favorite bean soups, simply puree some of the beans instead of adding heavy cream or sour cream.

Need a meal in minutes? Keep a few soups and stews in the freezer. Double the recipe the next time you make soup, then freeze the excess. You'll thank yourself on rushed evenings during the week. Soups travel well, too. All you need is a Thermos or microwave for hot, satisfying low-fat lunches away from home.

CREAMY TOMATO SOUP

Canned tomatoes and fresh basil make a quick soup. A modest amount of half-and-half lends a creamy, satisfying texture at a cost of only about 3.5 grams of fat per serving.

HANDS-ON TIME: 10 MINUTES
UNATTENDED TIME: 30 MINUTES

1	tablespoon olive oil
1	onion, chopped
5	cloves garlic, minced
2	cans (28 ounces each) diced or crushed tomatoes
1	cup fat-free chicken broth or vegetable broth
⅓	cup packed fresh basil, chopped
1	tablespoon sugar
½	teaspoon dried thyme
1	cup orzo or other small pasta
½	cup half-and-half
	Ground black pepper

MAKES 4 SERVINGS
PER SERVING
409   CALORIES
8.9 G.   TOTAL FAT
2.9 G.   SATURATED FAT
13 G.   PROTEIN
72.2 G. CARBOHYDRATES
3.5 G.   DIETARY FIBER
11 MG.   CHOLESTEROL
682 MG. SODIUM

Warm the oil in a large saucepan over medium heat. Add the onions and garlic and cook for 5 minutes. Add the tomatoes, broth, basil, sugar, and thyme. Bring to a boil. Reduce the heat to medium-low. Cover and simmer for 30 minutes, stirring occasionally.

Cook the pasta in a large pot of boiling water according to the package directions. Drain. Stir into the soup and remove the pot from the heat.

Place the half-and-half in a small bowl. Stir a small amount of the soup into the half-and-half. Stirring constantly, slowly pour the half-and-half mixture into the soup. Season with the pepper.

SWITCH TIP

Heavy cream has 11 grams of fat in a 2-tablespoon serving. Switch to half-and-half and you'll save about 8 grams of fat. Made with equal parts whole milk and heavy cream, half-and-half has 3 grams of fat in a 2-tablespoon serving. But the grams can add up quickly, so use half-and-half only in small quantities to add rich texture to soups, sauces, and casseroles.

COOKING HINTS

- To vary the texture of the soup, use 1 can diced tomatoes and 1 can crushed tomatoes.

- If desired, garnish the soup with sliced fresh basil leaves, grated Parmesan cheese, and low-fat croutons or Garlic Croutons (page 351).

POTATO-LEEK SOUP

Fresh fennel gives this soup lots of sophistication. For a more traditional potato-leek soup, omit the fennel and add an extra potato.

HANDS-ON TIME: 25 MINUTES
UNATTENDED TIME: 20 MINUTES

1	tablespoon unsalted butter or canola oil
1	small onion, chopped
1½	pounds leeks, trimmed and sliced
2	cups chopped fennel bulb
2	pounds potatoes, peeled and cubed
½	teaspoon dried marjoram
½	teaspoon dried dill
6	cups fat-free chicken broth or vegetable broth
½	cup half-and-half
2	teaspoons dry sherry or nonalcoholic white wine
1	teaspoon chopped fresh parsley
1	teaspoon chopped fresh basil
	Salt and ground black pepper

MAKES 6 SERVINGS

PER SERVING
242   CALORIES
4.7 G.   TOTAL FAT
2.8 G.   SATURATED FAT
5.3 G.   PROTEIN
46.4 G.   CARBOHYDRATES
3.8 G.   DIETARY FIBER
13 MG.   CHOLESTEROL
117 MG.   SODIUM

Warm the butter or oil in a large pot over medium heat. Add the onions, leeks, and fennel. Cook for 10 minutes. Stir in the potatoes, marjoram, and dill. Pour in the broth and bring to a boil. Reduce the heat to medium-low, partially cover, and cook for 20 minutes.

Transfer the soup to a food processor or blender (in batches, if necessary) and process until smooth. Return to the pot. Stir in the half-and-half, sherry or wine, parsley, and basil. Season with the salt and pepper.

COOKING HINT

• Fennel is a vegetable with a white bulb and very light green stalks. To use, trim the root end and cut off the top where the stalks become thin. Cut the bulb into quarters lengthwise, cut out the core, and slice as needed. Fennel is very aromatic with a mild licorice or anise flavor. It blends well with potatoes, fish, cheese, and poultry.

SWEET POTATO SOUP

Packed with vitamins, sweet potatoes are among the healthiest of all vegetables. Most of the ingredients in this soup are very low in fat, so I add some half-and-half to round out the texture.

HANDS-ON TIME: 20 MINUTES
UNATTENDED TIME: 20 MINUTES

MAKES 6 SERVINGS
PER SERVING
219   CALORIES
6.9 G.   TOTAL FAT
4.2 G.   SATURATED FAT
4.3 G.   PROTEIN
36.3 G. CARBOHYDRATES
3.5 G.   DIETARY FIBER
20 MG.   CHOLESTEROL
118 MG. SODIUM

1	tablespoon unsalted butter or canola oil
1	onion, chopped
1	carrot, chopped
1	stalk celery, chopped
½	teaspoon minced fresh ginger
8	cups peeled and cubed sweet potatoes (about 4 medium)
1	large potato, peeled and cubed
6	cups fat-free chicken broth or vegetable broth
1	cup half-and-half
½	teaspoon grated nutmeg
	Salt and ground black pepper

Warm the butter or oil in a large pot over medium heat. Add the onions, carrots, celery, and ginger. Cook for 5 minutes. Stir in the sweet potatoes and potatoes. Add the broth and bring to a boil over high heat. Reduce the heat to medium and simmer for 20 minutes, or until the vegetables are soft.

Transfer the soup to a food processor or blender (in batches, if necessary) and process until very smooth. Return the soup to the pot. Stir in the half-and-half and nutmeg. Season with the salt and pepper.

COOKING HINT

• Nutmeg is the seed of an Oriental tree. The outer covering is removed and used as another spice, mace. The "nut" is then sold whole or ground. The ground product loses flavor much more quickly than whole nutmeg, so buy whole nutmeg and grate it fresh on the small holes of a grater.

ROASTED GARLIC SOUP

Roasting mellows the flavor and eliminates the bite of raw garlic. If you're a die-hard garlic-lover, float a few Garlic Croutons (page 351) on top.

HANDS-ON TIME: 25 MINUTES
UNATTENDED TIME: 30 MINUTES

2	whole bulbs garlic, unpeeled
2	tablespoons water
1	tablespoon unsalted butter
1	tablespoon olive oil
1	small onion, chopped
2	cloves garlic, minced
1	large potato, peeled and cubed
3	slices French or Italian bread, torn into pieces
6	cups fat-free chicken broth or vegetable broth
1	can (12 ounces) evaporated skim milk
1	tablespoon dry sherry or nonalcoholic white wine
	Salt and ground black pepper
⅓	cup Garlic Croutons or other low-fat croutons (optional)

MAKES 6 SERVINGS

PER SERVING

184	CALORIES
4.9 G.	TOTAL FAT
1.7 G.	SATURATED FAT
10.8 G.	PROTEIN
24.1 G.	CARBOHYDRATES
0.8 G.	DIETARY FIBER
7 MG.	CHOLESTEROL
439 MG.	SODIUM

Preheat the oven to 500°F. Coat 2 custard cups with no-stick spray. Slice ½" off the top of each garlic bulb. Coat with no-stick spray and set in the prepared cups. Add 1 tablespoon of the water to each cup. Bake for 25 to 30 minutes, or until the garlic is soft. Remove from the oven and set aside to cool.

Warm the butter and oil in a large pot over medium heat. Add the onions and cook for 2 minutes. Mix in the minced garlic and cook for 1 minute. Stir in the potatoes and bread. Remove from the heat.

Peel the roasted garlic and add the cloves to the pot. Return to the heat and cook for 1 minute. Pour in the broth and milk. Bring to a boil. Reduce the heat to low and simmer for 10 to 15 minutes, or until the potatoes are soft.

Transfer the soup to a food processor or blender (in batches, if necessary) and process until very smooth. Return the soup to the pot and add the sherry or wine. Season with the salt and pepper. Serve sprinkled with the croutons (if using).

MISO SOUP

Miso is a fermented soybean paste available in large supermarkets, health food stores, and Asian grocery stores. Here, it forms the base for a classic Asian broth-style soup.

HANDS-ON TIME: 20 MINUTES
UNATTENDED TIME: 10 MINUTES

MAKES 6 SERVINGS
PER SERVING
253   CALORIES
3.9 G.   TOTAL FAT
0.4 G.   SATURATED FAT
9.5 G.   PROTEIN
45 G.   CARBOHYDRATES
2 G.   DIETARY FIBER
0 MG.   CHOLESTEROL
351 MG.   SODIUM

1	tablespoon toasted sesame oil
1	pound reduced-fat tofu, squeezed dry and cubed
8	ounces shiitake or other mushrooms, sliced
4	cloves garlic, minced
1	teaspoon minced fresh ginger
1	package (3¾ ounces) cellophane noodles
½	cup rice wine or nonalcoholic white wine
5	tablespoons brown rice miso
7	cups fat-free chicken broth or vegetable broth
1	tablespoon reduced-sodium soy sauce
1	tablespoon chili puree with garlic
1	carrot, chopped
1	can (8 ounces) sliced water chestnuts, drained
1½	cups broccoli florets
1½	teaspoons chopped fresh cilantro
	Red-pepper flakes

Warm the oil in a large pot over medium heat. Add the tofu, mushrooms, garlic, and ginger. Cook for 5 minutes, stirring continually but gently so that the tofu doesn't break apart. Spoon into a bowl.

Place the noodles in a large bowl and cover with hot water. Soak for 10 minutes.

Add the wine to the pot and place over medium heat. Cook and stir, scraping any bits from the bottom of the pot. Stir in the miso and 1 cup of the broth. Mix until the miso is creamy. Pour in the remaining 6 cups broth. Add the soy sauce, chili puree, and carrots. Bring to a boil. Reduce the heat to medium and cook for 5 minutes. Add the water chestnuts and broccoli. Cook for 3 minutes.

Drain the noodles and cut into pieces. Stir into the soup with the reserved tofu mixture. Cook for 2 minutes. Add the cilantro. Season with the red-pepper flakes.

SWISS BROCCOLI SOUP

My kids love the flavor of this smooth and creamy soup. I love it because it gives them vitamins A and C as well as B-complex vitamins, calcium, potassium, and fiber.

HANDS-ON TIME: 35 MINUTES
UNATTENDED TIME: NONE

1	large head broccoli
1	teaspoon canola oil
1	onion, chopped
1	large potato, cubed
4	cups fat-free chicken broth or vegetable broth
1	teaspoon dried basil
1	teaspoon dried Italian herb seasoning
2	cups shredded part-skim Jarlsberg cheese
1½	cups skim milk
1½	cups evaporated skim milk
	Salt and ground black pepper

MAKES 6 SERVINGS

PER SERVING
264 CALORIES
5.7 G. TOTAL FAT
3 G. SATURATED FAT
23.6 G. PROTEIN
28.8 G. CARBOHYDRATES
0.7 G. DIETARY FIBER
23 MG. CHOLESTEROL
845 MG. SODIUM

Cut the florets off the broccoli stems. Chop the florets. Separately chop the stems.

Coat a large pot with no-stick spray. Add the oil and onions. Cook over medium heat for 3 minutes. Add the potatoes and broccoli stems. Cook and stir for 2 minutes. Pour in the broth, basil, and Italian seasoning. Bring to a boil. Reduce the heat to medium-low, cover, and cook for 10 minutes. Add all but 2 cups of the broccoli florets and cook for 5 minutes.

Transfer the soup to a food processor or blender (in batches, if necessary). Process until smooth. Return to the pot. Add the remaining broccoli florets and cook over medium heat for 6 to 8 minutes, or until the broccoli is tender. Gradually add the Jarlsberg, stirring constantly, until the cheese is melted and no longer stringy. Gradually stir in the milk and evaporated milk. Season with the salt and pepper. Gently stir until heated through.

COOKING HINT

- Store leftover soup in the refrigerator for up to 4 days. Most cheese soups don't freeze well.

CAULIFLOWER-CHEESE SOUP

Evaporated skim milk is the trick to this rich soup. It replaces the heavy cream and whole milk found in traditional cheese-soup recipes.

HANDS-ON TIME: 40 MINUTES
UNATTENDED TIME: 5 MINUTES

1	tablespoon unsalted butter or canola oil
1	small onion, chopped
2	cloves garlic, chopped
1	large potato, peeled and cubed
1	head cauliflower, cut into florets
5	cups fat-free chicken broth or vegetable broth
2	cans (12 ounces each) evaporated skim milk
6	ounces part-skim sharp Cheddar cheese, shredded
2	tablespoons dry sherry or nonalcoholic white wine
	Salt and ground black pepper

MAKES 8 SERVINGS
PER SERVING

190	CALORIES
5 G.	TOTAL FAT
2.6 G.	SATURATED FAT
16.7 G.	PROTEIN
19.6 G.	CARBOHYDRATES
3.3 G.	DIETARY FIBER
18 MG.	CHOLESTEROL
635 MG.	SODIUM

SWITCH TIP

Evaporated skim milk has a thick, creamy consistency that mimics the mouthfeel of heavy cream in soups, sauces, and even coffee. By making the switch from heavy cream, you'll save 40 grams of fat and 300 calories for every ½ cup used.

Warm the butter or oil in a large pot over medium heat. Add the onions and cook for 3 minutes. Add the garlic and cook for 2 minutes. Stir in the potatoes and cauliflower. Pour in the broth and milk. Bring to a boil over medium heat, stirring often. Reduce the heat to low and simmer, stirring often, for 15 minutes, or until the cauliflower and potatoes are soft.

Transfer the soup to a food processor or blender (in batches, if necessary) and process until smooth. Return the soup to the pot. Add the Cheddar and sherry or wine. Stir constantly until the cheese is melted. Season with the salt and pepper.

COOKING HINT

• Store leftover soup in the refrigerator for up to 4 days. Most cheese soups don't freeze well.

MANHATTAN CLAM CHOWDER

This quick chowder makes a tasty alternative to Friday-night pizza. It needs only bread and salad to make it a meal. Buy fresh chopped clams from the seafood counter at your supermarket. Or use 3 cans (6½ ounces each) chopped clams with juice.

HANDS-ON TIME: 10 MINUTES
UNATTENDED TIME: 30 MINUTES

MAKES 6 SERVINGS
PER SERVING
187   CALORIES
5.7 G.   TOTAL FAT
0.7 G.   SATURATED FAT
13.5 G. PROTEIN
21.5 G. CARBOHYDRATES
2.9 G.   DIETARY FIBER
25 MG.   CHOLESTEROL
426 MG. SODIUM

2	tablespoons olive oil
1	onion, chopped
1	carrot, finely chopped
2	stalks celery, chopped
2	large potatoes, cubed
3	bottles (8 ounces each) clam juice
1	can (28 ounces) diced tomatoes (with juice)
2	tablespoons chopped fresh parsley
1	teaspoon dried thyme
1	teaspoon sugar
1	pound chopped clams
	Salt and ground black pepper

Warm the oil in a large pot over medium heat. Add the onions, carrots, and celery. Cook for 5 minutes. Stir in the potatoes and cook for 2 minutes. Add the clam juice, tomatoes (with juice), parsley , thyme, and sugar. Bring to a boil. Reduce the heat to medium-low and simmer for 15 to 20 minutes, or until the potatoes are just tender.

Stir in the clams. Season with the salt and pepper. Simmer for 10 minutes, or until the clams are tender.

New England Clam Chowder

Are you hankering for chowder that's thick enough to eat with a fork? This chowder won't blow your fat budget. Half-and-half and evaporated skim milk replace the heavy cream.

Hands-on time: 10 minutes
Unattended time: 20 minutes

1	tablespoon unsalted butter
1	onion, chopped
2	large potatoes, peeled and cubed
2	bottles (8 ounces each) clam juice
1	bay leaf
¼	teaspoon dried thyme
1	can (12 ounces) evaporated skim milk
1	pound chopped clams
¼	teaspoon grated lemon rind
2½	tablespoons arrowroot or cornstarch
½	cup half-and-half
1	teaspoon Worcestershire sauce
2	tablespoons minced fresh parsley
	Salt and ground black pepper
	Paprika

Makes 4 servings

Per serving

324	CALORIES
8 G.	TOTAL FAT
4.3 G.	SATURATED FAT
25.6 G.	PROTEIN
37 G.	CARBOHYDRATES
1.8 G.	DIETARY FIBER
60 MG.	CHOLESTEROL
353 MG.	SODIUM

Melt the butter in a large saucepan over medium heat. Add the onions and cook for 5 minutes. Add the potatoes and cook for 1 minute. Add the clam juice, bay leaf, and thyme. Cook for 10 minutes.

Stir in the milk, clams, and lemon rind. Reduce the heat to medium-low and cook for 10 minutes.

Place the arrowroot or cornstarch in a small bowl. Add the half-and-half and stir until smooth. Gradually stir into the soup. Add the Worcestershire sauce and parsley. Cook over low heat, stirring constantly, until slightly thickened. Season with the salt and pepper. Remove and discard the bay leaf. Serve dusted with the paprika.

Cooking Hint

- Chopped clams are available in the fresh seafood section of your supermarket. Most markets also carry chopped clams in 6½-ounce cans near the sardines and anchovies. If using the canned variety, use 3 cans (with juice).

CRAB AND CORN CHOWDER

Use fresh summer corn for the most flavor in this soup. Frozen works, but it's not nearly as good.

HANDS-ON TIME: 15 MINUTES
UNATTENDED TIME: 20 MINUTES

2	tablespoons unsalted butter or canola oil
1	onion, chopped
1	carrot, chopped
1	stalk celery, chopped
3	cloves garlic, minced
2	potatoes, cubed
½	teaspoon dried marjoram
¼	teaspoon dried thyme
¼	teaspoon ground coriander
¼	teaspoon ground nutmeg
3	cups fat-free chicken broth or vegetable broth
1½	cups evaporated skim milk
2½	cups corn kernels
8	ounces lump crabmeat
1	tablespoon chopped fresh parsley
1	teaspoon dry sherry or nonalcoholic white wine
¼	teaspoon grated lemon rind
	Salt and ground black pepper
	Ground red pepper

MAKES 6 SERVINGS
PER SERVING
252   CALORIES
5.1 G.   TOTAL FAT
2.7 G.   SATURATED FAT
18.3 G. PROTEIN
3 G.   DIETARY FIBER
35.6 G. CARBOHYDRATES
51 MG.   CHOLESTEROL
364 MG. SODIUM

Warm the butter or oil in a large saucepan over medium heat. Add the onions, carrots, celery, and garlic. Cook for 5 minutes. Stir in the potatoes, marjoram, thyme, coriander, and nutmeg. Pour in the broth and milk. Bring to a boil, then reduce the heat to low. Cook for 15 minutes, or until the potatoes are just tender.

In a food processor or blender, process 2 cups of the corn until smooth. Stir into the soup with the crab, parsley, sherry or wine, lemon rind, and the remaining ½ cup corn. Cook for 5 minutes. Season with the salt, black pepper, and red pepper.

QUICK SWITCH

Corn and Potato Chowder: For a vegetarian alternative, omit the crab and add ¾ cup more corn and another potato.

187

SHRIMP BISQUE

This soup is everything a bisque should be—minus the fat. Half-and-half gives it just the right texture without the full measure of fat that heavy cream would contribute. I like to serve the bisque with nonfat oyster crackers and a crisp green salad.

HANDS-ON TIME: 30 MINUTES
UNATTENDED TIME: 20 MINUTES

MAKES 6 SERVINGS
PER SERVING
247   CALORIES
5.6 G.   TOTAL FAT
3 G.   SATURATED FAT
24 G.   PROTEIN
25.1 G. CARBOHYDRATES
1.9 G.   DIETARY FIBER
189 MG. CHOLESTEROL
326 MG. SODIUM

6	cups water
1½	pounds unpeeled shrimp
1	tablespoon unsalted butter or margarine
2	leeks, trimmed and chopped (white part only)
1	carrot, finely chopped
3	cloves garlic, minced
2	potatoes, peeled and cubed
1	bottle (8 ounces) clam juice
1	tablespoon minced fresh dill
½	teaspoon dried tarragon
½	teaspoon dried fines herbes (see hint)
1	teaspoon grated lemon rind
3	tablespoons arrowroot or cornstarch
1	cup nonfat or low-fat buttermilk
½	cup nonfat sour cream
½	cup half-and-half
	Salt and ground black pepper

Bring the water to a boil in a medium saucepan over high heat. Add the shrimp. Reduce the heat to medium-high and cook for 2 minutes, or until the shrimp turn bright pink. Using a slotted spoon, transfer the shrimp to a bowl to cool. Reserve the cooking liquid.

Peel the shrimp and return to the bowl. Add the peels to the reserved cooking liquid and simmer over medium-low heat for 20 minutes.

Melt the butter or margarine in a large pot over medium heat. Add the leeks, carrots, and garlic. Cook for 5 minutes. Stir in the potatoes and clam juice.

Strain the shrimp stock into the pot; discard the shells. Bring to a boil over high heat. Reduce the heat to medium-low and simmer for 15 minutes, or until the potatoes are tender.

Chop the reserved shrimp and add to the pot. Stir in the dill, tarragon, fines herbes, and lemon rind.

Place the arrowroot or cornstarch in a small bowl. Add a few tablespoons of the buttermilk and stir to dissolve. Whisk in the sour cream, half-and-half, and the remaining buttermilk. Add a few tablespoons of the soup to the mixture. Mix well and stir back into the pot. Season with the salt and pepper. Reduce the heat to low and simmer for 5 minutes.

COOKING HINT

• Fines herbes is a blend of mild herbs used in French cooking. It usually includes parsley, chives, tarragon, and chervil. Fines herbes works well in most egg dishes and cheese dishes. Look for it in the spice section of your supermarket.

CHILLED SEAFOOD SOUP

Here's an elegant soup that travels well.

HANDS-ON TIME: 25 MINUTES
UNATTENDED TIME: 2 HOURS

- 3 cups water
- 1 cup dry white wine or nonalcoholic white wine
- 8 ounces medium shrimp, peeled and deveined
- 8 ounces scallops
- 8 ounces salmon fillet, skin removed, cut into bite-size pieces
- 1 tablespoon unsalted butter or margarine
- 1 shallot, chopped
- 1 clove garlic, chopped
- ½ sweet red or green pepper, chopped
- 1 small jalapeño pepper, seeded and chopped (wear plastic gloves when handling)
- 1 cup nonfat sour cream
- 3 tablespoons chopped fresh dill
  Grated rind of 1 lime
- 1 pound lump crabmeat
- 1 cup low-fat buttermilk
  Salt and ground black pepper
  Hot-pepper sauce

MAKES 6 SERVINGS
PER SERVING
211   CALORIES
4.7 G. TOTAL FAT
1.8 G. SATURATED FAT
27.2 G. PROTEIN
8.8 G. CARBOHYDRATES
0.4 G. DIETARY FIBER
112 MG. CHOLESTEROL
279 MG. SODIUM

Bring the water and wine to a boil in a medium saucepan over high heat. Add the shrimp, scallops, and salmon. Reduce the heat to medium and cook for 2 to 4 minutes, or until the shrimp and scallops are opaque and the salmon flakes easily when tested with a fork. Using a slotted spoon, remove the seafood from the water and transfer to a plate. Place both the seafood and the stock in the refrigerator to cool.

Warm the butter or margarine in a small no-stick skillet over medium heat. Add the shallots and garlic. Cook for 3 minutes.

Transfer to a food processor. Add the red or green peppers, jalapeño peppers, sour cream, dill, and lime rind. Process until smooth. Pour the mixture into a large bowl. Stir in the crab, buttermilk, reserved seafood, and reserved stock. Season with the salt, black pepper, and hot-pepper sauce. Refrigerate for at least 2 hours or up to 24 hours.

FRUITY GAZPACHO

Gazpacho is a cold, fresh tomato soup hailing from Spain. The spicy and fruity flavors in this version make it unique.

HANDS-ON TIME: 20 MINUTES
UNATTENDED TIME: 2 HOURS

½	honeydew melon, cubed
2½	cups green grapes
1	avocado, halved
1	cucumber, halved
1	green pepper, halved
1	jalapeño pepper, seeded (wear plastic gloves when handling)
	Grated rind and juice of 1 lime
¼	cup fresh basil leaves
3	tablespoons fresh dill
2	tablespoons fresh parsley leaves
4	scallions, chopped
2	tablespoons white-wine vinegar
	Salt and ground black pepper
	Hot-pepper sauce (optional)

MAKES 6 SERVINGS
PER SERVING
156	CALORIES
5.1 G.	TOTAL FAT
1 G.	SATURATED FAT
2.4 G.	PROTEIN
29.6 G.	CARBOHYDRATES
3.5 G.	DIETARY FIBER
0 MG.	CHOLESTEROL
29 MG.	SODIUM

Place the melon in a food processor. Add 2 cups of the grapes, half of the avocado, half of the cucumber, and half of the green pepper. Add the jalapeño peppers, lime rind, lime juice, basil, dill, and parsley. Process until smooth. Pour into a large bowl.

Cut the remaining ½ cup grapes into quarters and add to the bowl. Dice the remaining avocado, cucumber, and green pepper. Add to the bowl. Stir in the scallions and vinegar. Season with the salt, black pepper, and hot-pepper sauce (if using). Cover and refrigerate for at least 2 hours or up to 24 hours.

COOKING HINT

- For a pretty presentation, reserve ¼ cup of the chopped scallions. Sprinkle over each serving.

SPLIT PEA AND WILD RICE SOUP

Wild rice gives traditional split pea soup a nice twist. It also adds several B vitamins. This recipe makes a large amount so you can freeze some for a quick meal. Freeze it for up to 3 months.

HANDS-ON TIME: 15 MINUTES
UNATTENDED TIME: 55 MINUTES

MAKES 10 SERVINGS
PER SERVING
348   CALORIES
3.8 G.   TOTAL FAT
0.5 G.   SATURATED FAT
18.7 G. PROTEIN
62.6 G. CARBOHYDRATES
4.3 G.   DIETARY FIBER
0 MG.   CHOLESTEROL
118 MG. SODIUM

2½	cups water
1	cup wild rice, rinsed
2	tablespoons olive oil
2	onions, chopped
4	carrots, finely chopped
4	stalks celery, chopped
4	cloves garlic, minced
3	cups split peas
1	bay leaf
1	teaspoon dried thyme
1	teaspoon dry mustard
⅛	teaspoon dried sage
10	cups fat-free chicken broth or vegetable broth
2	tablespoons lemon juice
	Salt and ground black pepper

Bring the water to a boil in a medium saucepan over high heat. Add the wild rice and return to a boil. Reduce the heat to low. Cover and cook for 45 minutes, or until the liquid has been absorbed.

Warm the oil in a large pot over medium heat. Add the onions, carrots, celery, and garlic. Cook for 10 minutes. Stir in the peas, bay leaf, thyme, mustard, and sage. Add the broth. Bring to a boil. Reduce the heat to medium-low, cover, and cook for 45 minutes, stirring occasionally.

Add the wild rice and lemon juice. Season with the salt and pepper. Reduce the heat to low. Cook, stirring, for 5 minutes, or until the soup is thick and the peas are soft. Remove and discard the bay leaf.

SOUTHWEST BEAN SOUP

This soup is tailor-made for cool autumn afternoons. For extra flavor, sprinkle with shredded part-skim Cheddar cheese.

HANDS-ON TIME: 15 MINUTES
UNATTENDED TIME: 1¼ HOURS

1	pound dry pinto beans, soaked overnight
6	cups water
3	tablespoons canola or olive oil
1	onion, chopped
7	cloves garlic, chopped
1	green or sweet red pepper, chopped
1	carrot, chopped
1	stalk celery, chopped
3	small zucchini, cubed
3	ripe tomatoes, cubed
1	can (4½ ounces) chopped green chili peppers
1	bay leaf
1	teaspoon chili powder
1	teaspoon dried oregano
1	teaspoon sugar
¼	teaspoon ground cumin
3	tablespoons tomato paste
1	tablespoon chopped fresh cilantro
1	tablespoon lemon juice
	Salt and ground black pepper

MAKES 8 SERVINGS

PER SERVING
286   CALORIES
6.2 G. TOTAL FAT
0.6 G. SATURATED FAT
13.7 G. PROTEIN
46.4 G. CARBOHYDRATES
2.8 G. DIETARY FIBER
0 MG.   CHOLESTEROL
130 MG. SODIUM

Drain and rinse the beans. Place in a large saucepan. Add the water and bring to a boil over high heat. Reduce the heat to medium-low and simmer for 50 minutes, or until the beans are tender.

Warm the oil in a large pot over medium heat. Add the onions and cook for 2 minutes. Add the garlic, green or red peppers, carrots, and celery. Cook for 5 minutes. Stir in the zucchini, tomatoes, chili peppers, bay leaf, chili powder, oregano, sugar, and cumin. Cook for 5 minutes.

Stir in the tomato paste, cilantro, lemon juice, and beans with the cooking liquid. Season with the salt and black pepper. Bring to a boil, stirring often. Reduce the heat to medium-low and simmer for 20 minutes. Remove and discard the bay leaf.

WHITE BEAN MINESTRONE

Beans, pasta, and vegetables make a classic hearty soup. Thanks to the canned beans, you can make this one in a jiffy. For the pasta, I prefer rotini, fusilli, or cavatelli.

HANDS-ON TIME: 10 MINUTES
UNATTENDED TIME: 45 MINUTES

MAKES 6 SERVINGS
PER SERVING
475   CALORIES
7.9 G.   TOTAL FAT
2.2 G.   SATURATED FAT
24.1 G. PROTEIN
79.5 G. CARBOHYDRATES
2.2 G.   DIETARY FIBER
5 MG.   CHOLESTEROL
688 MG. SODIUM

4	ounces pasta
2	tablespoons olive oil
1	large onion, chopped
6	cloves garlic, minced
1	carrot, chopped
1	stalk celery, chopped
1	large potato, peeled and cubed
1	can (14½ ounces) diced tomatoes (with juice)
4	cups fat-free chicken broth or vegetable broth
1	teaspoon dried thyme
½	teaspoon dried marjoram
2	cups packed fresh spinach, torn
3	cans (15½ ounces each) Great Northern or navy beans, rinsed and drained
2	tablespoons chopped fresh basil
⅛	teaspoon crushed saffron threads
1	tablespoon lemon juice
	Ground black pepper
6	tablespoons grated Parmesan cheese

Cook the pasta in a large saucepan of boiling water according to the package directions. Drain and place in a medium bowl.

Warm the oil in a large pot over medium heat. Add the onions, garlic, carrots, and celery. Cook for 10 minutes. Stir in the potatoes, tomatoes (with juice), broth, thyme, and marjoram. Bring to a boil. Reduce the heat to medium-low and simmer for 10 minutes.

Stir in the spinach, beans, basil, saffron, and lemon juice. Season with the pepper. Stir in the pasta. Reduce the heat to low, cover, and simmer, stirring often, for 20 minutes. Serve sprinkled with the Parmesan.

WHITE BEAN AND ESCAROLE SOUP

Escarole is a member of the chicory family of lettuces. It's a good source of beta-carotene and calcium. The slightly bitter flavor of escarole mellows nicely in this light Italian bean soup.

HANDS-ON TIME: 15 MINUTES
UNATTENDED TIME: 40 MINUTES

2	tablespoons olive oil
1	onion, chopped
10	cloves garlic, chopped
1	head escarole, chopped
2	teaspoons sugar
½	teaspoon dried oregano
5	cups fat-free chicken broth or vegetable broth
½	cup grated Parmesan cheese
¼	teaspoon grated lemon rind
3	cans (15½ ounces each) Great Northern beans, with liquid
	Salt and ground black pepper

Warm the oil in a large pot over medium-low heat. Add the onions and garlic. Cook for 10 minutes. Stir in the escarole, sugar, and oregano. Cook for 10 minutes.

Add the broth and bring to a boil over medium-high heat. Reduce the heat to low. Stir in the Parmesan and lemon rind; stir until the cheese melts. Stir in the beans with liquid. Season with the salt and pepper. Simmer over low heat, stirring often, for 20 minutes.

MAKES 6 SERVINGS
PER SERVING
378   CALORIES
7.9 G.   TOTAL FAT
2.5 G.   SATURATED FAT
24.5 G. PROTEIN
54 G.   CARBOHYDRATES
1.4 G.   DIETARY FIBER
6.6 MG. CHOLESTEROL
947 MG. SODIUM

SWITCH TIP

Studies show that chicken soup can actually help relieve symptoms of the common cold. The soup helps break up congestion and ease the flow of nasal secretions, making it easier for cold sufferers to breathe. University of Nebraska researchers studied the extracts from a batch of homemade chicken soup and found that they inhibited the white blood cells that trigger inflammation, phlegm, and scratchy throats. Next time you're feeling stuffy, reach for a bowl of chicken soup before you load up on cold medicine.

CHICKEN CHILI

Some folks have strict guidelines about what makes chili authentic. Here, I've broken most of the rules. The base is a green sauce made with chili peppers and tomatillos, those small green fruits that look like unripe tomatoes with papery skins and are used often in Mexican cooking. The meat is chicken instead of beef. I like to use 2 jalapeño peppers for a fair amount of heat, but one will do for those who prefer a milder version.

HANDS-ON TIME: 15 MINUTES
UNATTENDED TIME: 45 MINUTES

MAKES 4 SERVINGS
PER SERVING
458   CALORIES
9.4 G.   TOTAL FAT
1.6 G.   SATURATED FAT
41.6 G.   PROTEIN
54.4 G.   CARBOHYDRATES
2.2 G.   DIETARY FIBER
69 MG.   CHOLESTEROL
1,008 MG.   SODIUM

1	teaspoon + 1 tablespoon olive oil
1	pound boneless, skinless chicken breasts, cubed
1	onion, chopped
10	tomatillos, husked and chopped
2	jalapeño peppers, seeded and chopped (wear plastic gloves when handling)
6	cloves garlic, minced
2	teaspoons chili powder
1	teaspoon dried oregano
1	teaspoon sugar
½	teaspoon ground cumin
	Salt
3	cups fat-free chicken broth or vegetable broth
2	cans (15 ounces each) pinto beans, rinsed and drained
1	cup corn kernels
1	tablespoon chopped fresh cilantro
1	tablespoon lime juice
	Ground black pepper
1	tablespoon arrowroot or cornstarch
1	tablespoon water
	Part-skim Monterey Jack or hot-pepper cheese (optional)

Warm 1 teaspoon of the oil in a large saucepan over medium heat. Add the chicken and cook, stirring, for 5 minutes, or until lightly browned. Transfer to a medium bowl.

Add the remaining 1 tablespoon oil to the saucepan. Stir in the onions, tomatillos, jalapeño peppers, and garlic. Cook for 5 minutes. Stir in the chili powder, oregano, sugar, and cumin. Season with the salt. Add the broth and bring to a boil over high heat. Reduce the heat to medium-low, cover, and simmer for 30 minutes.

Stir in the beans, corn, cilantro, lime juice, and the reserved chicken. Season with the black pepper.

Place the arrowroot or cornstarch in a cup. Add the water and stir to dissolve. Add a spoonful of the chili to the cup, then add to the saucepan. Stir until slightly thickened. Simmer for 15 minutes. Serve sprinkled with the Monterey Jack or hot-pepper cheese (if using).

QUICK SWITCH

Vegetarian Chili Verde: Replace the chicken with 1 pound tofu, drained and crumbled.

Super-Bowl Chili

This recipe is easy to make, keeps well on low heat for several hours, and can be doubled or tripled when needed.

Hands-on time: 15 minutes
Unattended time: 30 minutes

1	tablespoon canola or olive oil
2	onions, chopped
5	cloves garlic, minced
1	large jalapeño pepper, seeded and chopped (wear plastic gloves when handling)
1	pound ground turkey breast
6	ounces low-fat turkey sausage, casings removed
3	tablespoons chili powder
1	tablespoon paprika
2	teaspoons dried oregano
2	teaspoons ground cumin
2	teaspoons unsweetened cocoa powder
1	can (28 ounces) tomato puree
1	can (15½ ounces) kidney beans, rinsed and drained
	Salt and ground black pepper
1	tablespoon chopped fresh cilantro
1	tablespoon lime juice

Makes 6 servings

Per serving
311   CALORIES
7.8 G.   TOTAL FAT
1.3 G.   SATURATED FAT
28 G.   PROTEIN
37.9 G. CARBOHYDRATES
9.9 G.   DIETARY FIBER
47 MG.   CHOLESTEROL
505 MG. SODIUM

Warm the oil in a large pot over medium heat. Add the onions, garlic, and jalapeño peppers. Cook for 5 minutes. Crumble the ground turkey and turkey sausage into the pot. Cook, breaking up the meat with a spoon, for 5 minutes. Stir in the chili powder, paprika, oregano, cumin, and cocoa.

Add the tomato puree and beans. Season with the salt and black pepper. Reduce the heat to low, cover, and cook for 30 minutes or up to 2 hours. Stir in the cilantro and lime juice.

Cooking Hints

- Made the chili too hot? Here's how to put out the fire: Serve it with nonfat sour cream or shredded part skim–milk cheese. Dairy products neutralize the heat-producing substance in chili peppers.

- Chili is incredibly versatile. To vary the flavor, add corn kernels, chopped vegetables, or other varieties of chili peppers.

LENTIL AND PASTA STEW

Lentils are fast and healthy. Unlike most other legumes, they don't require soaking before cooking. Plus, they're a good source of protein, calcium, iron, zinc, and potassium.

HANDS-ON TIME: 25 MINUTES
UNATTENDED TIME: 30 MINUTES

MAKES 4 SERVINGS

PER SERVING

561	CALORIES
5.1 G.	TOTAL FAT
0.7 G.	SATURATED FAT
29.3 G.	PROTEIN
102.6 G.	CARBOHYDRATES
2.5 G.	DIETARY FIBER
0 MG.	CHOLESTEROL
150 MG.	SODIUM

1	tablespoon olive oil
1	onion, chopped
5	cloves garlic, minced
1	carrot, chopped
2	teaspoons minced ginger
2	cups lentils
1	teaspoon dried thyme
1	teaspoon dried coriander
1	teaspoon chili powder
6	cups fat-free chicken broth or vegetable broth
2	potatoes, peeled and cubed
1	cup bow-tie noodles or other pasta
2	tablespoons chopped fresh parsley and/or cilantro
1	tablespoon sherry vinegar or white-wine vinegar
1	teaspoon grated lemon rind
	Salt and ground black pepper
6	scallions, chopped
	Feta cheese, crumbled (optional)

Warm the oil in a large pot over medium heat. Add the onions, garlic, carrots, and ginger. Cook for 5 minutes. Stir in the lentils, thyme, coriander, and chili powder. Add the broth and bring to a boil. Partially cover and simmer, stirring occasionally, for 30 to 35 minutes.

Add the potatoes and pasta. Cook, stirring often, for 10 minutes, or until the potatoes and pasta are tender. Stir in the parsley and/or cilantro, vinegar, and lemon rind. Season with the salt and pepper.

Serve sprinkled with the scallions and feta (if using).

COOKING HINT

- To brighten the flavor of hearty bean soups and stews, add a splash of vinegar at the end of the cooking time. A tablespoon of lemon juice or lime juice has the same effect.

LENTIL AND SAUSAGE STEW

This hearty lentil stew needs only a salad and crusty whole-grain bread to make a meal. Leftovers are great for a quick lunch.

HANDS-ON TIME: 10 MINUTES
UNATTENDED TIME: 45 MINUTES

5	cups fat-free chicken broth or vegetable broth
1½	cups lentils
2	bay leaves
½	teaspoon fennel seeds
1	teaspoon crushed dried rosemary
12	ounces low-fat turkey sausage, cut into ½" slices
1½	tablespoons olive oil
2	red onions, sliced
2	carrots, chopped
1	sweet red pepper, chopped
8	cloves garlic, minced
1	teaspoon dried savory
1	teaspoon dried thyme
1	teaspoon dried marjoram or oregano
¼	cup chopped fresh basil and/or parsley
¼	cup dry red wine or nonalcoholic red wine
¼	cup tomato paste
2	teaspoons balsamic vinegar
	Salt and ground black pepper

MAKES 6 SERVINGS
PER SERVING
351 CALORIES
8.3 G. TOTAL FAT
1.7 G. SATURATED FAT
27.3 G. PROTEIN
42.6 G. CARBOHYDRATES
2.8 G. DIETARY FIBER
36 MG. CHOLESTEROL
864 MG. SODIUM

In a large pot, combine the broth, lentils, bay leaves, fennel seeds, and rosemary. Bring to a boil over high heat. Reduce the heat to low, cover, and cook for 35 to 40 minutes, or until the lentils are just tender.

Coat a large saucepan with no-stick spray and place over medium heat. Add the sausage and cook until brown. Transfer to a medium bowl.

Add the oil to the saucepan and warm over medium heat. Add the onions, carrots, red peppers, and garlic. Cook for 5 minutes. Add the savory, thyme, and marjoram or oregano. Stir in the lentil mixture, sausage, basil and/or parsley, wine, and tomato paste. Cook for 10 minutes, or until the lentils and carrots are tender. Stir in the vinegar. Season with the salt and black pepper. Remove and discard the bay leaves.

AFRICAN CHICKEN AND RICE STEW

This stew gets rave reviews, and it comes together quickly.

HANDS-ON TIME: 35 MINUTES
UNATTENDED TIME: NONE

1	teaspoon + 1 tablespoon canola oil
1	pound boneless, skinless chicken breasts, cubed
1	onion, chopped
4	cloves garlic, minced
1	tablespoon chopped fresh ginger
2	red chili peppers or jalapeño peppers, seeded and chopped (wear plastic gloves when handling)
14	mushrooms, halved or quartered
1	teaspoon ground cumin
1	teaspoon ground coriander
½	teaspoon ground cinnamon
¼	teaspoon turmeric
4	cups fat-free chicken broth or vegetable broth
2	tablespoons peanut butter
1	can (15 ounces) pumpkin puree
3	cups cooked brown rice
1½	cups corn kernels
1	can (15 ounces) black-eyed peas or chickpeas, rinsed and drained
1	tablespoon chopped fresh parsley
1	teaspoon lemon juice
	Salt and ground black pepper
	Chopped peanuts (optional)

MAKES 6 SERVINGS
PER SERVING
412   CALORIES
11.7 G. TOTAL FAT
2 G.   SATURATED FAT
29.6 G. PROTEIN
49.1 G. CARBOHYDRATES
8.2 G.   DIETARY FIBER
46 MG.   CHOLESTEROL
435 MG. SODIUM

Warm 1 teaspoon of the oil in a large pot over medium heat. Add the chicken and cook, stirring, for 5 minutes, or until lightly browned. Transfer to a medium bowl.

Add the remaining 1 tablespoon oil to the pot. Add the onions, garlic, ginger, chili peppers or jalapeño peppers, and mushrooms. Cook for 10 minutes. Stir in the cumin, coriander, cinnamon, and turmeric.

In a medium bowl, combine the broth and peanut butter. Stir until blended. Add to the pot. Stir in the pumpkin. Bring to a boil, then reduce the heat to medium-low. Add the chicken, rice, corn, black-eyed peas or chickpeas, parsley, and lemon juice. Season with the salt and black pepper. Cook for 5 minutes. Sprinkle with the peanuts (if using).

RECIPES

"The history of the world is the record of a man in quest of his daily bread."

—H. W. VAN LOON, DUTCH-AMERICAN HISTORIAN

FIBER UP WITH WHOLE GRAINS AND LEGUMES

Grains and legumes have long been the mainstay of healthful diets throughout the world. They're also a top source of nutrition in the Low-Fat Living Program. These foods contain little or no fat, and they're high in fiber and other essential nutrients. And the complex carbohydrates in grains give you long-lasting energy that's released in a steady supply throughout the day.

What's more, grains and beans fill you up so that you don't overeat high-fat foods. You can generally eat a greater volume of beans and grains than fatty foods (like butter and oil) without taking in any more calories. That's because beans and grains have only 4 calories per gram of food, while fats like butter and oil have 9 calories per gram.

Looking for a substantial side dish? Try Mushroom and Barley Pilaf or Easy Black Beans. For something on the lighter side, look to Couscous with Apricots and Pine Nuts. Better yet, put beans and grains at the center of your meal. On a cold winter night, nothing satisfies like a plate of well-seasoned Four Beans and Brown Rice. In the long days of summer, reach for cooling Corn and Chicken Risotto. For more grain and bean dishes, see the salad recipes beginning on page 150, the soup recipes beginning on page 178, the pasta recipes beginning on page 220, and the bakery recipes beginning on page 372.

MUSHROOM AND BARLEY PILAF

If you like mushroom-barley soup, you'll love this robust pilaf. Serve it with hearty chicken or vegetable dishes. Use a variety of wild mushrooms for a unique twist.

HANDS-ON TIME: 15 MINUTES
UNATTENDED TIME: 35 MINUTES

1	tablespoon unsalted butter or margarine
2	shallots, chopped
1	clove garlic, minced
2½	cups chopped mushrooms
2	tablespoons dry sherry or nonalcoholic white wine
1	teaspoon reduced-sodium soy sauce
½	teaspoon dried marjoram
½	teaspoon dried thyme
	Salt and ground black pepper
1½	cups pearl barley
3	cups fat-free chicken broth or vegetable broth

MAKES 6 SERVINGS

PER SERVING

224	CALORIES
2.7 G.	TOTAL FAT
1.4 G.	SATURATED FAT
8.1 G.	PROTEIN
42 G.	CARBOHYDRATES
8.2 G.	DIETARY FIBER
5 MG.	CHOLESTEROL
204 MG.	SODIUM

Melt the butter or margarine in a medium saucepan over medium heat. Add the shallots and garlic. Cook for 3 minutes. Add the mushrooms, sherry or wine, soy sauce, marjoram, and thyme. Season with the salt and pepper. Cook for 7 to 10 minutes, or until the liquid evaporates and the mushrooms begin to brown. Add the barley and cook, stirring occasionally, for 2 minutes.

Pour in the broth and bring to a boil. Reduce the heat to medium-low, cover, and cook for 20 to 25 minutes, or until all the liquid is absorbed. Remove from the heat, cover, and let stand for 10 minutes. Toss with a fork before serving.

COOKING HINT

• Pearl barley is used in this recipe because it's readily available and quick to fix. However, the pearling process removes much of the fiber, minerals, and protein. To get the most nutrients, use hulled (or hull-less) barley, which is available in most health food stores. Use 1½ cups hulled barley and 4 cups broth. Cook for 1 to 1½ hours.

BROWN BASMATI AND ORZO PILAF

Basmati rice, a long-grain rice from India, has a distinct aroma and nutty flavor. Most supermarkets carry both white and brown varieties. Here, brown basmati and orzo pasta come together with minimal fuss and little fat.

HANDS-ON TIME: 15 MINUTES
UNATTENDED TIME: 35 MINUTES

MAKES 6 SERVINGS
PER SERVING
167   CALORIES
2.9 G.   TOTAL FAT
1.3 G.   SATURATED FAT
4.3 G.   PROTEIN
31.3 G.   CARBOHYDRATES
0.3 G.   DIETARY FIBER
5 MG.   CHOLESTEROL
199 MG.   SODIUM

2	cups water
1	tablespoon unsalted butter or olive oil
1	teaspoon dried parsley
1	teaspoon dried chives
½	teaspoon grated lemon rind
½	teaspoon salt
¼	teaspoon ground black pepper
1	cup brown basmati rice
⅔	cup orzo pasta
½	cup finely chopped red onions

In a medium saucepan, combine the water, butter or oil, parsley, chives, lemon rind, salt, and pepper. Bring to a boil over high heat and stir in the rice. Reduce the heat to medium-low. Cover and cook for 35 to 45 minutes, or until all the liquid is absorbed and the rice is tender.

While the rice is cooking, cook the pasta in another medium saucepan of boiling water according to the package directions. Drain and transfer to a serving bowl.

Coat a small skillet with no-stick spray. Set over medium heat until warm. Add the onions and cook for 5 minutes, or until lightly browned. Remove from the heat and toss with the orzo.

Add the rice to the orzo and toss to mix.

COOKING HINT

• If you can't find brown basmati rice, substitute long-grain brown rice.

CORN AND CHICKEN RISOTTO

Summer corn is cooked just right in this delicious risotto.

HANDS-ON TIME: 1 HOUR
UNATTENDED TIME: NONE

5	cups fat-free chicken broth or vegetable broth
4	teaspoons olive oil
2	shallots, chopped
1	sweet red pepper, thinly sliced
2	cups Arborio rice
1	cup dry white wine or nonalcoholic white wine
1	pound boneless, skinless chicken breasts, sliced into bite-size pieces
	Salt and ground black pepper
	Garlic powder and paprika
6	ears fresh corn, kernels removed (about 5 cups)
3	tablespoons chopped fresh herbs (basil, chives, cilantro)
1	cup shredded part-skim provolone or smoked mozzarella cheese
¼	cup grated Parmesan cheese

MAKES 6 SERVINGS

PER SERVING
583   CALORIES
8.9 G. TOTAL FAT
2.9 G. SATURATED FAT
35.2 G. PROTEIN
86.3 G. CARBOHYDRATES
3.4 G. DIETARY FIBER
55 MG. CHOLESTEROL
507 MG. SODIUM

Bring the broth to a boil in a medium saucepan over high heat. Reduce the heat to low and keep warm.

Warm 3 teaspoons of the oil in a large saucepan over medium heat. Add the shallots and red peppers. Cook for 2 minutes. Stir in the rice and cook for 2 minutes. Pour in the wine and cook, stirring constantly, for 5 minutes, or until most of the liquid is absorbed. Gradually add 4 cups of the broth, 1 cup at a time. Stir frequently until each addition of broth is absorbed (a total of about 25 minutes).

Meanwhile, warm the remaining 1 teaspoon oil in a large no-stick skillet over medium heat. Add the chicken. Season with the salt, black pepper, garlic powder, and paprika. Cook, stirring frequently, for 5 minutes, or until the chicken is cooked through.

When the fourth cup of broth has been absorbed, stir in the corn and herbs. Add the remaining 1 cup broth. Cook and stir for 10 minutes, or until the rice is tender yet firm. Remove from the heat. Stir in the chicken, provolone or mozzarella, and Parmesan. Season with additional salt and pepper.

ASPARAGUS RISOTTO WITH SUN-DRIED TOMATOES

Constant stirring creates the creamy texture unique to risotto.

HANDS-ON TIME: 40 MINUTES
UNATTENDED TIME: NONE

2	cups fat-free chicken broth or vegetable broth
8	sun-dried tomatoes
1	tablespoon olive oil
2	shallots or 1 small onion, finely chopped
1	cup Arborio rice
½	cup dry white wine or nonalcoholic white wine
8	ounces asparagus, trimmed and cut into 1" pieces
2	tablespoons chopped fresh chives
½	teaspoon finely grated lemon rind
¼	cup grated Parmesan cheese
	Salt and ground black pepper

MAKES 4 SERVINGS

PER SERVING

317	CALORIES
6.1 G.	TOTAL FAT
1.8 G.	SATURATED FAT
11.6 G.	PROTEIN
50.5 G.	CARBOHYDRATES
0.2 G.	DIETARY FIBER
5 MG.	CHOLESTEROL
575 MG.	SODIUM

Bring the broth to a boil in a small saucepan. Reduce the heat to low and keep warm.

Place the tomatoes in a small bowl. Cover them with boiling water and let soak until needed.

Warm the oil in a large saucepan over medium heat. Add the shallots or onions and cook for 2 minutes. Stir in the rice and cook for 1 minute. Pour in the wine and cook, stirring constantly, for 4 minutes, or until most of the liquid is absorbed. Gradually add 1 cup of the broth, ½ cup at a time. Stir frequently until each addition of broth is absorbed (a total of about 10 minutes).

Stir in another ½ cup broth and the asparagus, chives, and lemon rind. Cook and stir until the broth is absorbed. Add the remaining ½ cup broth. Cook and stir for 5 minutes, or until the asparagus is tender and the rice is tender, yet firm.

Remove from the heat and stir in the Parmesan. Season with the salt and pepper. Drain the tomatoes and slice. Sprinkle over the risotto.

COOKING HINT

- Arborio rice is available in the grains section of most supermarkets. Or see the mail-order sources on page 416.

RICE AND BROCCOLI WITH WALNUTS AND ROQUEFORT

The distinctive flavors of broccoli and Roquefort cheese make this a unique side dish. Serve it with chicken or fish entrées. I also like leftovers rolled inside a tortilla for lunch. Try blue cheese or Gorgonzola in place of the Roquefort.

HANDS-ON TIME: 5 MINUTES
UNATTENDED TIME: 40 MINUTES

MAKES 6 servings	
PER SERVING	
136	CALORIES
5.6 G.	TOTAL FAT
2.4 G.	SATURATED FAT
7.2 G.	PROTEIN
15.1 G.	CARBOHYDRATES
2 G.	DIETARY FIBER
10 MG.	CHOLESTEROL
348 MG.	SODIUM

1	teaspoon unsalted butter or canola oil
1	shallot, chopped
1	clove garlic, minced
½	cup brown rice
3	cups fat-free chicken broth or vegetable broth
	Salt and ground black pepper
2	cups small broccoli florets
2	tablespoons chopped toasted walnuts
1	tablespoon chopped fresh parsley
½	teaspoon grated lemon rind
2	ounces Roquefort cheese, crumbled

Warm the butter or oil in a large saucepan over medium-high heat. Add the shallots and garlic. Cook for 4 minutes, or until lightly browned. Stir in the rice and broth. Season with salt and pepper. Bring to a boil. Reduce the heat to low, cover, and cook for 30 minutes.

Place the broccoli on top of the rice. Do not stir. Cover and cook for 10 to 15 minutes, or until the liquid has been absorbed and the rice is tender.

Gently stir in the walnuts, parsley, and lemon rind. Sprinkle on the Roquefort. Toss lightly before serving.

PERFECT POLENTA

Polenta is a soft porridge made by cooking cornmeal in water or flavored liquids. The secret to perfect polenta is constant stirring. Buy the coarsest cornmeal that you can find. It is sometimes labeled as "polenta" or "corn grits."

HANDS-ON TIME: 20 MINUTES
UNATTENDED TIME: NONE

5   **cups water**
1½   **cups coarsely ground cornmeal**
      Salt and ground black pepper

MAKES 4 SERVINGS
PER SERVING
166   CALORIES
1.6 G.   TOTAL FAT
0.2 G.   SATURATED FAT
3.7 G.   PROTEIN
35.2 G. CARBOHYDRATES
7 G.   DIETARY FIBER
0 MG.   CHOLESTEROL
16 MG.   SODIUM

Bring the water to a boil in a large saucepan over medium-high heat. Using a whisk, slowly add the cornmeal, whisking constantly.

Reduce the heat to medium-low. Using a spoon, continue stirring and bringing the mixture up from the bottom and away from the sides. Cook and stir for 15 to 20 minutes, or until the mixture is thick enough for the spoon to stand upright in the pot. Season with salt and pepper.

COOKING HINTS

- For more robust flavor, replace the water with fat-free chicken broth or vegetable broth. Add dried oregano and dried basil to the liquid. Stir grated Parmesan cheese into the finished polenta.

- Serve polenta with your favorite pasta sauce. Or try the pasta sauces from the following recipes: Pasta Puttanesca (page 220), Pasta and Seafood Marinara (page 221), and Shells with Lentil Sauce (page 233).

- When cooled, polenta becomes firm. It can then be cut into pieces for grilling or broiling. Pour the hot polenta into a baking dish and let it cool. Used this way, polenta can be served like pasta or layered in casseroles as you would lasagna noodles. For polenta pizza, spread the hot polenta in a thin circle on a baking sheet coated with no-stick spray. Let cool. Bake the polenta crust at 450°F for 5 to 8 minutes, or until the top is firm but not browned. Add your favorite toppings and bake for another 10 minutes.

Couscous with Apricots and Pine Nuts

Couscous is a tiny round pasta made from semolina flour that cooks up quick. Look for it near the rice in your grocery store. For a change of pace, replace the apricots and pine nuts with your favorite nuts and dried fruit.

1	tablespoon butter or canola oil
1½	cups couscous
3	tablespoons pine nuts
2¼	cups boiling water
6	dried apricots, diced
⅛	teaspoon ground cinnamon
1	tablespoon chopped fresh parsley
	Salt and ground black pepper

Hands-on time: 10 minutes
Unattended time: 10 minutes

Makes 4 servings
Per serving
361   CALORIES
7.2 G.   TOTAL FAT
2.4 G.   SATURATED FAT
11.3 G. PROTEIN
64.5 G. CARBOHYDRATES
11.9 G. DIETARY FIBER
8 MG.   CHOLESTEROL
38 MG.   SODIUM

In a medium saucepan, warm the butter or oil. Add the couscous and pine nuts. Cook, stirring often, over medium heat for 4 minutes, or until the nuts are lightly toasted and fragrant. Remove from the heat and add the water, apricots, and cinnamon. Stir once, cover tightly, and let stand for 10 to 15 minutes, or until the liquid is absorbed.

Gently fluff the couscous with a fork. Add the parsley and season with salt and pepper.

Cooking Hint

• For more fiber, try whole-wheat couscous. It's available in many grocery stores and health food stores.

White Beans with Roasted Peppers and Sage

This quick side dish makes a refreshing change from potatoes. It's also a nice appetizer with crackers or mini pita pockets. Leftovers keep in the refrigerator for up to 3 days.

1	tablespoon olive oil
1	shallot, sliced
2	cloves garlic, minced
¼–½	teaspoon dried sage
¾	cup sliced roasted red peppers
1	can (15½ ounces) white beans, rinsed and drained
2	teaspoons chopped fresh basil
2	teaspoons fresh lemon juice
	Salt and ground black pepper

Warm the oil in a medium no-stick skillet over medium heat. Add the shallots and garlic. Cook for 1 minute. Stir in the sage and cook for 1 minute. Add the red peppers, beans, basil, and lemon juice. Stir to combine well. Cook for 1 to 2 minutes, or until heated through. Remove from the heat. Season with salt and black pepper to taste. Serve warm or at room temperature.

COOKING HINT

- You can replace the roasted red peppers with sliced sweet red peppers sauteed in a small amount of olive oil.

HANDS-ON TIME: 10 MINUTES
UNATTENDED TIME: NONE

MAKES 4 SERVINGS

PER SERVING
170	CALORIES
3.8 G.	TOTAL FAT
0.5 G.	SATURATED FAT
8.4 G.	PROTEIN
27.2 G.	CARBOHYDRATES
0.8 G.	DIETARY FIBER
0 MG.	CHOLESTEROL
420 MG.	SODIUM

SWITCH TIP

Canned beans tend to be high in sodium. But you can reduce the sodium by up to 50 percent by draining the liquid and rinsing the beans. Pour the beans into a colander and rinse under cold water.

Easy Black Beans

Cilantro and lime juice give these speedy beans their Mexican flavor. Adjust the amount of chili peppers to suit your taste.

HANDS-ON TIME: 20 MINUTES
UNATTENDED TIME: NONE

1	tablespoon canola or olive oil
1	small onion, finely chopped
½	sweet red or green pepper, finely chopped
2	cloves garlic, minced
3	cans (15 ounces each) black beans, drained, not rinsed
1	can (4½ ounces) chopped green chili peppers
1	teaspoon ground cumin
1	teaspoon ground coriander
1	tablespoon chopped fresh cilantro
1	tablespoon lime juice or lemon juice
	Salt and ground black pepper

MAKES 6 SERVINGS

PER SERVING

210	CALORIES
4.3 G.	TOTAL FAT
0.2 G.	SATURATED FAT
17.7 G.	PROTEIN
40.2 G.	CARBOHYDRATES
13.6 G.	DIETARY FIBER
0 MG.	CHOLESTEROL
744 MG.	SODIUM

Warm the oil in a large no-stick skillet over medium heat. Add the onions, red or green peppers, and garlic. Cook for 5 minutes. Stir in the beans, chili peppers, cumin, and coriander. Cook for 10 minutes, stirring and mashing some of the beans as they cook.

Add the cilantro and lime juice or lemon juice. Season with the salt and black pepper. Continue to cook and mash the beans until the desired consistency is reached.

Cooking Hints

- For more heat, replace the canned green chili peppers with 1 seeded and finely chopped jalapeño pepper (wear plastic gloves when handling). Or use your favorite reconstituted and chopped dried chili peppers. I especially like the deep rich flavor of pasilla and chipotle chilies.

- Drain the beans in a colander because the liquid is quite thick. To retain a small amount of the canning liquid and help create a creamy consistency for this dish, do not rinse the beans after draining them.

MUSTARD BAKED BEANS

Boston baked beans usually take hours to cook, but my variation uses canned beans for a quick side dish. Try them with turkey burgers, chicken, fish, and casseroles.

HANDS-ON TIME: 10 MINUTES
UNATTENDED TIME: 35 MINUTES

1	teaspoon olive oil
1	onion, sliced
3	cans (15½ ounces each) white beans, drained and rinsed
¼	cup molasses
3	tablespoons Worcestershire sauce
2	tablespoons coarse mustard
2	tablespoons honey
1	tablespoon apple cider vinegar
2	teaspoons dry mustard
	Ground black pepper
	Red-pepper flakes

MAKES 6 SERVINGS

PER SERVING

339	CALORIES
2 G.	TOTAL FAT
0.3 G.	SATURATED FAT
16.9 G.	PROTEIN
65.6 G.	CARBOHYDRATES
0.9 G.	DIETARY FIBER
0 MG.	CHOLESTEROL
992 MG.	SODIUM

Preheat the oven to 375°F. Coat a 2-quart baking dish with no-stick spray.

Warm the oil in a large no-stick skillet over medium heat. Add the onions and cook for 5 minutes.

In a large bowl, mix the beans, molasses, Worcestershire sauce, coarse mustard, honey, vinegar, and dry mustard. Add the onions. Season with the black pepper and red-pepper flakes. Mix well. Transfer to the baking dish.

Cover and bake for 15 minutes. Uncover and stir. Cover and bake for 20 to 25 minutes, or until bubbling. Stir before serving.

COOKING HINT

• I like to use small white navy beans for this recipe. Other white beans also work. Try Great Northern or cannellini beans (white kidney beans).

SWITCH TIP

Go beyond white beans and chickpeas. Try lentils. They come in a variety of colors—including brown, red, green, and yellow—and they're one of the few legumes that cook quickly without presoaking. Lentils add protein, fiber, and minerals to your diet. Plus, they're incredibly versatile in the kitchen. Dress a lentil salad with your favorite vinaigrette, make lentil soup, or use lentils as the basis for pasta sauces.

CAJUN RED BEANS AND RICE

Here's a heart-warming main dish for bean-lovers. Go light on the hot sauce during cooking. You can always add more at the table.

HANDS-ON TIME: 35 MINUTES
UNATTENDED TIME: 50 MINUTES

MAKES 4 SERVINGS
PER SERVING
521   CALORIES
10.4 G. TOTAL FAT
0.8 G.   SATURATED FAT
24.3 G. PROTEIN
97.5 G. CARBOHYDRATES
18 G.   DIETARY FIBER
0 MG.   CHOLESTEROL
837 MG. SODIUM

2	tablespoons canola oil
2	small onions, chopped
1	sweet red or green pepper, chopped
10	cloves garlic, minced
1	stalk celery, chopped
1½	teaspoons dried oregano
½	teaspoon dried thyme
½	teaspoon ground cumin
	Hot-pepper sauce
	Salt and ground black pepper
2¼	cups fat-free chicken broth or vegetable broth
1	cup brown rice
1	can (14½ ounces) diced tomatoes (with juice)
1	tablespoon Worcestershire sauce
1	bay leaf
1	teaspoon paprika
1	teaspoon ground coriander
½	teaspoon sugar
2	cans (15 ounces each) red kidney beans, drained, not rinsed
1	teaspoon white-wine vinegar or lemon juice
	Baked tortilla chips (optional)

Warm 1 tablespoon of the oil in a medium saucepan over medium heat. Add the half of the onions, half of the red or green peppers, half of the garlic, and the celery. Cook for 10 minutes, stirring often. Add 1 teaspoon of the oregano, the thyme, and cumin. Season with hot-pepper sauce, salt, and black pepper. Pour in the broth and bring to a boil. Stir in the rice and return to a boil. Reduce the heat to medium-low. Cover and cook for 45 minutes, or until the liquid is absorbed and the rice is tender. Remove from the heat and set aside for 5 minutes. Fluff with a fork before serving.

Meanwhile, in a medium saucepan over medium heat, warm the remaining 1 tablespoon oil. Add the remaining onions, red or green peppers, and garlic. Cook for 5 minutes. Add the tomatoes (with juice), Worcestershire sauce, bay leaf, paprika, coriander, sugar, beans, and remaining ½ teaspoon oregano. Season with hot pepper sauce, salt, and black pepper. Reduce the heat to medium-low. Cook for 20 minutes, stirring frequently. Stir in the vinegar or lemon juice. Remove and discard the bay leaf before serving.

Serve over the rice. Top with the tortilla chips (if using).

MEXICAN BROWN RICE

Serve this easy rice dish with burritos, tacos, or your favorite Mexican meal.

HANDS-ON TIME: 5 MINUTES
UNATTENDED TIME: 40 MINUTES

1½	cups fat-free chicken broth or vegetable broth
¾	cup brown rice
1	teaspoon chili powder
½	teaspoon garlic powder
½	teaspoon sugar
¼	teaspoon ground cumin
	Salt and ground black pepper

MAKES 4 SERVINGS
PER SERVING
147	CALORIES
1.1 G.	TOTAL FAT
0.2 G.	SATURATED FAT
3.2 G.	PROTEIN
30.9 G.	CARBOHYDRATES
2.2 G.	DIETARY FIBER
0 MG.	CHOLESTEROL
40 MG.	SODIUM

Bring the broth to a boil in a medium saucepan over high heat. Stir in the rice, chili powder, garlic powder, sugar, and cumin. Season with the salt and pepper. Return to a boil. Reduce the heat to low. Cover and cook for 35 to 45 minutes, or until the liquid is absorbed and the rice is soft.

Remove from the heat and let stand for 5 minutes. Fluff with a fork before serving.

Four Beans and Brown Rice

Meatless meals aren't limited to pasta or cheese. This beany dish packs in flavor, protein, and fiber. And it's easy to put together. Most of the ingredients are spices.

Hands-on time: 30 minutes
Unattended time: 15 minutes

Makes 6 servings

Per serving

533	CALORIES
6.7 G.	TOTAL FAT
0.6 G.	SATURATED FAT
29.5 G.	PROTEIN
106.5 G.	CARBOHYDRATES
22.5 G.	DIETARY FIBER
0 MG.	CHOLESTEROL
952 MG.	SODIUM

3	cups fat-free chicken broth or vegetable broth
1½	cups brown rice
	Salt
1	tablespoon olive oil
1	red onion, sliced
6	cloves garlic, minced
1	tablespoon minced fresh ginger
1	carrot, chopped
1	sweet red pepper, chopped
2	jalapeño peppers, seeded and chopped (wear plastic gloves when handling)
2	teaspoons chili powder
2	teaspoons ground coriander
1	teaspoon dry mustard
½	teaspoon ground cumin
½	teaspoon dried oregano
½	teaspoon dried thyme
1	can (14½ ounces) diced tomatoes (with juice)
½	cup dry red wine or nonalcoholic red wine
3	tablespoons tomato paste
1	can (15½ ounces) red kidney beans, rinsed and drained
1	can (15½ ounces) black-eyed peas, rinsed and drained
1	can (15½ ounces) white beans, rinsed and drained
1	can (15½ ounces) black beans (with liquid)
¼	teaspoon liquid smoke
1	teaspoon grated lemon rind
1	tablespoon sherry vinegar or white-wine vinegar
	Nonfat sour cream (optional)
	Chopped fresh cilantro (optional)

Bring the broth to a boil in a medium saucepan over high heat. Add the rice and return to a boil. Season with the salt. Reduce the heat to low, cover, and cook for 45 minutes, or until the liquid is absorbed and the rice is tender.

Meanwhile, warm the oil in a large saucepan over medium heat. Add the onions, garlic, ginger, carrots, red peppers, and jalapeño peppers. Cook, stirring occasionally, for 7 minutes, or until the vegetables are tender. Stir in the chili powder, coriander, mustard, cumin, oregano, and thyme. Cook for 1 minute. Add the tomatoes (with juice), wine, tomato paste, kidney beans, black-eyed peas, white beans, black beans (with liquid), and liquid smoke. Reduce the heat to medium-low. Cover and cook, stirring occasionally, for 20 minutes. Stir in the lemon rind and vinegar.

Serve over the rice. Garnish with the sour cream (if using) and cilantro (if using).

COOKING HINT

- Liquid smoke can be found in the condiment section of most grocery stores. It makes a good substitute for the flavor of bacon and ham in soups, stews, and casseroles. Use it sparingly—a little goes a very long way.

Recipes

CHAPTER 17

"Appetite is the best sauce."

—FRENCH PROVERB

PASTA PERFECTO

Pasta is the perfect Low-Fat Living food. It's high in complex carbohydrates, low in fat, quick-cooking, and versatile. Plus, most pastas
are interchangeable. Just "keep it in the family," so to speak. If strand
pasta like linguine is called for, you can substitute another strand
pasta, like spaghetti or fettuccine. The same goes for the shaped
pastas. If you're out of ziti, try penne, rotini, or bow-ties.

To keep pasta from packing on the pounds, steer clear of high-fat
sauces—ones loaded with oil, butter, cream, or cheese. Of course, that
doesn't mean giving up all creamy sauces. I love a good cream sauce
on pasta, so I've come up with a few low-fat options. Ziti with Creamy
Walnut Sauce gets its luscious texture from low-fat ricotta cheese and
nonfat sour cream. In Fettuccine with Asparagus and Pea Sauce, the
vegetables are pureed with half-and-half to create a rich-flavored,
emerald-colored sauce that's lower in fat than one using heavy cream.

Don't forget the Parmesan. Just a touch of freshly grated Parmesan
or Romano cheese on a pasta dish can greatly improve its flavor
without blowing your fat budget. One tablespoon of grated Parmesan
cheese has only 23 calories and 1.5 grams of fat.

Most of the recipes here are done quickly on the stove top. For baked
pasta dishes like lasagna, see the recipes beginning on page 306.

219

PASTA PUTTANESCA

Most of what's needed for this traditional high-flavor Italian dish is no doubt already in your pantry.

HANDS-ON TIME: 15 MINUTES
UNATTENDED TIME: 30 MINUTES

1	tablespoon olive oil
1	can (2 ounces) anchovy fillets, rinsed and drained
6	cloves garlic, minced
1	can (28 ounces) peeled plum tomatoes (with juice)
1	cup chopped fresh parsley
2	teaspoons dried oregano
20	kalamata olives, pitted and coarsely chopped
⅓	cup drained capers
½	teaspoon grated lemon rind
	Ground black pepper
	Red-pepper flakes
1	pound fusilli or spaghetti
½	cup fat-free chicken broth or vegetable broth
	Grated Parmesan or crumbled feta cheese (optional)

MAKES 4 SERVINGS

PER SERVING
576   CALORIES
10.8 G. TOTAL FAT
1.5 G. SATURATED FAT
22.3 G. PROTEIN
99.7 G. CARBOHYDRATES
1.9 G. DIETARY FIBER
12 MG. CHOLESTEROL
964 MG. SODIUM

Warm the oil in a medium saucepan over medium heat. Add the anchovies and garlic. Mash into a paste with a wooden spoon.

Coarsely chop the tomatoes in the can. Add the tomatoes (with juice), parsley, oregano, olives, capers, and lemon rind to the saucepan. Bring to a boil. Reduce the heat to medium-low and simmer, stirring occasionally, for 30 minutes. Season with the black pepper and red-pepper flakes.

Cook the pasta in a large pot of boiling water according to the package directions. Drain and place in a large bowl. Toss with the broth. Top with the sauce and sprinkle with the Parmesan or feta (if using).

SWITCH TIP

Olives are great flavor-boosters. But they're loaded with fat. To slim them down a bit, buy the kind packed in brine or vinegar instead of oil. Look for lower-fat varieties, too. Black olives have the least fat. Greek olives are the next best, with green olives having the most fat. Chop olives finely so that the flavor distributes throughout the dish and you can use less.

PASTA AND SEAFOOD MARINARA

Use your favorite seafood for this dish. I like shrimp, scallops, clams, mussels, lobster, and crab.

HANDS-ON TIME: 15 MINUTES
UNATTENDED TIME: 30 MINUTES

1	tablespoon olive oil
1	onion, chopped
4	cloves garlic, minced
1	can (28 ounces) tomato puree
¼	cup dry red wine or nonalcoholic red wine
2	tablespoons chopped fresh parsley
2	tablespoons chopped fresh basil
½	teaspoon sugar
¼	teaspoon grated lemon rind
¼	teaspoon dried oregano
⅛	teaspoon dried sage
	Salt and ground black pepper
	Red-pepper flakes
10	ounces linguine or spaghetti
1	pound mixed seafood
	Grated Parmesan cheese (optional)

MAKES 4 SERVINGS

PER SERVING
534 CALORIES
6.3 G. TOTAL FAT
0.8 G. SATURATED FAT
33.7 G. PROTEIN
81.9 G. CARBOHYDRATES
5.3 G. DIETARY FIBER
112 MG. CHOLESTEROL
275 MG. SODIUM

Warm the oil in a medium saucepan over medium heat. Add the onions and garlic. Cook for 10 minutes. Stir in the tomato puree, wine, parsley, basil, sugar, lemon rind, oregano, and sage. Season with the salt, black pepper, and red-pepper flakes. Reduce the heat to low. Cover and cook for 25 minutes.

Cook the pasta in a large pot of boiling water according to the package directions. Drain and place in a large bowl.

Add the seafood to the sauce. Cook for 5 to 10 minutes, or until cooked through. Pour the sauce over the pasta. Sprinkle with the Parmesan (if using).

QUICK SWITCH

Spicy Pasta Marinara: For a vegetarian version, omit the seafood and add a variety of sautéed vegetables and more red-pepper flakes.

SPAGHETTI AND MEATBALLS

I lightened up a traditional favorite with ground turkey breast. If you like a more chunky sauce, add mushrooms, zucchini, or other vegetables along with the onions and garlic.

HANDS-ON TIME: 30 MINUTES
UNATTENDED TIME: 50 MINUTES

MAKES 8 SERVINGS
PER SERVING
471	CALORIES
8.8 G.	TOTAL FAT
2.2 G.	SATURATED FAT
25.3 G.	PROTEIN
71.6 G.	CARBOHYDRATES
2.8 G.	DIETARY FIBER
79 MG.	CHOLESTEROL
340 MG.	SODIUM

SAUCE

1   tablespoon olive oil
1   onion, chopped
4   cloves garlic, minced
1   green pepper, chopped
1   can (14½ ounces) diced tomatoes (with juice)
1   can (28 ounces) tomato puree
1½   tablespoons chopped fresh basil
1   tablespoon chopped fresh parsley
1½   teaspoons chopped fresh oregano
     Salt and ground black pepper

MEATBALLS

3   slices whole-grain bread, crusts removed
1   cup skim milk
2   eggs, lightly beaten
1   pound ground turkey breast
⅓   cup chopped fresh parsley
3   cloves garlic, minced
¼   cup grated Parmesan or Romano cheese
⅛   teaspoon allspice
     Salt and ground black pepper
1   tablespoon olive oil

SPAGHETTI

1   pound spaghetti
     Grated Parmesan cheese (optional)

To make the sauce: Warm the oil in a medium saucepan over medium heat. Add the onions, garlic, and green peppers. Cook for 10 to 12 minutes, or until well-browned. Stir in the diced tomatoes (with juice) and cook for 5 minutes. Add the tomato puree, basil, parsley, and oregano. Season with the salt and black pepper. Reduce the heat to low. Cover and cook for 30 minutes, stirring occasionally.

To make the meatballs: In a small bowl, combine the bread and milk.

In a medium bowl, combine the eggs, turkey, parsley, garlic, Parmesan or Romano, and allspice. Lightly squeeze some of the milk from the bread and crumble the bread into the bowl; discard the remaining milk. Season with the salt and pepper. Mix well. Form the turkey mixture into 16 balls.

Line a baking sheet with wax paper. Place the meatballs on the sheet and refrigerate for 15 minutes or up to 3 hours.

Warm the oil in a large no-stick skillet over medium heat. Add the meatballs and cook for 10 minutes; gently turn to brown on all sides. Add the sauce to the skillet. Reduce the heat to low, cover, and cook for 20 to 25 minutes, or until the meatballs are cooked through.

To make the spaghetti: Cook the pasta in a large pot of boiling water according to the package directions. Drain and place in a large bowl. Top with the sauce and meatballs. Sprinkle with the Parmesan (if using).

COOKING HINT

- Parsley comes in two varieties—Italian flat-leaf and curly leaf. Curly is often used as a garnish. The flat-leaf variety has a bit more flavor. When possible, use flat-leaf parsley for cooking.

CAPELLINI WITH SCALLOPS AND TOMATOES

Capellini is a very thin pasta that's thinner than vermicelli. It makes a perfect nest for tender sea scallops and a light tomato sauce.

HANDS-ON TIME: 15 MINUTES
UNATTENDED TIME: 20 MINUTES

1	tablespoon + 1 teaspoon olive oil
1	small onion, chopped
4	cloves garlic, minced
1	can (28 ounces) diced tomatoes (with juice)
¼	cup packed fresh basil leaves, chopped
½	teaspoon grated lemon rind
	Salt and ground black pepper
1	pound sea scallops, cut into bite-size pieces
10	ounces capellini
½	cup fat-free chicken broth or vegetable broth
¼	cup grated Parmesan or Romano cheese

MAKES 4 SERVINGS
PER SERVING
497   CALORIES
9.5 G.   TOTAL FAT
2.1 G.   SATURATED FAT
35.8 G. PROTEIN
68.2 G. CARBOHYDRATES
1.8 G.   DIETARY FIBER
53 MG.   CHOLESTEROL
725 MG. SODIUM

Warm 1 tablespoon of the oil in a medium saucepan over medium heat. Add the onions and garlic. Cook for 5 minutes, or until softened. Add the tomatoes (with juice) and cook for 15 minutes. Stir in the basil and lemon rind. Season with the salt and pepper. Reduce the heat to low.

Warm the remaining teaspoon of oil in a large no-stick skillet over medium-high heat. Add the scallops. Cook and stir for 2 to 4 minutes, or until no longer translucent. Do not overcook.

Cook the pasta in a large pot of boiling water according to the package directions. Drain and place in a large bowl. Toss with the broth. Pour the sauce over the pasta and top with the scallops. Sprinkle with the Parmesan or Romano.

COOKING HINTS

• Buy sea scallops instead of bay scallops for this dish. They tend to be higher in quality and have better flavor. To vary the dish, replace the scallops with shrimp or cubed fish.

• For added safety, all seafood should be rinsed in cool water and patted dry before cooking.

LINGUINE WITH WHITE CLAM SAUCE

Traditional versions of this dish are usually swimming in oil. I use extra clam juice to lower the fat. If you can find a flavored pasta, use it here. My favorites are parsley-garlic and lemon-garlic.

HANDS-ON TIME: 10 MINUTES
UNATTENDED TIME: 20 MINUTES

MAKES 4 SERVINGS
PER SERVING
560   CALORIES
11.1 G. TOTAL FAT
1.8 G. SATURATED FAT
42.4 G. PROTEIN
67.9 G. CARBOHYDRATES
0 G.   DIETARY FIBER
66 MG. CHOLESTEROL
552 MG. SODIUM

1	tablespoon olive oil
3	cloves garlic, minced
2	bottles (8 ounces each) clam juice
½	cup dry white wine or nonalcoholic white wine
½	teaspoon grated lemon rind
	Red-pepper flakes
2	cans (6½ ounces each) chopped clams (with juice)
1	tablespoon chopped fresh parsley
2	teaspoons arrowroot or cornstarch
1	tablespoon water
1	pound linguine
¼	cup grated Parmesan cheese
	Ground black pepper

Warm the oil in a medium saucepan over medium heat. Add the garlic. Cook and stir for 1 minute. Add the clam juice, wine, and lemon rind. Season with the red-pepper flakes. Drain the clams and add the liquid to the saucepan; set the clams aside. Bring to a boil. Reduce the heat to low and simmer for 20 minutes.

Chop the clams slightly and add to the saucepan. Add the parsley. Cook for 5 to 10 minutes.

Place the arrowroot or cornstarch in a cup. Add the water and stir to dissolve. Stir in 2 tablespoons of the sauce. Stir the mixture into the saucepan and stir until slightly thickened.

Cook the pasta in a large pot of boiling water according to the package directions. Drain and place in a large bowl. Pour the sauce over the pasta and sprinkle with the Parmesan. Season with the black pepper.

LEMON LINGUINE WITH SALMON

Here's an impressive meal that you can make in less than 30 minutes. Just add some bread and a crunchy salad with low-fat vinaigrette.

HANDS-ON TIME: 25 MINUTES
UNATTENDED TIME: NONE

1	tablespoon unsalted butter
1	tablespoon olive oil
1	clove garlic, minced
1½	cups fat-free chicken broth or vegetable broth
1	tablespoon chopped fresh basil
2	teaspoons drained capers
1	teaspoon grated lemon rind
3	tablespoons fresh lemon juice
	Salt and ground black pepper
12	ounces linguine
1	pound salmon fillet, skin removed, cut into 4 pieces
¼	cup half-and-half

MAKES 4 SERVINGS

PER SERVING
545   CALORIES
13.5 G. TOTAL FAT
4.3 G. SATURATED FAT
35.4 G. PROTEIN
68.2 G. CARBOHYDRATES
0.1 G. DIETARY FIBER
71 MG. CHOLESTEROL
260 MG. SODIUM

Preheat the broiler. Coat a broiler pan with no-stick spray.

Warm the butter and oil in a medium saucepan over medium heat. Add the garlic and cook for 2 minutes. Stir in the broth, basil, capers, lemon rind, and 2 tablespoons of the lemon juice. Season with the salt and pepper. Reduce the heat to low and cook for 5 minutes.

Cook the pasta in a large pot of boiling water according to the package directions. Drain and place in a large bowl.

Place the salmon on the prepared pan. Sprinkle with the remaining 1 tablespoon lemon juice. Broil 4" from the heat for 5 minutes per side, or until the fish flakes easily when tested with a fork.

Slowly stir the half-and-half into the saucepan. Pour half of the sauce over the pasta and toss lightly. Place the salmon over the pasta and pour the remaining sauce over top.

ASIAN NOODLES WITH CHICKEN

A little peanut butter and toasted sesame oil go a long way. Chili-garlic puree provides the spice. Look for chili-garlic puree in the international aisle of your supermarket or in Asian grocery stores.

HANDS-ON TIME: 20 MINUTES
UNATTENDED TIME: NONE

MAKES 6 SERVINGS
PER SERVING
364   CALORIES
8.6 G.   TOTAL FAT
1.5 G.   SATURATED FAT
24.7 G. PROTEIN
45.8G.   CARBOHYDRATES
1.5 G.   DIETARY FIBER
46 MG.   CHOLESTEROL
273 MG. SODIUM

10	ounces Chinese noodles or spaghetti
1	pound boneless, skinless chicken breasts, cut into thin strips
1	clove garlic, minced
1	teaspoon minced fresh ginger
	Salt and ground black pepper
¼	cup chopped peanuts
1	sweet red pepper, chopped
6	scallions, chopped
3	tablespoons dry sherry or nonalcoholic white wine
1	tablespoon peanut butter
1	tablespoon toasted sesame oil
1	cup fat-free chicken broth or vegetable broth
3	tablespoons rice vinegar
2	tablespoons reduced-sodium soy sauce
2	teaspoons honey
1	teaspoon chili-garlic puree
	Red-pepper flakes

Cook the noodles in a large pot of boiling water according to the package directions. Drain and place in a large bowl.

Coat a large no-stick skillet with no-stick spray. Place over medium-high heat. Add the chicken, garlic, and ginger. Season with the salt and black pepper. Cook, stirring, for 5 minutes, or until the chicken is no longer pink when tested with a sharp knife. Add to the noodles. Stir in the peanuts, red peppers, and scallions. Toss to mix.

Return the skillet to the heat and add the sherry or wine. Cook, stirring, for 1 minute to scrape up the browned bits on the bottom of the pan. Pour the liquid into a medium bowl. Add the peanut butter and oil. Mix until smooth. Stir in the broth, vinegar, soy sauce, honey, and chili-garlic puree. Season with the red-pepper flakes. Pour over the noodles and toss to coat.

FETTUCCINE WITH ASPARAGUS AND PEA SAUCE

Serve this dish in the spring, when fresh asparagus is at its best. Pureed with frozen peas and half-and-half, asparagus makes an elegant green sauce for pasta.

HANDS-ON TIME: 10 MINUTES
UNATTENDED TIME: 15 MINUTES

1	pound asparagus, trimmed
2	shallots, chopped
3	cloves garlic, minced
¾	cup half-and-half
¼	cup chopped fresh parsley and/or basil
¼	teaspoon grated lemon rind
1½	cups frozen peas, thawed
	Salt and ground black pepper
	Red-pepper flakes
12	ounces fettuccine
¼	cup sliced roasted red peppers
1	tablespoon chopped fresh chives

MAKES 4 SERVINGS

PER SERVING

395	CALORIES
8.8 G.	TOTAL FAT
3.4 G.	SATURATED FAT
18.8 G.	PROTEIN
65.1 G.	CARBOHYDRATES
2.6 G.	DIETARY FIBER
17 MG.	CHOLESTEROL
227 MG.	SODIUM

Place the asparagus in a steamer basket. Steam over boiling water in a large covered saucepan for 10 minutes, or until the asparagus is tender. Cut off the tips. Set the tips and stalks aside.

Coat a small no-stick skillet with no-stick spray and place over medium heat. Add the shallots and garlic. Cook for 2 to 3 minutes, or until softened. Transfer to a food processor or blender.

Add the half-and-half, parsley and/or basil, lemon rind, 1 cup of the peas, and the reserved asparagus stalks. Process until smooth. Season with the salt, black pepper, and red-pepper flakes.

Cook the pasta in a large pot of boiling water according to the package directions. Drain and place in a large bowl. Add the sauce and toss to mix. Top with the remaining ½ cup peas, reserved asparagus tips, roasted peppers, and chives.

CREAMY FETTUCCINE AND SEAFOOD

Dazzle your family or guests with this luxurious pasta and seafood combo. The French refer to it as fruits of the sea. I call it delicious! It's rich and creamy without a lot of fat. Take your choice of mixed seafood, such as scallops, peeled shrimp, salmon, chopped clams, and shelled mussels.

HANDS-ON TIME: 20 MINUTES
UNATTENDED TIME: NONE

MAKES 6 SERVINGS
PER SERVING
415   CALORIES
8.4 G.   TOTAL FAT
2.1 G.   SATURATED FAT
37.4 G.   PROTEIN
49.9 G.   CARBOHYDRATES
1.1 G.   DIETARY FIBER
60 MG.   CHOLESTEROL
694 MG.   SODIUM

1	tablespoon olive oil or unsalted butter
2	shallots, chopped
3	cloves garlic, minced
8	ounces mushrooms, sliced
2	cups evaporated skim milk
1	can (14½ ounces) whole peeled tomatoes, drained and chopped
2	tablespoons chopped fresh basil and/or parsley
1	teaspoon grated lemon rind
12	ounces fettuccine pasta
1	pound mixed seafood
1	can (4½ ounces) lump crabmeat, drained
2	tablespoons arrowroot or cornstarch
2	tablespoons water
½	cup grated Parmesan cheese
	Salt and ground black pepper

Warm the oil or butter in a medium saucepan over medium heat. Add the shallots and garlic. Cook for 2 minutes. Add the mushrooms and cook for 5 minutes, or until softened. Stir in the milk, tomatoes, basil or parsley, and lemon rind. Cook for 5 minutes.

Cook the pasta in a large pot of boiling water according to the package directions. Drain and place in a large bowl.

Add the seafood and crab to the sauce. Cook for 5 minutes, or until the seafood is cooked through.

Place the arrowroot or cornstarch in a cup. Add the water and stir to dissolve. Add a spoonful of the sauce to the cup. Stir into the saucepan and stir until slightly thickened. Stir in the Parmesan. Season with the salt and pepper.

Pour the sauce over the pasta. Toss to combine.

BOW-TIES WITH SALMON AND ROQUEFORT

Here's where a few higher-fat ingredients come in handy. Small amounts of pine nuts and Roquefort cheese make a big impact on taste without upsetting a low-fat lifestyle.

HANDS-ON TIME: 25 MINUTES
UNATTENDED TIME: NONE

1	tablespoon olive oil
4	cloves garlic, minced
¼	teaspoon dried sage
1	cup fat-free chicken broth or vegetable broth
¼	cup dry white wine or nonalcoholic white wine
	Ground black pepper
1	pound bow-tie pasta
1	pound salmon fillet
	Juice of ½ lemon
1½	ounces Roquefort or blue cheese, crumbled
3	tablespoons toasted pine nuts

MAKES 6 SERVINGS
PER SERVING
462 CALORIES
10.9 G. TOTAL FAT
2.7 G. SATURATED FAT
28.1 G. PROTEIN
60.7 G. CARBOHYDRATES
0.1 G. DIETARY FIBER
45 MG. CHOLESTEROL
235 MG. SODIUM

Preheat the broiler. Coat a broiler pan with no-stick spray.

Coat a small saucepan with no-stick spray. Place over medium heat. Add the oil, garlic, and sage. Cook for 30 seconds. Add the broth and wine. Season with the pepper. Reduce the heat to low and simmer for 5 minutes.

Cook the pasta in a large pot of boiling water according to the package directions.

Place the salmon on the prepared pan and sprinkle with the lemon juice. Broil 4" from the heat for 10 minutes per 1" thickness of fish, or until the fish flakes easily when tested with a fork.

Drain the pasta and place in a large bowl. Toss with the broth mixture. Flake the salmon into pieces and discard the skin. Place the salmon on top of the pasta. Add the Roquefort or blue cheese and pine nuts. Toss gently.

PENNE WITH SAUSAGE AND BROCCOLI

Hungry husbands and kids love this dish. Make it with hot, sweet, or flavored sausage. For the least fat, use turkey sausage or chicken sausage made from breast meat.

HANDS-ON TIME: 25 MINUTES
UNATTENDED TIME: NONE

1	**pound penne pasta**
3	**cups broccoli florets**
4	**cloves garlic, minced**
12	**ounces low-fat turkey sausage or chicken sausage, casings removed**
½	**cup fat-free chicken broth or vegetable broth**
½	**cup grated Parmesan cheese**
1	**tablespoon olive oil**
2	**tablespoons balsamic vinegar**
	Ground black pepper

MAKES 6 SERVINGS

PER SERVING

456	CALORIES
10.3 G.	TOTAL FAT
3.2 G.	SATURATED FAT
25.1 G.	PROTEIN
65 G.	CARBOHYDRATES
1.5 G.	DIETARY FIBER
42 MG.	CHOLESTEROL
675 MG.	SODIUM

Cook the pasta in a large pot of boiling water for 8 minutes. Add the broccoli and cook for 3 minutes, or until the pasta and broccoli are just tender. Drain and place in a large bowl.

Coat a large no-stick skillet with no-stick spray and place over medium heat. Add the garlic and cook for 1 minute. Crumble the sausage into the skillet. Cook, breaking up the pieces with a wooden spoon, for 5 minutes, or until browned. Pour over the pasta.

Add the broth, Parmesan, oil, and vinegar to the pasta. Toss to mix. Season with the pepper.

COOKING HINTS

- Check your local supermarket or butcher for flavored sausage. Some of my favorites are chicken and apple, Sante Fe–style, and sun-dried tomato and basil.

- Sprinkle this dish with red-pepper flakes for more kick.

QUICK SWITCH

Penne with Tofu Sausage and Broccoli: For a vegetarian rendition of this dish, replace the turkey sausage with tofu sausage. Tofu sausage is available in the frozen section of most supermarkets.

ZITI WITH CREAMY WALNUT SAUCE

This no-cook sauce is similar to pesto. Low-fat ricotta cheese, sour cream, and milk make it sinfully smooth and delicious—minus the guilt.

HANDS-ON TIME: 15 MINUTES
UNATTENDED TIME: NONE

1	pound ziti pasta
½	cup low-fat ricotta cheese
½	cup skim milk
½	cup toasted walnuts
¼	cup nonfat sour cream
1	small clove garlic
2	tablespoons fresh basil leaves
2	tablespoons fresh parsley leaves
¼	teaspoon grated lemon rind
	Salt and ground black pepper
¼	cup fat-free chicken broth or vegetable broth
6	tablespoons grated Parmesan cheese

MAKES 6 SERVINGS
PER SERVING
418   CALORIES
9.9 G.   TOTAL FAT
1.8 G.   SATURATED FAT
18.6 G. PROTEIN
63.6 G. CARBOHYDRATES
0.4 G.   DIETARY FIBER
5 MG.   CHOLESTEROL
237 MG. SODIUM

Cook the pasta in a large pot of boiling water according to the package directions.

In a food processor, combine the ricotta, milk, walnuts, sour cream, garlic, basil, parsley, and lemon rind. Process until smooth. Season with the salt and pepper.

Drain the pasta and place in a large bowl. Add the broth and toss to coat. Pour the sauce over the pasta and mix well. Sprinkle with the Parmesan.

SWITCH TIP

Don't want to give up the rich flavor of ricotta? Try low-fat ricotta. The quality varies from brand to brand, so shop around for one that you like. Avoid the nonfat varieties, though. They don't meet the flavor standards of most folks. Look for a ricotta with about 2 grams of fat per ¼ cup.

SHELLS WITH LENTIL SAUCE

Most folks are surprised by this pasta dish. It's light yet very satisfying. The lentils cook quickly and make a full-bodied sauce. Plus, they have only a trace of fat and are high in calcium, potassium, zinc, and iron.

2	tablespoons olive oil
1	onion, chopped
4	cloves garlic, minced
2¼	cups fat-free chicken broth or vegetable broth
2	cups dry red wine or nonalcoholic red wine
1	cup drained canned peeled tomatoes, chopped
1	carrot, shredded
¾	cup lentils
1½	tablespoons tomato paste
1	teaspoon dried oregano
1	tablespoon chopped fresh basil
1	teaspoon sugar
1	teaspoon lemon juice
	Salt and ground black pepper
12	ounces small pasta shells
¼	cup grated Parmesan cheese

Warm the oil in a medium saucepan over medium heat. Add the onions and garlic. Cook for 5 minutes. Stir in the broth, wine, tomatoes, carrots, lentils, tomato paste, and oregano. Bring to a boil. Reduce the heat to medium-low. Cover and cook, stirring occasionally, for 50 to 60 minutes, or until the lentils are very soft. Stir in the basil, sugar, and lemon juice. Season with the salt and pepper.

Cook the pasta in a large pot of boiling water according to the package directions. Drain and place in a large bowl. Pour the sauce over the top. Toss to mix. Serve sprinkled with the Parmesan.

HANDS-ON TIME: 10 MINUTES
UNATTENDED TIME: 50 MINUTES

MAKES 6 SERVINGS
PER SERVING
451 CALORIES
7.2 G. TOTAL FAT
1.6 G. SATURATED FAT
16.3 G. PROTEIN
68.1 G. CARBOHYDRATES
1.2 G. DIETARY FIBER
3 MG. CHOLESTEROL
217 MG. SODIUM

SWITCH TIP

Eat more lentils and less meat. While you're at it, include more leafy greens and orange juice in your diet. According to a report in the *Journal of the American Medical Association*, up to 50,000 deaths from heart disease could be prevented annually if Americans consumed more folate, which is abundant in lentils, orange juice, spinach, and other leafy greens.

TORTELLINI PRIMAVERA WITH GARLIC SAUCE

Don't shy away from the amount of garlic called for in this dish. The garlic flavor becomes quite mild after roasting. It blends well with evaporated skim milk to create a rich, buttery-tasting sauce.

HANDS-ON TIME: 40 MINUTES
UNATTENDED TIME: NONE

MAKES 6 SERVINGS
PER SERVING:
210   CALORIES
4.7 G.   TOTAL FAT
1.3 G.   SATURATED FAT
11.4 G. PROTEIN
32.6 G. CARBOHYDRATES
3.7 G.   DIETARY FIBER
6 MG.   CHOLESTEROL
229 MG. SODIUM

2	whole bulbs garlic, unpeeled
3	tablespoons water
1	red onion, chopped
2	cloves garlic, minced
1	sweet red pepper, sliced
1	zucchini, cut lengthwise and sliced
4	ounces mushrooms, sliced
1	cup cauliflower florets
2	cups broccoli florets
18	ounces low-fat cheese tortellini
1	tablespoon olive oil
1	can (12 ounces) evaporated skim milk
½	teaspoon dry mustard
1	tablespoon dry sherry or nonalcoholic white wine
	Salt and ground black pepper
1	tablespoon arrowroot or cornstarch

Preheat the oven to 500°F. Coat 2 custard cups with no-stick spray. Slice ½" off the top of each garlic bulb. Coat with no-stick spray and set in the prepared cups. Add 1 tablespoon of the water to each cup. Bake for 25 to 30 minutes, or until the garlic is soft. Remove from the oven and set aside to cool.

Coat a large no-stick skillet with no-stick spray. Place over medium heat until hot. Add the onions, minced garlic, and red peppers. Cook for 5 minutes. Stir in the zucchini and mushrooms. Cook for 5 minutes. Transfer to a large bowl.

Cook the cauliflower in a large pot of boiling water for 3 minutes. Add the broccoli and tortellini. Boil for 2 minutes, or until the tortellini is just cooked through. Drain and add to the bowl. Toss to mix.

Peel the roasted garlic and place in a blender. Add the oil and ½ cup of the milk. Process until smooth. Place the skillet over medium heat. Add the garlic mixture. Stir in the mustard, sherry or wine, and the remaining 1 cup milk. Season with the salt and black pepper. Heat until bubbling.

Place the arrowroot or cornstarch in a cup. Add the remaining 1 tablespoon water and stir to dissolve. Mix a little of the hot sauce into the cup. Stir into the skillet. Heat until slightly thickened. Pour over the tortellini and vegetables. Toss well.

COOKING HINT

- Look for low-fat cheese tortellini in the refrigerated or frozen section of your grocery store. The brand I use has only 3 grams of fat per cup. If you can't find it, regular cheese tortellini can be substituted.

Recipes

18

"The genius of love and the genius of hunger are the two moving forces behind all living things."
—IVAN TURGENEV, RUSSIAN WRITER

LOW-FAT CATCH OF THE DAY

If cooking fish and other seafood seems tricky to you, try the ultra-simple recipes in this chapter. Most of these dishes are ready in a flash and don't require fussy cooking methods. For special occasions, I've included more elegant recipes, too. The Salmon and Spinach in Phyllo with Caper Sauce makes a wonderful centerpiece for a romantic dinner.

Here is the number one ground rule for cooking up delicious fish: Let freshness be your guide. Don't be too picky about getting a partic-ular type on a particular day. Many varieties of fish can be substituted for one another. For instance, if salmon isn't fresh at the market, try another firm-fleshed fish like swordfish or tuna. Here's the second ground rule: Flavor it well. A good marinade or sauce will make your seafood sing on the plate. The real flavor secret to my no-fuss grilled red snapper is the peach salsa that goes along with it.

Even if you don't live on the coast or in the land of lakes, you can still enjoy a variety of fish, both fresh and frozen. Most types cook up quickly, and they're a lean source of protein. So dive right in and ex-periment with your favorite varieties. If you like fish and pasta dishes, turn to the recipes in chapter 17.

GRILLED RED SNAPPER WITH PEACH SALSA

If only every summer meal could be this easy. When peaches and sweet Vidalia onions are in season, invite company over for dinner to savor this unique fruity salsa. It's the perfect complement to grilled red snapper.

HANDS-ON TIME: 15 MINUTES
UNATTENDED TIME: NONE

MAKES 4 SERVINGS

PER SERVING
246   CALORIES
2.6 G. TOTAL FAT
0.5 G. SATURATED FAT
36.8 G. PROTEIN
19.1 G. CARBOHYDRATES
3.1 G. DIETARY FIBER
62 MG. CHOLESTEROL
76 MG. SODIUM

5	peaches, peeled, pitted, and chopped
½	Vidalia onion, chopped
1	sweet red pepper, chopped
¼	teaspoon ground cinnamon
⅛	teaspoon ground ginger
⅛	teaspoon ground red pepper
	Salt
1½	pounds skinless red snapper fillets
2	tablespoons lemon juice
	Ground black pepper

In a medium bowl, combine the peaches, onions, red peppers, cinnamon, ginger, and ground red pepper. Season with the salt.

Preheat the grill. Coat the grill rack with no-stick spray.

Sprinkle the fillets with the lemon juice. Season with the black pepper. Grill 4" from the heat for 5 to 6 minutes, or until the fish flakes easily when tested with a fork. Serve with the salsa.

COOKING HINTS

- Try salmon, halibut, or sole in place of the snapper. For the salsa, peaches can be replaced with apricots or other fruits.

- You can cook the fish under the broiler instead of on the grill. Broil 4" from the heat for 2 to 3 minutes per side, or until the fish flakes easily when tested with a fork.

- Here's a good rule of thumb for cooking fish to just the right doneness: Cook the fish for 10 minutes per 1" thickness of fish, or just until the fish begins to flake easily when tested with a fork (the fish will continue to cook slightly when removed from the heat). Turn the fish over halfway through the total cooking time.

SWORDFISH STUFFED WITH BASIL PESTO

Here's a quick way to flavor fish without marinating. The pesto is ready in a snap. The fish broils in minutes.

HANDS-ON TIME: 10 MINUTES
UNATTENDED TIME: 10 MINUTES

½   **cup packed fresh basil**
1   **clove garlic**
1   **tablespoon pine nuts**
1   **tablespoon grated Parmesan cheese**
1   **tablespoon chopped fresh parsley**
1   **tablespoon water**
2   **teaspoons olive oil**
    Salt and ground black pepper
6   **swordfish steaks (about 5½ ounces each)**

MAKES 6 SERVINGS
PER SERVING
212   CALORIES
8.7 G.   TOTAL FAT
2.2 G.   SATURATED FAT
30.8 G. PROTEIN
0.6 G.   CARBOHYDRATES
0 G.   DIETARY FIBER
60 MG.   CHOLESTEROL
156 MG. SODIUM

In a blender or food processor, combine the basil, garlic, pine nuts, Parmesan, parsley, water, and oil. Process until smooth. Season with the salt and pepper.

Preheat the broiler. Coat a broiler pan with no-stick spray.

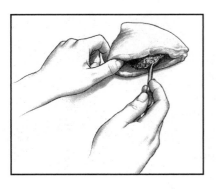

To make a pocket for the stuffing, slice the fish through its side, cutting nearly to the skin. Be careful not to cut the fish in half. Stuff the fish with the pesto, reserving a few tablespoons of pesto. Spread the reserved pesto on the top and bottom of the fish.

Place the fish on the prepared pan and broil 4" from the heat for 10 minutes per 1" thickness of fish, or until the fish flakes easily when tested with a fork; turn the fish over halfway through the cooking time.

COOKING HINT

• To intensify the flavor, cover and refrigerate the stuffed fish for up to 8 hours.

BROILED FISH WITH ITALIAN VEGETABLES

You can use any type of fish for this recipe. The vegetable topping has assertive flavors, so I like to use bold-flavored fish such as red snapper, mahi mahi, tilapia, or tuna. This is a good recipe to use when experimenting with types of fish that may be unfamiliar to you.

HANDS-ON TIME: 25 MINUTES
UNATTENDED TIME: NONE

MAKES 4 SERVINGS
PER SERVING
243   CALORIES
7.8 G.   TOTAL FAT
1.2 G.   SATURATED FAT
36.4 G. PROTEIN
7 G.   CARBOHYDRATES
1.8 G.   DIETARY FIBER
62 MG.   CHOLESTEROL
372 MG. SODIUM

1	tablespoon olive oil
1	red onion, finely chopped
4	cloves garlic, finely chopped
1	medium zucchini, finely chopped
½	cup finely chopped roasted red peppers
12	black or kalamata olives, pitted and finely chopped
3	tablespoons drained capers, finely chopped
1	tablespoon finely chopped fresh basil
1	teaspoon finely chopped fresh parsley
	Salt and ground black pepper
1½	pounds fish fillets
	Lemon juice

Coat a large no-stick skillet with no-stick spray. Add the oil and warm over medium heat. Add the onions and garlic. Cook for 2 minutes. Stir in the zucchini and cook for 5 minutes. Add the red peppers, olives, capers, basil, and parsley. Reduce the heat to medium-low. Cook, stirring frequently, for 5 minutes, or until the zucchini is soft and the mixture is well-blended. Season with the salt and black pepper.

Preheat the broiler. Coat a broiler pan with no-stick spray. Place the fish on the pan and sprinkle with the lemon juice. Broil 4" from the heat for 10 minutes per 1" thickness of fish, or until the fish flakes easily when tested with a fork (if using firm-fleshed fish, turn the fish over halfway through the cooking time).

Serve with the vegetable mixture spooned over the top.

COOKING HINT

• The vegetable mixture from this recipe makes a great spread for crackers, toasts, and bruschetta.

TERIYAKI TUNA STEAKS

If you have fussy fish-eaters to please, try this zesty-sweet raspberry marinade. It's perfect for tuna steaks. Or use it on other firm fish or even poultry.

HANDS-ON TIME: 15 MINUTES
UNATTENDED TIME: 2 HOURS

3 tablespoons raspberry vinegar
1 tablespoon reduced-sodium soy sauce
1 tablespoon honey
1 tablespoon water
1 clove garlic, minced
½ teaspoon minced fresh ginger
½ teaspoon toasted sesame oil
½ teaspoon unbleached flour
6 tuna steaks (about 5 ½ ounces each)

MAKES 6 SERVINGS
PER SERVING
169   CALORIES
1.6 G. TOTAL FAT
0.4 G. SATURATED FAT
34.2 G. PROTEIN
2.3 G. CARBOHYDRATES
0 G.   DIETARY FIBER
66 MG. CHOLESTEROL
108 MG. SODIUM

In a cup, mix the vinegar, soy sauce, honey, water, garlic, ginger, oil, and flour.

Place the tuna in a single layer in a large ceramic or glass baking dish. Pour the marinade over the fish and turn to coat evenly. Cover and refrigerate for 2 hours, turning the fish at least once.

Preheat the broiler or grill. Coat the broiler pan or grill rack with no-stick spray. Remove the fish from the marinade and cook 4" from the heat for about 10 minutes per 1" thickness of fish, or until the fish flakes easily when tested with a fork; turn the fish over halfway through the cooking time. Discard any remaining marinade.

MARINATED TUNA WITH CHERRY SAUCE

Bold-flavored cherry sauce is the crowning touch for these thick tuna steaks. I like the dish served over a bed of Garlic Mashed Potatoes (page 347). If tuna isn't fresh at the market, swordfish or even chicken makes a good substitute.

HANDS-ON TIME: 20 MINUTES
UNATTENDED TIME: 30 MINUTES

MAKES 6 SERVINGS
PER SERVING
217   CALORIES
3.2 G.   TOTAL FAT
1.5 G.   SATURATED FAT
27.3 G.   PROTEIN
12.3 G.   CARBOHYDRATES
0.1 G.   DIETARY FIBER
55 MG.   CHOLESTEROL
127 MG.   SODIUM

MARINADE

6	tuna steaks (4 ounces each)
½	cup dry red wine or nonalcoholic red wine
½	cup balsamic vinegar

SAUCE

1	tablespoon unsalted butter or canola oil
1	shallot, chopped
1	cup fat-free chicken broth or vegetable broth
½	cup dry red wine or nonalcoholic red wine
½	cup dried cherries
1	tablespoon chopped fresh parsley
½	teaspoon sugar
	Salt and ground black pepper

To make the marinade: Place the tuna in an 8" × 8" baking dish. Pour the wine and vinegar over the tuna. Cover and refrigerate for 30 minutes.

To make the sauce: Warm the butter or oil in a small saucepan over medium heat. Add the shallots and cook for 1 minute. Stir in the broth, wine, cherries, parsley, and sugar. Drain the marinade from the fish and add to the sauce.

Bring the sauce to a boil. Reduce the heat to medium-low. Cook for 20 minutes, or until the sauce is reduced by about half. Season with salt and pepper.

Meanwhile, preheat the broiler. Coat a broiler pan with no-stick spray. Place the tuna on the pan and broil 4" from the heat for about 10 minutes per 1" thickness of fish, or until slightly pink in the center when tested with a sharp knife (red is undercooked); turn the fish over halfway through the cooking time. Serve with the sauce.

GRILLED HALIBUT WITH AVOCADO SAUCE

Avocados are quite high in fat—about 30 grams each. But most of it is heart-healthy monounsaturated fat. This recipe uses a single avocado for 6 servings, so you can still enjoy the lush, creamy flavor without getting too much fat.

HANDS-ON TIME: 20 MINUTES
UNATTENDED TIME: NONE

MAKES 6 SERVINGS
PER SERVING
250 CALORIES
9 G.   TOTAL FAT
1.3 G.   SATURATED FAT
36.9 G. PROTEIN
5.1 G.   CARBOHYDRATES
1.4 G.   DIETARY FIBER
55 MG. CHOLESTEROL
104 MG. SODIUM

SAUCE

1	avocado
¼	cup water
¼	cup nonfat sour cream
4	teaspoons lime juice
3	tablespoons finely chopped scallions
¼	teaspoon ground cumin
	Hot-pepper sauce or ground red pepper
	Salt and ground black pepper

FISH

6	halibut fillets (6 ounces each)
3	tablespoons lime juice
1	tomato, finely chopped

Preheat the grill or broiler. Coat a grill rack or broiler pan with no-stick spray.

To make the sauce: In a food processor or blender, combine the avocado, water, sour cream, lime juice, scallions, and cumin. Process until smooth. Season with the hot-pepper sauce or red pepper, salt, and black pepper.

To make the fish: Sprinkle both sides of the halibut with the lime juice. Place on the grill rack or broiler pan. Cook 4" from the heat for 4 to 5 minutes per side, or until the fish flakes easily when tested with a fork. Serve with the sauce and tomatoes.

COOKING HINT

- Avocados have a green, buttery flesh that turns brown when exposed to air. To prevent browning, sprinkle the avocado with lemon juice or lime juice. When using only half an avocado, leave the pit in the unused half, cover with plastic wrap, and refrigerate. If any brown spots appear, simply scrape them away.

SALMON FILLETS WITH FRESH TOMATOES

Preparing this meal is as easy as wrapping up a sandwich.

HANDS-ON TIME: 15 MINUTES
UNATTENDED TIME: 10 MINUTES

1	clove garlic, minced
2	tomatoes, finely chopped
2	tablespoons finely chopped red onions
1	teaspoon olive oil
½	teaspoon grated lemon rind
1	tablespoon chopped fresh dill
1	teaspoon chopped fresh parsley
1	tablespoon drained capers
	Salt and ground black pepper
4	salmon fillets (6 ounces each), skin removed

MAKES 4 SERVINGS

PER SERVING
219	CALORIES
7 G.	TOTAL FAT
1.1 G.	SATURATED FAT
33.6 G.	PROTEIN
3.6 G.	CARBOHYDRATES
0.9 G.	DIETARY FIBER
86 MG.	CHOLESTEROL
195 MG.	SODIUM

Preheat the oven to 450°F. Cut 4 square pieces of parchment paper or foil and coat each with no-stick spray.

In a medium bowl, combine the garlic, tomatoes, onions, oil, lemon rind, dill, parsley, and capers. Season with the salt and pepper. Mix well.

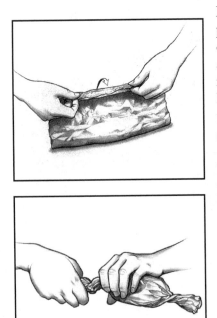

Place each fillet on the prepared parchment paper or foil. Top with equal amounts of the tomato mixture. For each packet, bring 2 opposite edges of the parchment or foil together on top of the fish and fold over several times. Twist the short ends in opposite directions to make a tight seal.

Place the packages on a baking sheet. Bake for 10 minutes per 1" thickness of fish, or until the fish flakes easily when tested with a fork.

SALMON CAKES WITH MUSTARD SAUCE

Serve these savory salmon cakes on buns or as a main dish.

HANDS-ON TIME: 20 MINUTES
UNATTENDED TIME: 10 MINUTES

CAKES

1	pound skinless salmon fillet
4	ounces smoked salmon, chopped
1	potato, finely shredded
5	scallions, finely chopped
½	sweet red or green pepper, finely chopped
¾	cup fat-free egg substitute
⅓	cup seasoned nonfat dry bread crumbs
3	tablespoons lemon juice
1	tablespoon chopped fresh parsley
1	tablespoon chopped fresh dill
½	teaspoon grated lemon rind
	Hot-pepper sauce

SAUCE

½	cup nonfat sour cream
½	cup nonfat or low-fat buttermilk
¼	cup low-fat mayonnaise
¼	cup coarse mustard
2	tablespoons lemon juice
¼	teaspoon dry mustard
	Salt and ground black pepper

MAKES 8 SERVINGS
PER SERVING

153	CALORIES
3.8 G.	TOTAL FAT
0.6 G.	SATURATED FAT
16.8 G.	PROTEIN
13 G.	CARBOHYDRATES
0.7 G.	DIETARY FIBER
31 MG.	CHOLESTEROL
411 MG.	SODIUM

SWITCH TIP

Packaged bread crumbs often contain added fats like cheese and oil. To eliminate these extra fat grams, make bread crumbs at home. They're super-easy, freeze well, and put day-old bread to good use. Cut any variety of bread into cubes, spread evenly on a baking sheet, and bake at 350°F for 10 minutes, or until dried. Let the bread cubes cool, then transfer them to a food processor or blender. Process into crumbs. For seasoned bread crumbs, mix dried herbs (such as thyme, basil, and oregano), ground pepper, and salt into the crumbs. Refrigerate or freeze the bread crumbs in an airtight container.

To make the cakes: Preheat the broiler. Coat the broiler pan with no-stick spray. Place the fillet on the pan. Broil 4" from the heat for 10 minutes per 1" thickness of fish, or until cooked through. Break the fillet into small pieces and place in a large bowl. Add the smoked salmon, potatoes, scallions, red or green peppers, egg substitute, bread crumbs, lemon juice, parsley, dill, and lemon rind. Season with the hot-pepper sauce. Mix well. Form into 8 patties.

Again coat the broiler pan with no-stick spray. Place the patties on the pan. Broil for 5 minutes per side, or until browned and heated through.

To make the sauce: In a blender or food processor, combine the sour cream, buttermilk, mayonnaise, coarse mustard, lemon juice, and dry mustard. Puree until smooth. Season with the salt and pepper. Serve with the salmon cakes.

SALMON AND SPINACH IN PHYLLO WITH CAPER SAUCE

This elegant French dish is tailor-made for special occasions. Salmon fillets are topped with sautéed spinach and baked inside layers of crispy phyllo dough. A smooth mushroom-flavored sauce is the crowning touch. If you have fish stock, use it in place of the broth.

HANDS-ON TIME: 30 MINUTES
UNATTENDED TIME: 20 MINUTES

MAKES 4 SERVINGS
PER SERVING
390 CALORIES
11.5 G. TOTAL FAT
3.7 G. SATURATED FAT
31.5 G. PROTEIN
39.2 G. CARBOHYDRATES
2.2 G. DIETARY FIBER
68 MG. CHOLESTEROL
652 MG. SODIUM

SAUCE

- 1 tablespoon unsalted butter or margarine
- 3 tablespoons unbleached flour
- 2 cups fat-free chicken broth or vegetable broth
- ¼ cup chopped mushrooms
- 1 tablespoon drained small capers
  Salt and ground black pepper

FISH

- 1 teaspoon unsalted butter or olive oil
- 5 cloves garlic, minced
- 10 ounces fresh spinach, torn
  Salt and ground black pepper
- 1 tablespoon lemon juice
- 1 pound salmon fillet, skin removed, cut into 4 pieces
- 8 ounces phyllo dough (see hint)

To make the sauce: Melt the butter or margarine in a small saucepan over medium heat. Add the flour and mix until incorporated. Slowly stir in the broth. Add the mushrooms and reduce the heat to low. Simmer for 30 minutes. Strain the sauce and discard the mushrooms. Return the sauce to the pan and add the capers. Season with the salt and pepper. Keep warm on very low heat until ready to use.

To make the fish: While the sauce is simmering, preheat the oven to 350°F. Coat a baking sheet with no-stick spray.

Coat a large no-stick skillet with no-stick spray and set over medium heat. Add the butter or oil and garlic. Cook for 1 minute. Add the spinach and cook, stirring often, for 5 minutes, or until just softened. Season with the salt and pepper.

Drizzle the lemon juice over the salmon.

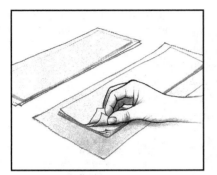

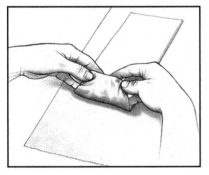

Separate the phyllo dough into 4 equal-size portions, each containing about 8 long rectangular sheets. Cover the dough not in use with plastic wrap to prevent it from drying out.

Working with 1 portion of dough at a time, coat each sheet with no-stick spray, then layer the sheets, one on top of the other. Spread one-eighth of the spinach mixture onto a short end of the dough. Place the fish on the spinach. Top with another one-eighth of the spinach.

Starting from the end with the spinach and fish, carefully roll the dough so that the spinach and fish are wrapped inside. Roll up halfway, then fold in the sides. Continue rolling to make a tight packet. Place the packet, seam side down, on the prepared baking sheet and coat with no-stick spray. Repeat with the remaining fish, spinach mixture, and phyllo.

Bake for 20 minutes, or until the phyllo is crisp. Serve with the sauce.

COOKING HINT

- To get 8 ounces of phyllo, cut a 1-pound package of phyllo dough in half crosswise (resulting in long rectangular sheets of dough). Use as directed. Freeze the remainder.

SWITCH TIP

Phyllo dough is a wonderful low-fat alternative to butter-laden pastry dough. The paper-thin sheets of dough crisp up nicely in the oven and make a great wrapping for savory or sweet fillings. Traditionally, the sheets are brushed with melted butter and layered one on top of the other. To reduce the fat and fuss, I use no-stick spray. For savory dishes, use olive oil spray; for desserts, try butter-flavored spray. Look for 1-pound packages of phyllo dough in the freezer section of your grocery store. I often cut the roll of dough in half crosswise to get 8 ounces of dough in a more manageable size. The remaining 8 ounces goes back in the freezer until I'm ready to use it. When working with phyllo dough, cover the unused portion of dough with plastic wrap to prevent the sheets from drying out as you work.

PAN-SEARED CRAB CAKES

Dense or light, flat or rounded, crab cakes have one thing in common: They're usually fried. Here's my take on the traditional seaside favorite. I use lots of crabmeat (use the best that you can find) and a small amount of whole-grain bread to hold them together, then I lightly pan-sear them. Try these with Zippy Tartar Sauce (page 368).

HANDS-ON TIME: 30 MINUTES
UNATTENDED TIME: NONE

MAKES 4 SERVINGS
PER SERVING
169   CALORIES
5.4 G.   TOTAL FAT
1.9 G.   SATURATED FAT
21.6 G.   PROTEIN
7.3 G.   CARBOHYDRATES
0.6 G.   DIETARY FIBER
154 MG.   CHOLESTEROL
818 MG.   SODIUM

1	pound crabmeat
½	cup fresh whole-grain bread crumbs
2	scallions, finely chopped
1	tablespoon chopped fresh parsley
1	egg, lightly beaten
5	tablespoons nonfat mayonnaise
1	teaspoon dry mustard
1	teaspoon lemon juice
½	teaspoon hot-pepper sauce
½	teaspoon salt
½	teaspoon ground black pepper
2	teaspoons unsalted butter or canola oil

In a medium bowl, gently combine the crab, bread crumbs, scallions, and parsley.

In a small bowl, combine the egg, mayonnaise, mustard, lemon juice, hot-pepper sauce, salt, and pepper. Gently stir the mayonnaise mixture into the crab mixture until well-combined. Shape the crab mixture into 8 compact cakes.

Coat a large no-stick skillet with no-stick spray. Set over medium heat until hot. Warm 1 teaspoon of the butter or oil. Place 4 of the cakes in the skillet and cook for 4 to 6 minutes per side, or until well-browned and cooked through. Remove from the skillet and keep warm. Add the remaining 1 teaspoon butter or oil to the skillet. Cook the remaining 4 cakes.

STEAMED MUSSELS IN BROTH

Mussels are in high demand in Europe, but not so here, where clams and oysters reign. I suggest this simple preparation to get better acquainted. Buy mussels with shells tightly shut and without any breaks.

HANDS-ON TIME: 15 MINUTES
UNATTENDED TIME: 25 MINUTES

MAKES 8 SERVINGS
PER SERVING
329   CALORIES
6.6 G.   TOTAL FAT
1.2 G.   SATURATED FAT
22.4 G.   PROTEIN
38.8 G.   CARBOHYDRATES
0.5 G.   DIETARY FIBER
37 MG.   CHOLESTEROL
687 MG.   SODIUM

4	quarts cold water
⅓	cup salt
5	pounds mussels
1	tablespoon olive oil
8	cloves garlic, minced
1	leek, chopped
2	stalks celery, thinly sliced
2	cups fat-free chicken broth or clam juice
1	cup dry white wine or nonalcoholic white wine
1	teaspoon dried thyme
9	sprigs fresh Italian parsley
½	teaspoon grated lemon rind
	Salt and ground black pepper
1	large loaf crusty whole-grain French or Italian bread, sliced

Place the water in a large pot. Add the ⅓ cup salt and stir to dissolve. Scrub the mussels under cold running water and add to the pot. Let soak for 15 to 20 minutes to remove any grit. Drain the mussels and discard the water. With scissors, cut off and discard any loose threadlike filaments hanging from the mussels. Set the mussels aside.

Warm the oil in a large soup pot over medium heat. Add the garlic, leeks, and celery. Cook for 2 minutes, or until lightly browned. Add the broth or juice, wine, thyme, parsley, and lemon rind. Season with the salt and pepper. Bring to a boil. Reduce the heat to low and simmer for 5 minutes.

Return to a boil and add the mussels. Cover and cook for 5 minutes, or until the shells are opened wide.

Divide the mussels among serving bowls and pour the broth over top. Discard any unopened mussels. Serve with the bread to dip in the broth.

CASHEW-CRUSTED SHRIMP WITH MANGO SAUCE

Heavy batter-dipped shrimp can't compare with this light nutty coating. The tropical fruit sauce is an upbeat replacement for fat-laden tartar sauce. As seafood entrées go, this one is a beauty.

HANDS-ON TIME: 30 MINUTES
UNATTENDED TIME: NONE

MAKES 4 SERVINGS
PER SERVING
243   CALORIES
6.8 G.   TOTAL FAT
1.6 G.   SATURATED FAT
30.2 G. PROTEIN
14.7 G. CARBOHYDRATES
1.7 G.   DIETARY FIBER
316 MG. CHOLESTEROL
491 MG. SODIUM

SAUCE

1	large ripe mango, peeled and pitted
1	hard-cooked egg yolk
¼	cup nonfat mayonnaise
1	tablespoon thinly sliced fresh basil
	Salt and ground black pepper
	Ground red pepper

SHRIMP

¼	cup cashew pieces, toasted
1½	pounds tiger shrimp or large shrimp, peeled, deveined, and butterflied, tails left on (see hint)
	Salt and ground black pepper

To make the sauce: In a blender or food processor, process the mango, egg yolk, and mayonnaise until smooth. Transfer to a small bowl and stir in the basil. Season with the salt, black pepper, and red pepper. Cover and refrigerate until ready to use. Bring the sauce to room temperature before serving.

To make the shrimp: Place 8 wooden skewers in a shallow dish and cover with water. Set aside to soak.

In a blender or food processor, grind the cashews into a fine powder. Spread on a large flat plate.

Flatten the shrimp so that the halves fan out slightly. Place the shrimp in a medium bowl. Season with the salt and pepper.

Drain the skewers. Divide the shrimp among the skewers. (Thread the tip and tail of each shrimp onto the skewers; leaving ¼" between each shrimp.) Dip each side of the skewered shrimp into the cashews to create a thin crust.

Preheat the broiler. Coat the broiler pan with no-stick

spray. Place the skewers on the pan and broil 2" from the heat for 2 to 3 minutes per side, or until the shrimp are no longer pink. Serve with the mango sauce.

COOKING HINTS

• To butterfly shrimp, slice down the center of the back of the shrimp from head to tail, as you would for deveining,

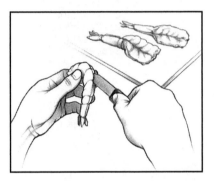

only cut a bit deeper. Cut about halfway through, being careful not to cut the shrimp in half. Then, flatten slightly. Leave the tails on the shrimp. The shrimp will fan out during cooking.

• To toast the cashews, place them in a dry no-stick skillet. Cook over medium heat, shaking the pan, for 3 to 5 minutes, or until the cashews are fragrant and golden.

• The sauce can be made ahead and refrigerated for up to 1 day.

• This dish tastes great served over cooked grains such as orzo, rice, or couscous.

• To serve the shrimp as an appetizer, thread one shrimp per toothpick and use the sauce as a dip.

QUICK SWITCHES

Almond-Crusted Scallops with Peach Sauce: Replace the mango with 2 large peaches (peeled, pitted, and chopped). Replace the cashews with ¼ cup toasted almonds. Replace the shrimp with 1½ pounds sea scallops.

Pecan-Crusted Tuna with Apricot Sauce: Replace the mango with 3 apricots (peeled, pitted, and chopped). Replace the cashews with ¼ cup toasted pecans. Replace the shrimp with 1½ pounds tuna steak, cut into 1" cubes.

SHRIMP CURRY WITH BROWN RICE

Reduced-fat coconut milk makes a creamy, tropical-tasting dish without truckloads of fat. Add more or less curry powder to suit your taste. Try hot curry powder if you like it spicy or mild curry powder for less heat.

HANDS-ON TIME: 45 MINUTES
UNATTENDED TIME: NONE

MAKES 6 SERVINGS
PER SERVING
476   CALORIES
10.4 G. TOTAL FAT
2.3 G. SATURATED FAT
27.8 G. PROTEIN
70.3 G. CARBOHYDRATES
6.9 G. DIETARY FIBER
180 MG. CHOLESTEROL
268 MG. SODIUM

1	tablespoon unsalted butter or canola oil
2	onions, chopped
1	sweet red pepper, sliced
5	cloves garlic, minced
2	teaspoons minced fresh ginger
1½	tablespoons curry powder
2	teaspoons paprika
1	teaspoon chili powder
1½	pounds shrimp, peeled, deveined, and butterflied (see hint)
1	tablespoon arrowroot or cornstarch
1	cup fat-free chicken broth or vegetable broth
1	tablespoon lemon juice
1–1½	cups light coconut milk
	Salt
6	cups cooked brown rice
1	banana, sliced
½	cup raisins
¼	cup chopped unsalted peanuts
2	tablespoons chopped fresh cilantro

Warm the butter or oil in a large no-stick skillet over medium heat. Add the onions, peppers, garlic, and ginger. Cook for 5 minutes. Stir in the curry powder, paprika, and chili powder. Cook, stirring, for 1 minute. Add the shrimp and stir to coat with the spices.

Place the arrowroot or cornstarch in a small bowl. Slowly stir in the broth to dissolve the arrowroot or cornstarch. Stir into the skillet. Add the lemon juice and 1 cup of the coconut milk. Season with the salt. Reduce the heat to low. Cook, stirring, until the shrimp are opaque and just cooked through. (Add up to ½ cup more coconut milk if the sauce is too thick.)

Serve the shrimp over the rice. Sprinkle with the bananas, raisins, peanuts, and cilantro.

COOKING HINT

- To butterfly shrimp, slice down the center of the back of the shrimp from head to tail, as you would for deveining, only cut a bit deeper. Cut about halfway through, being careful not to cut the shrimp in half. Flatten slightly (see illustration on page 251). The shrimp will fan out during cooking.

QUICK SWITCHES

Chicken Curry with Brown Rice: Replace the shrimp with 1½ pounds cubed boneless, skinless chicken breasts. Cook the chicken until no longer pink in the center.

Tofu Curry with Brown Rice: Replace the shrimp with 1½ pounds firm tofu that you've pressed the excess water from and cubed.

SWITCH TIP

Coconut milk is a key ingredient in warm-climate cuisines like Thai, Indonesian, African, and Indian. It has a thick, smooth texture that lends creamy richness to sauces and soups. Unfortunately, coconut milk is typically very high in fat (about 97 percent of calories), most of which is saturated. However, light coconut milk is available in most grocery stores today. This reduced-fat product has just 3 grams of fat per ¼ cup, compared with 12 grams for regular coconut milk. Look for it in the international aisle of your supermarket.

MEDITERRANEAN FISH STEW

This is a hearty seafood stew that originates from the Mediterranean region of France. Traditionally, leftover fish from the fishermen's nets were used. You can use the varieties that I've specified or choose whatever seafood is available—and fresh—at your market. The stew is served with lots of bread to soak up the saffron-scented broth.

HANDS-ON TIME: 25 MINUTES
UNATTENDED TIME: 20 MINUTES

MAKES 6 SERVINGS
PER SERVING
476   CALORIES
10.6 G. TOTAL FAT
1.8 G.   SATURATED FAT
50.8 G. PROTEIN
38.6 G. CARBOHYDRATES
3.2 G.   DIETARY FIBER
177 MG. CHOLESTEROL
756 MG. SODIUM

2	tablespoons olive oil
1	large leek, sliced
4	cloves garlic, sliced
½	sweet red pepper, finely chopped
1	carrot, finely chopped
1	can (28 ounces) low-sodium peeled tomatoes (with juice)
2	cups bottled clam juice or fish stock
2	cups low-sodium tomato sauce
2	cups fat-free chicken broth or vegetable broth
1	cup dry white wine or nonalcoholic white wine
¼	cup chopped fresh parsley
¼	cup chopped fresh basil
2	slices crusty whole-grain bread, crumbled
1	teaspoon crushed saffron threads
1	teaspoon fennel seeds
1	teaspoon dried thyme
1	teaspoon grated lemon rind
8	ounces halibut, cut into bite-size pieces
8	ounces swordfish, cut into bite-size pieces
1	pound shrimp, peeled and deveined
8	ounces scallops
5	ounces chopped clams
	Salt and ground black pepper
6	thick slices whole-grain bread

Warm the oil in a large soup pot over medium-high heat. Add the leeks, garlic, red peppers, and carrots. Cook for 5 minutes. Crush the tomatoes slightly in the can and add (with juice) to the pot. Stir in the clam juice or fish stock, tomato sauce, broth, wine, parsley, basil, crumbled bread, saffron, fennel seeds, thyme, and lemon rind. Bring to a boil. Reduce the heat to medium-low, cover, and simmer for 20 minutes, stirring occasionally.

Add the halibut and swordfish. Cook for 5 minutes. Add the shrimp, scallops, and clams. Cook for 3 minutes, or until the fish is just cooked through. Season with the salt and black pepper.

To serve, place a slice of bread in each bowl. Top with the stew.

COOKING HINT

- To vary the flavor, replace the halibut and swordfish with 1 pound firm fish such as tuna, salmon, sea bass, mahi mahi, or marlin.

RECIPES

"Poultry is for the cook what canvas is for the painter."
—ANTHELME BRILLAT-SAVARIN, FRENCH POLITICIAN AND FOOD
CONNOISSEUR

POULTRY WITH HIGH-FLAVOR
VARIETY

Poultry is a leading source of lean protein in the Low-Fat Living
Program. It's generally low in fat and high in important nutrients like
iron and zinc.

Poultry is also America's favorite entrée for fast meals. Boneless
cuts of chicken and turkey cook quickly, and the flavor possibilities
are endless. You can broil, grill, or poach a chicken breast in minutes.
Marinades and sauces allow you to create your family's favorite flavors. Add a simple vegetable topping and some rice or pasta, and the
meal is complete.

Most of the recipes here use boneless, skinless chicken breasts because they're convenient, versatile, and very low in fat. Turkey breast
is likewise extra-lean, and I use that for several recipes. Ground turkey
stands in for ground beef in moist and savory Southwest Turkey Meat
Loaf. When buying ground turkey, look for 100 percent ground turkey
breast. Sometimes ground turkey includes the dark meat and skin,
which can make the fat content soar.

For easy accompaniments to the poultry recipes in this chapter,
check out the grain side dishes beginning on page 204 and the vegetable side dishes beginning on page 332.

CHICKEN PARMESAN STRIPS

I created these chicken strips for my kids. Adults love them, too. Dip them in tomato sauce or Zippy Tartar Sauce (page 368). For a quick meal, serve the strips with a salad and Chili Fries (page 349).

HANDS-ON TIME: 10 MINUTES
UNATTENDED TIME: 35 MINUTES

1	pound boneless, skinless chicken breasts, cut into strips
½	cup skim milk
⅓	cup nonfat dry bread crumbs or cereal crumbs
3	tablespoons grated Parmesan cheese
2	teaspoons dried parsley
¼	teaspoon ground black pepper

MAKES 4 SERVINGS
PER SERVING
197   CALORIES
4.8 G.   TOTAL FAT
1.8 G.   SATURATED FAT
28.9 G. PROTEIN
7.6 G.   CARBOHYDRATES
0 G.   DIETARY FIBER
73 MG.   CHOLESTEROL
233 MG. SODIUM

Place the chicken in a shallow bowl and cover with the milk. Cover and refrigerate for at least 15 minutes or up to 4 hours.

Preheat the oven to 375°F. Coat a baking sheet with no-stick spray.

In a shallow bowl, combine the bread crumbs or cereal crumbs, Parmesan, parsley, and pepper.

Dip the chicken pieces into the crumb mixture to coat well. Place on the prepared baking sheet. Coat each piece of chicken with no-stick spray (use olive oil spray for the most flavor).

Bake for 20 minutes, or until the chicken is no longer pink in the center when tested with a sharp knife.

SKILLET CHICKEN WITH MUSHROOMS AND PEPPERS

Pull off a great meal in just 15 minutes. Serve this easy chicken entrée with mashed potatoes, rice, or whole-grain bread and a crisp salad.

HANDS-ON TIME: 15 MINUTES
UNATTENDED TIME: NONE

1	tablespoon olive oil
1	red onion, thickly sliced
10	cloves garlic, sliced
1	sweet red pepper, sliced
8	ounces mushrooms, sliced
1	pound boneless, skinless chicken breasts, cubed
1	tablespoon chopped fresh basil
	Salt and ground black pepper

MAKES 4 SERVINGS
PER SERVING

224	CALORIES
6.8 G.	TOTAL FAT
1.3 G.	SATURATED FAT
28.2 G.	PROTEIN
13 G.	CARBOHYDRATES
2.6 G.	DIETARY FIBER
69 MG.	CHOLESTEROL
63 MG.	SODIUM

Warm the oil in a large skillet over medium-high heat. Add the onions, garlic, red peppers, and mushrooms. Cook for 2 minutes.

Stir in the chicken and basil. Season with the salt and black pepper. Cook for 5 minutes, or until the chicken is no longer pink in the center when tested with a sharp knife.

SWITCH TIP

For the least fat, stick with white meat when eating poultry. A 3-ounce serving of dark meat (thigh and leg) has 5 grams more fat than the same amount of breast meat.

CHICKEN AND NOODLES WITH TOMATOES

This dish is like a chicken-noodle stew but less heavy. White beans, pasta, and herbed tomato sauce give it a light taste.

HANDS-ON TIME: 35 MINUTES
UNATTENDED TIME: NONE

2	teaspoons olive oil
1	pound boneless, skinless chicken breasts, cut into strips
	Salt and ground black pepper
1	onion, sliced
1	green pepper, chopped
6	cloves garlic, minced
1	teaspoon dried oregano
1	can (28 ounces) diced tomatoes (with juice)
¾	cup dry white wine or nonalcoholic white wine
8	ounces spaghetti
¼	cup chopped fresh basil and/or parsley
1	teaspoon grated lemon rind
1	can (15½ ounces) white beans, rinsed and drained
½	cup grated Parmesan cheese

MAKES 6 SERVINGS
PER SERVING
437   CALORIES
7.3 G.   TOTAL FAT
2.6 G.   SATURATED FAT
32.5 G. PROTEIN
55.9 G. CARBOHYDRATES
1.8 G.   DIETARY FIBER
53 MG.   CHOLESTEROL
693 MG. SODIUM

Warm 1 teaspoon of the oil in a large no-stick skillet over medium heat. Add the chicken and cook for 2 to 3 minutes, or until partially cooked. Season with the salt and black pepper. Transfer the chicken to a plate.

Warm the remaining 1 teaspoon oil in the same skillet over medium heat. Add the onions, green peppers, and garlic. Cook for 5 minutes. Stir in the oregano, tomatoes (with juice), and wine. Simmer for 10 minutes.

Cook the pasta in a large pot of boiling water according to the package directions. Drain and place in a large bowl.

Stir the basil and/or parsley and lemon rind into the sauce. Season with the salt and black pepper. Add the reserved chicken and the beans. Stir gently to cover the chicken with the sauce. Cook for 5 minutes, or until the chicken is no longer pink in the center when tested with a sharp knife.

Stir the Parmesan into the sauce and pour over the pasta.

HONEY-MUSTARD CURRY CHICKEN

Here's a dish for super-rushed evenings. It takes only 5 minutes of hands-on time. Marinating is optional, and you can either bake or grill the chicken.

HANDS-ON TIME: 5 MINUTES
UNATTENDED TIME: 35 MINUTES

3	tablespoons honey
3	tablespoons coarse mustard
1	tablespoon canola oil
1½	teaspoons curry powder
1	teaspoon chopped fresh chives
½	teaspoon salt (optional)
	Ground black pepper
6	boneless, skinless chicken breast halves (4 ounces each)

MAKES 6 SERVINGS
PER SERVING

345	CALORIES
9 G.	TOTAL FAT
2 G.	SATURATED FAT
53.9 G.	PROTEIN
9.2 G.	CARBOHYDRATES
0.3 G.	DIETARY FIBER
146 MG.	CHOLESTEROL
227 MG.	SODIUM

Preheat the oven to 400°F.

In a baking dish, mix together the honey, mustard, oil, curry powder, chives, and salt (if using). Season with the pepper. Add the chicken and coat with the sauce. Cover and refrigerate for at least 5 minutes or up to 24 hours.

Uncover and bake for 30 to 35 minutes, or until the chicken is no longer pink in the center when tested with a sharp knife.

COOKING HINTS

- To save time and boost flavor, marinate the chicken a day ahead of time.

- To grill the chicken, preheat the grill. Coat the grill rack with no-stick spray. Grill the chicken 4" from the heat for 3 to 4 minutes per side, or until no longer pink in the center when tested with a sharp knife.

SESAME CHICKEN SATAYS

These small kabobs are fun to make and eat as an appetizer or light meal. For more intense flavor, let the chicken marinate for up to 24 hours. Serve with Peanut Satay Sauce (facing page).

HANDS-ON TIME: 15 MINUTES
UNATTENDED TIME: 1 HOUR

1	tablespoon reduced-sodium soy sauce
1	tablespoon lime juice
1	tablespoon honey
2	teaspoons toasted sesame oil
1	teaspoon minced fresh ginger
1	clove garlic, minced
½	teaspoon ground coriander
1	tablespoon chopped fresh cilantro or parsley
1	pound boneless, skinless chicken breasts, cut into ½" strips
1	tablespoon sesame seeds

MAKES 4 SERVINGS
PER SERVING
160	CALORIES
4.8 G.	TOTAL FAT
1.1 G.	SATURATED FAT
26 G.	PROTEIN
1.9 G.	CARBOHYDRATES
0.2 G.	DIETARY FIBER
69 MG.	CHOLESTEROL
112 MG.	SODIUM

Place 8 bamboo skewers in a shallow dish and cover with water. Set aside to soak.

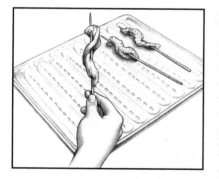

In a small bowl, mix together the soy sauce, lime juice, honey, oil, ginger, garlic, coriander, and cilantro or parsley. Add the chicken and coat with the marinade. Cover and refrigerate for at least 1 hour or up to 24 hours.

Preheat the grill or broiler. Coat the grill rack or broiler pan with no-stick spray. Drain the bamboo skewers. Thread the chicken on the skewers in an S pattern. Discard the remaining marinade.

Place the skewered chicken on the grill rack or broiler pan. Sprinkle with the sesame seeds. Cook 4" from the heat for 3 minutes per side, or until the chicken is no longer pink in the center when tested with a sharp knife.

COOKING HINT

- Bamboo skewers are available in most grocery stores. Check the international aisle or the utensil aisle. To prevent them from burning on the edges, soak the skewers in water for at least 10 to 20 minutes before using. If you substitute metal skewers, reduce the cooking time slightly because metal conducts heat and cooks the food more quickly.

QUICK SWITCH

Sesame Shrimp Satays: Replace the chicken with 1 pound shrimp, peeled and deveined. Serve with the Peanut Satay Sauce.

PEANUT SATAY SAUCE

Here's a delicious dipping sauce for Sesame Chicken Satays and other types of satay.

HANDS-ON TIME: 5 MINUTES
UNATTENDED TIME: NONE

¼	cup fat-free chicken broth or vegetable broth
2	tablespoons peanut butter
1	tablespoon toasted sesame oil
1	tablespoon reduced-sodium soy sauce
1	teaspoon sugar
¼	teaspoon red-pepper flakes

MAKES 6 TABLESPOONS

PER 1½ TABLESPOONS
72	CALORIES
5.7 G.	TOTAL FAT
0.9 G.	SATURATED FAT
2.9 G.	PROTEIN
2.9 G.	CARBOHYDRATES
1 G.	DIETARY FIBER
0 MG.	CHOLESTEROL
175 MG.	SODIUM

In a small bowl, combine the broth, peanut butter, oil, soy sauce, sugar, and red-pepper flakes. Mix well.

BUTTERMILK-BATTER BAKED CHICKEN

Buttermilk and three kinds of ground pepper make a savory batter for baked chicken. If you don't have white pepper, use more black. Garlic Mashed Potatoes (page 347) and steamed broccoli are delicious accompaniments.

¾	cup whole-wheat pastry flour or unbleached flour
1	teaspoon onion powder
½	teaspoon salt
	Ground black pepper
	Ground white pepper
	Ground red pepper
1	cup nonfat or low-fat buttermilk
2	tablespoons olive oil
6	skinless, bone-in chicken breast halves (4 ounces each)

Preheat the oven to 375°F. Coat a jelly-roll pan with no-stick spray.

In a small bowl, combine the flour, onion powder, and salt. Season with the black pepper, white pepper, and red pepper. Stir in the buttermilk and oil. Mix until smooth.

Dip the chicken in the batter to coat. Place on the prepared pan. Lightly coat each breast with no-stick spray. Bake for 45 minutes, or until the chicken is no longer pink in the center when tested with a sharp knife. If the crust needs a little browning, run under the broiler for 2 minutes.

HANDS-ON TIME: 5 MINUTES
UNATTENDED TIME: 45 MINUTES

MAKES 6 SERVINGS
PER SERVING

390	CALORIES
11 G.	TOTAL FAT
2.4 G.	SATURATED FAT
56.9 G.	PROTEIN
13.1 G.	CARBOHYDRATES
1.9 G.	DIETARY FIBER
147 MG.	CHOLESTEROL
347 MG.	SODIUM

SWITCH TIP

If you buy poultry with the skin on, cook it that way to keep the meat moist. Then remove the skin before eating. Removing the skin from poultry can save up to 5 grams of fat per 3-ounce serving.

Mexican Chicken in Tortillas

This is one of my favorite Mexican recipes. Guests love it. The sauce lends the chicken a dark, rich flavor. Here, it's served in tortillas, but it's equally good on baked potatoes or stuffed inside calzones. If desired, top with shredded Cheddar, salsa, and cilantro.

HANDS-ON TIME: 15 MINUTES
UNATTENDED TIME: 45 MINUTES

MAKES 6 SERVINGS
PER SERVING
379   CALORIES
8.5 G.   TOTAL FAT
1.4 G.   SATURATED FAT
26.3 G.   PROTEIN
57.2 G.   CARBOHYDRATES
16.8 G.   DIETARY FIBER
46 MG.   CHOLESTEROL
885 MG.   SODIUM

2	tablespoons olive oil
1	onion, chopped
1	sweet red pepper, chopped
4	cloves garlic, minced
3	cups cooked and shredded chicken breast
1	can (14½ ounces) diced tomatoes (with juice)
1	can (6 ounces) tomato paste
¾	cup Mexican Chili Sauce (page 266)
12	fat-free flour tortillas

Warm the oil in a large saucepan over medium heat. Add the onions, peppers, and garlic. Cook for 10 minutes. Stir in the chicken, tomatoes (with juice), tomato paste, and chili sauce. Cook for 15 minutes, stirring often. Reduce the heat to low, cover, and simmer for 30 minutes.

Serve wrapped inside the tortillas.

Cooking Hint

• For special occasions, serve this dish with Mango and Papaya Salsa (page 367) in place of tomato salsa.

Quick Switches

Mexican Chicken Nachos: Omit the tortillas. Layer the bottom of a 9" pie plate with baked tortilla chips. Top with half of the chicken. Layer on salsa, shredded cheese, and chopped cilantro. Add another layer of chips and the remaining chicken. Top with more salsa, cheese, and cilantro. Bake at 375°F for 15 minutes, or until the cheese melts.

Mexican Tofu in Tortillas: Replace the chicken with 1 pound firm tofu that you have pressed the excess water from and crumbled.

MEXICAN CHILI SAUCE

This sauce is called mole (MOH-lay) in Mexico. It's a rich blend of dried chili peppers, nuts, seeds, spices, and—surprise!—chocolate. The chocolate gives the sauce its characteristic deep, dark color. Use the sauce with Mexican Chicken in Tortillas (page 265) or stir it into soups, stews, or rice for a blast of flavor.

HANDS-ON TIME: 20 MINUTES
UNATTENDED TIME: NONE

MAKES 3 CUPS
PER 2 TABLESPOONS
28   CALORIES
1.4 G.   TOTAL FAT
0.2 G.   SATURATED FAT
0.9 G.   PROTEIN
3.4 G.   CARBOHYDRATES
0.9 G.   DIETARY FIBER
0 MG.   CHOLESTEROL
52 MG.   SODIUM

5   dried pasilla or ancho chili peppers, seeded and coarsely torn (wear plastic gloves when handling)
1   dried chipotle pepper, seeded and coarsely torn (wear plastic gloves when handling)
1   cup boiling water
2   tablespoons sesame seeds
2   tablespoons pumpkin seeds or chopped almonds
¼   teaspoon anise seeds
1   tablespoon olive oil
1   small onion, chopped
2   cloves garlic, chopped
3   tablespoons raisins
5   tomatillos, husked and chopped (see hint)
1   cup fat-free chicken broth or vegetable broth
¼   cup tomato paste
1   tablespoon unsweetened cocoa powder
¼   cup packed fresh cilantro
¼   teaspoon ground cloves
¼   teaspoon ground cinnamon
¼   teaspoon ground coriander
¼   teaspoon ground cumin
¼   teaspoon dried oregano
¼   teaspoon dried thyme
    Salt and ground black pepper

In a small bowl, combine the pasilla or ancho peppers, chipotle peppers, and water. Let stand until needed.

In a large no-stick skillet, combine the sesame seeds, pumpkin seeds or almonds, and anise seeds. Cook over medium heat, stirring, for 3 minutes, or until lightly browned. Transfer to a food processor or blender.

Add the oil to the skillet. Add the onions, garlic, raisins, and tomatillos. Cook for 5 minutes, or until the onions are tender. Transfer to the food processor.

Drain the chili peppers and add to the food processor; discard the water.

Add the broth, tomato paste, cocoa, cilantro, cloves, cinnamon, coriander, cumin, oregano, and thyme. Season with the salt and black pepper. Process until the mixture is very smooth. Store, covered, in the refrigerator.

Cooking Hints

- Tomatillos are small green vegetables with a thin, papery husk. They are available in many supermarkets. Remove the husk and stem before using.

- Chipotle, pasilla, and ancho peppers are dried chili peppers available in the produce aisle of many supermarkets. If you can't find them locally, check the mail-order resources on page 416.

- If you have any leftover sauce, freeze it in small plastic bags for up to 3 months.

CHICKEN WITH PEANUT SAUCE AND PINEAPPLE SALSA

Get ready for a flavor extravaganza. Fruity salsa and savory peanut sauce lend exotic tastes to grilled chicken. Despite the number of ingredients, this dish comes together in under an hour.

HANDS-ON TIME: 45 MINUTES
UNATTENDED TIME: NONE

MAKES 6 SERVINGS
PER SERVING
582   CALORIES
14.7 G. TOTAL FAT
2.8 G. SATURATED FAT
37.3 G. PROTEIN
77.4 G. CARBOHYDRATES
7.9 G. DIETARY FIBER
69 MG. CHOLESTEROL
304 MG. SODIUM

SALSA

1	pineapple, peeled, cored, and cut into small pieces
1	sweet red pepper, quartered
½	large red onion, quartered
1	jalapeño pepper, seeded (wear plastic gloves when handling)
1	clove garlic
¼	cup packed fresh cilantro
1	tablespoon lime juice
1	teaspoon grated lime rind
	Salt and ground black pepper
	Ground red pepper

SAUCE

¼	cup peanut butter
2	tablespoons reduced-sodium soy sauce
1¼	tablespoons rice vinegar or white-wine vinegar
1	tablespoon chopped fresh cilantro
1½	teaspoons sugar or honey
1½	teaspoons dry sherry or nonalcoholic white wine
1	clove garlic
½	teaspoon chopped fresh ginger
½	cup fat-free chicken broth or vegetable broth
	Salt and ground black pepper
	Ground red pepper

CHICKEN

6	boneless, skinless chicken breast halves (4 ounces each)
6	cups hot cooked brown rice
6	tablespoons chopped unsalted peanuts

To make the salsa: Preheat the oven to 500°F. Line a baking sheet with foil and coat with no-stick spray.

Place half of the pineapple in a large bowl. Place the remaining pineapple on the prepared baking sheet in an even layer and roast for 15 to 20 minutes, or until lightly browned. Transfer to the bowl.

In a food processor, combine the sweet red peppers, onions, jalapeño peppers, garlic, and cilantro. Process using on/off turns until the vegetables are finely chopped. Transfer to the bowl. Add the lime juice and lime rind to the bowl. Season with the salt, black pepper, and ground red pepper. Mix well.

To make the sauce: Rinse out the food processor. Add the peanut butter, soy sauce, vinegar, cilantro, sugar or honey, sherry or wine, garlic, and ginger. Process until smooth. Add the broth. Season with the salt, black pepper, and red pepper. Process until well-blended. Transfer to a medium bowl.

To make the chicken: Preheat the grill or broiler. Coat the grill rack or broiler pan with no-stick spray. Cook the chicken 4" from the heat for 5 minutes per side, or until no longer pink in the center when tested with a sharp knife.

Serve with the rice, peanut sauce, and salsa. Sprinkle with the peanuts.

COOKING HINT

- Pineapples don't ripen after they're picked, so choose one that's plump and soft with a sweet aroma at the bottom. To cut a pineapple, slice off the top and bottom first. Cut the pineapple lengthwise into quarters. Remove the core and slice the skin from each quarter.

MEDITERRANEAN SKILLET CHICKEN

Sun-dried tomatoes, olives, and capers provide big flavors.

HANDS-ON TIME: 30 MINUTES
UNATTENDED TIME: 30 MINUTES

20	sun-dried tomatoes
1	tablespoon olive oil
2	red onions, sliced
1	sweet red pepper, sliced
8	ounces mushrooms, sliced
6	large cloves garlic, sliced
6	small skinless, bone-in chicken breasts (4 ounces each)
1	can (28 ounces) peeled tomatoes (with juice)
¼	cup dry white wine or nonalcoholic white wine
18	small black or green Greek olives, pitted
2	tablespoons drained capers
1	tablespoon grated lemon rind
1	pound wide yolk-free egg noodles
½	cup chopped fresh parsley
¼	cup chopped fresh basil
4	ounces feta cheese, crumbled
	Ground black pepper
	Ground red pepper
¼	cup half-and-half

MAKES 6 SERVINGS
PER SERVING
544   CALORIES
12.4 G. TOTAL FAT
4.7 G.   SATURATED FAT
30.3 G. PROTEIN
79.9 G. CARBOHYDRATES
3.4 G.   DIETARY FIBER
66 MG.   CHOLESTEROL
734 MG. SODIUM

Soak the sun-dried tomatoes in 1 cup hot water until needed. Warm the oil in a Dutch oven over medium heat. Add the onions, sliced red peppers, mushrooms, and garlic. Cook for 5 minutes, or until soft. Spread the vegetables to the edge of the pan and add the chicken, breast side down. Cook for 5 minutes, or until lightly browned. Turn the chicken over and spoon the vegetables on top.

Chop the tomatoes in the can. Add the tomatoes (with juice), wine, olives, capers, and lemon rind to the pan. Drain the sun-dried tomatoes. Thinly slice and add to the pan. Cover and cook for 30 minutes.

Cook the noodles in a large pot of boiling water according to the package directions. Drain and transfer to a large bowl.

Stir the parsley, basil, and feta into the chicken mixture. Season with the black pepper and ground red pepper. Cook for 5 minutes. Remove from the heat and stir in the half-and-half. Serve over the noodles.

MOROCCAN CHICKEN

Recreate Morocco in your kitchen with figs, chickpeas, and aromatic spices. This dish requires minimal hands-on time and needs only cooked rice or couscous and a salad to complete the meal.

HANDS-ON TIME: 10 MINUTES
UNATTENDED TIME: 45 MINUTES

2	tablespoons olive oil
1	onion, chopped
6	cloves garlic, chopped
1	tablespoon minced fresh ginger
1	can (28 ounces) diced tomatoes (with juice)
1	cup fat-free chicken broth or vegetable broth
2	tablespoons chopped fresh parsley
1	teaspoon paprika
1	teaspoon ground coriander
½	teaspoon grated lemon rind
¼	teaspoon ground cinnamon
¼	teaspoon crushed saffron threads
6	skinless, bone-in chicken breast halves (4 ounces each)
1	can (15 ounces) chickpeas, rinsed and drained
6	dried figs, halved
	Salt and ground black pepper

MAKES 6 SERVINGS

PER SERVING
337	CALORIES
9.4 G.	TOTAL FAT
1.7 G.	SATURATED FAT
33 G.	PROTEIN
30.9 G.	CARBOHYDRATES
5.4 G.	DIETARY FIBER
73 MG.	CHOLESTEROL
668 MG.	SODIUM

Warm the oil in a Dutch oven over medium heat. Add the onions, garlic, and ginger. Cook for 5 minutes. Stir in the tomatoes (with juice), broth, parsley, paprika, coriander, lemon rind, cinnamon, and saffron. Add the chicken (breast side down), chickpeas, and figs. Season with the salt and pepper. Reduce the heat to medium-low. Cover and cook for 45 minutes, or until the chicken is no longer pink in the center when tested with a sharp knife.

STUFFED TURKEY PARMESAN

Cheese-lovers can indulge without guilt. Lean turkey tenderloin is stuffed with herbed cream cheese and baked with tomato sauce, mozzarella, and Parmesan. Leftovers—if you have any—make great sub sandwiches the next day.

HANDS-ON TIME: 25 MINUTES
UNATTENDED TIME: 45 MINUTES

MAKES 4 SERVINGS

PER SERVING
524	CALORIES
13.3 G.	TOTAL FAT
4.8 G.	SATURATED FAT
51.4 G.	PROTEIN
48.4 G.	CARBOHYDRATES
2.6 G.	DIETARY FIBER
83 MG.	CHOLESTEROL
571 MG.	SODIUM

1½ **pounds turkey breast tenderloin, cut into 4 pieces**
¼ **cup whole-wheat pastry flour or unbleached flour**
2 **teaspoons olive oil**
4 **ounces nonfat cream cheese**
1 **teaspoon dried parsley**
1 **teaspoon dried chives**
½ **teaspoon garlic powder**
   Salt and ground black pepper
2 **cups fat-free low-sodium tomato sauce**
¾ **cup shredded part-skim mozzarella cheese**
¼ **cup grated Parmesan cheese**
8 **ounces fettuccine**

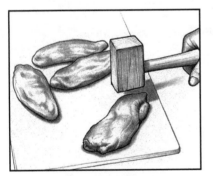

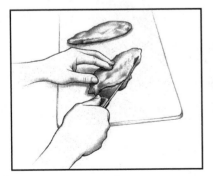

Preheat the oven to 350°F. Coat an 8" × 8" baking dish with no-stick spray.

Pound the turkey with a mallet to flatten slightly. To make a pocket for the stuffing, slice each piece lengthwise through the side, being careful not to cut all the way through.

Place the flour on a large plate. Dredge the turkey in the flour to coat both sides.

Warm the oil in a large no-stick skillet over medium heat. Add the turkey and cook for 2 to 4 minutes per side, or until lightly browned. Remove from the heat.

In a small bowl, mix the cream cheese, parsley, chives, and garlic powder. Season with the salt and pepper. Stuff the turkey pieces with the cream-cheese mixture and secure the opening with a toothpick.

Spread 1 cup of the tomato sauce over the bottom of the prepared dish. Add the turkey and top with the remaining 1 cup tomato sauce. Sprinkle with the mozzarella and Parmesan. Cover loosely with foil and bake for 30 minutes. Uncover and bake for 15 minutes.

Cook the pasta in a large pot of boiling water according to the package directions. Drain. Serve the turkey and sauce over the pasta.

QUICK SWITCH

Stuffed Tempeh Parmesan: For a vegetarian version of this dish, replace the turkey with 2 pounds tempeh, a soy food available in large supermarkets and health food stores. Spread the herbed cheese between two layers of tempeh and proceed as directed.

TURKEY PICCATA

Turkey cutlets replace the veal in this Italian classic. If possible, use a flavored pasta such as wild mushroom.

HANDS-ON TIME: 25 MINUTES
UNATTENDED TIME: NONE

1½	pounds fettuccine
1	cup fat-free chicken broth or vegetable broth
½	cup whole-wheat pastry flour or unbleached flour
	Salt and ground black pepper
1½	pounds thinly sliced turkey cutlets
1	tablespoon + 3 teaspoons unsalted butter
½	cup dry white wine or nonalcoholic white wine
	Juice of 1 large lemon
3	tablespoons drained capers
1	tablespoon chopped fresh parsley

MAKES 6 SERVINGS

PER SERVING
533   CALORIES
8.7 G.   TOTAL FAT
3.3 G.   SATURATED FAT
35.6 G. PROTEIN
74.1 G. CARBOHYDRATES
18.9 G. DIETARY FIBER
55 MG.   CHOLESTEROL
275 MG. SODIUM

Cook the pasta in a large pot of boiling water according to the package directions. Drain and return to the pot. Add the broth, toss to mix, and keep warm over low heat.

In a shallow bowl, mix the flour, salt, and pepper. Dredge the turkey in the mixture to coat both sides.

Warm 1 tablespoon of the butter in a large no-stick skillet over medium heat. Add enough turkey cutlets to fill the skillet. Cook for 2 to 3 minutes per side, or until cooked through. Transfer to a covered plate to keep warm. Repeat with the remaining turkey, using an additional 1½ teaspoons of the butter.

Return the skillet to medium heat. Add the wine, lemon juice, capers, and the remaining 1½ teaspoons butter. Cook for 2 minutes, stirring occasionally.

Serve the turkey over the pasta and top with the sauce. Sprinkle with the parsley.

COOKING HINT

- Turkey breast can be purchased in presliced medallion-size pieces at most grocery stores. To make your own, buy turkey cutlets and freeze them. Thaw slightly. Using a sharp knife, cut the turkey into ¼" slices. Thaw completely before cooking.

TURKEY CUTLETS WITH ARTICHOKE HEARTS

Looking for a touch of elegance? Fresh fennel, leeks, and artichoke hearts create a sophisticated sauce for turkey cutlets. Serve this dish with thin noodles or mashed potatoes.

HANDS-ON TIME: 25 MINUTES
UNATTENDED TIME: NONE

½	cup nonfat dry bread crumbs
1	pound turkey breast slices or cutlets
1	tablespoon unsalted butter or olive oil
2	leeks, halved lengthwise and thickly sliced
8	ounces fennel bulb, thinly sliced
4	ounces mushrooms, sliced
1	can (14 ounces) artichoke hearts, rinsed, drained, and quartered
1	cup fat-free chicken broth or vegetable broth
⅛	teaspoon grated lemon rind
¼	cup thinly sliced fresh basil
1	teaspoon arrowroot or cornstarch
1	tablespoon dry sherry or nonalcoholic white wine
¼	cup half-and-half
	Salt and ground black pepper

MAKES 4 SERVINGS

PER SERVING
330	CALORIES
8.7 G.	TOTAL FAT
4 G.	SATURATED FAT
28.5 G.	PROTEIN
37.1 G.	CARBOHYDRATES
6.6 G.	DIETARY FIBER
58 MG.	CHOLESTEROL
383 MG.	SODIUM

Place the bread crumbs in a shallow bowl. Dredge the turkey in the crumbs to coat both sides. Coat a large no-stick skillet with no-stick spray. Set over medium heat until hot. Add the turkey (in batches, if necessary) and cook for 2 minutes per side, or until just browned. Transfer to a plate.

Warm the butter or oil in the same skillet over medium heat. Add the leeks and fennel. Cook for 2 minutes. Stir in the mushrooms and artichokes. Cook for 2 minutes.

Stir in the broth and lemon rind. Add the basil and the reserved turkey. Stir gently, spooning the vegetables over the turkey. Cover and cook for 3 minutes, or until the turkey is no longer pink in the center when tested with a sharp knife.

Place the arrowroot or cornstarch in a small bowl. Add the sherry or wine and stir to dissolve. Stir in the half-and-half. Gradually add to the skillet, stirring constantly. Season with the salt and pepper. Stir gently to blend the sauce with the other ingredients. Cover and cook for 1 minute, or until the sauce is slightly thickened.

275

SOUTHWEST TURKEY MEAT LOAF

Here's a low-fat makeover with a shot of Southwestern seasonings. Spike some ketchup with chopped mild green chili peppers, hot-pepper sauce, and chili powder to pour over the top.

HANDS-ON TIME: 15 MINUTES
UNATTENDED TIME: 55 MINUTES

MAKES 4 SERVINGS
PER SERVING
254   CALORIES
7.9 G.   TOTAL FAT
1.4 G.   SATURATED FAT
24.8 G. PROTEIN
21.4 G. CARBOHYDRATES
3.3 G.   DIETARY FIBER
97 MG.   CHOLESTEROL
390 MG. SODIUM

1	tablespoon canola or olive oil
1	onion, chopped
1	sweet red or green pepper, chopped
6	cloves garlic, minced
1	large jalapeño pepper, seeded and chopped (wear plastic gloves when handling)
1	tablespoon chopped fresh parsley
2	teaspoons dried basil
1½	teaspoons dried oregano
1½	teaspoons dried thyme
½–1	teaspoon ground cumin
1	egg
⅓	cup crushed baked tortilla chips
1	tablespoon apple cider vinegar
1	cup tomato sauce
1	pound ground turkey breast
	Salt and ground black pepper
	Hot-pepper sauce

Add 1" of hot water to a 13" × 9" baking dish. Place on the middle rack of the oven. Preheat the oven to 350°F. Coat an 8" × 4" loaf pan with no-stick spray.

Warm the oil in a medium no-stick skillet over medium heat. Add the onions, red or green peppers, garlic, and jalapeño peppers. Cook for 5 minutes. Stir in the parsley, basil, oregano, thyme, and cumin.

Place the egg in a large bowl. Beat lightly. Add the tortilla chips, vinegar, tomato sauce, onion mixture, and turkey. Season with the salt, black pepper, and hot-pepper sauce. Mix well. ·

Spoon into the prepared loaf pan, smoothing out the top. Place the loaf pan in the baking dish containing water. Bake for 45 minutes. Remove from the oven and cool for 10 minutes on a wire rack.

TURKEY SAUSAGE SANDWICHES

Sausage sandwiches are notoriously high in fat. Low-fat meats and whole-grain bread make these wholesome.

HANDS-ON TIME: 20 MINUTES
UNATTENDED TIME: NONE

2   **large onions, sliced**
2   **sweet red, yellow, or green peppers, thickly sliced**
     Salt and ground black pepper
4   **links (3 ounces each) low-fat turkey or chicken sausage**
1   **large whole-grain baguette**

MAKES 4 SERVINGS
PER SERVING
325   CALORIES
8.5 G.   TOTAL FAT
2.1 G.   SATURATED FAT
22.6 G.   PROTEIN
41.9 G.   CARBOHYDRATES
2.7 G.   DIETARY FIBER
54 MG.   CHOLESTEROL
995 MG.   SODIUM

Coat a large no-stick skillet with no-stick spray and set over medium heat. Add the onions and cook for 3 minutes. Stir in the red, yellow, or green peppers. Season with the salt and black pepper. Cook for 5 minutes. Add the sausage and cook for 10 to 12 minutes, or until the sausage is browned and cooked through when tested with a sharp knife.

Cut the baguette into 4 equal pieces. Slice each piece lengthwise through the side, without cutting all the way through. Place a sausage link inside each piece of bread and top with the onions and peppers.

COOKING HINT

- If you like sauce on your sandwich, spoon a few table-spoons fat-free marinara sauce over each serving.

RECIPES

CHAPTER

"Don't be intimidated by foreign cookery. Tomatoes and oregano make it Italian. Wine and tarragon make it French. Sour cream makes it Russian. Lemon and cinnamon make it Greek. Soy sauce makes it Chinese. Garlic makes it good. Now you are an International Cook."
—ALICE MAY BROCK, AMERICAN AUTHOR AND RESTAURATEUR

PIZZA TO TACOS—FUN FOODS LAYERED AND STUFFED

Pizza, burritos, tacos, and dumplings are some of my favorite meals. They're bursting with the exciting flavors of herbs, spices, cheeses, or whatever else you choose to include. That's the wonderful thing about layered and stuffed foods—the fillings and toppings are open to end-less variations. I like to make these dishes on weekends when I have a bit more time. Then I fill the freezer with them for quick meals and lunches throughout the week. Here's how to make the perfect crust.

- For a crispy crust, use a hot oven. Preheat it to 500°F.

- For an extra-crispy crust, use a pizza stone. Preheat the stone in the oven, then put the pizza directly on it.

- For a super-crispy crust, substitute semolina flour for some or all of the unbleached flour.

- For an herb crust, add crushed oregano, basil, and garlic powder to the flour mixture.

- For a honey whole-wheat crust, substitute whole-wheat flour for the unbleached flour and use honey instead of sugar.

- For a cheese crust, add a small amount of grated Parmesan cheese to the flour mixture.

279

MULTIGRAIN PIZZA DOUGH

Pizza has become an American obsession. Kids and adults love to create signature pizzas with their favorite toppings. Here's a low-fat crust that will keep your special creations light and lean.

HANDS-ON TIME: 15 MINUTES
UNATTENDED TIME: 1 HOUR

MAKES 6 SERVINGS
PER SERVING
219   CALORIES
1.8 G.   TOTAL FAT
0.2 G.   SATURATED FAT
6.7 G.   PROTEIN
44.4 G.   CARBOHYDRATES
3.8 G.   DIETARY FIBER
0 MG.   CHOLESTEROL
360 MG.   SODIUM

1¼	cups warm water (110°–115°F)
1	tablespoon active dry yeast
1	teaspoon sugar or honey
½	cup whole-wheat flour
½	cup cornmeal
1	teaspoon salt
1	teaspoon olive oil
1¾–2	cups unbleached flour

In a large bowl, combine the water, yeast, and sugar or honey. Set aside for 5 minutes, or until foamy.

Add the whole-wheat flour, cornmeal, salt, and oil. Using an electric mixer, beat well for 3 minutes (or beat vigorously by hand for 5 minutes). Stir in 1¾ cups of the unbleached flour.

Turn out onto a floured surface and knead in enough of the remaining unbleached flour to form a soft dough (be careful not to add too much flour). Knead for 10 minutes, or until smooth and elastic. Form the dough into a ball.

Coat a large bowl with no-stick spray. Add the dough and turn to coat all sides. Cover and let rise in a warm place for about 1 hour, or until doubled in size.

Punch down the dough and refrigerate or freeze until ready to use. Let come to room temperature before using.

PIZZA WITH APPLES, WALNUTS, AND GORGONZOLA

This pizza features the rich flavors of autumn. Serve it with a light salad and low-fat dressing.

HANDS-ON TIME: 15 MINUTES
UNATTENDED TIME: 30 MINUTES

Cornmeal
1   **recipe Multigrain Pizza Dough (facing page) or 1 tube (10 ounces) low-fat refrigerated pizza dough**
2   **onions, sliced**
2   **apples, peeled and chopped**
6   **tablespoons chopped walnuts**
6   **tablespoons crumbled Roquefort cheese**
1   **cup shredded part-skim mozzarella cheese**
1½ **teaspoons dried oregano**

MAKES 6 SERVINGS
PER SERVING
412   CALORIES
13.8 G. TOTAL FAT
5.2 G. SATURATED FAT
17 G.   PROTEIN
57.3 G. CARBOHYDRATES
5.6 G. DIETARY FIBER
24 MG. CHOLESTEROL
706 MG. SODIUM

Preheat the oven to 500°F. Coat 3 baking sheets with no-stick spray and sprinkle with cornmeal.

Coat a large no-stick skillet with no-stick spray and set over medium heat until warm. Add the onions and cook for 5 to 8 minutes, or until brown and wilted.

Divide the dough into 6 pieces. On a floured work surface, roll or pat each piece into a 7" circle. Place on the prepared baking sheets.

Divide the onions, apples, walnuts, Roquefort, and mozzarella among the pizzas. Sprinkle with the oregano.

Bake 1 sheet at a time on the bottom rack of the oven for 10 to 15 minutes, or until the cheese is melted and the crust is lightly browned.

MEDITERRANEAN PIZZA

If you love pizza with the works, these individual pizzas are for you. With roasted red peppers and olives, you'll never miss the high-fat pepperoni or sausage.

HANDS-ON TIME: 10 MINUTES
UNATTENDED TIME: 30 MINUTES

Cornmeal

1	recipe Multigrain Pizza Dough (page 280) or 1 tube (10 ounces) low-fat refrigerated pizza dough
10	mushrooms, sliced
1	onion, chopped
1	cup chopped roasted red peppers or sweet red peppers
18	small black or kalamata olives, pitted and chopped
3	cloves garlic, minced
1½	cups shredded part-skim mozzarella cheese
1½	teaspoons dried oregano

MAKES 6 SERVINGS

PER SERVING
331   CALORIES
8.5 G.   TOTAL FAT
3.3 G.   SATURATED FAT
15 G.   PROTEIN
51.2 G. CARBOHYDRATES
5.7 G.   DIETARY FIBER
16 MG.   CHOLESTEROL
552 MG. SODIUM

Preheat the oven to 500°F. Coat 3 baking sheets with no-stick spray and sprinkle with cornmeal.

Divide the dough into 6 pieces. On a floured work surface, roll or pat each piece into a 7" circle. Place on the prepared baking sheets.

Divide the mushrooms, onions, red peppers, olives, garlic, and mozzarella among the pizzas. Sprinkle with the oregano.

Bake 1 sheet at a time on the bottom rack of the oven for 10 to 15 minutes, or until the cheese is melted and the crust is lightly browned.

TOP TOPPINGS

People love personalizing their pizzas. Put out small bowls of toppings and let everyone improvise. Or rely on these classic combinations.

- *Vegetarian:* tomato sauce, onions, green peppers, mushrooms, and a small amount of olives
- *Garden Harvest:* tomato sauce, small broccoli and cauliflower florets, crushed garlic, roasted peppers, and fresh spinach
- *Primavera:* tomatoes, peppers, scallions, mushrooms, zucchini, and asparagus
- *Spinach and Ricotta:* fresh or frozen spinach sautéed with a small amount of olive oil, oregano, and basil; tomatoes, part-skim ricotta cheese, and part-skim Swiss cheese
- *Broccoli and Cheddar:* broccoli florets and part-skim Cheddar cheese
- *Chicken Fajita:* chicken breast strips sautéed with onions, peppers, chili powder, oregano, and cumin; fresh cilantro, and part-skim hot-pepper Monterey Jack cheese
- *Spinach and Feta:* red onions, tomatoes, spinach, fresh basil, feta cheese, and Parmesan cheese
- *Wild Mushroom:* assorted mushrooms sautéed with shallots, garlic, thyme, and rosemary; Parmesan cheese and part-skim Swiss or Havarti cheese
- *Smoked Salmon:* low-fat or nonfat cream cheese, fresh dill, red onions, tomatoes, and part-skim Havarti or mozzarella cheese
- *Shrimp Scampi:* shrimp sautéed with onions, garlic, and lemon; fresh basil, part-skim mozzarella, and part-skim Havarti or provolone cheese
- *Barbecued Chicken:* chicken strips grilled with barbecue sauce, onions, peppers, and mushrooms; part-skim provolone cheese
- *Sun-Dried Tomato Pesto:* Sun-Dried Tomato Pesto (page 365), artichokes, goat cheese, and part-skim mozzarella cheese
- *Seafood Marinara:* marinara sauce, cooked mixed seafood, part-skim mozzarella cheese, and part-skim provolone cheese

STUFFED PIZZA

Two crusts, three cheeses, and a harvest of tasty vegetables—what could be better?

HANDS-ON TIME: 20 MINUTES
UNATTENDED TIME: 1 HOUR

DOUGH

2	cups warm water (110°–115°F)
1	tablespoon active dry yeast
1	tablespoon honey or sugar
1½	cups whole-wheat flour
1	teaspoon salt
3–4	cups semolina flour or unbleached flour
	Cornmeal

MAKES 8 SERVINGS
PER SERVING
535   CALORIES
10.7 G. TOTAL FAT
6.1 G. SATURATED FAT
35.1 G. PROTEIN
77.8 G. CARBOHYDRATES
5.5 G. DIETARY FIBER
33 MG. CHOLESTEROL
597 MG. SODIUM

FILLING

5	cloves garlic, minced
1	container (15 ounces) nonfat or low-fat ricotta cheese
2	cups small broccoli florets
2	cups fresh spinach, torn into pieces
1	red onion, sliced
2	large tomatoes, sliced
½	cup sliced roasted red peppers
4	cups shredded part-skim mozzarella or provolone cheese
1	teaspoon dried oregano
	Red-pepper flakes (optional)
1	tablespoon grated Parmesan cheese

To make the dough: In a large bowl, combine the water, yeast, and honey or sugar. Set aside for 5 minutes, or until foamy.

Add the whole-wheat flour and salt. Using an electric mixer, beat well for 3 minutes (or beat vigorously by hand for 5 minutes). Stir in 3 cups of the semolina or unbleached flour.

Turn out onto a floured surface and knead in enough of the remaining semolina or unbleached flour to form a very soft dough (be careful not to add too much flour). Knead for 10 minutes, or until smooth and elastic. Form the dough into a ball.

Coat a large bowl with no-stick spray. Add the dough and turn to coat all sides. Cover and let rise in a warm place for about 45 minutes, or until almost doubled in size.

Coat a baking sheet with no-stick spray and sprinkle with cornmeal.

Punch down the dough and divide in half. On a floured surface, roll 1 piece of dough into a 15" circle. Place on the prepared baking sheet.

Preheat the oven to 450°F.

To make the filling: Spread the garlic and the ricotta on the dough. Add the broccoli, spinach, onions, tomatoes, roasted peppers, and mozzarella or provolone. Sprinkle with the oregano and red-pepper flakes (if using).

Roll the remaining piece of dough into a 15" circle. Place over the filling and pinch the top and bottom crusts together. Coat the dough with no-stick spray and sprinkle with the Parmesan. Using a sharp knife, cut 4 slits in the top of the dough. Bake on the bottom rack of the oven for 20 to 30 minutes, or until the crust is lightly browned. Cool slightly before cutting.

SPINACH AND RICOTTA CALZONES

If you like pizza and turnovers, you'll love calzones. Serve these with warmed tomato sauce.

HANDS-ON TIME: 35 MINUTES
UNATTENDED TIME: 1½ HOURS

DOUGH

1⅔	cups warm water (110°–115°F)
1	tablespoon active dry yeast
2	teaspoons honey or sugar
2	cups whole-wheat flour or unbleached flour
1	teaspoon salt
1	teaspoon olive oil
2–3	cups unbleached flour

MAKES 6

PER CALZONE
429   CALORIES
7.4 G.   TOTAL FAT
3.3 G.   SATURATED FAT
22.6 G. PROTEIN
71.4 G. CARBOHYDRATES
7 G.   DIETARY FIBER
15 MG. CHOLESTEROL
587 MG. SODIUM

FILLING

1	package (10 ounces) frozen chopped spinach, thawed
1	teaspoon olive oil
1	cup chopped onions
3	cloves garlic, minced
1	teaspoon sugar
	Salt and ground black pepper
1	cup shredded part-skim mozzarella cheese
¾	cup nonfat or low-fat ricotta cheese
½	teaspoon grated lemon rind
¼	cup + 1 tablespoon grated Parmesan cheese

To make the dough: In a large bowl, combine the water, yeast, and honey or sugar. Set aside for 5 minutes, or until foamy.

Add the whole-wheat flour or unbleached flour, salt, and oil. Using an electric mixer, beat well for 3 minutes (or beat vigorously by hand for 5 minutes). Stir in 2 cups of the unbleached flour.

Turn out onto a floured surface and knead in enough of the remaining unbleached flour to form a very soft dough (be careful not to add too much flour). Knead for 10 minutes, or until smooth and elastic. Form the dough into a ball.

Coat a large bowl with no-stick spray. Add the dough and turn to coat all sides. Cover and let rise in a warm place for about 45 minutes, or until doubled in size.

Coat a baking sheet with no-stick spray.

Punch down the dough and divide into 6 pieces. Roll or pat each piece into a 7" circle.

To make the filling: Drain the spinach and squeeze out the excess liquid.

Warm the oil in a large no-stick skillet over medium heat. Add the onions and garlic. Cook for 5 minutes. Add the

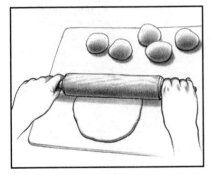

spinach and sugar. Season with the salt and pepper. Cook for 10 minutes, or until most of the liquid has evaporated. Cool slightly.

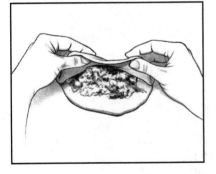

In a medium bowl, combine the mozzarella, ricotta, lemon rind, and ¼ cup of the Parmesan. Add the spinach mixture and stir until well-combined.

Preheat the oven to 375°F.

Spread an equal amount of the filling on half of each piece of dough. Fold the dough over the filling and pinch the edges to seal.

Place the calzones on the prepared baking sheet and cut 2 slits on the top of each one. Coat each with no-stick spray and sprinkle with the remaining 1 tablespoon Parmesan. Bake on the bottom rack of the oven for 30 minutes, or until the crust is lightly browned. Cool slightly before serving.

Mushroom Calzones

The hands-on time for these calzones is less than a half-hour. After the dough rises, simply stuff the calzones with the mushroom and cheese filling and pop them in the oven. I like to use an assortment of mushrooms, such as portobello, cremini, and shiitake.

HANDS-ON TIME: 25 MINUTES
UNATTENDED TIME: 1½ HOURS

MAKES 6
PER CALZONE
451   CALORIES
8.9 G.   TOTAL FAT
4.5 G.   SATURATED FAT
20.2 G. PROTEIN
74 G.   CARBOHYDRATES
8.4 G.   DIETARY FIBER
21 MG.   CHOLESTEROL
500 MG. SODIUM

DOUGH

1⅔	cups warm water (110°–115°F)
1	tablespoon active dry yeast
2	teaspoons honey or sugar
2	cups whole-wheat flour or unbleached flour
1	teaspoon salt
1	teaspoon olive oil
2–3	cups unbleached flour

FILLING

1	tablespoon unsalted butter or margarine
1	onion, sliced
4	cloves garlic, chopped
1	pound mushrooms, chopped
1	teaspoon dried thyme
	Salt and ground black pepper
2	tablespoons unbleached flour
3	tablespoons nonfat sour cream
3	tablespoons dry sherry or nonalcoholic white wine
1½	cups shredded part-skim provolone, Swiss, or mozzarella cheese

To make the dough: In a large bowl, combine the water, yeast, and honey or sugar. Set aside for 5 minutes, or until foamy.

Add the whole-wheat flour or unbleached flour, salt, and oil. Using an electric mixer, beat well for 3 minutes (or beat vigorously by hand for 5 minutes). Stir in 2 cups of the unbleached flour.

Turn out onto a floured surface and knead in enough of the remaining unbleached flour to form a very soft dough (be careful not to add too much flour). Knead for 10 minutes, or until smooth and elastic. Form the dough into a ball.

Coat a large bowl with no-stick spray. Add the dough and turn to coat all sides. Cover and let rise in a warm place for about 45 minutes, or until doubled in size.

Coat a baking sheet with no-stick spray.

Punch down the dough and divide into 6 pieces. On a floured work surface, roll or pat each piece into a 7" circle (see top illustration on page 287).

To make the filling: Melt the butter or margarine in a large no-stick skillet over medium heat. Add the onions and garlic. Cook for 3 minutes. Add the mushrooms and thyme. Season with the salt and pepper. Cook for 15 minutes, or until all of the liquid has evaporated. Stir in the flour. Remove from the heat and stir in the sour cream. Transfer to a bowl and set aside to cool.

Return the skillet to the heat and add the sherry or wine. Cook and stir for 2 minutes to deglaze the pan. Pour the pan juices over the mushrooms. Stir in the provolone, Swiss, or mozzarella and mix well.

Preheat the oven to 375°F.

Spread an equal amount of the filling on half of each piece of dough. Fold the dough over the filling and pinch the edges to seal (see middle illustration on page 287).

Place the calzones on the prepared baking sheet and cut 2 slits on the top of each one (see bottom illustration on page 287). Coat each with no-stick spray. Bake on the bottom rack of the oven for 30 minutes, or until the crust is lightly browned. Cool slightly before serving.

COOKING HINT

- Keep these calzones on hand for no-fuss lunches or suppers. Wrap extra calzones in foil and refrigerate for up to 1 week or freeze for up to 1 month. If frozen, thaw the calzones. Reheat in a 350°F oven for 20 minutes, or until the filling is hot.

ROASTED EGGPLANT AND POLENTA PARMESAN

Polenta is an Italian porridge made from cornmeal and water. It firms up while cooling, so I spread it into a baking dish to make a soft-bottom crust for low-fat eggplant Parmesan. Rather than fry the eggplant in oceans of oil, I roast it.

HANDS-ON TIME: 45 MINUTES
UNATTENDED TIME: 50 MINUTES

MAKES 6 SERVINGS
PER SERVING
321	CALORIES
10.1 G.	TOTAL FAT
4.3 G.	SATURATED FAT
22 G.	PROTEIN
39.4 G.	CARBOHYDRATES
4.8 G.	DIETARY FIBER
53 MG.	CHOLESTEROL
837 MG.	SODIUM

3⅓	cups water
1	cup coarse cornmeal
	Salt
2	medium eggplants, peeled and cut into ½" slices
1	tablespoon olive oil
1	onion, chopped
5	cloves garlic, minced
1	can (28 ounces) crushed tomatoes
½	cup packed fresh basil, chopped
2	tablespoons chopped fresh parsley
2	tablespoons tomato paste
	Ground black pepper
1	cup nonfat or low-fat ricotta cheese
4	ounces nonfat cream cheese
1	egg
½	cup grated Parmesan cheese
1	cup shredded part–skim milk mozzarella cheese

Coat an 11" × 7" baking dish with no-stick spray.

Bring the water to a boil in a large saucepan. Gradually whisk in the cornmeal and ½ teaspoon salt. Reduce the heat to medium-low. Cook and stir with a wooden spoon for 10 to 15 minutes, or until the mixture is thick enough for the spoon to stand upright. Spread half of the polenta in the bottom of the prepared baking dish. Refrigerate until ready to use. On a piece of foil coated with no-stick spray, spread the remaining polenta into a flat 11" × 7" rectangle. Refrigerate until ready to use.

Preheat the oven to 500°F. Coat 2 baking sheets with no-stick spray. Place the eggplant in a single layer on the prepared baking sheets. Coat with no-stick spray and sprinkle lightly with salt. Bake for 10 minutes. Turn the slices, coat with no-stick spray, and bake for 10 minutes.

Reduce the oven temperature to 375°F.

Warm the oil in a medium saucepan over medium heat. Add the onions and garlic. Cook for 5 minutes. Add the tomatoes, basil, parsley, and tomato paste. Season with the salt and pepper. Reduce the heat to low. Cover and cook for 10 minutes.

In a medium bowl, combine the ricotta, cream cheese, egg, and Parmesan. Using an electric mixer, beat until smooth.

Remove the baking dish from the refrigerator. Spread 1 cup of the tomato sauce over the polenta. Layer with half of the eggplant. Top with half of the ricotta mixture. Spread with another 1 cup of the sauce. Continue layering with the remaining eggplant and ricotta mixture. Carefully slide the reserved polenta on top. Discard the foil. Spread with the remaining sauce and sprinkle with the mozzarella.

Bake for 35 minutes, or until the cheese is melted and the sauce is bubbling. Cool for 15 minutes before serving.

COOKING HINT

- Cornmeal for polenta is more coarse than the type used for cornbread. It's available near the rice and grains in your grocery store and may be labeled "polenta," "corn grits," or "coarsely ground cornmeal."

SEAFOOD CANNELLONI WITH PINK SAUCE

Seafood and cheeses make a delicious stuffing for cannelloni. Fresh lasagna sheets taste best here, but you can substitute dry cannelloni or manicotti shells. Cook the shells according to the package directions before stuffing.

HANDS-ON TIME: 35 MINUTES
UNATTENDED TIME: 30 MINUTES

MAKES 10 SERVINGS
PER SERVING
286   CALORIES
4.6 G.   TOTAL FAT
1.5 G.   SATURATED FAT
31 G.   PROTEIN
31 G.   CARBOHYDRATES
2.5 G.   DIETARY FIBER
85 MG.   CHOLESTEROL
650 MG.   SODIUM

3   cups fat-free tomato sauce
2   cans (12 ounces each) evaporated skim milk
1   salmon fillet (8 ounces)
    Lemon juice
8   ounces sea scallops
8   ounces rock shrimp or small shrimp, peeled and deveined
1   egg
1   container (15 ounces) nonfat or low-fat ricotta cheese
½   cup shredded reduced-fat Havarti or mozzarella cheese
2   tablespoons chopped fresh parsley
1   teaspoon grated lemon rind
½   teaspoon garlic powder
    Salt and ground black pepper
12 ounces fresh lasagna sheets (about ten 7" × 4" sheets)
¼   cup grated Parmesan cheese

In a medium saucepan, combine the tomato sauce and milk. Cook and stir over low heat until heated through.

Preheat the broiler. Coat the broiler pan with no-stick spray. Place the salmon on the prepared pan and sprinkle with lemon juice. Cook for 10 minutes per 1" thickness of fish, or until the fish just begins to flake when tested with a fork. Keep the salmon on the pan and finish cooking with the shellfish. Sprinkle the scallops and shrimp with lemon juice and place on the broiler pan with the salmon. Cook for 2 to 3 minutes, or until the scallops and shrimp are cooked through. Transfer the seafood to a plate.

Place the egg in a large bowl. Stir with a fork to beat lightly. Add the ricotta, Havarti or mozzarella, parsley, lemon rind, and garlic powder. Season with the salt and

pepper. Mix well. Cut the seafood into bite-size pieces and stir into the ricotta mixture.

Spread 2 cups of the sauce over the bottom of a 10" × 15" baking dish.

Place about 1 cup of the seafood mixture down the center of 1 lasagna sheet. Gently roll up the sheet crosswise to make a large tube. If necessary, spoon additional filling into the ends of the tube. Place the cannelloni, seam side down, in the prepared baking dish. Repeat with the remaining pasta and filling. Allow a small space between the cannelloni as you place them in the dish.

Reduce the oven temperature to 350°F. Pour the remaining sauce over the cannelloni. Sprinkle with the Parmesan and bake for 30 minutes. Cool slightly before serving.

ROASTED VEGETABLE QUESADILLAS

Quesadillas are Mexico's answer to American grilled cheese. Here, they're filled with roasted vegetables and cheese, then topped with lime-spiked nonfat sour cream.

HANDS-ON TIME: 20 MINUTES
UNATTENDED TIME: 30 MINUTES

TOPPING

½	cup nonfat sour cream
1	teaspoon lime juice
½	teaspoon ground cumin
¼	teaspoon grated lime rind

FILLING

1⅓	cups chopped asparagus
1⅓	cups chopped sweet red pepper
1⅓	cups chopped yellow squash or zucchini
1	large red onion, sliced
1	teaspoon olive oil
	Salt and ground black pepper

QUESADILLAS

8	fat-free flour tortillas (6" diameter)
8	ounces shredded reduced-fat hot-pepper Monterey Jack or Cheddar cheese
4	teaspoons finely chopped cilantro (optional)

MAKES 4 SERVINGS
PER SERVING

386	CALORIES
11.8 G.	TOTAL FAT
6.3 G.	SATURATED FAT
29.1 G.	PROTEIN
49.9 G.	CARBOHYDRATES
13.3 G.	DIETARY FIBER
40 MG.	CHOLESTEROL
1,036 MG.	SODIUM

To make the topping: In a small bowl, combine the sour cream, lime juice, cumin, and lime rind. Cover and refrigerate for 30 minutes or up to 24 hours.

To make the filling: Preheat the oven to 500°F. Coat a jelly-roll pan with no-stick spray.

In a medium bowl, mix together the asparagus, red peppers, squash or zucchini, onions, and oil. Season with the salt and black pepper. Spread in a single layer in the prepared pan. Bake for 15 minutes, or until tender and lightly browned; shake the pan halfway through cooking to turn the vegetables. Remove from the oven.

To make the quesadillas: Preheat the broiler. Coat a baking sheet with no-stick spray.

Place 2 tortillas, side by side, on the prepared sheet. Layer each with one-quarter of the vegetable mixture, 2 ounces

of the Monterey Jack or Cheddar, and 1 teaspoon of the cilantro (if using). Top each with 1 tortilla. Coat with no-stick spray. Broil 4" from the heat for about 2 minutes. Using a large spatula, carefully turn the quesadillas over and broil for another 2 minutes, or until the cheese has melted and the quesadillas are lightly browned (watch carefully to prevent them from burning). Remove from the oven and transfer to a plate. Keep warm.

Repeat with the remaining 4 tortillas, vegetable mixture, 4 ounces cheese and 2 teaspoons cilantro (if using).

Cut each quesadilla into wedges and serve with the topping.

COOKING HINTS

• If you've looked everywhere and still can't locate reduced-fat hot-pepper Monterey Jack cheese, use reduced-fat Monterey Jack and add 1 teaspoon chopped canned green chili or jalapeño peppers to each quesadilla.

• To cut the quesadillas easily, use a pizza cutter.

CORN AND POTATO ENCHILADAS

Tomatillo means "little tomato" in Spanish. These tasty green vegetables make a wonderful sauce for enchiladas. Look for them in the produce aisle of your supermarket. Or check the ethnic aisle for canned tomatillos. If you can't find them, replace the tomatillo sauce with your favorite salsa.

HANDS-ON TIME: 30 MINUTES
UNATTENDED TIME: 25 MINUTES

MAKES 6 SERVINGS
PER SERVING
352   CALORIES
11.2 G.   TOTAL FAT
4.4 G.   SATURATED FAT
18.6 G.   PROTEIN
47.9 G.   CARBOHYDRATES
2.1 G.   DIETARY FIBER
27 MG.   CHOLESTEROL
400 MG.   SODIUM

SAUCE

1   **tablespoon canola or olive oil**
1   **pound tomatillos, chopped**
1   **onion, chopped**
1   **green pepper, chopped**
2   **cloves garlic, chopped**
1   **jalapeño pepper, chopped (wear plastic gloves when handling)**
½   **teaspoon dried oregano**
     Sugar
     Salt and ground black pepper

ENCHILADAS

2   **potatoes, peeled and diced**
2   **cups part-skim hot-pepper or sharp Cheddar cheese**
1   **cup frozen corn kernels, thawed**
½   **red onion, finely chopped**
1   **tablespoon chopped fresh cilantro**
1   **small jalapeño pepper, chopped (wear plastic gloves when handling), optional**
¼   **cup nonfat sour cream**
12   **fat-free corn tortillas (6" diameter)**
     Low-fat sour cream (optional)

To make the sauce: Warm the oil in a medium saucepan over medium heat. Add the tomatillos, onions, green peppers, garlic, jalapeño peppers, and oregano. Cook for 10 to 15 minutes, or until the tomatillos are soft.

Transfer the sauce to a food processor or blender and process until smooth. Transfer back to the saucepan. Season with the sugar, salt, and black pepper.

To make the enchiladas: Place the potatoes in a medium

saucepan. Add cold water to cover. Bring to a boil over high heat. Reduce the heat to medium and cook for 10 minutes, or until just soft. Drain and place in a medium bowl. Add the hot-pepper cheese or Cheddar, corn, onions, cilantro, and jalapeño peppers (if using). Toss to combine.

Preheat the oven to 375°F. Spread ½ cup of the sauce on the bottom of a 10" × 15" baking dish.

Spread 1 tablespoon of sauce over each tortilla. Divide the ¼ cup sour cream among the tortillas, spreading it down the center of each. Top with the potato filling. Fold the sides of each tortilla over the filling and seal closed with a toothpick (see illustration on page 298). Place the tortillas, seam side up, in the prepared baking dish. Pour the remaining sauce over top, being sure to wet each enchilada. Remove the toothpicks. Cover with foil and bake for 25 minutes. Serve topped with the sour cream (if using).

SMOTHERED BURRITOS

Here's one of my favorite quick Mexican meals. Beans and vegetables are tucked inside tortillas, then blanketed with a lightly spiced tomato sauce. For variety, fill the burritos with whatever you have on hand—leftover chili and rice, cooked chicken, or cooked beans.

HANDS-ON TIME: 15 MINUTES
UNATTENDED TIME: 10 MINUTES

MAKES 6 SERVINGS
PER SERVING
317   CALORIES
5.9 G.   TOTAL FAT
2.1 G.   SATURATED FAT
19.1 G.   PROTEIN
55.7 G.   CARBOHYDRATES
11.1 G.   DIETARY FIBER
15 MG.   CHOLESTEROL
1,727 G.   SODIUM

SAUCE

1	cup water
¾	cup salsa
¼	cup tomato paste
¼	cup coarse cornmeal
¼	teaspoon chili powder
¼	teaspoon garlic powder
1	cup fat-free tomato sauce

BURRITOS

1	can (15½ ounces) reduced-fat chili beans
1	can (15 ounces) nonfat refried beans
¾	cup nonfat sour cream
6	fat-free flour tortillas (8" diameter)
2	cups chopped romaine lettuce
2	tomatoes, chopped
6	scallions, chopped
1½	cups shredded part-skim Cheddar cheese

To make the sauce: In a medium saucepan, combine the water, salsa, tomato paste, cornmeal, chili powder, and garlic powder. Mix until smooth. Stir in the tomato sauce. Cover and cook over medium heat for 10 minutes.

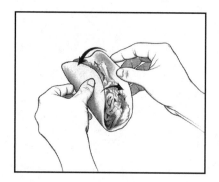

To make the burritos: In a small microwave-safe bowl, combine the chili beans and refried beans. Microwave on high power for 1 to 2 minutes, or until warm; stop and stir after 1 minute.

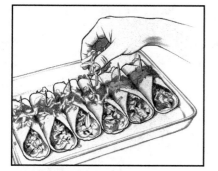

Preheat the oven to 350°F. Divide the sour cream among the tortillas, spreading it down the center of each. Top with the bean mixture, lettuce, tomatoes, scallions, and ¾ cup of the Cheddar. Fold the sides of each tortilla over the filling and seal closed with a toothpick. Place the filled tortillas, seam side up, in a jelly-roll pan. Top with the sauce. Sprinkle with the remaining ¾ cup Cheddar. Remove the toothpicks. Bake for 10 minutes, or until the cheese is melted.

SWITCH TIP

Two tablespoons of regular sour cream have about 60 calories and 6 grams of fat. Switch to nonfat sour cream and you'll dodge 30 calories and all the fat. Nonfat sour cream has the same creamy texture as the original, making it an easy switch for dishes where it's mixed in with other ingredients. Try a few different brands to find your favorite. If you're using nonfat sour cream as a stand-alone ingredient (on baked potatoes or nachos, for instance), spice it up with your favorite herbs and seasonings.

ASIAN POTATO DUMPLINGS

These savory dumplings are filled with spicy mashed potatoes, then steamed. Serve them with Asian Dipping Sauce (page 302). For a full meal, add to the menu some brown rice, sautéed spinach, and Asian Coleslaw with Orange-Ginger Dressing (page 165).

HANDS-ON TIME: 1 HOUR
UNATTENDED TIME: 30 MINUTES

MAKES 20
PER 5 DUMPLINGS
420   CALORIES
4 G.   TOTAL FAT
2.1 G.   SATURATED FAT
11.3 G.   PROTEIN
83.7 G.   CARBOHYDRATES
2.6 G.   DIETARY FIBER
9 MG.   CHOLESTEROL
441 MG.   SODIUM

DOUGH

2½	cups unbleached flour
¼	teaspoon baking powder
¼	teaspoon salt
¾	cup water

FILLING

1	pound potatoes, peeled and cubed
⅓	cup skim milk, warmed
1	tablespoon chopped fresh cilantro
2	scallions, finely chopped
1	tablespoon unsalted butter or canola oil
¼	cup chopped red onions
3	cloves garlic, minced
1½	teaspoons minced fresh ginger
1	tablespoon reduced-sodium soy sauce
½	teaspoon chili powder
¼	teaspoon salt
¼	teaspoon ground black pepper

To make the dough: In a medium bowl, combine the flour, baking powder, and salt. Make a well in the center. Slowly pour in the water while mixing the dough with a spoon. Add water as needed to form a smooth dough. Turn the dough out onto a floured surface and knead for 5 minutes. Cover with plastic wrap. Set aside for 30 minutes.

To make the filling: Place the potatoes in a medium saucepan. Add cold water to cover. Bring to a boil over high heat. Reduce the heat to medium and cook for 10 minutes, or until just soft. Drain and place in a medium bowl. Add the milk, cilantro, and scallions. Mash until smooth.

Warm the butter or oil in a small skillet over medium heat. Add the onions, garlic, and ginger. Cook for 5 minutes. Stir in the soy sauce, chili powder, salt, and pepper. Add to the potato mixture and mix well.

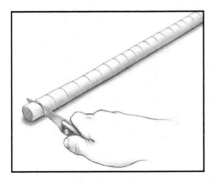

Shape the dough into a long log about 1" in diameter. Using a sharp knife, cut the log into 20 pieces. Cover the pieces of dough with plastic wrap. Roll or pat each piece of dough into a 3" to 3½" circle. The circle of dough should be thinner at the edges and thicker in the middle.

Place about 1 tablespoon filling in the center of each circle. Pull the sides of the dough up and around the filling and pinch closed in the center.

Place the dumplings in a single layer in a steamer basket (work in batches). Steam over boiling water in a large covered saucepan for 15 minutes. Remove the cooked dumplings and keep warm. Repeat until all the dumplings have been cooked.

COOKING HINT

- To save time, replace the dumpling dough with wonton wrappers. Look for them in your supermarket's produce section.

ASIAN DIPPING SAUCE

This mildly spicy sauce tastes great with Asian Potato Dumplings (page 300). It can also be used as an Oriental-style marinade for chicken. Or splash it over cooked rice or potatoes for a flavor boost. Customize the sauce to satisfy your own heat barometer by adding more or less of the chili-garlic puree.

HANDS-ON TIME: 10 MINUTES
UNATTENDED TIME: NONE

MAKES 1 CUP

PER TABLESPOON
20   CALORIES
1.8 G.   TOTAL FAT
0.2 G.   SATURATED FAT
0.3 G.   PROTEIN
0.8 G.   CARBOHYDRATES
0.1 G.   DIETARY FIBER
0 MG.   CHOLESTEROL
131 MG.   SODIUM

1	tablespoon canola or olive oil
3	tablespoons chopped onions
3	cloves garlic, minced
1	teaspoon minced fresh ginger
⅓	cup water
2	scallions, finely chopped
3	tablespoons reduced-sodium soy sauce
1	tablespoon toasted sesame oil
1	tablespoon rice vinegar
1	tablespoon chili-garlic puree
1	tablespoon chopped fresh cilantro
½	teaspoon sugar

Warm the oil in a small no-stick skillet over medium heat. Add the onions, garlic, and ginger. Cook for 5 minutes. Transfer to a small bowl.

Add the water, scallions, soy sauce, sesame oil, vinegar, chili-garlic puree, cilantro, and sugar to the bowl. Mix well. Store, covered, in the refrigerator for up to 1 week. Mix well before using.

CHICKEN TACOS

Tacos are fun to make and eat—my whole family loves them. We put the tortillas and fillings on the table so that we can each create our own. Try both the hard and soft-shell types of tortillas. These tacos taste great with Mango and Papaya Salsa (page 367).

HANDS-ON TIME: 20 MINUTES
UNATTENDED TIME: NONE

MAKES 12 SERVINGS
PER SERVING
202   CALORIES
5.2 G.   TOTAL FAT
1.4 G.   SATURATED FAT
14.8 G.   PROTEIN
23.7 G.   CARBOHYDRATES
1.2 G.   DIETARY FIBER
28 MG.   CHOLESTEROL
187 MG.   SODIUM

1	tablespoon olive oil
1	onion, finely chopped
2	cloves garlic, minced
1	jalapeño pepper, finely chopped (wear plastic gloves when handling)
3	cups shredded cooked chicken breast
¾	cup fat-free chicken broth or vegetable broth
½	teaspoon ground cumin
	Salt and ground black pepper
12	flour tortillas (6" diameter) or taco shells, warmed
2	cups chopped romaine lettuce
1	cup shredded part-skim sharp Cheddar cheese
3	tomatoes, chopped
¼	cup nonfat sour cream
	Salsa (optional)

Warm the oil in a large no-stick skillet over medium heat. Add the onions, garlic, and jalapeño peppers. Cook for 5 minutes. Add the chicken, broth, and cumin. Season with the salt and black pepper. Cook for 10 minutes, or until most of the liquid has been absorbed and the chicken mixture is fairly dry. Place in a medium bowl.

Fill the tortillas or taco shells with the chicken. Top with the lettuce, Cheddar, tomatoes, sour cream, and salsa (if using).

QUICK SWITCH

Vegetarian Tacos: Replace the chicken with 1 can (15 ounces) vegetarian refried beans. Include 2 cups cooked rice with the toppings.

Recipes

21

"Cooking is at once one of the simplest and most gratifying of the arts, but to cook well one must love and respect food."

—CRAIG CLAIBORNE, AMERICAN COOKBOOK AUTHOR

SLIM AND SAVORY CASSEROLES AND PIES

Casseroles and pies are synonymous with homestyle cooking. They make satisfying one-dish meals. They're the perfect way to use up left-over vegetables, pasta, grains, beans, fish, or poultry. And the steps are straightforward: Mix it up, pop it in a dish, and bake.

The best thing about pies and casseroles is that kids love them. My kids smile big when I tell them we're having Chicken and Chili Casserole, Baked Ziti, or Chili-Cheese Pie. Big-batch main dishes like these are comfort food for the whole family. If the dinner hour is the rushed hour, assemble the casserole ahead of time—even the night before—and refrigerate it until you're ready. Then just pop it in the oven. And leftovers make great lunches the next day.

Most of the recipes in this chapter are meals in themselves. A loaf of crusty bread may be all you need to complete the dinner menu. For extra-hearty appetites, round out the meal with one of the salads beginning on page 150.

BAKED ZITI

Here's a basic recipe that's open to endless variations. You can replace the ziti with rigatoni, penne, or other pasta shapes. Use whatever low-fat shredded cheeses and tomato sauce you prefer. And feel free to add things like spinach, roasted peppers, and herbs.

HANDS-ON TIME: 15 MINUTES
UNATTENDED TIME: 30 MINUTES

MAKES 8 SERVINGS
PER SERVING
366   CALORIES
7.2 G.   TOTAL FAT
4.8 G.   SATURATED FAT
28.6 G. PROTEIN
46.7 G. CARBOHYDRATES
2 G.   DIETARY FIBER
25 MG.   CHOLESTEROL
855 MG. SODIUM

12	ounces ziti
1	container (15 ounces) nonfat or low-fat ricotta cheese
¼	cup skim milk
1	tablespoon chopped fresh basil
1	teaspoon garlic powder
2½	cups shredded part-skim provolone cheese
¼	cup + 2 tablespoons grated Parmesan cheese
	Salt and ground black pepper
4	cups fat-free tomato sauce
	Dried oregano

Preheat the oven to 375°F. Cook the pasta in a large pot of boiling water according to the package directions. Drain.

In a large bowl, combine the ricotta, milk, basil, garlic powder, 1½ cups of the provolone, and ¼ cup of the Parmesan. Mix well. Season with the salt and pepper. Add the pasta and toss to mix.

Place 2 cups of the tomato sauce in the bottom of a 13" × 9" baking dish. Spread the ziti mixture on top. Add the remaining 2 cups sauce. Sprinkle with the remaining 1 cup provolone and the remaining 2 tablespoons Parmesan. Sprinkle with the oregano.

Cover with foil, tenting the foil to prevent the cheese from sticking. Bake for 30 to 40 minutes, or until the cheese is melted and the casserole is bubbling.

QUICK SWITCH

Baked Ziti with Turkey Sausage: Remove 8 ounces of turkey sausage from their casings and crumble into a large no-stick skillet. Cook until lightly browned and stir into the ricotta mixture. Proceed as directed.

ANGEL HAIR TORTE

This pasta dish looks impressive, and it's easy to make. Angel hair pasta is mixed with three cheeses, baked in a springform pan, then cut into wedges. It has a mild flavor that's perfect for brunch, lunch, or a light dinner.

HANDS-ON TIME: 15 MINUTES
UNATTENDED TIME: 35 MINUTES

MAKES 8 SERVINGS
PER SERVING
368   CALORIES
10.5 G. TOTAL FAT
4.5 G.   SATURATED FAT
27.6 G. PROTEIN
42.3 G. CARBOHYDRATES
0.8 G.   DIETARY FIBER
19 MG.   CHOLESTEROL
457 MG. SODIUM

1	red onion, chopped
4	cloves garlic, minced
12	ounces angel hair pasta
1	cup fat-free chicken broth or vegetable broth
1½	cups nonfat cottage cheese
1½	cups nonfat or low-fat ricotta cheese
¾	cup grated Parmesan cheese
½	cup chopped fresh parsley
2	tablespoons olive oil
2	teaspoons dried oregano
1½	cups shredded part-skim mozzarella cheese
	Ground black pepper
2	large tomatoes, sliced

Preheat the oven to 350°F. Coat a 10" springform pan with no-stick spray.

Coat a medium no-stick skillet with no-stick spray. Set over medium heat. Add the onions and garlic. Cook for 3 minutes, or until the onions are lightly browned and soft.

Cook the pasta in a large pot of boiling water according to the package directions. Drain and transfer to a large bowl. Add the onions, broth, cottage cheese, ricotta, Parmesan, parsley, oil, oregano, and ½ cup of the mozzarella. Season with the pepper. Mix well and pour into the prepared pan. Lay the tomatoes on top and sprinkle with the remaining 1 cup mozzarella.

Bake for 25 minutes, or until the cheese is melted. Cool on a wire rack for 10 minutes. Remove from the pan and cut into wedges.

BAKED GNOCCHI WITH PROVOLONE

Gnocchi are small Italian dumplings that you cook like pasta. They're usually served as a side dish with melted butter and grated cheese. But the gnocchi themselves are quite low in fat. Here, I use them as the basis for a quick casserole with tomatoes, basil, and cheese. Serve this dish with plenty of crusty whole-grain bread for dipping into the sauce.

HANDS-ON TIME: 20 MINUTES
UNATTENDED TIME: 25 MINUTES

MAKES 4 SERVINGS
PER SERVING
545   CALORIES
7.9 G.   TOTAL FAT
3.5 G.   SATURATED FAT
30 G.   PROTEIN
90.8 G.   CARBOHYDRATES
3.1 G.   DIETARY FIBER
17 MG.   CHOLESTEROL
611 MG.   SODIUM

1	tablespoon olive oil
2	shallots, chopped
4	cloves garlic, minced
1	can (28 ounces) diced tomatoes (with juice)
⅔	cup fat-free chicken broth or vegetable broth
½	cup dry white wine or nonalcoholic white wine
¼	cup chopped fresh basil
1	teaspoon sugar
	Ground black pepper
1½	pounds frozen or refrigerated gnocchi
1	cup shredded part-skim provolone or mozzarella cheese

Preheat the oven to 350°F. Coat a 2-quart baking dish with no-stick spray.

Warm the oil in a large saucepan over medium heat. Add the shallots and garlic; cook for 2 minutes. Add the tomatoes (with juice), broth, wine, basil, and sugar. Bring to a boil. Reduce the heat to medium-low and simmer for 10 minutes. Season with the pepper.

Cook the gnocchi in a large pot of boiling water according to the package directions. Drain and transfer to the prepared baking dish. Sprinkle with the provolone or mozzarella and toss lightly. Add the sauce and toss to mix. Cover with foil and bake for 25 minutes, or until the casserole is hot and bubbling.

SWITCH TIP

Among hard cheeses, provolone reigns supreme. Ounce for ounce, provolone has less fat than American, Cheddar, Colby, Monterey Jack, Swiss, and Muenster. And its pronounced flavor goes a long way in sandwiches and pasta dishes, so you don't need to use as much. Pick up some provolone to keep fat to a minimum while still enjoying the satisfying flavor of cheese. For the least fat, choose reduced-fat provolone.

Rustic Italian Pasta Bake

Most of these Italian pantry staples will be on your shelves.

Hands-on time: 20 minutes
Unattended time: 30 minutes

10	**sun-dried tomatoes**
1	**teaspoon olive oil**
1	**onion, chopped**
1	**green pepper, chopped**
8	**cloves garlic, minced**
1	**can (28 ounces) reduced-sodium tomato puree**
¾	**cup chopped roasted red peppers**
⅓	**cup chopped fresh parsley and/or basil**
2	**tablespoons dry red wine or nonalcoholic red wine**
2	**tablespoons drained capers**
1	**teaspoon dried oregano**
	Ground black pepper
12	**ounces ziti or penne**
1	**container (15 ounces) nonfat or low-fat ricotta cheese**
1	**can (15 ounces) artichoke hearts, rinsed, drained, and quartered**
1	**can (15½ ounces) navy beans, rinsed and drained**
2	**cups shredded part-skim provolone cheese**
2	**tablespoons grated Parmesan cheese**

Makes 8 servings
Per serving
455	CALORIES
6.5 G.	TOTAL FAT
3.6 G.	SATURATED FAT
31.5 G.	PROTEIN
71.8 G.	CARBOHYDRATES
6.1 G.	DIETARY FIBER
18 MG.	CHOLESTEROL
541 MG.	SODIUM

SWITCH TIP

Sun-dried tomatoes are fabulous flavor-boosters. They have a deep, concentrated tomato flavor and no fat—as long as they aren't packed in oil. Use them in pasta dishes, on pizza, or pureed in dips and spreads. Most grocery stores keep them in the produce section. Just soak the leathery tomatoes in hot water for 15 minutes, or until they're rehydrated. Then chop, slice, and use the tomatoes as directed. The soaking liquid can be used for soups, sauces, and dips.

Soak the sun-dried tomatoes in hot water for 5 to 10 minutes, or until softened. Drain and slice.

Warm the oil in a medium saucepan over medium heat. Add the onions, green peppers, and garlic. Cook for 5 minutes. Stir in the sun-dried tomatoes, tomato puree, red peppers, parsley and/or basil, wine, capers, and oregano. Season with the black pepper. Cook for 15 minutes.

Preheat the oven to 375°F. Coat a 4-quart baking dish with no-stick spray.

Cook the pasta in a large pot of boiling water according to the package directions. Drain and transfer to a large bowl. Add the sauce and mix well. Stir in the ricotta, artichokes, beans, and 1 cup of the provolone. Transfer to the prepared baking dish and sprinkle with the remaining 1 cup provolone and the Parmesan. Cover with foil and bake for 15 to 25 minutes, or until bubbly.

BROCCOLI AND CHEDDAR QUICHE

Ahh...to have the satisfaction of quiche without the fat. But who wants to give up on the homey smooth taste of eggs and cream? I certainly don't. So I use a combination of eggs, egg substitute, and evaporated skim milk. Sourdough bread stands in for the typical crust. The flavor is fantastic.

HANDS-ON TIME: 20 MINUTES
UNATTENDED TIME: 40 MINUTES

MAKES 6 SERVINGS
PER SERVING
219   CALORIES
7.3 G. TOTAL FAT
3 G.   SATURATED FAT
18.7 G. PROTEIN
19.1 G. CARBOHYDRATES
1.4 G. DIETARY FIBER
123 MG. CHOLESTEROL
648 MG. SODIUM

4	ounces sourdough or French bread, cut into ¼"-thick slices
1½	cups shredded part-skim sharp Cheddar cheese
3	cups broccoli florets
1	teaspoon dried fines herbes (see hint)
½	teaspoon garlic powder
3	eggs
1	cup fat-free egg substitute
1	cup evaporated skim milk
	Salt and ground black pepper

Preheat the oven to 350°F. Coat a 10" deep-dish pie plate with no-stick spray.

Line the pie plate with the bread, cutting the slices to fit and using small pieces to fill any empty spaces. Sprinkle with ¼ cup of the Cheddar.

Place the broccoli in a steamer basket. Steam over boiling water in a large covered saucepan for 3 to 5 minutes, or until bright green and crisp-tender.

Arrange the broccoli in the pie plate. Sprinkle with the fines herbes, garlic powder, and the remaining 1¼ cups Cheddar.

Place the eggs in a medium bowl. Whisk well to combine. Whisk in the egg substitute and milk. Season with the salt and pepper. Pour over the broccoli.

Bake for 30 to 35 minutes, or until the eggs are set. Cool on a wire rack for 10 to 15 minutes before slicing.

COOKING HINT

- Fines herbes is a classic French combination of herbs, including parsley, chives, tarragon, and chervil. If you have all these herbs, make up a batch of fines herbes to keep on hand. Otherwise, look for fines herbes in the spice aisle of your supermarket.

QUICK SWITCHES

Cauliflower and Swiss Quiche: Replace the broccoli with cauliflower florets and the Cheddar cheese with part-skim Swiss.

Chicken and Roasted-Pepper Quiche: Replace the broccoli with 2 cups diced cooked chicken. Add 1 cup roasted red pepper slices along with the fines herbes and garlic powder.

SWITCH TIP

A slice of traditional quiche contains about 48 grams of fat—28 of which are artery-clogging saturated fat. That's more than half a day's worth of total fat and more than a whole day's worth of saturated fat for most people. Quiche also has more than 500 calories and about 258 milligrams of cholesterol (almost a day's worth). But you don't have to give up quiche. This Broccoli and Cheddar Quiche has only 200 calories and 7 grams of fat per generous serving. I reduced fat and cholesterol by using a combination of whole eggs, fat-free egg substitute, evaporated skim milk, part-skim Cheddar cheese, and soudough bread instead of the usual high-fat pie crust. To slim down your favorite egg-cream-and-cheese casseroles, replace some of the eggs with egg substitute, switch from heavy cream to creamy evaporated skim milk, and use part skim–milk cheese.

WHITE VEGETABLE LASAGNA

A clever combination of low-fat cheese, nonfat sour cream, and skim milk saves a load of fat in this creamy entrée. Your taste buds will swear that they are in Little Italy.

HANDS-ON TIME: 35 MINUTES
UNATTENDED TIME: 1 HOUR

1	package (10 ounces) frozen chopped spinach, thawed
1	container (15 ounces) nonfat or low-fat ricotta cheese
1	cup fat-free egg substitute
¼	cup chopped fresh basil
1	teaspoon grated lemon rind
1	onion, chopped
8	ounces mushrooms, chopped
2	cups chopped zucchini
1	cup small broccoli florets
4	cloves garlic, minced
	Salt and ground black pepper
¼	cup whole-wheat pastry flour or unbleached flour
1	can (12 ounces) evaporated skim milk
¼	cup nonfat sour cream
1½	pounds fresh lasagna noodles (about twenty 7" × 4" sheets); see hint
2	cups shredded part-skim mozzarella cheese
¼	cup grated Parmesan cheese

MAKES 8 SERVINGS
PER SERVING
426   CALORIES
10.8 G. TOTAL FAT
3.6 G. SATURATED FAT
29.9 G. PROTEIN
54.1 G. CARBOHYDRATES
5.2 G. DIETARY FIBER
20 MG. CHOLESTEROL
595 MG. SODIUM

Preheat the oven to 350°F. Coat a 13" × 9" baking dish with no-stick spray.

Drain the spinach and squeeze out the excess liquid. Transfer to a medium bowl. Add the ricotta, egg substitute, basil, and lemon rind. Mix well.

Coat a large no-stick skillet with no-stick spray. Add the onions and cook over medium heat for 2 minutes. Stir in the mushrooms, zucchini, broccoli, and garlic. Season with the salt and pepper. Cook, stirring occasionally, for 5 minutes, or until the mushrooms begin to release their liquid. Stir in the flour and mix well.

In a small bowl, combine the milk and sour cream. Whisk to combine. Stir into the skillet. Reduce the heat to medium-low and cook, stirring, for 2 minutes, or until the mixture begins to thicken. Do not boil.

Spread a thin layer of the vegetable sauce in the prepared baking dish. Place a double layer of noodles on top of the sauce. Top with one-third of the ricotta mixture. Sprinkle with ½ cup of the mozzarella. Top with one-fourth of the remaining vegetable sauce. Repeat the layering, ending with 1 layer of noodles, sauce, and mozzarella (the top layer will use more mozzarella and sauces than the bottom layers). Sprinkle with the Parmesan.

Cover with foil and bake for 50 minutes. Remove the foil and bake for 10 minutes. Let cool slightly before cutting.

COOKING HINT

- Fresh lasagna noodles are available in the refrigerator section of many large supermarkets. You can replace 1½ pounds fresh lasagna noodles with 1 box (16 ounces) dry lasagna noodles. Cook the dry noodles according to the package directions before layering in the baking dish.

SWITCH TIP

One whole egg contains 5 grams of fat and over 200 milligrams of cholesterol (more than two-thirds of the recommended daily limit of 300 milligrams). Egg whites, on the other hand, are fat-free and cholesterol-free. Egg whites also offer the binding and leavening properties found in whole eggs. When only a few eggs are called for, particularly in a crust or baked good, use just the whites. That simple act can considerably reduce your consumption of cholesterol.

TURKEY SAUSAGE AND SPAGHETTI CASSEROLE

This casserole is just as good as the original version, which featured pork sausage. Some taste-testers said that it was even better.

HANDS-ON TIME: 20 MINUTES
UNATTENDED TIME: 1 HOUR

12	ounces spaghetti
1	tablespoon olive oil
12	ounces turkey sausage, casings removed
3	cans (14 ounces each) diced tomatoes (with juice)
½	cup grated Parmesan cheese
2	teaspoons dried basil
1	teaspoon garlic powder
1	teaspoon dried oregano
	Ground black pepper
	Red-pepper flakes
½	cup nonfat cracker crumbs

MAKES 6 SERVINGS
PER SERVING
449   CALORIES
9.2 G. TOTAL FAT
2.4 G. SATURATED FAT
22.8 G. PROTEIN
68.6 G. CARBOHYDRATES
1.4 G. DIETARY FIBER
39 MG. CHOLESTEROL
879 MG. SODIUM

Preheat the oven to 350°F. Coat a 3-quart baking dish with no-stick spray.

Cook the pasta in a large pot of boiling water according to the package directions. Drain and transfer to a large bowl.

Warm the oil in a large no-stick skillet over medium heat. Crumble the sausage into the skillet. Cook and stir for 5 minutes, or until browned. Add to the spaghetti.

Stir in the tomatoes (with juice), Parmesan, basil, garlic powder, and oregano. Season with the black pepper and red-pepper flakes.

Pour into the prepared baking dish and top with the cracker crumbs. Coat the cracker crumbs with no-stick spray.

Bake for 1 hour, or until the crumbs are browned and the casserole is bubbling.

CHILI-CHEESE PIE

Serve this creamy pie in the Mexican tradition with Easy Black Beans (page 212) and Mexican Brown Rice (page 215).

HANDS-ON TIME: 15 MINUTES
UNATTENDED TIME: 35 MINUTES

1 cup corn kernels
1 cup shredded part-skim hot-pepper cheese or sharp Cheddar cheese
1 cup fat-free egg substitute or 4 eggs, beaten
6 scallions, chopped
2 teaspoons chopped fresh cilantro
2 fat-free flour tortillas (8" diameter)
2 cans (4½ ounces each) whole green chili peppers, drained

MAKES 4 SERVINGS
PER SERVING
177   CALORIES
4.1 G.   TOTAL FAT
2 G.   SATURATED FAT
14.1 G.   PROTEIN
22.5 G.   CARBOHYDRATES
5.9 G.   DIETARY FIBER
15 MG.   CHOLESTEROL
866 MG.   SODIUM

Preheat the oven to 350°F. Coat a 9" pie plate with no-stick spray.

In a medium bowl, combine the corn, hot-pepper cheese or Cheddar, egg substitute or eggs, scallions, and cilantro.

Place 1 tortilla in the pie plate. Top with 1 can of the chili peppers and half of the egg mixture. Top with the remaining tortilla, the remaining 1 can chili peppers, and the remaining egg mixture. Cover with foil and bake for 35 to 40 minutes, or until almost set. Allow to cool for 5 minutes before slicing into wedges.

GREEK MACARONI AND CHEESE

Traditional Greek baked macaroni, *pastitsio*, contains whole eggs, ground beef, butter, and whole milk. With the use of creamy evaporated skim milk, egg substitute, and ground turkey, you can avoid much of the saturated fat of the original and still enjoy delicious *pastitsio*. Add a salad with nonfat dressing to complete the meal.

HANDS-ON TIME: 20 MINUTES
UNATTENDED TIME: 45 MINUTES

MAKES 6 SERVINGS
PER SERVING
436   CALORIES
8 G.   TOTAL FAT
3.8 G.   SATURATED FAT
36.4 G. PROTEIN
52.8 G. CARBOHYDRATES
1.2 G.   DIETARY FIBER
46 MG.   CHOLESTEROL
592 MG. SODIUM

8	ounces macaroni
½	cup skim milk
1	cup fat-free egg substitute
1	teaspoon olive oil
1	small onion, chopped
1	pound ground turkey breast
2	tablespoons steak sauce
1	tablespoon chopped fresh parsley
¼	teaspoon ground cinnamon
½	cup fat-free tomato sauce
1	tablespoon unsalted butter or margarine
¼	cup whole-wheat pastry flour or unbleached flour
2	cans (12 ounces each) evaporated skim milk
	Salt and ground black pepper
½	cup grated Parmesan cheese

Preheat the oven to 350°F. Coat a 3-quart baking dish with no-stick spray.

Cook the macaroni in a large pot of boiling water according to the package directions. Drain and transfer to a medium bowl. Stir in the skim milk and ½ cup of the egg substitute.

Coat a large no-stick skillet with no-stick spray and place over medium heat. Add the oil and onions; cook for 3 minutes, or until the onions are lightly browned and soft. Crumble the turkey into the skillet. Add the steak sauce, parsley, and cinnamon. Cook for 5 minutes, stirring often to break the turkey into small pieces. Add the tomato sauce and bring to a boil. Remove from the heat.

Melt the butter or margarine in a small saucepan over medium heat. Stir in the flour until incorporated. Gradually whisk in the evaporated milk. Cook, whisking, until the mixture is slightly thickened. Remove from the heat and gradually whisk in the remaining ½ cup egg substitute. Season with the salt and pepper.

Spoon half of the macaroni mixture into the prepared baking dish. Sprinkle with ¼ cup of the Parmesan. Top with the turkey mixture. Add half of the sauce, the remaining macaroni mixture, and the remaining ¼ cup Parmesan. Top with the remaining sauce. Bake for 45 to 55 minutes, or until the casserole is heated through and bubbling.

COOKING HINT

• You can replace the ground turkey, steak sauce, and cinnamon with crumbled turkey sausage or chicken sausage.

CHICKEN POTPIE

Chicken potpie is the ultimate comfort food, but it's typically sky-high in fat. I've kept its soothing creamy sauce and satisfying crust by using evaporated skim milk instead of cream and layering a low-fat biscuit on top.

HANDS-ON TIME: 30 MINUTES
UNATTENDED TIME: 25 MINUTES

MAKES 6 SERVINGS
PER SERVING
436   CALORIES
9.5 G.   TOTAL FAT
4.7 G.   SATURATED FAT
34.3 G.   PROTEIN
55.8 G.   CARBOHYDRATES
8.9 G.   DIETARY FIBER
65 MG.   CHOLESTEROL
598 MG.   SODIUM

FILLING

1	tablespoon unsalted butter or canola oil
1	onion, chopped
1	sweet red or green pepper, chopped
4	cloves garlic, crushed
2	stalks celery, chopped
2	carrots, thinly sliced
8	ounces mushrooms, sliced
1	pound boneless, skinless chicken breasts, cubed
1½	teaspoons dried Italian herb seasoning
½	teaspoon dry mustard
5	tablespoons whole-wheat pastry flour or unbleached flour
1	can (12 ounces) evaporated skim milk
2½	cups fat-free chicken broth or vegetable broth
1	tablespoon dry sherry or nonalcoholic white wine
1	cup peas
	Salt and ground black pepper

CRUST

1¾	cups whole-wheat pastry flour or unbleached flour
1	tablespoon baking powder
1	teaspoon sugar
¼	teaspoon salt
2	tablespoons unsalted butter or margarine
1	cup nonfat or low-fat buttermilk

To make the filling: Coat six 2-cup baking dishes with no-stick spray. Place on a baking sheet.

Warm the butter or oil in a large saucepan over medium heat. Add the onions, red or green peppers, garlic, celery, carrots, and mushrooms. Cook for 5 minutes. Mix in the chicken, Italian herb seasoning, and mustard. Cook for 2 minutes. Stir in the flour until well-combined. Gradually stir in the milk and broth. Cook, stirring, for 5 to 10 minutes, or until the mixture has thickened. Stir in the sherry or wine and peas. Season with the salt and black pepper. Spoon the filling into the prepared baking dishes.

To make the crust: Preheat the oven to 400°F.

In a large bowl, mix the flour, baking powder, sugar, and salt. Using a pastry blender, blend in the butter or margarine until the mixture resembles fine crumbs. Using a fork, stir in the buttermilk until the mixture is just moistened. Drop the batter over the filling in the baking dishes.

Bake for 20 minutes, or until the filling is bubbling and the crust is lightly browned. Cool on a wire rack for 5 minutes before serving.

QUICK SWITCHES

Seafood Potpie: Replace the chicken with 1 to 1½ pounds mixed seafood. Shrimp, scallops, crab, lobster, cubed tuna, halibut, salmon, and whitefish work well.

Vegetable Potpie: Replace the chicken with 3 cups mixed vegetables or cooked beans. Potatoes, sweet potatoes, broccoli, cauliflower, green beans, corn, cooked white beans, and tofu work well. Replace the chicken broth with vegetable broth.

ROASTED ROOT-VEGETABLE PIE

This cool-weather entrée appeals to meat-eaters and vegetarians alike. Mashed potatoes surround a harvest of hearty root vegetables. Vary the vegetables to suit your tastes—you'll need about 6 cups. Serve with Fresh Cran-Raspberry Relish (page 366) for a note of sweetness.

HANDS-ON TIME: 45 MINUTES
UNATTENDED TIME: 45 MINUTES

MAKES 6 SERVINGS
PER SERVING
413	CALORIES
9.4 G.	TOTAL FAT
3.3 G.	SATURATED FAT
12.2 G.	PROTEIN
71.7 G.	CARBOHYDRATES
8.9 G.	DIETARY FIBER
13 MG.	CHOLESTEROL
224 MG.	SODIUM

PIE

2	sweet potatoes, peeled and cubed
2	parsnips, peeled and cubed
6	medium beets, peeled and cubed
2	onions, quartered
6	cloves garlic, halved
2	tablespoons olive oil
1	teaspoon dried thyme
	Salt and ground black pepper
5	baking potatoes, peeled and cubed
½	cup skim milk
2	tablespoons nonfat sour cream
1	tablespoon fat-free mayonnaise
1	tablespoon unsalted butter or margarine

GRAVY

1	tablespoon unsalted butter or margarine
1	cup finely chopped mushrooms
1	shallot, chopped
1	teaspoon dried thyme
3	tablespoons unbleached flour
1	can (12 ounces) evaporated skim milk
2	tablespoons dry sherry or nonalcoholic white wine
	Salt and ground black pepper

To make the pie: Preheat the oven to 500°F. Coat 2 jelly-roll pans with no-stick spray.

In a large bowl, combine the sweet potatoes, parsnips, beets, onions, garlic, oil, and thyme. Season with the salt and pepper. Divide between the prepared pans and spread evenly. Bake for 15 minutes. Stir and bake for another 15 minutes.

Meanwhile, place the baking potatoes in a large saucepan and add cold water to cover. Bring to a boil over high heat. Reduce the heat to medium-high and cook for 15 minutes, or until the potatoes are soft when tested with a sharp knife. Drain and place in a large bowl. Add the milk, sour cream, mayonnaise, and butter or margarine. Using an electric mixer or potato masher, mash the potatoes until smooth. Season with salt and pepper.

Reduce the oven temperature to 350°F. Coat an 8" × 8" baking dish with no-stick spray.

Spread a thin layer of mashed potatoes in the bottom of the prepared dish. Add the roasted vegetables and top with the remaining mashed potatoes. Bake for 30 minutes.

To make the gravy: Melt the butter or margarine in a small saucepan over medium heat. Add the mushrooms, shallots, and thyme. Cook for 10 minutes. Stir in the flour. Gradually whisk in the milk and sherry or wine. Cook, stirring, for 5 minutes, or until thickened. Season with salt and pepper. Serve with the pie.

COOKING HINT

- For the mushroom gravy, try a combination of portobello and button mushrooms.

SPAGHETTI SQUASH CASSEROLE

Never had spaghetti squash? Try it in this creamy vegetable-rich casserole. This dish is perfect for potlucks and makes a satisfying vegetarian entrée when served with a salad and crusty bread. Or have it as a side dish with chicken or fish.

1	medium spaghetti squash (about 4 pounds)
1	onion, chopped
1	sweet red or green pepper, chopped
6	cloves garlic, minced
8	ounces mushrooms, sliced
3	teaspoons dried Italian herb seasoning
½	teaspoon chili powder
2	cups shredded part-skim Cheddar, hot-pepper, or Swiss cheese
1	cup reduced-fat cottage cheese or nonfat ricotta cheese
½	cup nonfat sour cream
2	tomatoes, chopped
1	can (4 ounces) chopped green chili peppers, drained
½	cup corn kernels
	Salt and ground black pepper
½	cup nonfat dry bread crumbs
3	tablespoons grated Parmesan cheese
	Paprika

HANDS-ON TIME: 30 MINUTES
UNATTENDED TIME: 1 HOUR 5 MINUTES

MAKES 6 SERVINGS

PER SERVING
291	CALORIES
8.1 G.	TOTAL FAT
3.8 G.	SATURATED FAT
21.1 G.	PROTEIN
36 G.	CARBOHYDRATES
3.8 G.	DIETARY FIBER
24 MG.	CHOLESTEROL
824 MG.	SODIUM

Using a fork, pierce the squash in several places. Place on a microwave-safe plate. Microwave on high power for 20 to 25 minutes, or until the interior is soft when tested with a fork. Carefully cut in half. Set aside to cool.

Preheat the oven to 375°F. Coat a 3-quart baking dish with no-stick spray.

Coat a large no-stick skillet with no-stick spray and set over medium heat until warm. Add the onions, red or green peppers, and garlic. Cook for 5 minutes. Add the mushrooms. Cook for 10 minutes, stirring often. Mix in the Italian herb seasoning and chili powder. Transfer to a large bowl.

Stir in the shredded cheese, cottage cheese or ricotta, sour cream, tomatoes, chili peppers, and corn.

Scoop out and discard the seeds and stringy membranes. Using a fork, scrape the squash from the shell to create spaghetti-like strands. Add the squash to the cheese mixture and stir until well-blended. Season with the salt and black pepper. Transfer to the prepared baking dish.

In a small bowl, combine the bread crumbs and Parmesan. Spread over the top of the casserole and sprinkle with the paprika.

Bake for 35 to 40 minutes, or until bubbling. Cool on a wire rack for 10 to 15 minutes before serving.

TOSTADA PIE

This pie is a meal in itself. Make it as spicy as you like by using hot or mild salsa.

HANDS-ON TIME: 25 MINUTES
UNATTENDED TIME: 25 MINUTES

4	fat-free flour tortillas (8" diameter)
1	onion, chopped
2	cloves garlic, minced
1	teaspoon olive oil
1	pound ground turkey breast
1	teaspoon chili powder
1	teaspoon dried oregano
¼	teaspoon ground cumin
1	can (15 ounces) nonfat refried beans
1	can (4½ ounces) chopped green chili peppers
⅓	cup salsa
1½	cups shredded part-skim sharp Cheddar cheese
2	cups chopped romaine lettuce
2	tomatoes, diced
6	scallions, chopped
	Pickled hot or mild peppers (optional)
4	tablespoons nonfat sour cream
	Salsa (optional)

MAKES 4 SERVINGS
PER SERVING
477   CALORIES
10.1 G. TOTAL FAT
3.9 G. SATURATED FAT
39 G.   PROTEIN
48.1 G. CARBOHYDRATES
11.4 G. DIETARY FIBER
67 MG. CHOLESTEROL
851 MG. SODIUM

Coat a large no-stick skillet with no-stick spray. Place over medium heat until hot. Add 1 tortilla and cook for 1 minute per side, or until the tortilla is browned and firm. Remove to a covered plate to keep warm. Repeat with the remaining 3 tortillas.

Preheat the oven to 350°F. Coat a 9" pie plate with no-stick spray.

Coat the same skillet with no-stick spray. Add the onions, garlic, and oil. Cook over medium heat for 2 minutes. Crumble the turkey into the skillet. Cook, breaking up the pieces with a spoon, for 5 minutes, or until browned. Add the chili powder, oregano, and cumin. Mix well. Add the beans, chili peppers, and ⅓ cup salsa. Mix well.

Place 1 tortilla in the pie plate. Top with one-fourth of the bean mixture and one-fourth of the Cheddar. Repeat 3 times to use all the tortillas, bean mixture, and Cheddar.

Bake for 25 minutes, or until heated through. Using a large spatula, carefully transfer the pie onto a large serving plate. Sprinkle the lettuce around the sides of the plate. Top the pie with the tomatoes, scallions, and pickled peppers (if using). Cut into wedges. Serve with the sour cream and additional salsa (if using).

CHICKEN AND CHILI CASSEROLE

In the mood for a filling Tex-Mex meal? Try this tasty casserole of beans, vegetables, and chicken baked in a cornbread crust. While the casserole bakes, toss together a mixed salad to round out the meal.

HANDS-ON TIME: 25 MINUTES
UNATTENDED TIME: 35 MINUTES

MAKES 6 SERVINGS
PER SERVING
523   CALORIES
13.8 G.   TOTAL FAT
4 G.   SATURATED FAT
40.3 G.   PROTEIN
64.9 G.   CARBOHYDRATES
8.4 G.   DIETARY FIBER
75 MG.   CHOLESTEROL
935 MG.   SODIUM

FILLING

1	pound boneless, skinless chicken breasts, cut into bite-size pieces
½	cup water
1	onion, sliced
1	sweet red or green pepper, sliced
1	can (15½ ounces) low-fat chili beans or 2 cups vegetarian chili
1	can (4½ ounces) chopped green chili peppers

CRUST

1	cup whole-wheat pastry flour or unbleached flour
¾	cup cornmeal
⅓	cup sugar
1	tablespoon baking powder
½	teaspoon salt
1	cup skim milk
2	egg whites, lightly beaten
2	tablespoons canola oil
1	cup corn kernels
1½	cups shredded part-skim sharp Cheddar cheese

To make the filling: Coat a large no-stick skillet with no-stick spray and set over medium-high heat. Add the chicken. Cook, stirring, for 5 minutes, or until lightly browned. Add the water. Cover and cook for 10 minutes, or until the chicken is cooked through. Transfer to a large bowl.

Preheat oven to 425°F. Lightly coat a 2-quart baking dish with no-stick spray.

Wipe out the skillet and coat with no-stick spray. Set over medium heat. Add the onions and cook for 3 minutes. Stir in the sliced peppers and cook for 5 minutes, or until the vegetables are softened. Add the vegetables to the chicken

in the large bowl. Add the beans or chili and chili peppers and mix well.

To make the crust: In another large bowl, combine the flour, cornmeal, sugar, baking powder, and salt. Mix well.

In a small bowl, combine the milk, egg whites, and oil. Mix well. Stir into the flour mixture until the dry ingredients are just moistened. Fold in the corn.

Pour half of the crust batter into the bottom of the prepared baking dish. Sprinkle with ½ cup of the Cheddar. Add the chicken and bean mixture. Sprinkle with the remaining 1 cup cheese and top with the remaining batter.

Bake for 25 minutes, or until the crust is lightly browned. Cool on a wire rack for 10 minutes before serving.

COOKING HINT

- You can replace the chicken breasts with turkey or turkey sausage.

QUICK SWITCH

Vegetarian Chili Casserole: Replace the chicken with 1 pound cubed or crumbled tofu or tempeh. Homemade or canned meatless chili can replace the chili beans.

SWITCH TIP

Ground turkey breast makes a great low-fat alternative to ground beef. For meatballs and meat loaf, you can replace up to half of the ground beef with ground turkey without a noticeable flavor difference. Look for 100 percent ground turkey breast to get the leanest ground turkey available. Some packages of ground turkey contain the fatty dark meat and even some skin.

MEXICAN TORTILLA CASSEROLE

This is my version of what the Mexicans call chilaquiles (chee-lah-KEE-lays), a highly seasoned homestyle casserole. I use nonfat refried beans and a creamy tomato sauce, which I layer with baked corn tortilla chips. Serve this one-dish meal with crunchy vegetables.

HANDS-ON TIME: 50 MINUTES
UNATTENDED TIME: 30 MINUTES

MAKES 6 SERVINGS
PER SERVING
419   CALORIES
8.5 G.   TOTAL FAT
3.1 G.   SATURATED FAT
20 G.   PROTEIN
67.7 G.   CARBOHYDRATES
5.1 G.   DIETARY FIBER
20 MG.   CHOLESTEROL
995 MG.   SODIUM

RICE AND SAUCE

- 2¼ cups cooked brown rice
- ¼ teaspoon garlic powder
- 1 tablespoon chopped fresh cilantro
- ¾ teaspoon ground cumin
  Salt and ground black pepper
- 1 teaspoon canola or olive oil
- ½ onion, chopped
- 1 clove garlic, minced
- 1 can (14½ ounces) low-sodium diced tomatoes (with juice)
- ½ cup fat-free chicken broth or vegetable broth
- 5 tablespoons low-sodium tomato paste
- 2 teaspoons chili powder
- 1 teaspoon arrowroot or cornstarch
- 1 teaspoon water
- 1 cup nonfat sour cream
- 1 can (4½ ounces) chopped green chili peppers

FILLING

- 12 corn tortillas (6" diameter), halved and cut into 1" strips
  Salt
- 1 can (15 ounces) nonfat refried beans, warmed
- 2 cups shredded part-skim sharp Cheddar cheese
- 1 tablespoon chopped fresh cilantro

To make the rice and sauce: Place the rice in a medium bowl. Stir in the garlic powder, cilantro, and ½ teaspoon of the cumin. Season with the salt and black pepper.

Warm the oil in a medium saucepan over medium heat. Add the onions and minced garlic. Cook for 2 minutes. Add the tomatoes (with juice), broth, tomato paste, chili powder, and the remaining ¼ teaspoon cumin. Partially cover and cook for 10 minutes. Reduce the heat to low.

Place the arrowroot or cornstarch in a small bowl. Stir in the water to dissolve. Stir in the sour cream. Stir a small amount of the tomato sauce into the sour-cream mixture to warm it. Slowly stir the sour-cream mixture into the saucepan. Mix in the chili peppers. Season with the salt and black pepper. Cook just until heated through. Remove from the heat.

To make the filling: Preheat the oven to 500°F. Coat a baking sheet with no-stick spray. Place the tortilla strips in a single layer on the baking sheet. Coat with no-stick spray and lightly sprinkle with salt. Bake for 5 minutes, or until lightly browned and crisp. Remove from the oven and reduce the oven temperature to 375°F.

Coat a 2-quart baking dish with no-stick spray. Place half of the chips in the bottom of the dish. Spread half the beans over the chips. Top with half of the rice, ¾ cup of the Cheddar, and half of the sauce. Make another layer with the remaining chips, beans, rice, and sauce. Sprinkle with the remaining ¾ cup Cheddar. Bake for 30 minutes. Sprinkle with the cilantro.

COOKING HINT

- To make 2¼ cups cooked brown rice, bring 1½ cups water to a boil in a medium saucepan. Add ¾ cup brown rice and return to a boil. Reduce the heat to low, cover, and simmer for 30 to 40 minutes, or until the rice is tender.

RECIPES

"Cooking is like matrimony—two things served together must match."
—YUAN MEI, CHINESE POET AND SCHOLAR

EASY ADD-ONS

Side dishes are an important part of a low-fat meal. They help complement flavors, add color, and balance the meal nutritionally. Picking the side dish is sometimes half the fun of creating a menu. Here are a few matchups to get you started.

- Roasted Shallot Mashed Potatoes (page 347) have a deep, hearty flavor and a light brown color. They're best served with substantial dishes like Southwest Turkey Meat Loaf (page 276) or Marinated Tuna with Cherry Sauce (page 242).

- Light and soft Saffron Buttered Noodles (page 344) combine well with the mild flavors of Swordfish Stuffed with Basil Pesto (page 239) or Buttermilk-Batter Baked Chicken (page 264).

- Asparagus with Lemon-Hazelnut Sauce (page 336) has a subtle yet distinctive flavor. It works well alongside light dishes like Capellini with Scallops and Tomatoes (page 224).

- Italian Broccoli (page 332) is a perfect match to Pasta and Seafood Marinara (page 221).

For bean and grain side dishes, see the recipes beginning on page 204. If you're hankering for a savory snack, check out the recipes toward the end of this chapter, beginning on page 352.

ITALIAN BROCCOLI

Garlic and sweet red peppers breathe new life into steamed broccoli. This colorful dish goes with just about any entrée.

HANDS-ON TIME: 15 MINUTES
UNATTENDED TIME: NONE

1	large head broccoli, cut into florets
1	tablespoon olive oil
4	cloves garlic, thinly sliced
1	sweet red pepper, sliced
	Salt and ground black pepper
	Red-pepper flakes

MAKES 4 SERVINGS

PER SERVING

94	CALORIES
4.1 G.	TOTAL FAT
0.5 G.	SATURATED FAT
5.4 G.	PROTEIN
12.7 G.	CARBOHYDRATES
1.1 G.	DIETARY FIBER
0 MG.	CHOLESTEROL
37 MG.	SODIUM

Place the broccoli in a steamer basket. Steam over boiling water in a large covered saucepan for 3 to 5 minutes, or until bright green and crisp-tender. Transfer to a large bowl.

Coat a large no-stick skillet with no-stick spray. Add the oil and place over medium heat. Stir in the garlic and red peppers. Cook for 3 minutes. Add the broccoli and mix well.

Season with the salt, black pepper, and red-pepper flakes.

SESAME GREEN BEANS

These green beans have an Asian flair from the sesame oil and soy sauce.

HANDS-ON TIME: 20 MINUTES
UNATTENDED TIME: NONE

1	pound green beans, trimmed
2	teaspoons toasted sesame oil
1	clove garlic, minced
2	teaspoons reduced-sodium soy sauce
1	tablespoon sesame seeds
	Red-pepper flakes.

MAKES 4 SERVINGS

PER SERVING

61	CALORIES
3.5 G.	TOTAL FAT
0.5 G.	SATURATED FAT
2.2 G.	PROTEIN
6.8 G.	CARBOHYDRATES
0.2 G.	DIETARY FIBER
0 MG.	CHOLESTEROL
102 MG.	SODIUM

Place the beans in a steamer basket. Steam over boiling water in a large covered saucepan for 8 to 10 minutes, or until just tender.

Warm the oil in a large no-stick skillet over medium heat. Add the garlic and cook for 1 minute. Add the beans, soy sauce, and sesame seeds. Season with the red-pepper flakes. Cook for 4 to 5 minutes, stirring often.

GREEN BEANS WITH FETA AND WALNUTS

Many fat-watchers avoid cheese and nuts altogether. But what they save in fat they may lose in satisfying flavor. Here, just a touch of feta cheese and walnuts does wonders for steamed green beans.

HANDS-ON TIME: 15 MINUTES
UNATTENDED TIME: NONE

1   pound green beans, trimmed
1   tablespoon fat-free chicken broth or vegetable broth
1   ounce feta cheese, crumbled
2   tablespoons toasted walnut pieces

MAKES 4 SERVINGS
PER SERVING
69	CALORIES
3.8 G.	TOTAL FAT
1.2 G.	SATURATED FAT
3.4 G.	PROTEIN
7 G.	CARBOHYDRATES
0.1 G.	DIETARY FIBER
6 MG.	CHOLESTEROL
97 MG.	SODIUM

Place the beans in a steamer basket. Steam over boiling water in a large covered saucepan for 8 to 10 minutes, or until just tender. Transfer to a large bowl. Toss with the broth. Sprinkle with the feta and walnuts.

COOKING HINTS

- To toast the walnuts, place them in a dry skillet over medium heat. Cook, shaking the pan often, for 3 to 5 minutes, or until fragrant and golden.

- Here's how to trim green beans quickly. Line up the ends of 5 to 8 beans at a time. Using a large knife, slice off the ends of all the beans at once. Turn the beans around and repeat with the other ends.

Zucchini with Tomato and Herbs

You can never have enough zucchini recipes—especially during harvest time. Here, zukes are stewed in an Italian-style tomato sauce. This dish makes a great pasta sauce, too.

HANDS-ON TIME: 35 MINUTES
UNATTENDED TIME: NONE

1	tablespoon olive oil
1	onion, sliced
8	cloves garlic, chopped
4	medium zucchini, thickly sliced
¼	cup chopped fresh basil
1	teaspoon dried oregano
1	teaspoon dried Italian seasoning
1	can (14½ ounces) diced tomatoes (with juice)
1	cup tomato sauce
1	teaspoon sugar
½	teaspoon grated lemon rind
	Ground black pepper
	Grated Parmesan cheese (optional)

MAKES 6 SERVINGS

PER SERVING

79	CALORIES
2.6 G.	TOTAL FAT
0.4 G.	SATURATED FAT
2.9 G.	PROTEIN
12.7 G.	CARBOHYDRATES
2.5 G.	DIETARY FIBER
0 MG.	CHOLESTEROL
303 MG.	SODIUM

Warm the oil in a large no-stick skillet over medium heat. Add the onions and garlic. Cook for 3 minutes. Stir in the zucchini, basil, oregano, and Italian seasoning. Cook for 15 minutes, stirring often.

Add the tomatoes (with juice), tomato sauce, sugar, and lemon rind. Cook for 15 to 30 minutes, stirring occasionally. Season with the pepper. Sprinkle with the Parmesan (if using).

Cooking Hint

- A small amount of sugar can mellow bitter flavors. Add ½ to 1 teaspoon sugar to tomato sauces, cooked spinach, or some soups and stews to round out the taste.

ZUCCHINI-PARMESAN FRITTERS

Fritters are usually deep-fried, but a no-stick skillet and a small amount of butter or margarine make them golden and crispy with a lot less fat. For a main dish, serve the fritters with warm tomato sauce and side dishes of salad and bread.

HANDS-ON TIME: 10 MINUTES
UNATTENDED TIME: 20 MINUTES

MAKES 15
PER FRITTER

34	CALORIES
1.2 G.	TOTAL FAT
0.6 G.	SATURATED FAT
1.2 G.	PROTEIN
4.1 G.	CARBOHYDRATES
0.7 G.	DIETARY FIBER
16 MG.	CHOLESTEROL
71 MG.	SODIUM

3	cups shredded zucchini
	Salt
1	egg
¼	cup skim milk
¼	cup grated Parmesan cheese
½	cup whole-wheat pastry flour or unbleached flour
1½	teaspoons baking powder
¼	teaspoon ground black pepper
1	teaspoon unsalted butter or margarine

Place the zucchini in a colander and sprinkle with salt. Set aside to drain for 20 minutes. Rinse well with cold water. Press to remove any excess liquid from the zucchini.

Place the egg in a large bowl. Whisk lightly. Add the milk and Parmesan. Mix well.

In a cup, combine the flour, baking powder, and pepper. Mix well and stir into the egg mixture. Stir in the zucchini.

Coat a large no-stick skillet with no-stick spray and set over medium-high heat. Add the butter or margarine and allow to melt. Drop the batter into the skillet by rounded tablespoons. Smooth out the tops and cook for 2 to 4 minutes per side, or until lightly browned and cooked through.

ASPARAGUS WITH LEMON-HAZELNUT SAUCE

Asparagus is one of spring's first vegetables. This lemony sauce is a refreshing change from the heavy butter-and-cheese sauces that often accompany asparagus.

HANDS-ON TIME: 15 MINUTES
UNATTENDED TIME: NONE

15	hazelnuts
½	teaspoon grated lemon rind
¼	cup nonfat or low-fat mayonnaise
2	tablespoons lemon juice
2	tablespoons skim milk
1	teaspoon white-wine vinegar
	Salt and ground black pepper
1	pound asparagus

MAKES 4 SERVINGS

PER SERVING
64   CALORIES
2.7 G.   TOTAL FAT
0.3 G.   SATURATED FAT
3.5 G.   PROTEIN
9.2 G.   CARBOHYDRATES
0.5 G.   DIETARY FIBER
0 MG.   CHOLESTEROL
206 MG.   SODIUM

In a food processor or blender, combine the hazelnuts and lemon rind. Process until finely ground. Add the mayonnaise, lemon juice, milk, and vinegar. Season with the salt and pepper. Mix well. Pour into a small bowl.

Place the asparagus in a steamer basket. Steam over boiling water in a large covered saucepan for 5 to 10 minutes, or until tender. Transfer to a serving plate. Serve with the sauce.

COOKING HINTS

- Personal preference defines whether thick or thin asparagus spears are best. Both types should be bright green and straight with firm, compact tips.

- For a festive appetizer, steam the asparagus until bright green and crisp-tender. Serve the whole stalks standing in a tall glass with the sauce in a bowl for dipping.

FRESH CORN RELISH

This is a great end-of-the-summer recipe when fresh corn is plentiful. Its bright flavor pairs well with sandwiches, casseroles, and chicken or fish dishes. This relish keeps in the refrigerator for up to 3 weeks.

1	small red onion, quartered
½	sweet red pepper, sliced
1	small jalapeño pepper, seeded and chopped (wear plastic gloves when handling)
¼	cup fresh cilantro leaves
¼	cup fresh parsley leaves
¼	cup fresh basil leaves
1	tablespoon fresh dill
2	cloves garlic
4½	cups corn kernels
½	cup white-wine vinegar
¼	teaspoon ground cumin
¼	teaspoon ground turmeric
	Salt and ground black pepper

HANDS-ON TIME: 10 MINUTES
UNATTENDED TIME: 10 MINUTES

MAKES 4 CUPS
PER ½ CUP

33	CALORIES
0.4 G.	TOTAL FAT
0 G.	SATURATED FAT
1.1 G.	PROTEIN
7.8 G.	CARBOHYDRATES
1.2 G.	DIETARY FIBER
0 MG.	CHOLESTEROL
9 MG.	SODIUM

In a food processor, combine the onions, red peppers, jalapeño peppers, cilantro, parsley, basil, dill, and garlic. Process using on/off turns until finely chopped. Transfer to a large saucepan. Add the corn. Stir in the vinegar, cumin, and turmeric. Season with the salt and black pepper.

Cook over medium heat for 10 minutes, or until heated through. Serve hot or cold.

COOKING HINT

• If using fresh corn, you'll need about 5 ears.

BAKED WHOLE CAULIFLOWER

This dish makes a stunning presentation. Cruciferous vegetables like cauliflower (and broccoli, Brussels sprouts, cabbage, turnips, and radishes) deserve an extra-special place on your table since they're thought to play a role in reducing cancer risk.

HANDS-ON TIME: 10 MINUTES
UNATTENDED TIME: 1 HOUR

MAKES 4 SERVINGS
PER SERVING
74   CALORIES
4 G.   TOTAL FAT
2.2 G.   SATURATED FAT
5.8 G.   PROTEIN
6.4 G.   CARBOHYDRATES
5.5 G.   DIETARY FIBER
9 MG.   CHOLESTEROL
274 MG.   SODIUM

1	head cauliflower
½	cup fat-free chicken broth or vegetable broth
1	tablespoon unsalted butter or margarine, melted
1	clove garlic, minced
1	teaspoon dried basil
½	teaspoon grated lemon rind
¼	teaspoon salt
1	tablespoon grated Parmesan cheese
	Ground black pepper

Preheat the oven to 375°F.

Trim the cauliflower and cut out the core with a sharp knife. Place the head, right side up, in a glass or ceramic baking dish just large enough to hold it.

In a small bowl, combine the broth, butter or margarine, garlic, basil, lemon rind, and salt. Pour over the cauliflower, covering the top and sides. Sprinkle with the Parmesan. Season with the pepper.

Cover tightly with foil and bake for 1 to 1¼ hours, or until soft when tested with a sharp knife.

COOKING HINT

• Avoid cooking cauliflower in aluminum bakeware, which imparts a yellowish cast to the vegetable.

GLAZED BRUSSELS SPROUTS

Small, fresh brussels sprouts taste best. The larger they are and the longer they're stored, the stronger the "cabbagey" flavor becomes.

1   pound small brussels sprouts, trimmed
1   cup fat-free chicken broth or vegetable broth
½   cup dry white wine or nonalcoholic white wine
1   tablespoon unsalted butter or margarine
    Salt and ground black pepper

Cut an × into the root side of each brussels sprout.

In a large saucepan, combine the broth, wine, and butter or margarine. Season with the salt and pepper. Add the brussels sprouts in as much of a single layer as possible. Bring to a boil over high heat. Reduce the heat to medium-low. Simmer for 10 to 15 minutes, or until tender and most of the liquid has been reduced. Stir occasionally to coat the sprouts with the glaze.

HANDS-ON TIME: 20 MINUTES
UNATTENDED TIME: NONE

MAKES 4 SERVINGS

PER SERVING
100   CALORIES
3.7 G.   TOTAL FAT
2 G.   SATURATED FAT
4.4 G.   PROTEIN
11.3 G.   CARBOHYDRATES
0.1 G.   DIETARY FIBER
8 MG.   CHOLESTEROL
112 MG.   SODIUM

BRAISED RED CABBAGE

Parboiling red cabbage mellows its strong flavor. Here, it's braised with vinegar and brown sugar for a pleasant sweet-and-sour taste. For variety, add a teaspoon of caraway seeds.

1	head red cabbage, thinly sliced
1	tablespoon canola oil
1	red onion, chopped
¼	cup red wine vinegar
¼	cup dry red wine or nonalcoholic red wine
¼	cup packed brown sugar
1	tablespoon chopped fresh parsley
1	bay leaf
½	teaspoon dried thyme
	Salt and ground black pepper
	Balsamic vinegar

Cook the cabbage in a large pot of boiling water for 2 to 3 minutes. Drain.

Warm the oil in a large no-stick skillet over medium heat. Add the onions and cook for 5 minutes. Stir in the cabbage, vinegar, wine, brown sugar, parsley, bay leaf, and thyme. Cover and cook, stirring often, for 30 minutes, or until the cabbage is soft. Season with the salt, pepper, and balsamic vinegar. Remove and discard the bay leaf.

HANDS-ON TIME: 45 MINUTES
UNATTENDED TIME: NONE

MAKES 6 SERVINGS
PER SERVING
96	CALORIES
2.5 G.	TOTAL FAT
0.2 G.	SATURATED FAT
1.5 G.	PROTEIN
17.1 G.	CARBOHYDRATES
0.4 G.	DIETARY FIBER
0 MG.	CHOLESTEROL
19 MG.	SODIUM

ORANGE-GINGER BEETS

These beets grab "best of show" honors for color and flavor. They're served over their greens and topped with a spicy-sweet orange sauce.

HANDS-ON TIME: 15 MINUTES
UNATTENDED TIME: 25 MINUTES

1¾	pounds small beets with greens
1	tablespoon unsalted butter or olive oil
1	onion, thickly sliced
1	teaspoon minced fresh ginger
4	large cloves garlic, minced
¼	cup orange juice
1	teaspoon grated lime rind
1	teaspoon sugar
	Salt and ground black pepper

MAKES 4 SERVINGS
PER SERVING
111 CALORIES
3.2 G. TOTAL FAT
1.9 G. SATURATED FAT
2.6 G. PROTEIN
18.6 G. CARBOHYDRATES
0.9 G. DIETARY FIBER
8 MG. CHOLESTEROL
85 MG. SODIUM

Trim the greens from the beets leaving a ½" stem. Rinse and drain the greens.

Scrub the beets and place in a large saucepan. Add cold water to cover and bring to a boil over high heat. Reduce the heat to medium-low and simmer for 25 minutes, or until the beets are tender when pierced with a sharp knife. Drain and rinse under cold water, rubbing to remove the skins. Cut off the stems and discard. Cut the beets into cubes and place in a medium bowl.

Warm 1½ teaspoons of the butter or oil in a large no-stick skillet. Add the onions, ginger, and about one-quarter of the garlic. Cook for 5 minutes. Add the orange juice, lime rind, and cubed beets. Simmer for 5 minutes.

Warm the remaining 1½ teaspoons butter or oil in another large skillet over medium heat. Add the beet greens, sugar, and the remaining garlic. Cook until the greens are just wilted. Place the greens on the bottom of a shallow bowl. Top with the beet mixture. Season with the salt and pepper.

COOKING HINT

• If you can't find beets with their greens in your grocery store, use 1 pound beets and 10 ounces spinach.

SAVORY MUSHROOM PIE

Use a variety of mushrooms for the most flavor.

2	tablespoons unsalted butter or margarine
1	onion, finely chopped
2	pounds mushrooms, thinly sliced
2	teaspoons dried thyme
2	tablespoons dry sherry or nonalcoholic white wine
	Salt and ground black pepper
¼	cup unbleached flour
8	ounces phyllo dough (see hint)
2	egg whites, lightly beaten
4	tablespoons grated Parmesan cheese

HANDS-ON TIME: 30 MINUTES
UNATTENDED TIME: 45 MINUTES

MAKES 8 SERVINGS

PER SERVING

187	CALORIES
6.2 G.	TOTAL FAT
2.8 G.	SATURATED FAT
7.3 G.	PROTEIN
25.7 G.	CARBOHYDRATES
2 G.	DIETARY FIBER
11 MG.	CHOLESTEROL
215 MG.	SODIUM

Melt the butter or margarine in a large skillet over medium heat. Add the onions, mushrooms, and thyme. Cook for 10 minutes, stirring occasionally. Add the sherry or wine. Season with the salt and pepper. Cook for 2 minutes. Stir in the flour. Cook and stir for 5 minutes.

Preheat the oven to 350°F. Coat an 8" × 8" baking dish with no-stick spray.

Unroll the phyllo dough and cut the sheets in half to make 2 piles of square sheets. Cover one pile with plastic to keep it from drying out. Remove 1 sheet from the other pile and place it in the baking dish. Coat with no-stick spray. Top with another sheet and brush with a little of the egg white. Continue to layer the sheets, alternately coating each sheet with no-stick spray or egg white. Sprinkle with 2 table-spoons of the Parmesan.

Spread the mushroom mixture evenly over the phyllo. Sprinkle with the remaining 2 tablespoons Parmesan.

Uncover the remaining pile of phyllo. Layer over the mushroom mixture, alternately coating each sheet with no-stick spray or egg white. Tuck the edges of the dough down the sides of the pan. Coat the top with no-stick spray. Bake for 45 minutes, or until brown and crispy. Cool slightly before serving.

COOKING HINT

- To get 8 ounces of phyllo dough, cut 1 package (1 pound) of phyllo in half crosswise and freeze the remainder.

CHESTNUT STUFFING WITH TURKEY SAUSAGE

This stuffing fills a 2-quart casserole and an 18- to 20-pound turkey. Divide the recipe in half when you're not feeding a crowd.

HANDS-ON TIME: 15 MINUTES
UNATTENDED TIME: 30 MINUTES

1	loaf day-old bread, cubed
1	package (1 pound) cornbread stuffing crumbs
12	ounces turkey sausage, cooked and crumbled
2	tablespoons canola oil
2	onions, chopped
2	stalks celery, chopped
3	cups cooked chestnuts, coarsely chopped
1	cup dried cherries or cranberries
3	tablespoons chopped fresh parsley
1	tablespoon dried sage
	Salt and ground black pepper
4–6	cups fat-free chicken broth or vegetable broth

MAKES 12 SERVINGS
PER SERVING
371   CALORIES
6.2 G.   TOTAL FAT
1.2 G.   SATURATED FAT
13.3 G. PROTEIN
65.4 G. CARBOHYDRATES
2.5 G.   DIETARY FIBER
13 MG.   CHOLESTEROL
892 MG. SODIUM

Preheat the oven to 350°F. Coat a 2-quart baking dish with no-stick spray.

In a large bowl, combine the bread, cornbread crumbs, and sausage.

Warm the oil in a large no-stick skillet over medium heat. Add the onions and celery. Cook for 5 minutes. Stir in the chestnuts, cherries or cranberries, parsley, and sage. Season with the salt and pepper. Stir into the bread mixture.

Pour in enough broth to moisten the stuffing. Toss gently. Stuff the turkey and transfer the remaining stuffing to the prepared baking dish. Cover and bake for 30 to 40 minutes, or until heated through and lightly browned on top.

SWITCH TIP

Chestnuts are unique in the nut family because they are low in fat. One ounce of chestnuts has only 70 calories and half a gram of fat. Most nuts have about 170 calories and 15 grams of fat per ounce. To keep your holiday meals healthy, use chestnuts in place of other nuts in stuffings and casseroles.

COOKING HINTS

• If you're stuffing a turkey, use a little less broth because the bird will keep the stuffing moist. Place the stuffing in loosely so that it cooks all the way through. Do not stuff the bird until you're ready to roast it.

• If you don't have day-old bread, cut fresh bread into cubes and bake on a baking sheet in a 300°F oven for 15 to 20 minutes, or until dry.

• Shelled roasted chestnuts are available during the holiday season in many supermarkets.

SAFFRON BUTTERED NOODLES

Buttered noodles can pack a wallop of fat. Here, no-yolk egg noodles bathe in a rich-tasting sauce made with a small amount of butter or margarine and saffron. Add a few toasted pine nuts, if desired.

8	ounces no-yolk egg noodles
1	cup fat-free chicken broth or vegetable broth
1	tablespoon unsalted butter or margarine
2	teaspoons chopped fresh parsley
¼	teaspoon crushed saffron threads
	Salt and ground black pepper

Cook the noodles in a large pot of boiling water according to the package directions. Drain and place in a large bowl.

In a small saucepan, combine the broth, butter or margarine, parsley, and saffron. Cook over medium heat for 5 minutes. Pour over the noodles. Season with the salt and pepper. Toss well.

HANDS-ON TIME: 15 MINUTES
UNATTENDED TIME: NONE

MAKES 6 SERVINGS
PER SERVING

153	CALORIES
2.1 G.	TOTAL FAT
1.3 G.	SATURATED FAT
3.8 G.	PROTEIN
29.9 G.	CARBOHYDRATES
0 G.	DIETARY FIBER
5 MG.	CHOLESTEROL
57 MG.	SODIUM

SWITCH TIP

Egg noodles have 2.5 grams of fat per cup. That's not especially high, but if you add butter, sour cream, or cheese, the fat grams can add up quickly. Switching to yolk-free egg noodles saves those extra fat grams. (Topping the noodles with reduced-fat products helps keep the noodles healthy.)

ROASTED WINTER VEGETABLES

All side dishes should be this easy. You toss the vegetables with oil, salt, and pepper—then bake. Cut the vegetables into same-size pieces so they're done at the same time. For a more aromatic flavor, add sprigs of fresh thyme or rosemary to the mix.

HANDS-ON TIME: 15 MINUTES
UNATTENDED TIME: 30 MINUTES

MAKES 4 SERVINGS
PER SERVING
238   CALORIES
3.7 G.   TOTAL FAT
0.5 G.   SATURATED FAT
5.1 G.   PROTEIN
48.2 G. CARBOHYDRATES
7.9 G.   DIETARY FIBER
0 MG.   CHOLESTEROL
367 MG. SODIUM

2 potatoes, cubed
2 beets, peeled and cubed
1 large sweet potato or yam, peeled and cubed
1 onion, chopped
1 tablespoon olive oil
½ teaspoon dried rosemary
½ teaspoon dried thyme
½ teaspoon salt
   Ground black pepper

Preheat the oven to 500°F. Coat a 13" × 9" baking dish with no-stick spray.

Place the potatoes, beets, sweet potatoes or yams, and onions in the prepared baking dish. Add the oil, rosemary, thyme, and salt. Season with the pepper. Toss well. Bake, stirring occasionally, for 30 minutes, or until the vegetables are tender.

ROASTED NEW POTATOES

There's a secret ingredient in this recipe: your oven. Oven-roasting mellows the flavor of garlic and heightens the flavor of potatoes. Thyme adds a savory note. If you don't have thyme, use rosemary.

1½	pounds small potatoes, halved if large
8	cloves garlic, peeled
12	sprigs fresh thyme
1	teaspoon olive oil
	Salt and ground black pepper

Preheat the oven to 500°F. Coat a 13" × 9" baking dish with no-stick spray.

Place the potatoes and garlic in a single layer in the prepared baking dish. Add the thyme and oil. Season with the salt and pepper. Toss gently.

Cover the pan tightly with foil. Bake for 20 minutes. Shake the pan to turn the ingredients. Bake for 20 minutes, or until tender.

HANDS-ON TIME: 10 MINUTES
UNATTENDED TIME: 40 MINUTES

MAKES 4 SERVINGS

PER SERVING

190	CALORIES
1.4 G.	TOTAL FAT
0.2 G.	SATURATED FAT
4.4 G.	PROTEIN
41.2 G.	CARBOHYDRATES
0.1 G.	DIETARY FIBER
0 MG.	CHOLESTEROL
14 MG.	SODIUM

GARLIC MASHED POTATOES

Gobs of butter and cream can turn innocent potatoes into a side dish that you'd rather sidestep. To reduce the fat, use nonfat sour cream and skim milk for creaminess. Garlic adds a wonderful flavor. Adjust the amount of garlic to suit your tastes.

2½	pounds potatoes, cubed
4–8	large cloves garlic, minced
¼	cup skim milk, warmed
2	tablespoons nonfat sour cream
1	tablespoon unsalted butter or margarine
	Salt and ground black pepper

Place the potatoes in a large saucepan. Add cold water to cover. Bring to a boil over high heat. Reduce the heat to medium and cook for 15 minutes, or until the potatoes are tender when tested with a knife. Drain and place in a large bowl.

Add the garlic, milk, sour cream, and butter or margarine. Mash or beat with an electric mixer until smooth. Season with the salt and pepper.

COOKING HINTS

- For a more mellow garlic flavor, roast the garlic in a 500°F oven for 15 minutes before adding to the potatoes. Or add the peeled cloves of garlic to the boiling potatoes 5 minutes before the end of their cooking time.

- For more buttery-tasting mashed potatoes, use yellow-flesh potatoes such as Yukon gold.

QUICK SWITCH

Roasted Shallot Mashed Potatoes: Replace the garlic with 7 peeled shallots. Place the shallots on a small baking sheet and coat with no-stick spray. Roast in a 500°F oven for 10 minutes. Shake the pan and roast for 10 minutes more. Add to the potatoes along with the sour cream.

HANDS-ON TIME: 15 MINUTES
UNATTENDED TIME: 15 MINUTES

MAKES 4 SERVINGS
PER SERVING

315	CALORIES
3.4 G.	TOTAL FAT
2 G.	SATURATED FAT
7 G.	PROTEIN
66 G.	CARBOHYDRATES
0.1 G.	DIETARY FIBER
8 MG.	CHOLESTEROL
29 MG.	SODIUM

POTATO PANCAKES

These potato cakes are traditionally served during Hanukkah. They're also traditionally fried in oil. Here, the cakes are cooked in a no-stick skillet with just a smidgen of oil for substantial fat savings. Enjoy them any time of year.

HANDS-ON TIME: 10 MINUTES
UNATTENDED TIME: 15 MINUTES

MAKES 16

PER PANCAKE
72	CALORIES
0.7 G.	TOTAL FAT
0.2 G.	SATURATED FAT
2.2 G.	PROTEIN
14.7 G.	CARBOHYDRATES
2.1 G.	DIETARY FIBER
27 MG.	CHOLESTEROL
24 MG.	SODIUM

1	pound potatoes, peeled and shredded
2	eggs
1	onion, grated
2	tablespoons whole-wheat pastry flour or unbleached flour
½	teaspoon baking powder
	Salt and ground black pepper
1	tablespoon canola or olive oil (optional)
	Unsweetened applesauce (optional)
	Nonfat sour cream (optional)

Place the potatoes in a colander and drain for 15 minutes. Rinse under cold water and press out the excess liquid.

Place the eggs in a large bowl. Whisk lightly. Stir in the potatoes, onions, flour, and baking powder. Season with the salt and pepper.

Coat a large no-stick skillet with no-stick spray. Add the oil (if using). Place over medium heat until warm.

Drop tablespoonfuls of batter into the skillet. Spread the pancakes into 3" circles. Cook for 2 to 4 minutes per side, or until lightly browned.

Serve warm with the applesauce and nonfat sour cream (if using).

QUICK SWITCH

Sweet Potato Pancakes: Replace the potatoes with 1 pound sweet potatoes, peeled and shredded.

CHILI FRIES

These oven-baked fries can be made as hot or mild as you like. Adjust the amount of ground red pepper to match your flame factor.

HANDS-ON TIME: 10 MINUTES
UNATTENDED TIME: 25 MINUTES

1	tablespoon olive or canola oil
1	teaspoon garlic powder
1	teaspoon paprika
1	teaspoon chili powder
½	teaspoon sugar
	Salt and ground black pepper
	Ground red pepper
5	baking potatoes, cut into thin strips

MAKES 4 SERVINGS
PER SERVING
312   CALORIES
3.8 G.   TOTAL FAT
0.5 G.   SATURATED FAT
6.1 G.   PROTEIN
65.4 G. CARBOHYDRATES
6.5 G.   DIETARY FIBER
0 MG.   CHOLESTEROL
27 MG.   SODIUM

Preheat the oven to 475°F. Coat a jelly-roll pan with no-stick spray.

In a large bowl, combine the oil, garlic powder, paprika, chili powder, and sugar. Season with the salt, black pepper, and ground red pepper. Add the potatoes and toss to coat.

Spread the potatoes in a single layer on the prepared pan. Bake for 25 to 30 minutes, or until lightly browned.

Line a large serving bowl with several layers of paper towels. Transfer the potatoes to the bowl and serve warm.

COOKING HINT

- For extra-crispy fries, broil the cooked potatoes 4" from the heat, turning occasionally, for 2 to 3 minutes, or until browned and crisp.

QUICK SWITCHES

Herbed Fries: Replace the garlic powder, paprika, chili powder, sugar, and ground red pepper with 1 to 2 tablespoons chopped fresh thyme or rosemary.

Sweet Potato Fries: Replace some or all of the baking potatoes with sweet potatoes.

Tomato, Basil, and Roasted Pepper Toasts

These toasts are called bruschetta in Italy. They're topped with an Italian-style salsa and a sprinkling of mozzarella, then served warm. Try them as an appetizer or snack.

HANDS-ON TIME: 10 MINUTES
UNATTENDED TIME: 10 MINUTES

2	tomatoes, diced
¼	cup chopped roasted red peppers
2	tablespoons grated Parmesan cheese
2	tablespoons chopped fresh basil and/or parsley
1	tablespoon olive oil
1	clove garlic, minced
	Salt and ground black pepper
12	slices ½" thick whole-grain or sourdough Italian bread
¾	cup shredded part-skim mozzarella cheese

MAKES 12

PER TOAST
88	CALORIES
3.1 G.	TOTAL FAT
1.2 G.	SATURATED FAT
4 G.	PROTEIN
11.4 G.	CARBOHYDRATES
1.4 G.	DIETARY FIBER
5 MG.	CHOLESTEROL
154 MG.	SODIUM

Preheat the oven to 375°F.

In a small bowl, combine the tomatoes, red peppers, Parmesan, basil and/or parsley, oil, and garlic. Season with the salt and black pepper. Mix well.

Place the bread on a baking sheet in a single layer and bake for 10 minutes, or until the edges begin to brown.

Preheat the broiler.

Spoon the tomato mixture onto the bread. Sprinkle with the mozzarella. Broil 4" from the heat for 2 to 4 minutes, or until the cheese is melted.

COOKING HINT

• These nibbles are incredibly versatile. Here are a few possibilities: Substitute crumbled feta cheese and capers for the roasted peppers and Parmesan cheese. Or substitute goat cheese for the roasted peppers and Parmesan cheese. Or substitute chopped roasted vegetables for the tomatoes and roasted peppers.

GARLIC CROUTONS

Looking to perk up that salad or soup? Here's a low-fat crouton that'll do the trick. I've been a miser with the oil, keeping fat down to about 1 gram per serving. Store the croutons in an airtight container and they'll last for weeks. For variety, add grated Parmesan cheese and crumbled dried herbs before baking.

HANDS-ON TIME: 10 MINUTES
UNATTENDED TIME: 15 MINUTES

MAKES 14 CUPS
PER ⅓ CUP

35	CALORIES
1.3 G.	TOTAL FAT
0.2 G.	SATURATED FAT
0.8 G.	PROTEIN
5 G.	CARBOHYDRATES
0 G.	DIETARY FIBER
0 MG.	CHOLESTEROL
57 MG.	SODIUM

3   **tablespoons olive oil**
5   **cloves garlic, crushed**
14   **cups cubed day-old sourdough baguette**

Preheat the oven to 375°F. Coat 2 jelly-roll pans with no-stick spray.

In a cup, combine the oil and garlic.

Place the bread in a very large bowl. Slowly drizzle the oil and garlic mixture over the bread, using a fork to toss as you mix. Toss until well-coated.

Spread the bread onto the prepared pans and coat with no-stick spray. Bake, stirring often, for 15 to 20 minutes, or until lightly browned. Cool completely.

COOKING HINT

• To use fresh bread, cut it into cubes and bake it on baking sheets in a 300°F oven for 15 to 20 minutes, or until dry.

CRUNCHY PITA STRIPS

Here's a nifty snack to munch on or dunk into your favorite dip. My kids love them straight from the jar. To vary the flavor, replace the garlic with chili powder, cumin, curry powder, Parmesan cheese, or ground red pepper. They're good plain, too.

HANDS-ON TIME: 15 MINUTES
UNATTENDED TIME: NONE

MAKES ABOUT 3 CUPS
PER ¼ CUP

38	CALORIES
1.4 G.	TOTAL FAT
0.2 G.	SATURATED FAT
1 G.	PROTEIN
0 G.	DIETARY FIBER
5.9 G.	CARBOHYDRATES
0 MG.	CHOLESTEROL
57 MG.	SODIUM

2	whole-wheat pita breads, halved
1	tablespoon olive oil
	Garlic powder
	Salt and ground black pepper

Preheat the oven to 350°F. Coat a baking sheet with no-stick spray.

Using a sharp knife, cut the pita breads apart at their outer edges to form 8 half-circles. Slice into ¼" strips, cutting the longer strips in half. Place in a large bowl.

Drizzle with the oil and toss well. Season with the garlic powder, salt, and pepper.

Spread the strips in a single layer on the prepared baking sheet. Coat the strips with no-stick spray. Bake for 5 minutes. Turn the strips over and bake for 5 minutes, or until just beginning to brown. Cool completely. Store in airtight containers.

SEASONED TORTILLA CHIPS

Chip-aholics unite! Here's a low-fat alternative to greasy, oversalted packaged snacks. Add a pinch or two of ground red pepper for more punch.

HANDS-ON TIME: 10 MINUTES
UNATTENDED TIME: NONE

10	**corn tortillas (6" diameter), halved and cut into 1" strips**
1	**teaspoon canola oil**
½	**teaspoon chili powder**
½	**teaspoon paprika**
¼	**teaspoon ground cumin**
¼	**teaspoon garlic powder**
¼	**teaspoon salt**
¼	**teaspoon ground black pepper**

MAKES 4 SERVINGS
PER SERVING
153 CALORIES
2.8 G. TOTAL FAT
0.3 G. SATURATED FAT
3.6 G. PROTEIN
29.6 G. CARBOHYDRATES
0.1 G. DIETARY FIBER
0 MG. CHOLESTEROL
237 MG. SODIUM

Preheat the oven to 500°F. Coat a large baking sheet with no-stick spray.

Place the tortilla strips in a large bowl. Drizzle with the oil, tossing to coat the strips.

In a cup, combine the chili powder, paprika, cumin, garlic powder, salt, and pepper. Sprinkle over the tortilla strips. Toss until well-coated.

Spread the strips in a single layer (they may overlap slightly) on the prepared baking sheet. Coat with no-stick spray. Bake for 5 minutes. Serve warm or cool completely and store in airtight containers.

QUICK SWITCHES

Cajun Tortilla Chips: Replace the chili powder and cumin with ground red pepper, onion powder, dried oregano, and dried thyme.

Curried Tortilla Chips: Replace the chili powder, cumin, and pepper with curry powder.

Indian Tortilla Chips: Replace the chili powder and pepper with coriander and ginger.

Italian Tortilla Chips: Replace the chili powder, paprika, cumin, garlic powder, and pepper with Parmesan cheese, garlic powder, dried oregano, and dried basil.

354

RECIPES

"The full use of taste is an act of genius."

—John La Farge, American artist and writer

Fat-Burning Dips, Spreads, and Sauces

Americans love to dip, dunk, slather, and splash. But most dips and spreads get their rich texture from high-fat butter, sour cream, cheese, or oil. To save the sauce and dodge the fat, look for lighter alternatives. Most salsas are naturally fat-free and high in flavor. Low-fat dairy products are also a tremendous help. They can create creamy dips and spreads that won't pack on the pounds. Nonfat cream cheese and a small amount of butter are the secrets to my low-fat butter spreads. They provide the rich, luscious texture of pure butter without all the saturated fat. Try these spreads on toast, crackers, steamed vegetables, pasta, or anywhere you'd normally use herbed butter.

To perk up sandwiches, try replacing the high-fat mayonnaise with savory spreads like Artichoke and Olive Spread or Roasted Red Pepper Hummus. If you need a little something to take to a friend's house, Smoked Salmon Mousse, White Bean and Walnut Dip, and Spicy Black Bean Dip can be prepared in minutes.

Looking for tasty, low-fat dippers to accompany these spreads and dips? Take a peek at the quick snacks in chapter 22.

HERB BUTTER SPREAD

My flavored "butter" spreads are a great low-fat alternative to butter. They have about half the fat of real butter and taste delicious. Spread them on bread, potatoes, or pasta. Or use them in place of butter to flavor rice and other grains.

HANDS-ON TIME: 5 MINUTES
UNATTENDED TIME: NONE

MAKES ½ CUP
PER 1 TEASPOON

27	CALORIES
2 G.	TOTAL FAT
1.3 G.	SATURATED FAT
1.4 G.	PROTEIN
0.5 G.	CARBOHYDRATES
0 G.	DIETARY FIBER
5 MG.	CHOLESTEROL
57 MG.	SODIUM

4	ounces nonfat cream cheese, at room temperature
2	tablespoons unsalted butter, at room temperature
2	teaspoons chopped fresh basil
2	teaspoons chopped fresh parsley
1	teaspoon chopped fresh dill
1	small clove garlic, minced
	Salt

In a food processor or blender, combine the cream cheese, butter, basil, parsley, dill, and garlic. Season with the salt. Process until smooth. Transfer to an airtight container and chill for up to 7 days. The spread will become firm as it chills.

PESTO BUTTER SPREAD

Fresh basil, nuts, and Parmesan cheese flavor this quick, savory spread. Slather it on crusty Italian bread. Or stir it into soups or pasta sauces for added flavor.

HANDS-ON TIME: 5 MINUTES
UNATTENDED TIME: NONE

MAKES ⅔ CUP
PER 1 TEASPOON

8	CALORIES
0.5 G.	TOTAL FAT
0.3 G.	SATURATED FAT
0.6 G.	PROTEIN
0.2 G.	CARBOHYDRATES
0 G.	DIETARY FIBER
1 MG.	CHOLESTEROL
24 MG.	SODIUM

4	ounces nonfat cream cheese, at room temperature
¼	cup chopped fresh basil
1	tablespoon chopped fresh parsley
1	tablespoon grated Parmesan cheese
1	tablespoon unsalted butter, at room temperature
2	teaspoons walnuts or pine nuts
1	small clove garlic
	Salt

In a food processor or blender, combine the cream cheese, basil, parsley, Parmesan, butter, walnuts or pine nuts, and garlic. Season with the salt. Process until smooth. Transfer to an airtight container and chill for up to 7 days. The spread will become firm as it chills.

MUSHROOM SPREAD

You can use mild button mushrooms in this spread. But why not go wild with flavorful varieties like porcini, portobello, shiitake, and cremini mushrooms? Use the spread with fresh bread, crackers, pita chips, or bagel chips. Neufchâtel cheese is a type of reduced-fat cream cheese.

HANDS-ON TIME: 15 MINUTES
UNATTENDED TIME: NONE

MAKES 1¾ CUPS
PER 1 TABLESPOON
43   CALORIES
2.2 G.   TOTAL FAT
1.4 G.   SATURATED FAT
3.6 G.   PROTEIN
1.7 G.   CARBOHYDRATES
0.1 G.   DIETARY FIBER
7 MG.   CHOLESTEROL
134 MG.   SODIUM

4   ounces mushrooms
1   teaspoon unsalted butter or margarine
1   shallot, finely chopped
      Salt
1   package (8 ounces) nonfat cream cheese
4   ounces Neufchâtel cheese
½   cup skim milk

Place the mushrooms in a food processor and chop finely.

Melt the butter or margarine in a large no-stick skillet over medium heat. Add the shallots and cook for 1 minute. Add the mushrooms and season with the salt. Cook for 10 minutes, or until all the liquid has evaporated.

In the food processor, combine the nonfat cream cheese, Neufchâtel cheese, milk, and mushrooms. Process until smooth. Transfer to an airtight container and chill for up to 4 days. The spread will become firm as it chills.

SWITCH TIP

Do you drink whole milk? Switching to low-fat varieties could save you up to 6 grams of fat per cup. A cup of whole milk has 8.9 grams of fat. Two percent milk has 4.7 grams. One percent milk has just 2.6 grams. For the most savings, go straight for skim milk. It has less than half a gram of fat per cup.

LEMON SPREAD

Trying to kick the peanut butter habit? Give this light, re-freshing lemon spread a try. It tastes great on fresh bread, bagels, and crackers.

HANDS-ON TIME: 5 MINUTES
UNATTENDED TIME: NONE

4	ounces nonfat cream cheese, at room temperature
2	tablespoons honey
1	tablespoon unsalted butter or margarine
1	tablespoon grated lemon rind
1	tablespoon lemon juice

MAKES ¾ CUP

PER 1 TABLESPOON

38	CALORIES
1.4 G.	TOTAL FAT
0.8 G.	SATURATED FAT
1.8 G.	PROTEIN
4.5 G.	CARBOHYDRATES
0 G.	DIETARY FIBER
4 MG.	CHOLESTEROL
76 MG.	SODIUM

In a food processor or blender, combine the cream cheese, honey, butter or margarine, lemon rind, and lemon juice. Process until smooth. Transfer to an airtight container and chill for up to 4 days. The spread will become firm as it chills.

COOKING HINT

- This spread really perks up a tuna fish sandwich. Spread it on the bread before adding the tuna.

ARTICHOKE AND OLIVE SPREAD

This is my version of a spread made with crushed olives that's popular in the Provence region of France. My lightened rendition uses high-flavor artichoke hearts and roasted peppers to cut the fat. With a food processor, you can make it in minutes.

HANDS-ON TIME: 10 MINUTES
UNATTENDED TIME: NONE

MAKES 2½ CUPS
PER 1 TABLESPOON

17	CALORIES
1.2 G.	TOTAL FAT
0.1 G.	SATURATED FAT
0.4 G.	PROTEIN
1.6 G.	CARBOHYDRATES
0.5 G.	DIETARY FIBER
0 MG.	CHOLESTEROL
135 MG.	SODIUM

1   tablespoon chopped fresh parsley
1   large clove garlic
1   cup pitted black or green olives
1   can (14 ounces) water-packed artichoke hearts, drained
½   cup finely chopped roasted red peppers
2   tablespoons drained capers
1   tablespoon lemon juice
    Ground black pepper

Place the parsley and garlic in a food processor or blender. Process using on/off turns until finely chopped. Add the olives and process until finely chopped but not pureed. Transfer to a medium bowl.

Place the artichokes in the food processor and process until finely chopped but not pureed. Add to the olive mixture. Stir in the red peppers, capers, and lemon juice. Season with the black pepper. Serve at room temperature. Store tightly covered in the refrigerator for up to 7 days.

ROASTED EGGPLANT SPREAD

Roasted eggplant has a smoky, mellow flavor. Fresh garlic gives it a little kick.

HANDS-ON TIME: 25 MINUTES
UNATTENDED TIME: NONE

1	medium eggplant, peeled and cut into 1" slices
1	clove garlic
¼	cup low-fat or nonfat mayonnaise
	Salt and ground black pepper

MAKES 1¼ CUPS
PER 1 TABLESPOON

14	CALORIES
0.8 G.	TOTAL FAT
0.1 G.	SATURATED FAT
0.2 G.	PROTEIN
1.7 G.	CARBOHYDRATES
0 G.	DIETARY FIBER
1 MG.	CHOLESTEROL
4 MG.	SODIUM

Preheat the oven to 500°F. Coat a baking sheet with no-stick spray.

Place the eggplant on the prepared baking sheet. Coat with no-stick spray and sprinkle with salt. Bake for 10 minutes. Turn the slices over and coat with no-stick spray. Salt lightly. Bake for 10 minutes.

Place the garlic in a food processor or blender. Process using on/off turns until finely chopped. Add the mayonnaise and eggplant. Process until smooth. Season with the salt and pepper.

Transfer to a medium bowl. Store tightly covered in the refrigerator for up to 4 days.

ROASTED RED PEPPER HUMMUS

Hummus, or chickpea spread, gets a whole new look—and taste—when the olive oil is replaced with naturally fat-free roasted peppers. For a satisfying snack, spread some hummus inside a split pita and stuff with tomatoes, thinly sliced onions, and sprouts.

HANDS-ON TIME: 10 MINUTES
UNATTENDED TIME: NONE

MAKES 2 CUPS
PER 1 TABLESPOON
83   CALORIES
3.4 G.   TOTAL FAT
0.1 G.   SATURATED FAT
3.6 G.   PROTEIN
10.1 G. CARBOHYDRATES
2.9 G.   DIETARY FIBER
0 MG.   CHOLESTEROL
160 MG. SODIUM

1   can (15 ounces) chickpeas, rinsed and drained
½   cup roasted red peppers
¼   cup packed fresh cilantro or parsley leaves
3   tablespoons lemon juice
2   tablespoons tahini
1   large clove garlic
⅛   teaspoon ground cumin
⅛   teaspoon ground coriander
     Salt and ground black pepper
     Hot-pepper sauce

In a food processor or blender, combine the chickpeas, red peppers, cilantro or parsley, lemon juice, tahini, garlic, cumin, and coriander. Process until smooth. Season with the salt, black pepper, and hot-pepper sauce.

Transfer to a medium bowl. Store tightly covered in the refrigerator for up to 4 days.

COOKING HINTS

- Tahini is a smooth paste made from ground sesame seeds. It's available in the international section of many supermarkets. Or look for it in Middle Eastern grocery stores.

- To roast your own peppers, see the tip on page 160.

- To use the hummus as a dip, thin it with 1 to 2 tablespoons of the chickpea canning liquid, defatted broth, or nonfat sour cream.

SMOKED SALMON MOUSSE

Mousse usually gets its silky richness from heavy cream. To trim the fat, I use a combination of nonfat and low-fat dairy products and plain gelatin. Try this high-protein snack with crackers, bread cubes, or crisp raw vegetables.

HANDS-ON TIME: 25 MINUTES
UNATTENDED TIME: 1 HOUR

MAKES 2 CUPS
PER 3 TABLESPOONS
41	CALORIES
0.7 G.	TOTAL FAT
0.2 G.	SATURATED FAT
6.7 G.	PROTEIN
1.4 G.	CARBOHYDRATES
0 G.	DIETARY FIBER
3 MG.	CHOLESTEROL
230 MG.	SODIUM

4	ounces smoked salmon
4	ounces nonfat cream cheese, at room temperature
2	scallions, chopped
8	chives, chopped
1	tablespoon lemon juice
¼	teaspoon grated lemon rind
	Ground black pepper
1	cup 1% low-fat cottage cheese
¼	cup skim milk
1	envelope unflavored gelatin

In a food processor or blender, combine the salmon, cream cheese, scallions, chives, lemon juice, and lemon rind. Season with the pepper. Process until smooth. Transfer to a small bowl. Cover and place in the freezer.

Place the cottage cheese in the food processor or blender. Process until smooth. Transfer to a large bowl.

Place the milk in a small saucepan. Sprinkle the gelatin over top and let stand for 5 minutes. Cook, stirring constantly, over medium heat for 1 minute, or until the gelatin dissolves. Remove from the heat and whisk in a few tablespoons of the pureed cottage cheese. Pour into the bowl with the cottage cheese. Using an electric mixer, beat on high speed for 8 minutes, or until the mixture is whipped.

Add the salmon mixture and beat on low speed until well-blended. Spoon into a bowl or decorative mold. Cover and refrigerate for at least 1 hour.

Invert the bowl or mold onto a serving plate. Shake gently to loosen. (If the mousse doesn't slip out easily, run warm water over the bottom of the bowl or mold.) The mousse can also be served directly from the container.

SWITCH TIP

Most varieties of cheese, like American, Cheddar, Swiss, Monterey Jack, Muenster, and Gouda, have between 8 and 11 grams of fat per ounce. Reduced-fat varieties have between 3 and 6 grams—about 6 grams less. Considering that 1 ounce is about 1 slice or a 1" cube, switching to reduced-fat cheese could add up to a significant fat savings in the long run.

WHITE BEAN AND WALNUT DIP

This spread is reminiscent of pâté, which is usually made with high-fat ground liver, pork, or veal. Fiber-rich beans, nuts, and mushrooms offer a similar texture and flavor—minus all the fat.

HANDS-ON TIME: 15 MINUTES
UNATTENDED TIME: NONE

MAKES 3½ CUPS
PER ¼ CUP
70   CALORIES
2.7 G.   TOTAL FAT
0.2 G.   SATURATED FAT
3.9 G.   PROTEIN
8.5 G.   CARBOHYDRATES
0.5 G.   DIETARY FIBER
0 MG.   CHOLESTEROL
149 MG. SODIUM

8	ounces mushrooms, chopped
1	small onion, chopped
1	clove garlic, minced
1	can (15½ ounces) navy or Great Northern beans
½	cup toasted walnuts
1	tablespoon chopped fresh parsley
1	tablespoon chopped fresh basil
1	tablespoon sherry vinegar
2	teaspoons Worcestershire sauce
	Hot-pepper sauce
	Salt and ground black pepper

Coat a large no-stick skillet with no-stick spray. Set over medium heat until warm. Add the mushrooms, onions, and garlic. Cook for 10 minutes, or until the most of the liquid has evaporated. Transfer to a food processor or blender.

Add the beans, walnuts, parsley, basil, vinegar, and Worcestershire sauce. Process until smooth. Season with the hot-pepper sauce, salt, and black pepper. Transfer to a medium bowl. Store tightly covered in the refrigerator for up to 2 days.

COOKING HINT

• You can use regular Worcestershire sauce for this recipe. Or try the white-wine variety for a more sophisticated flavor.

SPICY BLACK BEAN DIP

No high-fat sour cream here—so dig in and enjoy this light, fresh dip. It tastes great with Seasoned Tortilla Chips (page 353). Make it as hot or mild as you like by altering the amount of jalapeño peppers.

HANDS-ON TIME: 10 MINUTES
UNATTENDED TIME: NONE

MAKES 1¾ CUPS
PER 7 TABLESPOONS
111   CALORIES
2.4 G.   TOTAL FAT
0.1 G.   SATURATED FAT
9.1 G.   PROTEIN
21.2 G. CARBOHYDRATES
6.7 G.   DIETARY FIBER
0 MG.   CHOLESTEROL
461 MG. SODIUM

2	jalapeño peppers, halved and seeded (wear plastic gloves when handling)
½	small onion, halved
¼	cup chopped fresh cilantro
1	clove garlic
1	can (15 ounces) black beans, drained but not rinsed
1	tablespoon lime juice
2	teaspoons tomato paste
1	teaspoon grated lime rind
1	teaspoon canola oil
1½	teaspoons chili powder
½	teaspoon ground cumin
½	teaspoon paprika
¼	teaspoon dried oregano
	Salt and ground black pepper

Place the jalapeño peppers, onions, cilantro, and garlic in a food processor. Process using on/off turns until finely chopped. Add the beans, lime juice, tomato paste, lime rind, oil, chili powder, cumin, paprika, and oregano. Process until smooth. Season with the salt and pepper. Store tightly covered in the refrigerator for up to 4 days.

Sun-Dried Tomato Pesto

This powerhouse of a pesto has only 1.6 grams of fat per tablespoon—and its bold flavor makes a little go a long way. Toss a few tablespoons with pasta. Spread it over pizza crust in place of tomato sauce. Slather it on sandwiches as a condiment. Stir it into soups for a last-minute blast of flavor. Or use it as a thick marinade for grilled chicken, fish, turkey, or tofu.

HANDS-ON TIME: 5 MINUTES
UNATTENDED TIME: 15 MINUTES

MAKES 1¾ CUPS
PER 1 TABLESPOON
27   CALORIES
1.6 G.   TOTAL FAT
0.4 G.   SATURATED FAT
1.2 G.   PROTEIN
2.6 G.   CARBOHYDRATES
0.2 G.   DIETARY FIBER
1 MG.   CHOLESTEROL
39 MG.   SODIUM

1½	cups fat-free chicken broth or vegetable broth
3	ounces sun-dried tomatoes
½	cup packed fresh basil leaves
½	cup packed fresh parsley leaves
¼	cup grated Parmesan cheese
2	tablespoons pine nuts or walnuts
2	cloves garlic
1	teaspoon honey or sugar
2	tablespoons olive oil
	Salt and ground black pepper

Place the broth in a small saucepan and bring to a boil over high heat. Add the tomatoes. Remove from the heat and let soak for 15 minutes.

In a food processor or blender, combine the basil, parsley, Parmesan, pine nuts or walnuts, garlic, and honey or sugar. Process using on/off turns until finely chopped. Add the oil and reserved tomatoes with their soaking liquid. Process until smooth. Season with the salt and pepper. Transfer to a medium bowl. Store tightly covered in the refrigerator for up to 4 days.

Cooking Hint

• Pesto freezes well. Spoon ¼-cup portions into small resealable freezer bags. Freeze for up to 4 months. Or spoon the pesto into a standard-size plastic ice-cube tray. Place the tray in a large resealable freezer bag and freeze overnight. Then pop out the pesto cubes and freeze them in the bag for up to 4 months.

FRESH CRAN-RASPBERRY RELISH

My family uses this sweet-tart relish like jam—spread on bread, spooned over nonfat vanilla ice cream, and stirred into yogurt. Over the holidays, it makes a great low-calorie alternative to sugary canned cranberry sauce.

HANDS-ON TIME: 20 MINUTES
UNATTENDED TIME: NONE

1	package (12 ounces) cranberries
1	cup sugar
½	cup dried cranberries
1	cup + 1 tablespoon water
½	teaspoon grated orange rind
2	teaspoons arrowroot or cornstarch
¾	cup raspberries

MAKES ABOUT 3½ CUPS
PER ¼ CUP
75   CALORIES
0.1 G.   TOTAL FAT
0 G.   SATURATED FAT
0.2 G.   PROTEIN
19.3 G. CARBOHYDRATES
1.6 G.   DIETARY FIBER
0 MG.   CHOLESTEROL
0.5 MG. SODIUM

In a medium saucepan, combine the cranberries, sugar, dried cranberries, and 1 cup of the water. Bring to a boil over high heat. Reduce the heat to medium-low and simmer, stirring occasionally, for 15 minutes, or until slightly thickened. Add the orange rind.

Place the arrowroot or cornstarch in a cup. Add the remaining 1 tablespoon water and stir to dissolve. Stir in a spoonful of the cranberry relish. Stir the mixture into the saucepan and cook for several minutes, or until thickened. Gently stir in the raspberries.

Transfer to a medium bowl. Cover and store in the refrigerator for up to 3 weeks.

MANGO AND PAPAYA SALSA

Get set for a taste of the tropics. This salsa dresses up everything from beans and rice to broiled chicken and fish. I love it with Mexican Chicken in Tortillas (page 265).

HANDS-ON TIME: 10 MINUTES
UNATTENDED TIME: NONE

1	ripe papaya, chopped
1	ripe mango, chopped
	Juice of 1 lime
1	sweet red or green pepper, quartered
1	red onion, quartered
¼	cup packed fresh cilantro leaves
1	jalapeño pepper, seeded (wear plastic gloves when handling)
1	clove garlic
	Salt

MAKES 4 CUPS
PER ½ CUP
68   CALORIES
0.3 G.   TOTAL FAT
0 G.   SATURATED FAT
1.1 G.   PROTEIN
16.3 G. CARBOHYDRATES
2.5 G.   DIETARY FIBER
0 MG.   CHOLESTEROL
14 MG.   SODIUM

In a medium bowl, combine the papaya, mango, and lime juice. Mix well.

In a food processor or blender, combine the red or green peppers, onions, cilantro, jalapeño peppers, and garlic. Process using on/off turns until coarsely chopped. Add to the papaya mixture. Season with the salt. Cover and refrigerate for up to 4 days.

QUICK SWITCH

Pineapple and Peach Salsa: Replace the mango and papaya with 1½ cups chopped pineapple and 1½ cups chopped peaches.

ZIPPY TARTAR SAUCE

This condiment is not too spicy, not too sweet. It's perfect for Pan-Seared Crab Cakes (page 248).

HANDS-ON TIME: 5 MINUTES
UNATTENDED TIME: 1 HOUR

½   cup low-fat mayonnaise
1   shallot, finely chopped
2   tablespoons chopped green chili peppers
1½ tablespoons chopped dill pickles
1   tablespoon chopped fresh parsley
1   tablespoon lemon juice
½   teaspoon Worcestershire sauce
    Hot-pepper sauce
    Salt and ground black pepper

MAKES ¾ CUP

PER 1 TABLESPOON

12	CALORIES
0.7 G.	TOTAL FAT
0.1 G.	SATURATED FAT
0.1 G.	PROTEIN
2.1 G.	CARBOHYDRATES
0.1 G.	DIETARY FIBER
1 MG.	CHOLESTEROL
105 MG.	SODIUM

In a small bowl, combine the mayonnaise, shallots, chili peppers, pickles, parsley, lemon juice, and Worcestershire sauce. Season with the hot-pepper sauce, salt, and black pepper. Mix well. Cover and refrigerate for at least 1 hour or up to 2 days.

SWITCH TIP

Yogurt has more than twice as much calcium as cottage cheese. It even has more calcium than milk. Yogurt has between 300 and 450 milligrams of calcium per cup. That's between 25 and 50 percent of the daily requirement for most folks. Pick up some yogurt to snack on or use it in your favorite sauces, dips, and spreads. It'll boost your calcium intake and help keep your bones strong.

ROASTED TOMATO AND PEPPER SAUCE

Use this smoky-tasting sauce to top broiled fish or chicken breasts. Or toss it with pasta and cooked grains.

HANDS-ON TIME: 15 MINUTES
UNATTENDED TIME: 30 MINUTES

1½	**pounds plum tomatoes, halved lengthwise**
1	**tablespoon olive oil**
1	**shallot, chopped**
2	**cloves garlic, minced**
1	**cup chopped roasted red peppers**
1	**tablespoon chopped fresh basil**
1	**teaspoon balsamic vinegar**
¼	**teaspoon grated lemon rind**
	Salt and ground black pepper

MAKES ABOUT 4 CUPS
PER ⅔ CUP
54	CALORIES
2.7 G.	TOTAL FAT
0.4 G.	SATURATED FAT
1.3 G.	PROTEIN
7.8 G.	CARBOHYDRATES
2.2 G.	DIETARY FIBER
0 MG.	CHOLESTEROL
11 MG.	SODIUM

Preheat the oven to 500°F. Coat an 8" × 8" baking dish with no-stick spray. Place the tomatoes, cut side up, in a single layer in the baking dish. Bake for 30 to 40 minutes, or until the tomatoes are soft and lightly browned. Cool slightly. Remove and discard the peels. Chop the tomatoes.

Warm the oil in a medium saucepan over medium heat. Add the shallots and garlic. Cook for 2 minutes. Remove from the heat and stir in the red peppers, basil, vinegar, lemon rind, and tomatoes. Season with the salt and black pepper.

Transfer to a medium bowl. Cover and store in the refrigerator for up to 4 days. Serve warm, cold, or at room temperature.

RECIPES

"Bread is better than the song of birds."
—DANISH PROVERB

THE LOW-FAT LIVING BAKERY

Nothing beats the taste of homemade bread. In our home, the scent of a freshly baked loaf brings the family running to the kitchen. I feel good knowing that my family is getting high-quality whole-grain bread made without preservatives. You might think that homemade bread requires hours of hard work in the kitchen. Not true. One 20-minute stretch and a few extra 5-minute stints is all it takes. Once it's kneaded, bread dough can be refrigerated overnight, then risen and baked in the morning. Or you can freeze the kneaded dough for up to 4 months so that it's ready to rise and bake when you are.

And baking isn't something that you need to do each day. I like to make several loaves at a time. After all, it takes just as long to make three loaves as it does one. This leaves one loaf to be eaten as soon as it cools, another for the next few days, and one to wrap up for the freezer.

Of course, not everyone will delve into making yeast dough. So I've included recipes for quick breads like biscuits and cornbread, too. There's even a superfast herb bread that uses store-bought bread dough.

WHOLE-WHEAT BUTTERMILK BISCUITS

If you've forgotten what homemade biscuits taste like, you'll want to try this quick and easy recipe. The biscuits are light and flaky, and they go well with almost any meal.

HANDS-ON TIME: 10 MINUTES
UNATTENDED TIME: 10 MINUTES

¾ cup unbleached flour
1 teaspoon baking powder
½ teaspoon baking soda
¼ teaspoon sugar
⅛ teaspoon salt
8 tablespoons whole-wheat pastry flour
1 egg white
½ cup low-fat or nonfat buttermilk
1 tablespoon unsalted butter or margarine, melted

MAKES ABOUT 6
PER BISCUIT
121 CALORIES
2.5 G. TOTAL FAT
1.4 G. SATURATED FAT
4.3 G. PROTEIN
20.6 G. CARBOHYDRATES
1.7 G. DIETARY FIBER
6 MG. CHOLESTEROL
236 MG. SODIUM

Preheat the oven to 450°F. Coat a baking sheet with no-stick spray.

In a medium bowl, combine the unbleached flour, baking powder, baking soda, sugar, salt, and 6 tablespoons of the whole-wheat flour. Mix well.

Place the egg white in a small bowl and whisk lightly. Whisk in the buttermilk and butter or margarine. Pour into the flour mixture. Using a fork, stir just until combined.

Lightly flour a work surface with the remaining 2 table-spoons whole-wheat flour. Place the dough on the surface and gently knead into a ½"-thick circle. Using a 2" biscuit cutter or the rim of a glass, cut the dough into biscuits. Place on the prepared baking sheet. Gently gather together the scraps of dough to make more biscuits.

Bake for 7 to 10 minutes, or until lightly browned.

COOKING HINT

• For light and tender biscuits, handle the dough as little as possible. To help them rise, cut straight down into the dough with a biscuit cutter without twisting.

COTTAGE CHEESE AND DILL BISCUITS

These savory drop biscuits have a fraction of the fat of traditional butter biscuits. Serve them hot from the oven with soups and stews.

HANDS-ON TIME: 10 MINUTES
UNATTENDED TIME: 10 MINUTES

½	cup nonfat or low-fat cottage cheese
½	cup nonfat or low-fat buttermilk
2	teaspoons chopped fresh dill
1¾	cups whole-wheat pastry flour or unbleached flour
1	tablespoon baking powder
1	teaspoon sugar
¼	teaspoon baking soda
¼	teaspoon salt
3	tablespoons unsalted butter or margarine

MAKES 15
PER BISCUIT
79   CALORIES
2.8 G. TOTAL FAT
1.6 G. SATURATED FAT
3.2 G. PROTEIN
11.3 G. CARBOHYDRATES
1.8 G. DIETARY FIBER
7 MG.   CHOLESTEROL
152 MG. SODIUM

Preheat the oven to 450°F. Coat a baking sheet with no-stick spray.

In a small bowl, combine the cottage cheese, buttermilk, and dill. Mix well.

In a large bowl, combine the flour, baking powder, sugar, baking soda, and salt. Mix well. Using a pastry blender or fork, cut the butter or margarine into the flour mixture until fine crumbs form.

Gently stir the cottage-cheese mixture into the flour until just moistened. Using a large spoon, drop the batter into 15 mounds on the prepared baking sheet. Bake for 10 to 12 minutes, or until lightly browned.

GREEN CHILI AND ROASTED PEPPER CORNBREAD

Instead of adding full-fat cheese or bacon for flavor, I use part-skim Cheddar, roasted red peppers, and green chili peppers.

HANDS-ON TIME: 15 MINUTES
UNATTENDED TIME: 35 MINUTES

1	cup cornmeal
1½	cups whole-wheat pastry flour or unbleached flour
1½	cups shredded part-skim sharp Cheddar cheese
½	cup sugar
1	tablespoon baking powder
1	teaspoon baking soda
1	teaspoon salt
1	teaspoon chili powder
1	cup fat-free egg substitute
½	cup nonfat sour cream
1	tablespoon canola oil
1	can (4½ ounces) chopped green chili peppers
¼	cup chopped roasted red peppers or pimentos
1	cup corn kernels

MAKES 12 SERVINGS

PER SERVING
195   CALORIES
2.8 G.   TOTAL FAT
0.2 G.   SATURATED FAT
9.3 G.   PROTEIN
34.3 G. CARBOHYDRATES
3.4 G.   DIETARY FIBER
13.4 MG. CHOLESTEROL
697 MG. SODIUM

Preheat the oven to 425°F. Coat a 10" pie plate with no-stick spray.

In a large bowl, combine the cornmeal, flour, Cheddar, sugar, baking powder, baking soda, salt, and chili powder. Mix well.

In a small bowl, combine the egg substitute, sour cream, and oil. Mix well. Stir in the chili peppers and red peppers or pimentos. Pour over the flour mixture and mix until just moistened. Fold in the corn.

Transfer to the prepared pie plate. Reduce the oven temperature to 375°F. Bake for 35 to 40 minutes, or until lightly browned on top and a toothpick inserted into the center comes out clean. Cool on a wire rack.

COOKING HINTS

- Look for coarse cornmeal in your supermarket. It yields the best texture for cornbread.

- If using jarred roasted red peppers, choose the water-packed variety and drain them well before measuring.

WILD BLUEBERRY CORNBREAD

This cornbread is "double blue" from the blueberries and blue cornmeal, which is a favorite in the Southwest. Blue cornmeal contains more minerals and 20 percent more protein than yellow. Look for it in health food stores and large supermarkets.

1	cup blue or yellow cornmeal
1	cup whole-wheat pastry flour or unbleached flour
⅔	cup sugar
2	teaspoons baking powder
¼	teaspoon ground cinnamon
¼	teaspoon ground nutmeg
⅛	teaspoon salt
2	egg whites
1	egg
⅓	cup skim milk
¼	cup unsweetened applesauce
2	tablespoons unsalted butter, melted, or canola oil
1	teaspoon vanilla
1	teaspoon grated lemon rind
1½	cups wild blueberries (see hint)

Preheat the oven to 350°F. Coat a 8" × 4" loaf pan with no-stick spray.

In a medium bowl, combine the cornmeal, flour, sugar, baking powder, cinnamon, nutmeg, and salt. Mix well.

In a small bowl, lightly whisk the egg whites and egg. Whisk in the milk, applesauce, butter or oil, vanilla, and lemon rind. Pour into the flour mixture. Stir until just moistened. Gently fold in the blueberries.

Transfer to the prepared loaf pan and bake for 1 hour, or until a toothpick inserted into the center comes out moist but not wet. Cool on a wire rack.

COOKING HINT

- Wild blueberries are smaller and more intensely flavored than cultivated blueberries. Canned wild berries are available year round. You can also use fresh or frozen cultivated blueberries.

HANDS-ON TIME: 10 MINUTES
UNATTENDED TIME: 1 HOUR

MAKES 1 LOAF;
10 SLICES
PER SLICE
190 CALORIES
3.7 G. TOTAL FAT
1.8 G. SATURATED FAT
4.4 G. PROTEIN
36.2 G. CARBOHYDRATES
4.1 G. DIETARY FIBER
28 MG. CHOLESTEROL
121 MG. SODIUM

WHEAT AND BRAN SODA BREAD

This bread uses baking soda instead of yeast for the rise.

HANDS-ON TIME: 15 MINUTES
UNATTENDED TIME: 30 MINUTES

1¼   **cups whole-wheat pastry flour**
1¼   **cups unbleached flour**
⅓   **cup oat bran or wheat bran**
¼   **cup sugar**
½   **teaspoon salt**
½   **teaspoon baking soda**
½   **teaspoon cream of tartar**
1   **egg white**
1   **egg**
⅔   **cups low-fat buttermilk**
1   **tablespoon unsalted butter or margarine, melted**

MAKES 1 LOAF;
8 WEDGES
PER WEDGE
202   CALORIES
3.1 G.   TOTAL FAT
1.4 G.   SATURATED FAT
7.2 G.   PROTEIN
38.6 G.   CARBOHYDRATES
3.4 G.   DIETARY FIBER
31 MG.   CHOLESTEROL
250 MG.   SODIUM

Preheat the oven to 375°F. Coat a baking sheet with no-stick spray and sprinkle lightly with flour.

Place the pastry flour in a large bowl. Add 1 cup of the unbleached flour. Add the oat bran or wheat bran, sugar, salt, baking soda, and cream of tartar. Mix well. Make a well in the center.

In a small bowl, lightly whisk the egg white and egg. Whisk in the buttermilk and butter or margarine. Pour into the bowl with the flour. Stir until just moistened.

Spread the remaining ¼ cup unbleached flour on a work surface. Turn the dough out onto the surface and gently knead until coated with flour (the dough will be very soft and slightly sticky). Shape into a ball and transfer to the prepared baking sheet. Brush the top of the dough with a little extra buttermilk and dust with flour. Using a sharp knife, score the top of the loaf with an X.

Bake for 30 minutes, or until browned. Cool on a wire rack.

COOKING HINT

- If you don't use buttermilk often, look for dried cultured buttermilk in the baking section of your supermarket (near the dry milk). Add water according to the directions and you'll use only as much as you need.

BANANA-WALNUT WHEAT BREAD

Overripe bananas don't have to be mashed into a fat-laden cake or quick bread. They can be used in a low-fat yeast bread like this, which is perfect for breakfast or a snack. The bread keeps well in the freezer, so make both loaves and store one for later.

1 cup warm water (110°–115°F)
1 tablespoon active dry yeast
1 tablespoon + ½ cup honey
4 cups whole-wheat flour
3 very ripe bananas, mashed
½ cup chopped walnuts
1 teaspoon salt
2–3 cups unbleached flour

HANDS-ON TIME: 20 MINUTES
UNATTENDED TIME: 2¼ HOURS

MAKES 2 LOAVES;
24 SLICES
PER SLICE
160 CALORIES
2 G. TOTAL FAT
0.2 G. SATURATED FAT
4.8 G. PROTEIN
32.7 G. CARBOHYDRATES
3.3 G. DIETARY FIBER
0 MG. CHOLESTEROL
91 MG. SODIUM

In a large bowl, combine the water, yeast, and 1 tablespoon of the honey. Set aside for 5 minutes, or until foamy.

Add 2 cups of the whole-wheat flour. Using an electric mixer, beat well for 3 minutes (or beat vigorously by hand for 5 minutes). Stir in the bananas, walnuts, salt, and the remaining ½ cup honey. Stir in 1½ cups of the unbleached flour and the remaining 2 cups whole-wheat flour.

Turn out onto a floured surface and knead in enough of the remaining 1½ cups unbleached flour to form a soft dough (be careful not to add too much flour). Knead for 10 minutes, or until smooth and elastic. Form the dough into a ball.

Coat a large bowl with no-stick spray. Add the dough and turn to coat all sides. Cover and let rise in a warm place for about 1 hour, or until doubled in size.

Coat two 9" × 5" loaf pans with no-stick spray.

Punch down the dough and divide into 2 pieces. Shape into 2 loaves and place in the prepared loaf pans. Coat the tops of the loaves with no-stick spray. Cover and let rise in a warm place for about 35 minutes, or until doubled in size.

Preheat the oven to 350°F. Bake for 40 minutes, or until the loaves are brown on top and sound hollow when tapped on the bottom.

Cool on a wire rack.

QUICK HERB-CRUSTED BREAD

Frozen dough is the ultimate convenience food for folks who love fresh-baked bread. Be sure to shop for dough that is low in fat and includes at least some whole-grain flour. Here, I've coated the dough with herbs, oil, and a sprinkling of salt and poppy seeds.

HANDS-ON TIME: 15 MINUTES
UNATTENDED TIME: 20 MINUTES

MAKES 2 LOAVES;
28 SLICES
PER SLICE
92   CALORIES
2.1 G.   TOTAL FAT
0.5 G.   SATURATED FAT
2.5 G.   PROTEIN
15.3 G.   CARBOHYDRATES
0 G.   DIETARY FIBER
1 MG.   CHOLESTEROL
194 G.   SODIUM

1	tablespoon olive oil
¼	teaspoon dried oregano
¼	teaspoon dried basil
⅛	teaspoon dried thyme
⅛	teaspoon garlic powder
2	pounds frozen low-fat whole-grain bread dough, thawed
½	teaspoon salt
1	teaspoon poppy seeds

Preheat the oven to 350°F. Coat a baking sheet with no-stick spray.

In a cup, combine the oil, oregano, basil, thyme, and garlic powder.

On a floured surface, roll the dough into two logs, each about 12" to 14" long. Place the logs on the prepared baking sheet

about 4" apart and with the long sides stretching away from you. Flatten each log slightly. Using a sharp knife, make 6 angled cuts through each side of each dough log. Cut from just off-center through to the outside edge to make each cut. Make 1 vertical cut on the bottom of each log. The cut loaves should resemble a Christmas tree.

Brush the loaves with the oil mixture. Sprinkle evenly with the salt and poppy seeds. (If desired, coat the loaves with a misting of olive oil no-stick spray.)

Bake for 20 to 25 minutes, or until lightly browned.

SOFT SEMOLINA ROLLS

Semolina flour is normally used for pasta and pizza dough. Look for it in the baking aisle of large supermarkets and Italian grocery stores. Here, the high-protein flour creates a soft, light dinner roll perfect for dipping into tomato sauce.

HANDS-ON TIME: 20 MINUTES
UNATTENDED TIME: 2 HOURS

MAKES 16
PER ROLL

113	CALORIES
0.6 G.	TOTAL FAT
0.1 G.	SATURATED FAT
4.1 G.	PROTEIN
22.3 G.	CARBOHYDRATES
0.4 G.	DIETARY FIBER
13 MG.	CHOLESTEROL
205 MG.	SODIUM

1	cup warm water (110°–115°F)
1	tablespoon active dry yeast
1	tablespoon sugar
2	cups semolina flour
1	egg, lightly beaten
1½	teaspoons salt
1–1½	cups unbleached flour

In a large bowl, combine the water, yeast, and sugar. Set aside for 5 minutes, or until foamy.

Add 1 cup of the semolina flour. Using an electric mixer, beat well for 3 minutes (or beat vigorously by hand for 5 minutes). Stir in the egg and salt. Stir in ½ cup of the unbleached flour and the remaining 1 cup semolina flour.

Turn out onto a floured surface and knead in enough of the remaining 1 cup unbleached flour to form a very soft dough (be careful not to add too much flour). Knead for 10 minutes, or until smooth and elastic. Form the dough into a ball.

Coat a large bowl with no-stick spray. Add the dough and turn to coat all sides. Cover and let rise in a warm place for about 1 hour, or until doubled in size.

Coat a baking sheet with no-stick spray.

Punch down the dough and divide into 16 pieces. Shape each piece into a ball, roll in unbleached flour and place on the prepared sheet, leaving at least 2" between balls. Coat the tops of the balls with no-stick spray. Cover and let rise in a warm place for about 30 minutes, or until doubled in size.

Preheat the oven to 400°F. Bake for 20 minutes, or until the rolls are lightly browned.

Remove the rolls from the baking sheet. Cool on a wire rack.

WHOLE-WHEAT ROSEMARY-ONION ROLLS

Here's a hearty roll for hearty soups.

HANDS-ON TIME: 20 MINUTES
UNATTENDED TIME: 2 HOURS

1	cup warm water (110°–115°F)
1	tablespoon active dry yeast
1	tablespoon sugar
2	cups unbleached flour
½	cup fat-free egg substitute
1	tablespoon olive oil
1	teaspoon crushed dried rosemary
1	teaspoon salt
1	small onion, finely chopped
2–3	cups whole-wheat flour

MAKES 10
PER ROLL
201   CALORIES
2.1 G. TOTAL FAT
0.3 G. SATURATED FAT
7.5 G. PROTEIN
39.2 G. CARBOHYDRATES
3.8 G. DIETARY FIBER
0 MG.   CHOLESTEROL
236 MG. SODIUM

In a large bowl, combine the water, yeast, and sugar. Set aside for 5 minutes, or until foamy.

Add 1 cup of the unbleached flour. Using an electric mixer, beat well for 3 minutes (or beat vigorously by hand for 5 minutes). Stir in the egg substitute, oil, rosemary, salt, and all but ¼ cup of the onions. Stir in the remaining 1 cup unbleached flour and 1½ cups of the whole-wheat flour.

Turn out onto a floured surface and knead in enough of the remaining whole-wheat flour to form a soft dough (be careful not to add too much flour). Knead for 10 minutes, or until smooth, elastic, and a little sticky. Form into a ball.

Coat a large bowl with no-stick spray. Add the dough and turn to coat all sides. Cover and let rise in a warm place for about 1 hour, or until doubled in size.

Coat a baking sheet with no-stick spray.

Punch down the dough and divide into 10 pieces. Shape each piece into a disk-shaped roll. Place the remaining ¼ cup onions on a plate. Dip the top of each roll into the onions. Place the rolls, onion side up, on the prepared baking sheet, leaving at least 2" between rolls. Coat the tops of the rolls with no-stick spray. Cover and let rise in a warm place for about 30 minutes, or until almost doubled in size.

Preheat the oven to 375°F. Bake for 20 minutes, or until the rolls are until lightly browned. Remove the rolls from the baking sheet and cool on a wire rack.

MULTIGRAIN ITALIAN HERB BREAD

This puffy, somewhat flat Italian bread is known as fo-caccia (foe-KOTCH-a). I like to use a mixture of flours, such as whole-wheat, oat, rye, and semolina. The recipe also works if made entirely with unbleached flour.

HANDS-ON TIME: 25 MINUTES
UNATTENDED TIME: 1¼ HOURS

1	cup warm water (110°–115°F)
1	tablespoon active dry yeast
1	teaspoon sugar
2–2¼	cups unbleached flour
1	teaspoon salt
¼	teaspoon dried oregano
⅛	teaspoon garlic powder
½	cup multigrain flour
	Cornmeal
2	teaspoons olive oil
2	tablespoons grated Parmesan cheese

MAKES 8 SLICES
PER SLICE
164	CALORIES
2.2 G.	TOTAL FAT
0.6 G.	SATURATED FAT
5.1 G.	PROTEIN
30.7 G.	CARBOHYDRATES
2.1 G.	DIETARY FIBER
1 MG.	CHOLESTEROL
298 MG.	SODIUM

In a large bowl, combine the water, yeast, and sugar. Set aside for 5 minutes, or until foamy.

Add 1 cup of the unbleached flour. Using an electric mixer, beat well for 3 minutes (or beat vigorously by hand for 5 minutes). Stir in the salt, oregano, and garlic powder. Stir in the multigrain flour and 1 cup of the remaining unbleached flour.

Turn out onto a floured surface and knead in enough of the remaining ¼ cup unbleached flour to form a soft dough (be careful not to add too much flour). Knead for 5 minutes, or until smooth and elastic. Form the dough into a ball.

Coat a large bowl with no-stick spray. Add the dough and turn to coat all sides. Cover and let rise in a warm place for about 45 minutes, or until doubled in size.

Coat a baking sheet with no-stick spray and sprinkle with cornmeal.

Punch down the dough. Place on the prepared baking sheet. Press into a 10" to 12" circle with your fingers. Spread the oil evenly over the dough and sprinkle with the Parmesan. Cover and let rise in a warm place for 15 minutes.

Preheat the oven to 425°F. Bake on the bottom rack of the oven for 10 minutes, or until just barely browned. Remove from the baking sheet and cool on a wire rack.

MULTIGRAIN SUNFLOWER BREAD

This moist yet dense bread uses seven hearty grains and is topped with a crust of toasted sunflower seeds. You can vary the flours according to what you have on hand or what's available in your area.

1½	cups cold water
½	cup millet
½	cup bulgur or cracked wheat
1½	cups warm water (110°–115°F)
1½	tablespoons active dry yeast
1	tablespoon + ½ cup honey
2	cups whole-wheat flour
¼	cup sesame seeds
2	teaspoons salt
½	cup rolled oats
½	cup coarse cornmeal
½	cup rye flour
½	cup brown rice flour
½	cup barley flour
2–3	cups unbleached flour
¾	cup toasted sunflower seeds
1	egg white, lightly beaten

HANDS-ON TIME: 20 MINUTES
UNATTENDED TIME: 2½ HOURS

MAKES 2 LOAVES;
30 SLICES
PER SLICE
161   CALORIES
3.1 G.   TOTAL FAT
0.4 G.   SATURATED FAT
4.9 G.   PROTEIN
29.7 G. CARBOHYDRATES
3.8 G.   DIETARY FIBER
0 MG.   CHOLESTEROL
147 MG. SODIUM

Bring the cold water to a boil in a medium saucepan over high heat. Stir in the millet and bulgur or cracked wheat. Remove from the heat. Let stand until needed.

In a large bowl, combine the warm water, yeast, and 1 tablespoon of the honey. Set aside for 5 minutes, or until foamy.

Add the whole-wheat flour to the bowl. Using an electric mixer, beat well for 3 minutes (or beat vigorously by hand for 5 minutes). Stir in the sesame seeds, salt, and the remaining ½ cup honey. Drain the millet mixture and stir into the bowl. Stir in the oats, cornmeal, rye flour, brown rice flour, and barley flour.

Turn out onto a floured surface and knead in enough of the unbleached flour to form a soft dough (be careful not to add too much flour). Knead for 10 minutes, or until smooth and elastic. (The dough will remain slightly stiff and sticky because of the multigrain flours.) Form the dough into a ball.

Coat a large bowl with no-stick spray. Add the dough and turn to coat all sides. Cover and let rise in a warm place for about 1 hour, or until doubled in size.

Coat a baking sheet with no-stick spray.

Punch down the dough and divide in half. Shape each half into an oblong loaf.

Spread the sunflower seeds on a large piece of foil. Brush 1 loaf with the egg white, covering the entire surface. Roll the loaf in the sunflower seeds using the foil to help press the seeds around the entire loaf. Place on the prepared sheet. Repeat with the remaining loaf. Place on the prepared baking sheet, leaving at least 3" between loaves. Cut a long slit in the top of each loaf with a sharp knife.

Cover and let rise in a warm place for about 50 minutes, or until almost doubled in size.

Preheat the oven to 350°F. Bake for 40 minutes, or until the loaves are brown on top and sound hollow when tapped on the bottom.

Remove the loaves from the baking sheet and cool on a wire rack.

RAISIN-PECAN WHEAT BREAD

This recipe makes 3 loaves. It's so good, I like to freeze 2 loaves for ready-made snacks. If you want only 2 small loaves, just cut the recipe in half. Try serving the bread with low-fat cream cheese for a sweet snack or breakfast.

HANDS-ON TIME: 25 MINUTES
UNATTENDED TIME: 2¼ HOURS

MAKES 3 LOAVES;
45 SLICES
PER SLICE
184   CALORIES
3.7 G.   TOTAL FAT
0.3 G.   SATURATED FAT
4.5 G.   PROTEIN
35.3 G.   CARBOHYDRATES
3.2 G.   DIETARY FIBER
0 MG.   CHOLESTEROL
99 MG.   SODIUM

3	cups cold water
3	cups raisins
3	cups warm water (110°–115°F)
2	tablespoons active dry yeast
1	tablespoon + ½ cup honey
6	cups whole-wheat flour
¼	cup molasses
2	teaspoons salt
2	cups toasted pecans, coarsely broken
5–5½	cups unbleached flour

Bring the cold water to a boil in a medium saucepan over high heat. Stir in the raisins and remove from the heat. Let stand until needed.

In a large bowl, combine the warm water, yeast, and 1 table-spoon of the honey. Set aside for 5 minutes, or until foamy.

Add 3 cups of the whole-wheat flour. Using an electric mixer, beat well for 3 minutes (or beat vigorously by hand for 5 minutes). Stir in the molasses, salt, and the re-maining ½ cup honey.

Drain the raisins and add to the bowl. Stir in the pecans, 4 cups of the unbleached flour, and the remaining 3 cups whole-wheat flour.

Turn out onto a floured surface and knead in enough of the remaining 1½ cups unbleached flour to form a soft dough (be careful not to add too much flour). Knead for 10 minutes, or until smooth and elastic. (The dough will remain slightly sticky.) Form the dough into a ball.

Coat a large bowl with no-stick spray. Add the dough and turn to coat all sides. Cover and let rise in a warm place for about 1 hour, or until doubled in size.

Coat two baking sheets with no-stick spray.

Punch down the dough and divide it into 3 pieces. Shape each piece into a long loaf and place on the prepared baking sheets. Coat the tops of the loaves with no-stick spray. Cover and let rise in a warm place for 35 minutes, or until doubled in size.

Preheat the oven to 350°F. Cut a long slit (¼" deep) down the center of each loaf with a sharp knife. Bake for 40 to 45 minutes, or until the loaves are brown on top and sound hollow when tapped on the bottom.

Remove the loaves from the baking sheets and cool on a wire rack.

COOKING HINT

• Molasses is rich in minerals such as potassium, iron, and calcium. It also contains a good range of B vitamins.

SWITCH TIP

Nuts enhance the flavor and texture of breads, cookies, and muffins. But most nuts are about 75 percent fat. To use nuts in smaller quantities, toast them first to bring out their flavors. That way you don't need to use as much. Toast the nuts in a dry skillet over medium-low heat for 3 to 5 minutes, or until golden and fragrant. Shake the pan often to ensure even toasting. You can also toast nuts in a 300°F oven for 5 to 10 minutes.

385

APRICOT-ALMOND OATMEAL BREAD

This bread is great for snacks, breakfasts, and even sandwiches. The apricots provide additional fiber and vitamin A, and the almonds provide calcium and other minerals.

HANDS-ON TIME: 15 MINUTES
UNATTENDED TIME: 2½ HOURS

2¼	cups water
⅔	cup dried apricots
1	tablespoon active dry yeast
2	cups whole-wheat flour
¼	cup honey
1	teaspoon salt
1	cup rolled oats
½	cup roasted almonds, chopped
2–2½	cups unbleached flour

MAKES 2 LOAVES;
24 SLICES
PER SLICE
122   CALORIES
2 G.   TOTAL FAT
0.2 G.   SATURATED FAT
3.8 G.   PROTEIN
23.3 G.   CARBOHYDRATES
2.4 G.   DIETARY FIBER
0 MG.   CHOLESTEROL
90 MG.   SODIUM

Bring the water to a boil in a medium saucepan over high heat. Stir in the apricots and remove from the heat. Set aside for 15 to 20 minutes, or until the apricots are plump and softened. Remove the apricots from the water with a slotted spoon; leave the water in the saucepan. Coarsely chop the apricots.

Place the saucepan over medium-low heat for 1 minute, or until the water is warm (110° to 115°F). Transfer to a large bowl. Add the yeast and set aside for 5 minutes, or until foamy.

Add the whole-wheat flour. Using an electric mixer, beat well for 3 minutes (or beat vigorously by hand for 5 minutes). Stir in the honey and salt. Stir in the oats, almonds, apricots, and 1½ cups of the unbleached flour.

Turn out onto a floured surface and knead in enough of the remaining 1 cup unbleached flour to form a soft dough (be careful not to add too much flour). Knead for 10 minutes, or until smooth and elastic. (The dough will remain slightly sticky.) Form the dough into a ball.

Coat a large bowl with no-stick spray. Add the dough and turn to coat all sides. Cover and let rise in a warm place for about 1 hour, or until doubled in size.

Coat two 9" × 5" loaf pans with no-stick spray.

Punch down the dough and divide into 2 pieces. Shape into 2 loaves and place in the prepared loaf pans. Coat the tops of the loaves with no-stick spray. Cover and let rise in a warm place for about 35 minutes, or until doubled in size.

Preheat the oven to 350°F. Bake for 40 minutes, or until the loaves are brown on top. Remove from the pans and tap the loaves on the bottom. They should sound hollow; if not, return them to the oven for a few minutes.

Cool on a wire rack.

CINNAMON AND SUGAR TWISTS

These twists are like baked doughnuts—light, sweet, and airy. They perfume the kitchen with an intoxicating cinnamon aroma. And they take only 25 minutes of hands-on time.

HANDS-ON TIME: 25 MINUTES
UNATTENDED TIME: 1¾ HOURS

1½	cups skim milk
3	tablespoons unsalted butter or margarine
¼	cup warm water (110°–115°F)
1½	tablespoons active dry yeast
2	eggs, lightly beaten
1	teaspoon salt
½	cup + ⅔ cup sugar
½	teaspoon + 1 tablespoon ground cinnamon
2	cups whole-wheat flour
4	cups unbleached flour
2	egg whites, lightly beaten

MAKES 16
PER TWIST
265   CALORIES
3.6 G.   TOTAL FAT
1.7 G.   SATURATED FAT
7.7 G.   PROTEIN
51.4 G. CARBOHYDRATES
3 G.   DIETARY FIBER
33 MG.   CHOLESTEROL
162 MG. SODIUM

In a medium microwave-safe bowl, combine the milk and butter or margarine. Microwave on high power for 1 minute, or until the butter or margarine melts.

In a large bowl, combine the water and yeast. Set aside for 5 minutes, or until foamy.

Stir in the milk mixture. Stir in the eggs, salt, ½ cup of the sugar, and ½ teaspoon of the cinnamon. Add the whole-wheat flour. Using an electric mixer, beat well for 3 minutes (or beat vigorously by hand for 5 minutes). Stir in 2 cups of the unbleached flour.

Turn out onto a floured surface and knead in enough of the remaining 2 cups unbleached flour to form a soft dough (be careful not to add too much flour). Knead for 10 minutes, or until smooth and elastic. (The dough will be soft and sticky.)

Coat a large bowl with no-stick spray. With floured hands, form the dough into a ball and transfer to the bowl. Turn the dough to coat all sides. Cover and let rise in a warm place for about 1 hour, or until doubled in size.

Coat 2 baking sheets with no-stick spray and sprinkle lightly with flour.

In a cup, combine the remaining ⅔ cup sugar and the remaining 1 tablespoon cinnamon. Mix well.

Punch down the dough and turn it out onto a generously floured surface (the dough will be very soft and sticky). With a floured rolling pin, roll the dough into an 8" × 18" rectangle. With a floured knife, cut the dough into sixteen 8"-long strips.

S W I T C H   T I P

Want to get more fiber and complex carbohydrates? Switch from white flour, white rice, and white bread to whole-wheat flour, brown rice, and whole-grain breads. When buying bread, look at the ingredient list on the package. It's not whole-grain if the first ingredient is wheat flour (which means white flour). The first ingredient in whole-grain breads is whole-wheat flour, rye flour, or other whole-grain flours.

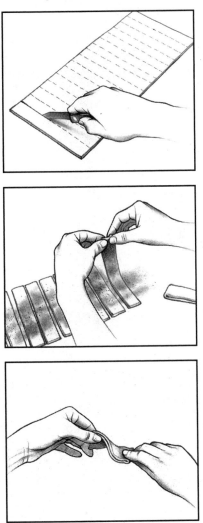

Brush the strips with the egg whites and sprinkle with some of the sugar mixture. Fold each strip back over on itself to bring the short ends together. Pinch the ends together. With two hands, grab the pinched end and the opposite end. Twist the ends in opposite directions to form a long spiral shape with the cinnamon and sugar swirled inside. Place on the prepared baking sheets, leaving at least 1" between pieces. Sprinkle with any remaining sugar mixture.

Cover and let rise in a warm place for 25 minutes, or until almost doubled in size (the dough will untwist slightly as it rises).

Preheat the oven to 350°F. Bake for 15 to 20 minutes, or until the twists are lightly browned. Remove the twists from the baking sheets and cool on a wire rack.

RECIPES

"Never eat more than you can lift."

—MISS PIGGY, AMERICAN MUPPET AND MOVIE STAR

LIGHT DESSERTS THAT QUELL CRAVINGS

Desserts are no longer off-limits in a low-fat lifestyle. Chocolate-Mocha Bundt Cake and Cappuccino Cheesecake can be perfectly healthy additions to the evening menu. And here's how to fully enjoy these desserts without a trace of the after-dinner slump: Leave a little time between dinner and dessert. In our home, we make it a point to do some moderate activity before indulging in the after-meal treat. We may enjoy an evening walk together, finish cleaning the dishes, or do some light exercise to give our metabolisms a boost. That way, dessert is even more satisfying and helps quell evening snack cravings.

But don't limit these treats to just the evening hours. Many of them make great afternoon snacks as well. Top off a satisfying lunch with a slice of Carrot Cake or Mocha Angel Food Cake. If your kids like after-school snacks, give them a bite of Sour Cream Apple Crumb Kuchen or Banana-Walnut Cake with Lemon Icing.

For more sweet snacks, like cookies, bars, and puddings, see the recipes beginning on page 124.

DOUBLE-BLUEBERRY CRISP

Fresh and dried blueberries make a rich but low-fat treat. Most supermarkets carry dried berries in the produce section.

HANDS-ON TIME: 15 MINUTES
UNATTENDED TIME: 45 MINUTES

FILLING

4	cups fresh blueberries
1	cup dried blueberries
⅔	cup sugar
¼	cup quick-cooking tapioca
3	tablespoons lemon juice
½	teaspoon ground cinnamon
¼	teaspoon ground nutmeg

TOPPING

½	cup whole-wheat pastry flour or unbleached flour
½	cup packed brown sugar
½	teaspoon ground cinnamon
1	tablespoon unsalted butter or margarine
1	tablespoon honey

CRUST

⅔	cup crushed nonfat or low-fat graham crackers

MAKES 9 SERVINGS
PER SERVING
259   CALORIES
2 G.   TOTAL FAT
0.9 G. SATURATED FAT
2.8 G. PROTEIN
62 G.   CARBOHYDRATES
4.2 G. DIETARY FIBER
4 MG.   CHOLESTEROL
20 MG. SODIUM

Preheat the oven to 375°F. Coat an 8" × 8" baking dish with no-stick spray.

To make the filling: In a large bowl, combine the fresh blueberries, dried blueberries, sugar, tapioca, lemon juice, cinnamon, and nutmeg. Mix well.

To make the topping: In a small bowl, combine the flour, brown sugar, and cinnamon. Mix well.

In a small microwave-safe cup, combine the butter or margarine and honey. Microwave on high power for 15 seconds, or until melted. Pour over the flour mixture and stir until moistened.

To make the crust: Spread the graham-cracker crumbs evenly over the bottom of the prepared baking dish. Mist the crumbs with no-stick spray. Pour in the filling. Sprinkle with the topping, pressing down slightly. Bake for 45 minutes, or until bubbly and browned.

APPLE-CHERRY CRISP

Graham crackers make a scrumptious topping in this easy version of apple crisp. For individual servings, use small baking dishes.

HANDS-ON TIME: 20 MINUTES
UNATTENDED TIME: 1 HOUR

FILLING

1	cup sugar
2	tablespoons arrowroot or cornstarch
¾	teaspoon ground cinnamon
½	teaspoon ground nutmeg
4	cups peeled and thinly sliced apples
1	can (16 ounces) pitted sour cherries packed in water, drained

TOPPING

4	whole low-fat or nonfat graham crackers
3	tablespoons slivered almonds
2	tablespoons packed brown sugar
2	tablespoons unsalted butter or margarine, melted

MAKES 6 SERVINGS
PER SERVING

382	CALORIES
7.4 G.	TOTAL FAT
2.8 G.	SATURATED FAT
3.5 G.	PROTEIN
77.8 G.	CARBOHYDRATES
2.5 G.	DIETARY FIBER
11 MG.	CHOLESTEROL
107 MG.	SODIUM

Preheat the oven to 350°F. Coat an 8" × 8" baking dish with no-stick spray.

To make the filling: In a small bowl, combine the sugar, arrowroot or cornstarch, cinnamon, and nutmeg. Mix well.

In a large bowl, combine the apples, cherries, and sugar mixture. Toss to mix. Spread in the prepared baking dish.

To make the topping: Place the crackers in a food processor or blender. Process into crumbs. Add the almonds, brown sugar, and butter or margarine. Process until moistened. Sprinkle over the apple mixture.

Bake for 1 hour, or until the apples are tender.

Peach and Pecan Crumble

Crumbles and crisps lose their healthy status when the toppings get too fatty. I've limited the fat to just a few tablespoons in this recipe. Sweet spices and toasted nuts round out the flavor. If the peaches aren't nice and sweet, add a little more brown sugar.

HANDS-ON TIME: 15 MINUTES
UNATTENDED TIME: 40 MINUTES

MAKES 9 SERVINGS
PER SERVING
230   CALORIES
5.7 G.   TOTAL FAT
2 G.   SATURATED FAT
4.4 G.   PROTEIN
43.7 G.   CARBOHYDRATES
4.7 G.   DIETARY FIBER
7 MG.   CHOLESTEROL
65 MG.   SODIUM

TOPPING

1	cup rolled oats
1	cup whole-wheat pastry flour or unbleached flour
¼	cup chopped toasted pecans
2	tablespoons packed brown sugar
1	teaspoon ground cinnamon
¼	teaspoon ground nutmeg
¼	teaspoon salt
⅛	teaspoon ground allspice
2	tablespoons unsalted butter or margarine
2	tablespoons honey

FILLING

12	peaches, peeled and sliced
¼	cup packed brown sugar
2	tablespoons lemon juice
2	tablespoons arrowroot or cornstarch

Preheat the oven to 375°F. Coat an 8" × 8" baking dish with no-stick spray.

To make the topping: In a medium bowl, combine the oats, flour, pecans, brown sugar, cinnamon, nutmeg, salt, and allspice. Mix well.

In a microwave-safe cup, combine the butter or margarine and honey. Microwave on high power for 30 seconds, or until melted. Pour over the oat mixture and stir until moistened.

To make the filling: In a large bowl, combine the peaches, brown sugar, lemon juice, and arrowroot or cornstarch. Toss to mix. Pour into the prepared baking dish. Sprinkle with the topping, pressing down firmly.

Bake for 40 to 45 minutes, or until bubbly and browned.

CHERRY CRUMBLE

A crunchy double crust encases sweet cherry filling in this quick-to-fix treat. Try it served à la mode with nonfat vanilla frozen yogurt or ice cream.

HANDS-ON TIME: 15 MINUTES
UNATTENDED TIME: 45 MINUTES

CRUST

2½	cups rolled oats
¾	cup whole-wheat pastry flour or unbleached flour
¾	cup packed brown sugar
2	teaspoons ground cinnamon
3	tablespoons unsalted butter or margarine
2	tablespoons honey

FILLING

½	cup arrowroot or cornstarch
⅔	cup sugar
2	cans (16 ounces each) pitted sour cherries packed in juice
½	cup dried cherries

MAKES 9 SERVINGS
PER SERVING

418	CALORIES
5.9 G.	TOTAL FAT
2.8 G.	SATURATED FAT
6.1 G.	PROTEIN
89.7 G.	CARBOHYDRATES
4.6 G.	DIETARY FIBER
11 MG.	CHOLESTEROL
18 MG.	SODIUM

Preheat the oven to 375°F. Coat an 8" × 8" baking dish with no-stick spray.

To make the crust: In a medium bowl, combine the oats, flour, brown sugar, and cinnamon. Mix well.

In a microwave-safe cup, combine the butter or margarine and honey. Microwave on high power for 30 seconds, or until melted. Pour over the oat mixture and stir until moistened. Press half of the mixture into the bottom and slightly up the sides of the prepared baking dish.

To make the filling: In a medium saucepan, combine the arrowroot or cornstarch and ⅓ cup of the sugar. Drain the cherry juice into the pan. Cook over medium heat, stirring constantly, until thick and bubbly. Remove from the heat and stir in the canned cherries, dried cherries, and the remaining ⅓ cup sugar. Pour into the baking dish.

Top with the remaining crust mixture and pat firmly into place.

Bake for 45 minutes, or until the filling is bubbly and the crust is browned.

PISTACHIO CUPS FILLED WITH ICE CREAM AND BERRIES

These are delicate, buttery cookies that are shaped into little cups while they're hot. When cooled, fill them with nonfat ice cream and fresh berries—or whatever else you desire.

HANDS-ON TIME: 10 MINUTES
UNATTENDED TIME: 1¼ HOURS

1	egg white
¼	cup sugar
3	tablespoons whole-wheat pastry flour or unbleached flour
¼	cup unsalted butter or margarine, melted
2	teaspoons vanilla
¼	teaspoon ground cinnamon
⅛	teaspoon salt
2	tablespoons pistachio nuts, finely chopped
4	cups nonfat or low-fat ice cream or frozen yogurt
4	cups fresh raspberries

MAKES 8 SERVINGS

PER SERVING
225	CALORIES
7.9 G.	TOTAL FAT
3.9 G.	SATURATED FAT
4.9 G.	PROTEIN
36.5 G.	CARBOHYDRATES
3.4 G.	DIETARY FIBER
16 MG.	CHOLESTEROL
111 MG.	SODIUM

Preheat the oven to 325°F. Line a baking sheet with parchment paper.

In a medium bowl, whisk together the egg white, sugar, flour, butter or margarine, vanilla, cinnamon, and salt. Stir in the pistachios. Cover and refrigerate for 1 hour.

For each cookie, drop 1 teaspoon of batter onto the prepared baking sheet, leaving several inches between cookies. Spread each into a thin circle with a knife.

Bake for 10 to 12 minutes, or until the edges are lightly brown. Remove from the oven. One at a time, remove from the baking sheet while still hot and immediately mold around an overturned small bowl. Remove from the bowl and transfer to a wire rack to cool completely.

Fill the cups with the ice cream or frozen yogurt and raspberries. Serve immediately.

COOKING HINT

- Create your own variations by replacing the pistachios with walnuts, almonds, pecans, or other nuts. In place of ice cream or frozen yogurt, use sorbet, pudding, or fresh chopped fruit.

PEACH AND MAPLE CUSTARD

Here's a creamy dessert that takes only 10 minutes of hands-on time. You can easily replace the peaches with ripe pears, plums, berries, or cherries.

HANDS-ON TIME: 10 MINUTES
UNATTENDED TIME: 40 MINUTES

4	cups peeled and diced peaches
2	ounces nonfat cream cheese, softened
2	ounces Neufchâtel cheese, softened
½	cup nonfat sour cream
½	cup maple syrup
1	cup fat-free egg substitute
1	tablespoon vanilla
½	teaspoon ground cinnamon
¼	teaspoon ground nutmeg
¼	teaspoon salt (optional)
4	teaspoons packed brown sugar

MAKES 6 SERVINGS
PER SERVING
194   CALORIES
2.3 G. TOTAL FAT
1.4 G. SATURATED FAT
7.8 G. PROTEIN
36.2 G. CARBOHYDRATES
1.8 G. DIETARY FIBER
7 MG.   CHOLESTEROL
179 MG. SODIUM

Preheat the oven to 375°F. Fill a 9" × 13" baking dish with ½" of water. Coat six 6- to 8-ounce oven-safe dessert cups with no-stick spray. Divide the peaches among the cups and set in the baking dish.

In a medium bowl, combine the cream cheese and Neufchâtel cheese. Using an electric mixer, beat until creamy. Add the sour cream and beat until smooth. Add the maple syrup, egg substitute, vanilla, cinnamon, nutmeg, and salt (if using). Beat until foamy.

Divide the mixture among the dessert cups. Sprinkle with the brown sugar. Carefully place the baking dish in the oven.

Bake for 40 minutes, or until the custard is set and slightly browned. Carefully transfer the cups to a wire rack. Serve warm or at room temperature.

COOKING HINT

- If you prefer the custard chilled, wrap the cups in plastic and refrigerate until serving time. The custard will keep for up to 3 days.

397

MERINGUE CUPS WITH CREAMY LEMON FILLING

You'll love this dessert for serving to company—it's light, refreshing, and easy to fix. The meringue cups are fat-free, and the filling is low in fat.

HANDS-ON TIME: 25 MINUTES
UNATTENDED TIME: 1¾ HOURS

MERINGUE CUPS

3	egg whites
¼	teaspoon cream of tartar
⅛	teaspoon salt
1	cup sugar
2	teaspoons vanilla

FILLING

3	egg yolks
¼	cup sugar
¼	cup lemon juice
1	tablespoon grated lemon rind
4	ounces nonfat cream cheese, softened
4	ounces Neufchâtel cheese, softened

MAKES 16

PER MERINGUE CUP
102	CALORIES
2.6 G.	TOTAL FAT
1.3 G.	SATURATED FAT
2.9 G.	PROTEIN
16.8 G.	CARBOHYDRATES
0 G.	DIETARY FIBER
45 MG.	CHOLESTEROL
99 MG.	SODIUM

Preheat the oven to 300°F. Line a baking sheet with parchment paper.

To make the meringue cups: Place the egg whites in a medium bowl. Using an electric mixer, beat until foamy. Add the cream of tartar and salt. Beat until soft peaks form. Gradually beat in the sugar until the mixture is stiff and glossy. Beat in the vanilla.

Drop 16 heaping tablespoons of meringue onto the prepared baking sheet, leaving at least 1" between mounds. Using the back of a spoon, press into the center of each meringue to form a cup.

Bake for 40 minutes; do not open the oven door during this time. Turn the oven off and let the meringues dry in the oven for 1 hour; do not open the oven door during this time.

To make the filling: In a small saucepan, combine the egg yolks, sugar, lemon juice, and lemon rind. Whisk to mix well. Cook over medium-low heat, whisking constantly, for 7 minutes, or until thickened. Remove from the heat and transfer to a medium bowl. Refrigerate until cool.

Using an electric mixer, beat in the cream cheese and Neufchâtel cheese until smooth and creamy. Refrigerate until ready to serve.

Divide the filling among the meringue cups.

COOKING HINTS

- The meringues can be made in advance and stored in a covered container until ready to use.

- Neufchâtel cheese is a type of lower-fat cream cheese; you may substitute reduced-fat cream cheese.

QUICK SWITCH

Meringue Cups with Creamy Lime Filling: Replace the lemon juice and lemon rind with lime juice and lime rind.

CRANBERRY-PUMPKIN PIE WITH PECANS

This dessert is a refreshing change from the plain pumpkin pies that turn up around the holidays. The recipe makes two pies, so you can freeze one for later. That ensures you won't have leftover canned pumpkin or berries.

HANDS-ON TIME: 15 MINUTES
UNATTENDED TIME: 1 HOUR

1	orange
1	package (12 ounces) cranberries
1	cup + ¾ cup sugar
1	tablespoon arrowroot or cornstarch
1	tablespoon water
1	can (15 ounces) unsweetened pumpkin
1	can (12 ounces) evaporated skim milk
½	cup fat-free egg substitute
1	teaspoon ground cinnamon
½	teaspoon ground ginger
½	teaspoon salt
¼	teaspoon ground nutmeg
¼	teaspoon ground cloves
2	unbaked low-fat deep-dish pie crusts
½	cup chopped pecans

MAKES 2 PIES;
16 SERVINGS
PER SERVING
253   CALORIES
8.6 G. TOTAL FAT
1.8 G. SATURATED FAT
4.3 G. PROTEIN
41.4 G. CARBOHYDRATES
2 G.   DIETARY FIBER
1 MG.   CHOLESTEROL
252 MG. SODIUM

Preheat the oven to 425°F.

Grate ¼ teaspoon rind from the orange into a medium saucepan. Squeeze ½ cup juice into the pan. Add the cranberries and 1 cup of the sugar. Cook over medium heat, stirring often, for 5 minutes.

Place the arrowroot or cornstarch in a small bowl. Add the water and stir to dissolve. Stir ¼ cup of the cranberries into the bowl. Pour the mixture into the saucepan. Cook, stirring, until thickened. Remove from the heat.

In a large bowl, combine the pumpkin, milk, egg substitute, cinnamon, ginger, salt, nutmeg, cloves, and the remaining ¾ cup sugar. Mix well.

Divide the cranberry mixture evenly between the pie crusts. Divide the pumpkin mixture between the crusts. Sprinkle with the pecans.

Bake for 15 minutes. Reduce the oven temperature to 350°F and bake for 45 to 50 minutes, or until the filling is set and the crust is lightly browned. Cool on a wire rack.

SWITCH TIP

The pie crusts found in most grocery stores are made with lard. But many stores now carry crusts made with vegetable oil. Some even carry whole-wheat pie crusts. A reduced-fat whole-wheat pie crust is your healthiest choice. If that's not available, look for a reduced-fat white-flour crust made with vegetable oil.

CHOCOLATE MARBLE CHEESECAKE

Serve this dessert to company. They'll be amazed that it's low-fat.

HANDS-ON TIME: 15 MINUTES
UNATTENDED TIME: 8 HOURS

½   **cup crushed low-fat chocolate graham crackers**
1½   **cups 1% low-fat cottage cheese**
2   **packages (8 ounces each) nonfat cream cheese, softened**
1   **package (8 ounces) Neufchâtel cheese, softened**
1   **cup nonfat sour cream**
1   **cup sugar**
1   **cup fat-free egg substitute**
1   **tablespoon vanilla**
6   **tablespoons milk chocolate chips, melted**
2   **tablespoons unsweetened cocoa powder**
1   **teaspoon finely grated lemon rind**

MAKES 16 SERVINGS

PER SERVING	
181	CALORIES
5.5 G.	TOTAL FAT
2.4 G.	SATURATED FAT
10.9 G.	PROTEIN
21.5 G.	CARBOHYDRATES
0.1 G.	DIETARY FIBER
13 MG.	CHOLESTEROL
365 MG.	SODIUM

Preheat the oven to 325°F. Coat a 10" springform pan with no-stick spray. Sprinkle the graham cracker crumbs on the bottom and slightly up the sides of the pan.

Place the cottage cheese in a food processor or blender. Process until smooth. In separate additions, add the cream cheese, Neufchâtel cheese, sour cream, sugar, egg substitute, and vanilla. Process until smooth after each addition; scrape down the sides of the container as necessary.

Pour half of the mixture into a medium bowl. Add the melted chocolate and cocoa. Stir until well-blended.

Add the lemon rind to the batter in the food processor or blender. Process until smooth. Spoon into the prepared pan.

Drop the chocolate batter in dollops into the pan. Using a knife, create a swirl pattern by gently drawing the knife once through both batters.

Bake for 1 hour without opening the oven door. Turn off the heat, open the oven door slightly, and let the cheesecake stand for 1 hour. Remove from the oven and cool on a wire rack. Cover and refrigerate for at least 6 hours or overnight.

COOKING HINT

• To melt chocolate chips, place them in a glass measuring cup. Microwave on high for 30 seconds. Stir. Repeat until the chocolate is just melted.

CARROT CAKE

A lot of oil and plenty of eggs give traditional carrot cake its moist texture. To unload the excess fat and retain the flavor, I used a combination of applesauce and fat-free egg substitute. The result is a moist and delicious cake that my family begs for.

HANDS-ON TIME: 25 MINUTES
UNATTENDED TIME: 45 MINUTES

MAKES 16 SERVINGS
PER SERVING
314   CALORIES
7.7 G.   TOTAL FAT
1.5 G.   SATURATED FAT
8.2 G.   PROTEIN
54.5 G.   CARBOHYDRATES
2.9 G.   DIETARY FIBER
5 MG.   CHOLESTEROL
329 MG.   SODIUM

CAKE

2	cups whole-wheat pastry flour or unbleached flour
½	cup chopped walnuts
1	tablespoon baking powder
1	teaspoon ground cinnamon
1	teaspoon ground nutmeg
½	teaspoon salt
¾	cup unsweetened applesauce
¼	cup canola oil
2	cups packed brown sugar
1	cup fat-free egg substitute
3	cups packed shredded carrots
½	teaspoon grated orange rind

FROSTING

12	ounces nonfat cream cheese, softened
4	ounces Neufchâtel cheese, softened
1	tablespoon vanilla
½	teaspoon orange or lemon extract
1½	cups confectioners' sugar
2	tablespoons finely chopped walnuts (optional)

To make the cake: Preheat the oven to 350°F. Coat two 8" round cake pans with no-stick spray and dust with flour, tapping out the excess.

In a medium bowl, combine the flour, walnuts, baking powder, cinnamon, nutmeg, and salt. Mix well.

In a large bowl, combine the applesauce, oil, brown sugar, egg substitute, carrots, and orange rind. Mix well.

Add the flour mixture to the applesauce mixture and stir until well-combined. Pour into the prepared pans.

Bake for 45 minutes, or until a toothpick inserted into the center comes out moist but not wet. Cool for 10 minutes on a wire rack. Remove from the pans and place on the rack until fully cooled.

To make the frosting: In a medium bowl, combine the cream cheese, Neufchâtel cheese, vanilla, and orange or lemon extract. Using an electric mixer, beat until smooth. Add the confectioners' sugar and beat until smooth.

Place 1 cake layer on a serving plate. Spread one-fourth of the frosting over the surface. Add the second cake layer and spread the remaining frosting over the top and sides. Sprinkle with the walnuts (if using).

COOKING HINT

- Neufchâtel cheese is a type of lower-fat cream cheese; you can substitute reduced-fat cream cheese.

Tangerine and Chocolate Layer Cake

If you dream of indulging in a Viennese coffeehouse dessert, this cake will take you there. The cake has an intense orange flavor that is mellowed by the chocolate icing. Although low in fat, this cake is dense and very rich-tasting.

Hands-on time: 35 minutes
Unattended time: 30 minutes

Makes 18 servings

Per serving
238	CALORIES
5.7 G.	TOTAL FAT
1.5 G.	SATURATED FAT
7.3 G.	PROTEIN
41.8 G.	CARBOHYDRATES
2.2 G.	DIETARY FIBER
29 MG.	CHOLESTEROL
279 MG.	SODIUM

Cake

2⅓	cups whole-wheat pastry flour or unbleached flour
1¾	teaspoons baking soda
¼	teaspoon salt (optional)
1	cup honey
¼	cup canola oil
¼	cup unsweetened applesauce
1	cup skim milk
2	eggs, separated
1	tablespoon vanilla
	Grated rind and juice of 2 honey tangerines

Frosting

12	ounces nonfat cream cheese, softened
4	ounces Neufchâtel cheese, softened
¾	cup unsweetened Dutch process cocoa powder
1½	cups confectioners' sugar
¾	cup finely chopped pecans (optional)

To make the cake: Preheat the oven to 350°F. Coat three 8" round cake pans with no-stick spray and dust with flour, tapping out the excess.

In a small bowl, combine the flour, baking soda, and salt (if using).

In a large bowl, combine the honey, oil, and applesauce. Mix well. Add the milk, egg yolks, vanilla, tangerine rind, and tangerine juice. Mix well.

Place the egg whites in a medium bowl. Using an electric mixer, beat until stiff peaks form.

Pour the flour mixture into the honey mixture and mix

well. Gently fold in the egg whites. Pour the batter into the prepared pans.

Bake for 20 to 25 minutes, or until a toothpick inserted into the center comes out moist but not wet.

Cool for 10 minutes on a wire rack. Remove from the pans and place on the rack until fully cooled. The layers will fall slightly as they cool.

To make the frosting: In a medium bowl, combine the cream cheese, Neufchâtel cheese, and cocoa. Using an electric mixer, beat until smooth. Add the confectioners' sugar and beat until smooth.

Place 1 cake layer on a serving plate. Spread a little less than one-fourth of the frosting evenly over the surface. Add the second cake layer and top with frosting. Add the third cake layer and spread the remaining frosting evenly over the top and sides. Sprinkle the pecans on the sides and top edges of the cake (if using).

COOKING HINTS

- You can substitute regular tangerines, mandarin oranges, or navel oranges for the honey tangerines.

- Dutch process cocoa powder has a richer chocolate flavor than regular unsweetened cocoa powder. Look for it next to the regular cocoa powder in the baking aisle of your grocery store. If necessary, regular unsweetened cocoa powder can be substituted.

- Neufchâtel cheese is a type of lower-fat cream cheese; you may substitute reduced-fat cream cheese.

Sour Cream Apple Crumb Kuchen

Kids (and adults) love the apple filling and the sweet crunchy topping in this cake. It makes a great dessert, snack, or grab-and-go breakfast.

HANDS-ON TIME: 20 MINUTES
UNATTENDED TIME: 50 MINUTES

TOPPING

½	cup packed brown sugar
¼	cup whole-wheat pastry flour or unbleached flour
½	cup chopped walnuts
2	tablespoons unsalted butter or margarine
1	teaspoon ground cinnamon

FILLING

3	cups coarsely chopped peeled apples
1	tablespoon sugar
1	teaspoon ground cinnamon

CAKE

2¼	cups whole-wheat pastry flour or unbleached flour
1½	cups sugar
1	tablespoon baking powder
1½	teaspoons baking soda
1½	cups nonfat sour cream
1	cup fat-free egg substitute
1	tablespoon vanilla

MAKES 15 SERVINGS
PER SERVING
259   CALORIES
4.5 G.   TOTAL FAT
1.3 G.   SATURATED FAT
6.8 G.   PROTEIN
50.9 G.   CARBOHYDRATES
3.1 G.   DIETARY FIBER
4 MG.   CHOLESTEROL
239 MG.   SODIUM

Preheat the oven to 350°F. Coat a 13" × 9" baking dish with no-stick spray.

To make the topping: In a food processor or blender, combine the brown sugar, flour, walnuts, butter or margarine, and cinnamon. Process until the mixture forms fine crumbs.

To make the filling: In a medium bowl, combine the apples, sugar, and cinnamon. Toss to combine.

To make the cake: In a large bowl, combine the flour, sugar, baking powder, and baking soda. Mix well.

In a small bowl, combine the sour cream, egg substitute, and vanilla. Using an electric mixer, beat until smooth.

Pour into the flour mixture and stir until combined. Spread a thin layer of batter on the bottom of the prepared baking dish. Top with the filling. Spread the remaining batter on top. Sprinkle the topping over the batter and pat down gently.

Bake for 50 to 60 minutes, or until a toothpick inserted into the center comes out almost clean.

ALMOND-SCENTED PEACH SAUCE

This sauce is an irresistible topping for frozen vanilla yogurt, reduced-fat ice cream, angel food cake, or pound cake. For great sundaes, sprinkle each serving with 1 tablespoon chopped pecans or almonds. Be sure to make the sauce ahead so that the flavors have time to blend. If you don't have amaretto, which is almond liqueur—or if you prefer not to use alcohol—use 1 teaspoon amaretto extract plus 2 tablespoons water.

HANDS-ON TIME: 5 MINUTES
UNATTENDED TIME: 30 MINUTES

MAKES 6 SERVINGS
PER SERVING
155   CALORIES
0.1 G.   TOTAL FAT
0 G.   SATURATED FAT
0.6 G.   PROTEIN
35.9 G.   CARBOHYDRATES
1.4 G.   DIETARY FIBER
0 MG.   CHOLESTEROL
1 MG.   SODIUM

⅓   cup sugar
¼   cup almond-flavored liqueur
¼   cup honey
¼   cup water
1   tablespoon lemon juice
8   peaches, peeled and thinly sliced

In a large bowl, combine the sugar, liqueur, honey, water, and lemon juice. Mix well. Add the peaches and toss gently. Set aside to marinate for at least 30 minutes.

QUICK SWITCH

Almond-Scented Strawberry Sauce: Replace the peaches with 4 cups sliced fresh strawberries.

CAPPUCCINO CHEESECAKE

Reminiscent of a cup of cappuccino, this dessert has a layer of rich coffee cheesecake topped with a layer of light cream cheese. Chocolate graham crackers form the crust.

HANDS-ON TIME: 15 MINUTES
UNATTENDED TIME: 8 HOURS

¼	cup finely crushed low-fat chocolate graham crackers
1	package (8 ounces) nonfat cream cheese, softened
12	ounces Neufchâtel cheese, softened
1	cup sugar
1	cup fat-free egg substitute
1	cup nonfat sour cream
2	teaspoons vanilla
6	tablespoons hot water
1½	teaspoons instant espresso powder or 1 tablespoon instant coffee powder
1½	teaspoons unsweetened Dutch process cocoa powder
	Ground cinnamon
	Unsweetened cocoa powder

MAKES 12 SERVINGS

PER SERVING

186	CALORIES
6.8 G.	TOTAL FAT
4.2 G.	SATURATED FAT
8.7 G.	PROTEIN
22.2 G.	CARBOHYDRATES
0.2 G.	DIETARY FIBER
22 MG.	CHOLESTEROL
280 MG.	SODIUM

Preheat the oven to 325°F. Coat an 8" springform pan with no-stick spray. Sprinkle the graham cracker crumbs on the bottom and slightly up the sides of the pan.

In a large bowl, combine the cream cheese and Neufchâtel cheese. Using an electric mixer, beat until smooth. In separate additions, beat in the sugar, egg substitute, sour cream, and vanilla. Beat until smooth after each addition; scrape down the sides of the bowl as necessary.

Pour 2 cups of the batter into a small bowl.

In a cup, combine the water and espresso or coffee powder. Stir until dissolved. Beat into the large bowl. Beat in the 1½ teaspoons cocoa.

Pour the coffee batter from the large bowl into the prepared pan. Carefully spoon the reserved batter from the small bowl evenly over the top, being careful not to mix the two layers. Sprinkle lightly with the cinnamon and the additional cocoa.

Bake for 1 hour without opening the oven door. Turn off the oven, open the door slightly, and let the cheesecake stand for 1 hour. Remove from the oven and cool on a wire rack. Cover and refrigerate for at least 6 hours or overnight.

CHOCOLATE-MOCHA BUNDT CAKE

Here's a rich dessert with only 4 grams of fat per serving. Cocoa powder, strong coffee, and prune puree give it a deep flavor without a lot of fat. I serve the cake with a dusting of confectioners' sugar. For special occasions, try it with frozen yogurt, fresh berries, or Raspberry Sauce (page 120).

2	cups whole-wheat pastry flour or unbleached flour
1½	cups sugar
1	cup unsweetened cocoa powder
½	cup packed brown sugar
2	teaspoons baking soda
1	teaspoon baking powder
¼	teaspoon salt
4	egg whites
1¼	cups brewed espresso or very strong coffee
½	cup coffee-flavored liqueur or strong coffee
2	tablespoons canola oil
1	tablespoon vanilla
1½	cups prune puree (see tip)

Preheat the oven to 350°F. Coat a 12-cup Bundt pan with no-stick spray.

In a large bowl, combine the flour, sugar, cocoa, brown sugar, baking soda, baking powder, and salt. Mix well.

In a medium bowl, lightly whisk the egg whites. Whisk in the espresso or coffee, liqueur or coffee, oil, and vanilla. Add the prune puree and mix well.

Make a well in the flour mixture and pour in the coffee mixture. Stir just until the ingredients are combined. Pour into the prepared pan.

Bake for 1 hour, or until a toothpick inserted into the center comes out moist but not wet.

Cool for 15 minutes on a wire rack. Remove from the pan and place on the rack until fully cooled.

HANDS-ON TIME: 15 MINUTES
UNATTENDED TIME: 1¼ HOURS

MAKES 12 SERVINGS
PER SERVING

396	CALORIES
4.2 G.	TOTAL FAT
0.5 G.	SATURATED FAT
7 G.	PROTEIN
4.8 G.	DIETARY FIBER
85.4 G.	CARBOHYDRATES
0 MG.	CHOLESTEROL
374 MG.	SODIUM

SWITCH TIP

Fat gives baked goods texture and tenderness. But it's possible to replace up to 50 percent of the fat in chocolate recipes with prune puree, which adds nutrients and a significant amount of soluble fiber (which may help lower blood cholesterol). You can use pureed baby food prunes. Or make it at home. To make 1½ cups prune puree, soak 1¼ cups pitted prunes in 1 cup hot water for 5 minutes, or until plump. Transfer to a food processor or blender and process until smooth. Use as directed in the recipe. Homemade prune puree will keep refrigerated for about 2 months in an airtight container.

409

ORANGE-CRANBERRY-NUT RING

Every cook likes to hear "oohs" and "ahhs" as she brings her specialty to the table. For the holidays, this oversized wreath-shaped bread is one of my most festive and beautiful offerings. Serve the bread with low-fat cream cheese for a delightful cool-weather dessert. If you aren't baking for a crowd, cut the recipe in half and make miniature wreaths. You can also bake the bread in loaf pans.

HANDS-ON TIME: 35 MINUTES
UNATTENDED TIME: 2¼ HOURS

MAKES 1 LOAF;
40 SLICES

PER SLICE
154	CALORIES
2.5 G.	TOTAL FAT
0.3 G.	SATURATED FAT
3.7 G.	PROTEIN
29.8 G.	CARBOHYDRATES
1.4 G.	DIETARY FIBER
16 MG.	CHOLESTEROL
59 MG.	SODIUM

BREAD

2	cups cold water
2	cups dried cranberries
2	cups warm water (110°–115°F)
2	tablespoons active dry yeast
1	teaspoon + 1 cup sugar
2	cups whole-wheat flour
2	eggs
2	teaspoons grated fresh orange rind
1	teaspoon salt
1	cup chopped pecans or walnuts
6–7	cups unbleached flour

GLAZE

1	egg, lightly beaten
1	tablespoon sugar

To make the bread: Bring the cold water to a boil in a medium saucepan over high heat. Stir in the cranberries and remove from the heat. Let soak until needed.

In a large bowl, combine the warm water, yeast, and 1 teaspoon of the sugar. Set aside for 5 minutes, or until foamy.

Stir in the whole-wheat flour, eggs, orange rind, salt, and the remaining 1 cup sugar. Using an electric mixer, beat well for 3 minutes (or beat vigorously by hand for 5 minutes).

Drain the cranberries and stir into the dough. Stir in the pecans or walnuts. Stir in 5 cups of the unbleached flour.

Turn out onto a floured surface and knead in enough of the remaining 2 cups unbleached flour to form a soft dough (be careful not to add too much flour). Knead for 10 minutes, or until smooth and elastic. (The dough will remain soft and sticky.) Form the dough into a ball.

Coat a large bowl with no-stick spray. Add the dough and turn to coat all sides. Cover and let rise in a warm place for 1 to 1½ hours, or until doubled in size.

Coat a large baking sheet with no-stick spray.

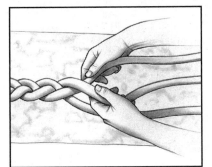

Punch down the dough and divide into 3 pieces. Shape each piece into a 3-foot-long strand. Lightly flour a very large piece of plastic wrap. Braid the strands together on the plastic wrap.

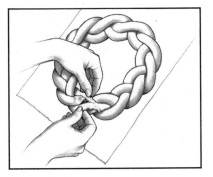

Connect the ends of the braid and pinch together to form a large wreath. Pick up the plastic wrap and transfer the wreath to the prepared baking sheet. Slide out the plastic wrap. Cover and let rise in a warm place for 30 minutes.

Preheat the oven to 350°F.

To make the glaze: Brush the dough with the egg. Sprinkle with the sugar.

Bake for 40 minutes, or until browned on top.

Remove the wreath from the baking sheet and cool on a wire rack.

BANANA-WALNUT CAKE WITH LEMON ICING

In less than 2 hours, you can magically transform overripe bananas into a gloriously moist and delicious dessert. The tangy lemon icing perfectly complements the sweet cake.

HANDS-ON TIME: 20 MINUTES
UNATTENDED TIME: 1½ HOURS

CAKE

3½	cups whole-wheat pastry flour or unbleached flour
½	cup chopped walnuts
2½	teaspoons baking soda
¼	teaspoon salt
2½	cups sugar
¾	cup unsweetened applesauce
1	cup fat-free egg substitute
½	cup nonfat sour cream
2	tablespoons unsalted butter or margarine, softened
1	tablespoon vanilla
5	ripe bananas, mashed

ICING

2	cups confectioners' sugar
3	tablespoons lemon juice
½	teaspoon finely grated lemon rind

MAKES 20 SERVINGS
PER SERVING
286   CALORIES
3.5 G.   TOTAL FAT
1 G.   SATURATED FAT
5.4 G.   PROTEIN
61.4 G. CARBOHYDRATES
3.4 G.   DIETARY FIBER
3 MG.   CHOLESTEROL
211 MG. SODIUM

To make the cake: Preheat the oven to 350°F. Coat a 12-cup Bundt pan with no-stick spray.

In a medium bowl, combine the flour, walnuts, baking soda, and salt. Mix well.

In a large bowl, combine the sugar, applesauce, egg substitute, sour cream, butter or margarine, and vanilla. Mix well.

Pour the flour mixture into the applesauce mixture. Stir until well-combined. Stir in the bananas. Pour into the prepared pan.

Bake for 1¼ hours, or until a toothpick inserted into the center comes out moist but not wet.

Cool for 10 minutes on a wire rack. Remove from the pan and place on the rack until fully cooled.

To make the icing: In a small bowl, combine the confectioners' sugar, lemon juice, and lemon rind. Mix until smooth. Using a rubber spatula, smooth the icing over the top of the cake, spreading it just over the edges so it drips slightly down the sides.

COOKING HINT

- You can replace the egg substitute with ½ cup egg substitute and 2 eggs.

QUICK SWITCHES

Banana-Nut Bread: Replace the 12-cup Bundt pan with two 9" × 5" loaf pans. Reduce the baking time to 1 hour.

Banana-Nut Muffins: Replace the Bundt pan with two 12-cup muffin pans. Reduce the baking time to 30 to 45 minutes.

MOCHA ANGEL FOOD CAKE

Cocoa powder and Kahlua make this cake a devilishly good version of a low-fat classic. Top with fresh berries and confectioners' sugar.

¾	cup whole-wheat pastry flour or unbleached flour
¼	cup unsweetened cocoa powder
¼	teaspoon salt (optional)
1¼	cups sugar
12	egg whites
1	teaspoon cream of tartar
¼	cup coffee-flavored liqueur or strong brewed coffee
1	teaspoon vanilla

Preheat the oven to 350°F.

Combine the flour, cocoa, salt (if using), and ¼ cup of the sugar in a sifter. Sift onto a piece of wax paper. Repeat the sifting 3 times. Return the mixture to the sifter.

Place the egg whites in a large bowl. Using an electric mixer, beat until foamy. Add the cream of tartar and beat until the whites are stiff but not dry.

Gradually fold in the remaining 1 cup sugar. Gradually sift the flour mixture over the batter, folding after each addition, until all the flour is incorporated.

In a small bowl, combine the liqueur or coffee and vanilla. Gently stir in 1 cup of the batter. Pour over the remaining batter and fold until incorporated.

Pour the batter into a dry 10" straight-sided tube pan. Bake for 55 minutes, or until the top springs back when lightly touched.

Remove the pan from the oven and invert it over the neck of a sturdy bottle to cool. Let stand for 1½ hours. When the cake is fully cool, run a knife around the edges of the pan to remove the cake.

HANDS-ON TIME: 25 MINUTES
UNATTENDED TIME: 2½ HOURS

MAKES 16 SERVINGS
PER SERVING

111	CALORIES
0.2 G.	TOTAL FAT
0 G.	SATURATED FAT
3.7 G.	PROTEIN
23 G.	CARBOHYDRATES
0.7 G.	DIETARY FIBER
0 MG.	CHOLESTEROL
43 MG.	SODIUM

SWITCH TIP

To get the flavors of your favorite liqueurs without the alcohol, try liqueur extracts. They work wonders in baked goods and sauces. Nonalcoholic liqueur extracts such as amaretto, Kahlua, and Grand Marnier are available in coffee shops and specialty stores. Or try the mail-order sources on page 416.

VANILLA CREAM TOPPING

This nonfat topping can be the crowning glory for your favorite cakes, tarts, and fruit desserts. Flavored and plain yogurt are drained to remove the liquid whey. The result is yogurt cheese that's slightly sweet, creamy, and open to many variations.

HANDS-ON TIME: 5 MINUTES
UNATTENDED TIME: 4 HOURS

MAKES ABOUT 1 CUP
PER TABLESPOON

34	CALORIES
0 G.	TOTAL FAT
0 G.	SATURATED FAT
2 G.	PROTEIN
7 G.	CARBOHYDRATES
0 G.	DIETARY FIBER
0 MG.	CHOLESTEROL
12 MG.	SODIUM

2	**containers (8 ounces each) nonfat vanilla yogurt**
1	**container (8 ounces) nonfat plain yogurt**
¼	**cup sugar**

In a medium bowl, combine the vanilla yogurt and plain yogurt. Mix well.

Line a sieve or colander with a large double-layer piece of cheesecloth. Spoon in the yogurt. Place over a large bowl. Cover and refrigerate for at least 4 hours, or overnight. (The longer the yogurt drains, the thicker the cream will be.)

Transfer to a medium bowl. Stir in the sugar. Store, tightly covered, in the refrigerator.

COOKING HINT

- If you don't have cheesecloth, use a large coffee filter to drain the yogurt. Place it in the sieve or colander.

QUICK SWITCHES

Fresh Fruit Cream: In a food processor or blender, process ½ cup strawberries, raspberries, blueberries, peaches, or pears until slightly chunky. Stir the fruit mixture into the yogurt before draining.

Lemon Cream: Replace the vanilla yogurt with nonfat lemon yogurt.

Nutmeg Cream: Stir ¼ teaspoon ground nutmeg into the yogurt mixture before draining.

Resources

Most of the recipes in this book use ingredients that are available in any grocery store. But some things, like whole-wheat pastry flour or walnut oil, may not be available in your favorite market. Check with your local health food store for these and other slightly unusual ingredients. If they can't help, the following mail-order sources surely can.

- AMERICAN SPOON FOODS, INC.
  P.O. Box 566
  Petosky, MI 49770

  Tucked away in rural northern Michigan, this company offers an array of fruits, fruit preserves, jellies, conserves, fruit butters, dried fruits, honeys, nut meats, and dried mushrooms.

- CHEF'S CATALOG
  3215 Commercial Avenue
  Northbrook, IL 60062-1900

  This catalog offers page after page of kitchen equipment, utensils, and gadgets. You'll find knives, pasta machines, food processors, garlic presses, and much more.

- DEAN AND DELUCA
  560 Broadway
  New York, NY 10012

  Here's where to find those specialty foods that you can't find anywhere else. They offer high-flavor foods from around the world, including pastas, grains, beans, teas, oils, and vinegars as well as cookware and kitchen tools.

- DIAMOND ORGANICS
  P.O. Box 2159
  Freedom, CA 95019-2159

  Order by credit card and you can expect overnight delivery of freshly picked organic herbs, fruits, vegetables, and greens. There's no minimum order. Split an order with friends to keep shipping costs down.

- GOURMET TRADING COMPANY
  1071 Avenida Acaso
  Camarillo, CA 93012

  This is my favorite mail-order source for flavor-packed salsas, hot sauces, Southwestern marinades, mustards, spice mixes, and dried chili peppers.

- PENN VALLEY FARMS
  6851 West Irving Park Road
  Chicago, IL 60634

  Penn Valley Farms offers low-fat turkey and chicken sausages in a variety of flavors. Only specially fed, all-natural poultry is used, and it's available raw or cooked.

- WALNUT ACRES
  Penns Creek, PA 17862

  More than 500 items are grown on the farm or selected from reputable suppliers. Products include nonfat granolas, flours, grains, bread and cookie mixes, canned and dried fruits, preserves, legumes, nuts, nut butters, cheeses, oils, pastas, spices, sweeteners, soups, and sauces.

- WILLIAMS-SONOMA
  Mail-Order Department, P.O. Box 7456
  San Francisco, CA 94120-7456

  Here you'll find appliances and gadgets, such as pots, pans, dishes, bread machines, salad spinners, pea shellers, ginger graters, seasonal foods, and much more.

INDEX

International Conversion Chart

These equivalents have been slightly rounded to make measuring easier.

VOLUME MEASUREMENTS

U.S.	Imperial	Metric
¼ tsp.	–	1.25 ml.
½ tsp.	–	2.5 ml.
1 tsp.	–	5 ml.
1 Tbsp.	–	15 ml.
2 Tbsp. (1 oz.)	1 fl. oz.	30 ml.
¼ cup (2 oz.)	2 fl. oz.	60 ml.
⅓ cup (3 oz.)	3 fl. oz.	80 ml.
½ cup (4 oz.)	4 fl. oz.	120 ml.
⅔ cup (5 oz.)	5 fl. oz.	160 ml.
¾ cup (6 oz.)	6 fl. oz.	180 ml.
1 cup (8 oz.)	8 fl. oz.	240 ml.

WEIGHT MEASUREMENTS

U.S.	Metric
1 oz.	30 g.
2 oz.	60 g.
4 oz. (¼ lb.)	115 g.
5 oz. (⅓ lb.)	145 g.
6 oz.	170 g.
7 oz.	200 g.
8 oz. (½ lb.)	230 g.
10 oz.	285 g.
12 oz. (¾ lb.)	340 g.
14 oz.	400 g.
16 oz. (1 lb.)	455 g.
2.2 lb.	1 kg.

LENGTH MEASUREMENTS

U.S.	Metric
¼″	0.6 cm.
½″	1.25 cm.
1″	2.5 cm.
2″	5 cm.
4″	11 cm.
6″	15 cm.
8″	20 cm.
10″	25 cm.
12″ (1′)	30 cm.

PAN SIZES

U.S.	Metric
8″ cake pan	20 x 4-cm. sandwich or cake tin
9″ cake pan	23 x 3.5-cm. sandwich or cake tin
11″ x 7″ baking pan	28 x 18-cm. baking pan
13″ x 9″ baking pan	32.5 x 23-cm. baking pan
2-qt. rectangular baking dish	30 x 19-cm. baking pan
15″ x 10″ baking pan	38 x 25.5-cm. baking pan (Swiss roll tin)
9″ pie plate	22 x 4 or 23 x 4-cm. pie plate
7″ or 8″ springform pan	18 or 20-cm. springform or loose-bottom cake tin
9″ x 5″ loaf pan	23 x 13-cm. or 2-lb. narrow loaf pan or paté tin
1½-qt. casserole	1.5-liter casserole
2-qt. casserole	2-liter casserole

TEMPERATURES

Farenheit	Centigrade	Gas
140°	60°	–
160°	70°	–
180°	80°	–
225°	110°	–
250°	120°	½
300°	150°	2
325°	160°	3
350°	180°	4
375°	190°	5
400°	200°	6
450°	230°	8
500°	260°	–